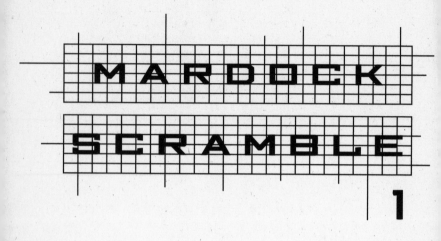

MARDOCK SCRAMBLE

1

Translated and adapted by
Andria Cheng

Lettered by
North Market Street Graphics

KODANSHA
COMICS

A Kodansha Comics Trade Paperback Original

Mardock Scramble volume 1 copyright © 2010 Tow Ubukata and Yoshitoki Oima
English translation copyright © 2011 Tow Ubukata and Yoshitoki Oima

Published in the United States by Kodansha Comics, an imprint of Kodansha USA Publishing, LLC, New York.

Publication rights for this English edition arranged through Kodansha Ltd., Tokyo.

First published in Japan in 2010 by Kodansha Ltd., Tokyo.

ISBN 978-1-935-42953-1

Printed in the United States of America.

www.kodanshacomics.com

1 2 3 4 5 6 7 8 9

Translator/Adapter: Andria Cheng
Lettering: North Market Street Graphics

MARDOCK SCRAMBLE 1

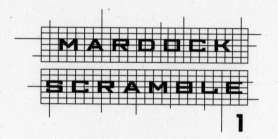

CONTENTS

HONORIFICS EXPLAINED

Throughout the Kodansha Comics books, you will find Japanese honorifics left intact in the translations. For those not familiar with how the Japanese use honorifics and, more important, how they differ from American honorifics, we present this brief overview.

Politeness has always been a critical facet of Japanese culture. Ever since the feudal era, when Japan was a highly stratified society, use of honorifics—which can be defined as polite speech that indicates relationship or status—has played an essential role in the Japanese language. When addressing someone in Japanese, an honorific usually takes the form of a suffix attached to one's name (example: "Asuna-san"), is used as a title at the end of one's name, or appears in place of the name itself (example: "Negi-sensei," or simply "Sensei!").

Honorifics can be expressions of respect or endearment. In the context of manga and anime, honorifics give insight into the nature of the relationship between characters. Many English translations leave out these important honorifics and therefore distort the feel of the original Japanese. Because Japanese honorifics contain nuances that English honorifics lack, it is our policy at Kodansha Comics not to translate them. Here, instead, is a guide to some of the honorifics you may encounter in Kodansha Comics books.

-san: This is the most common honorific and is equivalent to Mr., Miss, Ms., or Mrs. It is the all-purpose honorific and can be used in any situation where politeness is required.

-sama: This is one level higher than "-san" and is used to confer great respect.

-dono: This comes from the word "tono," which means "lord." It is an even higher level than "-sama" and confers utmost respect.

-kun: This suffix is used at the end of boys' names to express familiarity or endearment. It is also sometimes used by men among friends, or when addressing someone younger or of a lower station.

-chan: This is used to express endearment, mostly toward girls. It is also used for little boys, pets, and even among lovers. It gives a sense of childish cuteness.

Bozu: This is an informal way to refer to a boy, similar to the English terms "kid" and "squirt."

Sempai/ Senpai: This title suggests that the addressee is one's senior in a group or organization. It is most often used in a school setting, where underclassmen refer to their upperclassmen as "sempai." It can also be used in the workplace, such as when a newer employee addresses an employee who has seniority in the company.

Kohai: This is the opposite of "sempai" and is used toward underclassmen in school or newcomers in the workplace. It connotes that the addressee is of a lower station.

Sensei: Literally meaning "one who has come before," this title is used for teachers, doctors, or masters of any profession or art.

-[blank]: This is usually forgotten in these lists, but it is perhaps the most significant difference between Japanese and English. The lack of honorific means that the speaker has permission to address the person in a very intimate way. Usually, only family, spouses, or very close friends have this kind of permission. Known as yobisute, it can be gratifying when someone who has earned the intimacy starts to call one by one's name without an honorific. But when that intimacy hasn't been earned, it can be very insulting.

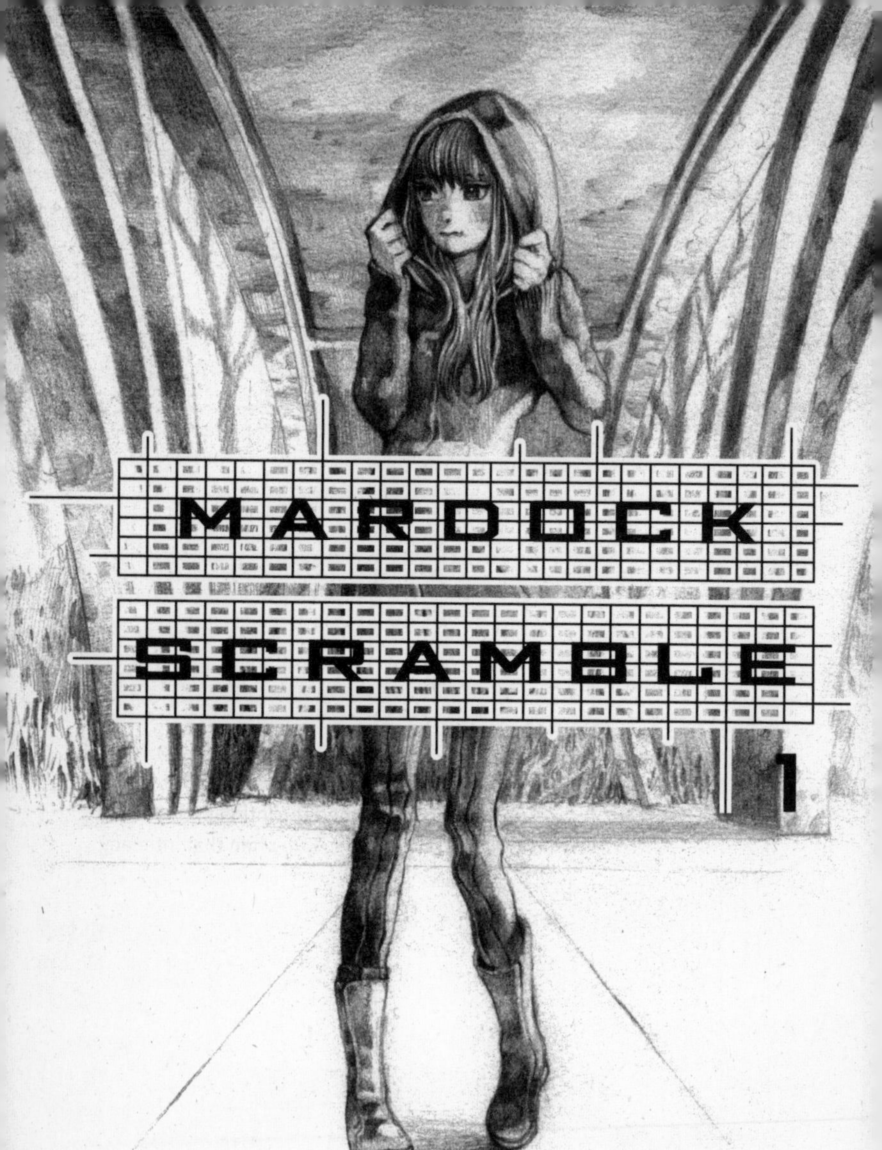
MARDOCK
SCRAMBLE
1

Created by
Tow Ubukata

Manga by
Yoshitoki Oima

MARDOCK SCRAMBLE

contents

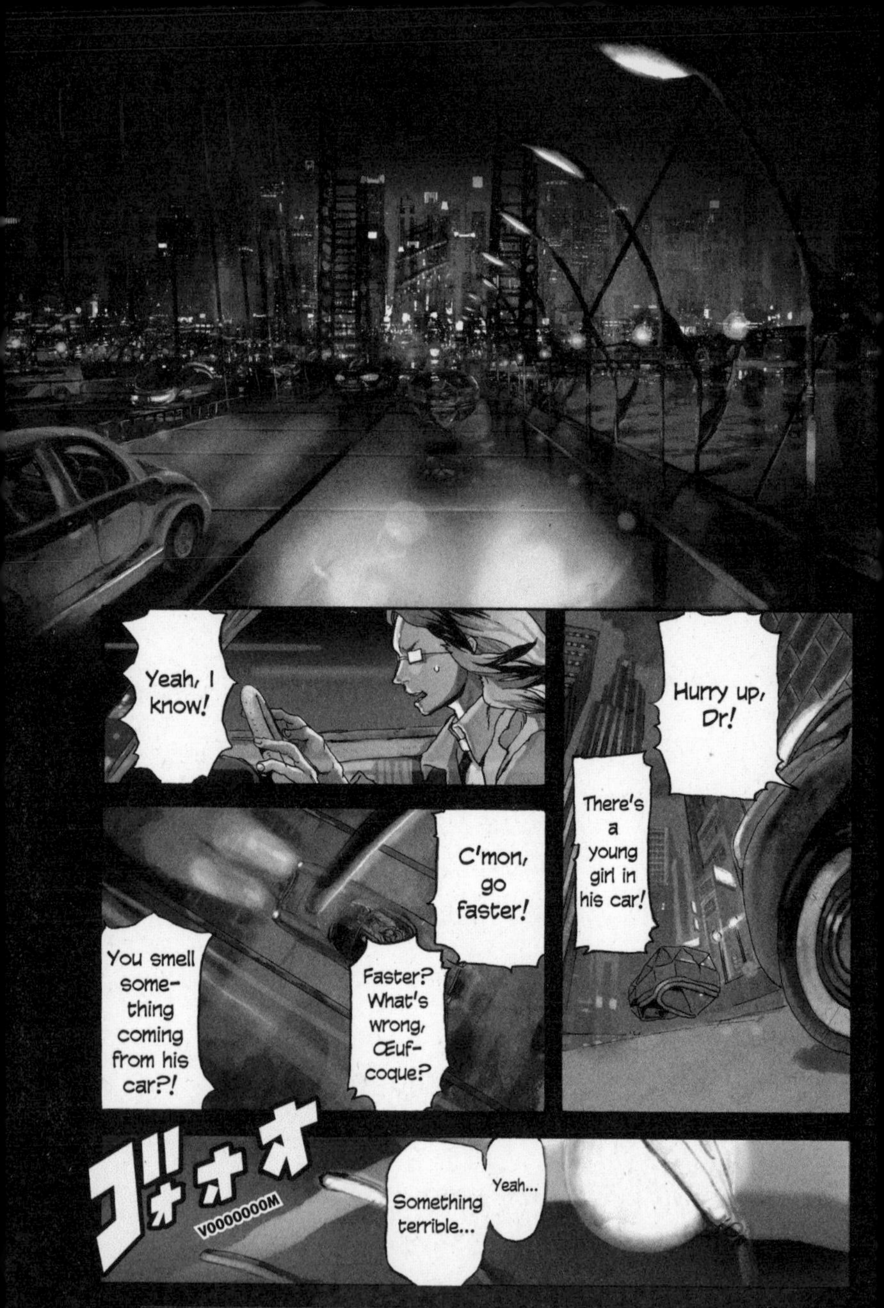
Hurry up, Dr!
There's a young girl in his car!
Yeah, I know!
C'mon, go faster!
Faster? What's wrong, Œuf-coque?
You smell some-thing coming from his car?!
Yeah...
Something terrible...
VOOOOOOOM

The smell of malice...!!

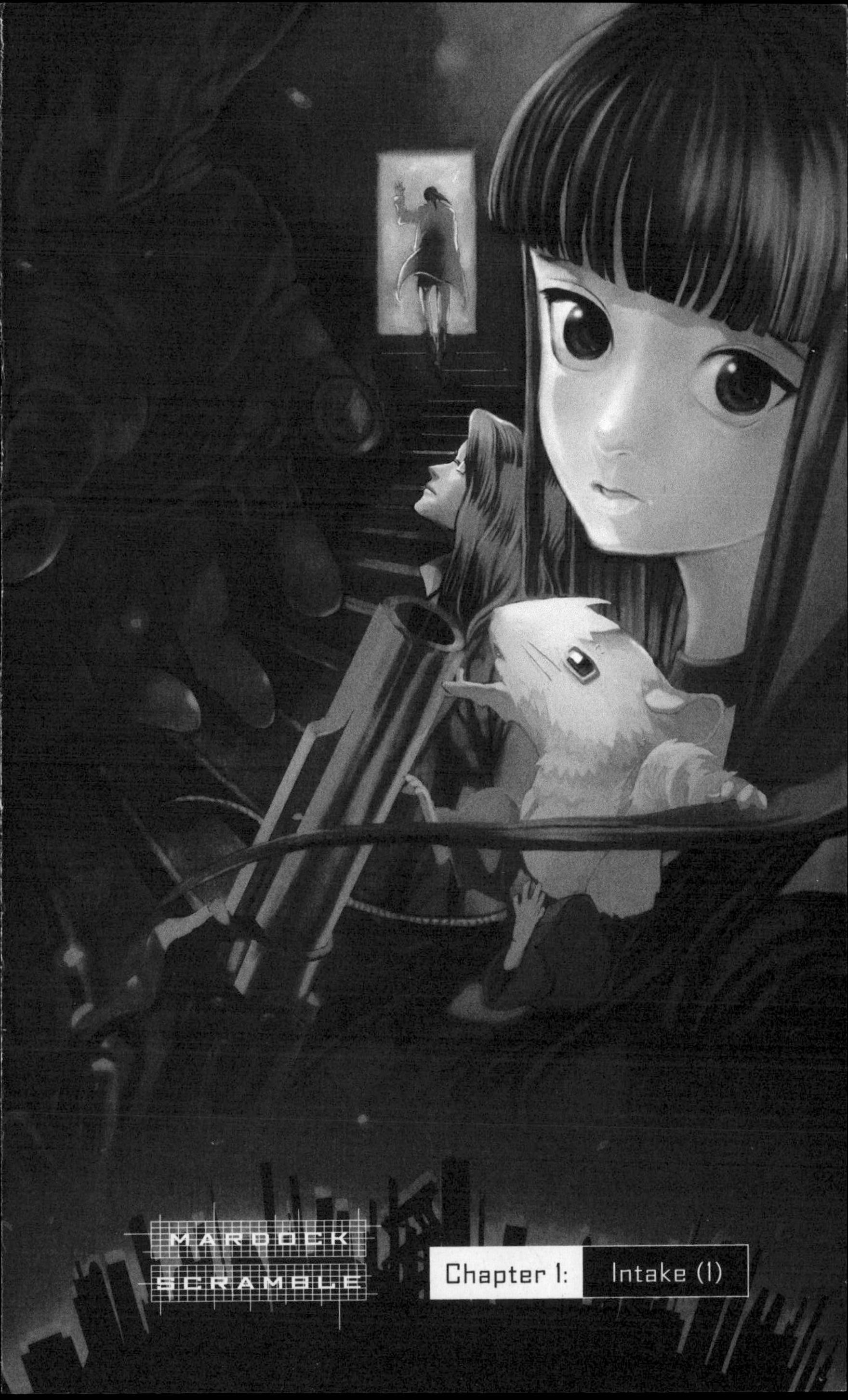
MARDOCK
SCRAMBLE
Chapter 1: Intake (1)

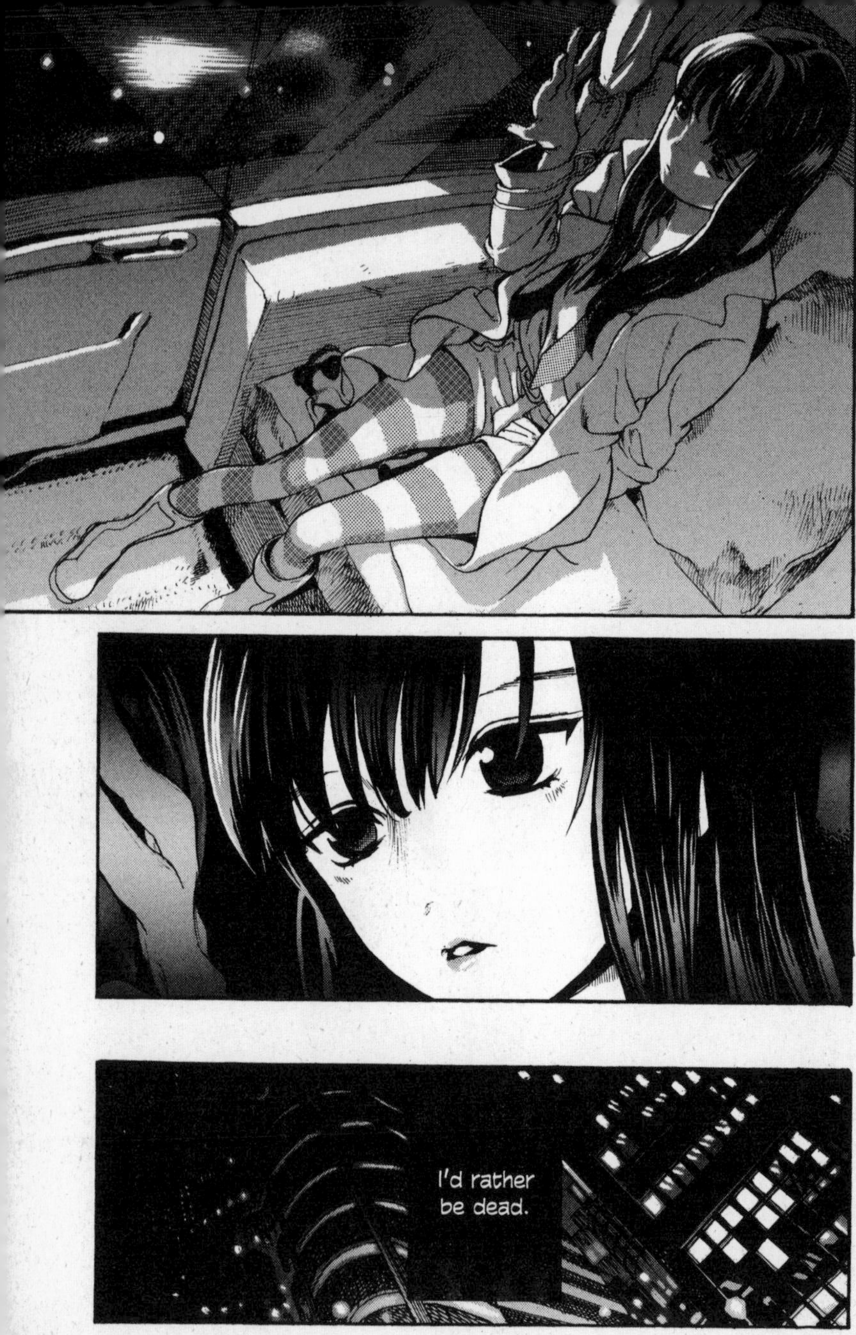
I'd rather
be dead.

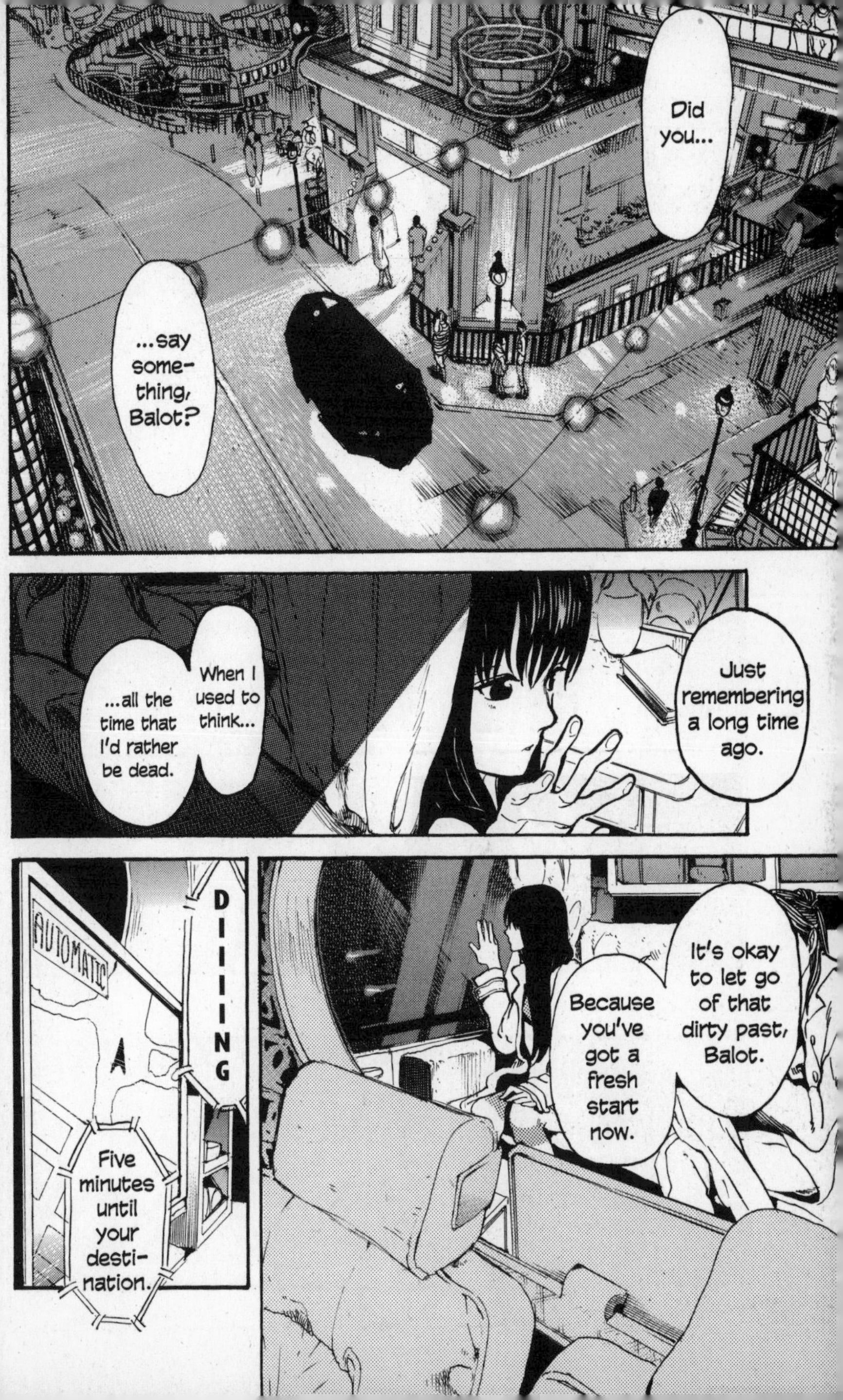
Did you...
...say something, Balot?
Just remembering a long time ago.
When I used to think...
...all the time that I'd rather be dead.
It's okay to let go of that dirty past, Balot.
Because you've got a fresh start now.
AUTOMATIC
DIIIING
Five minutes until your destination.

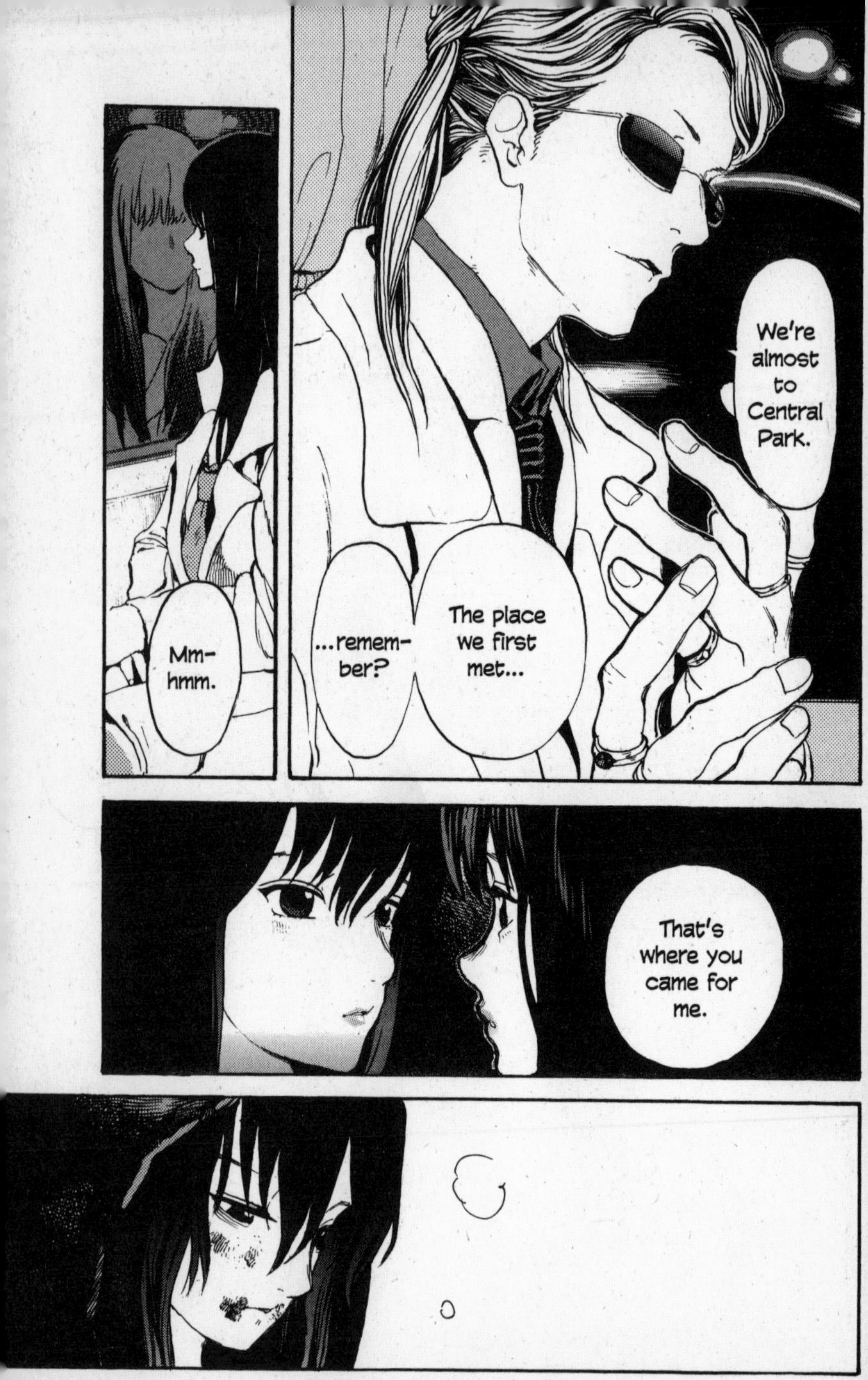
We're almost to Central Park.
The place we first met...
...remember?
Mm-hmm.
That's where you came for me.

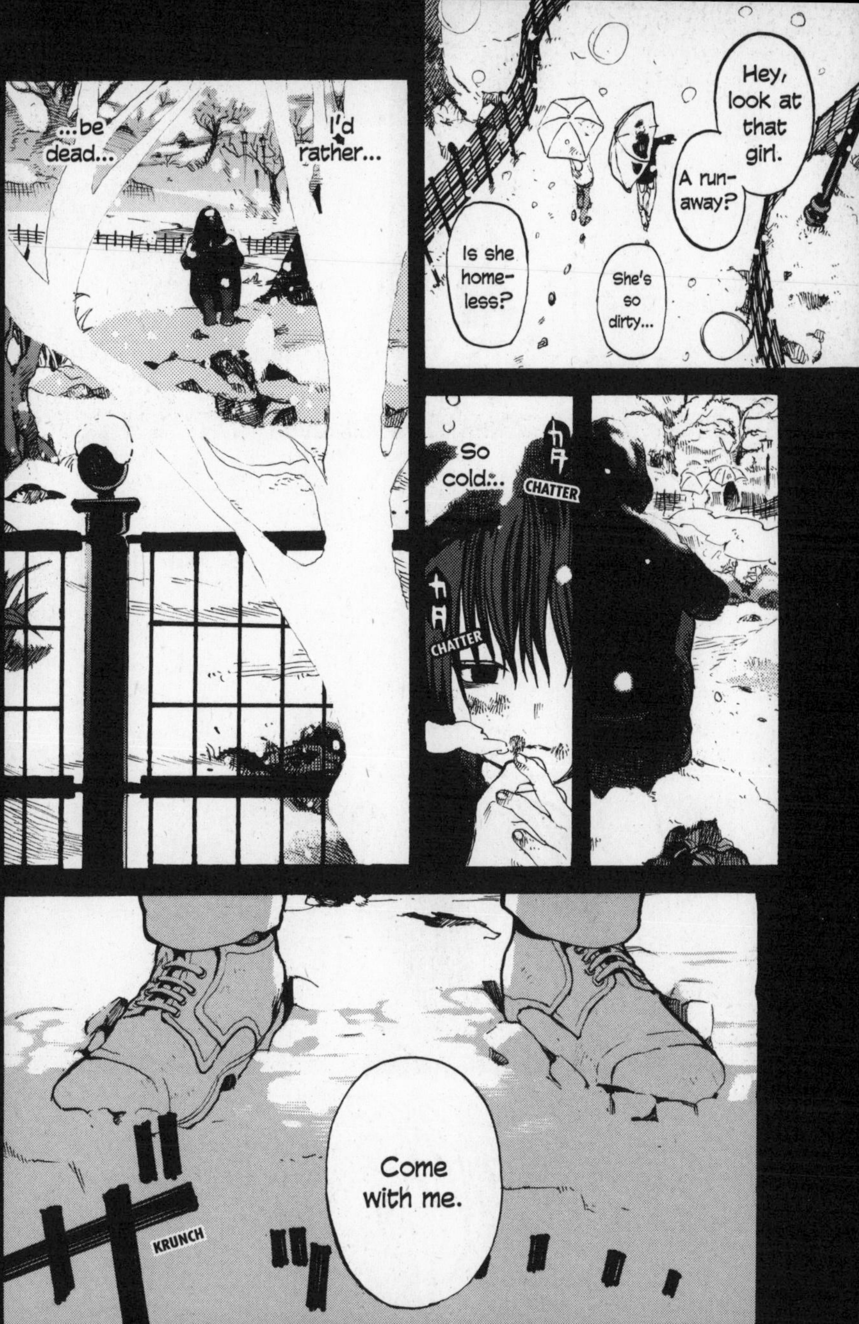
Hey, look at that girl.
A run-away?
She's so dirty...
Is she homeless?
So cold...
カチ CHATTER
カチ CHATTER
I'd rather...
...be dead...
Come with me.
KRUNCH

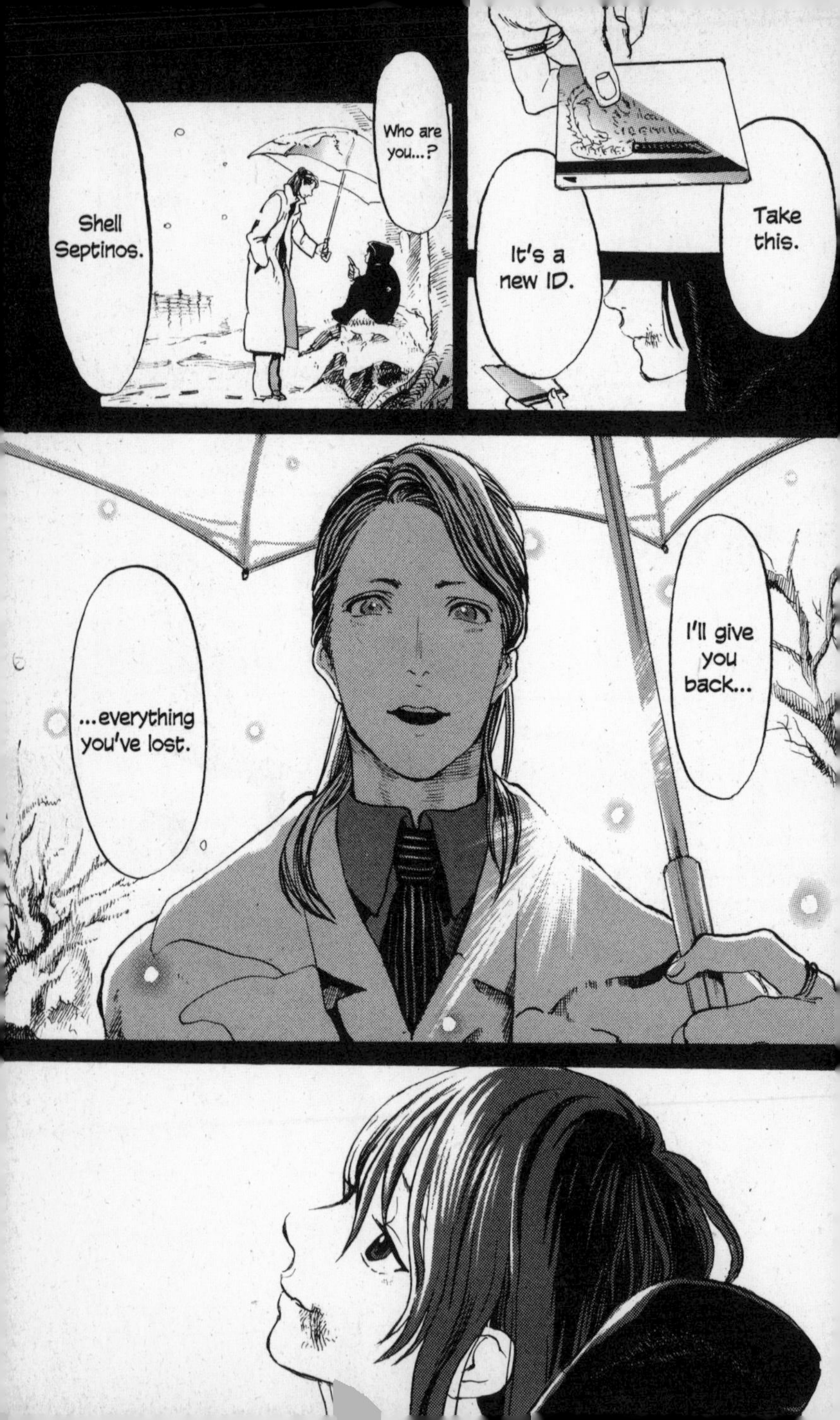
Take this.
It's a new ID.
Who are you...?
Shell Septinos.
I'll give you back...
...everything you've lost.

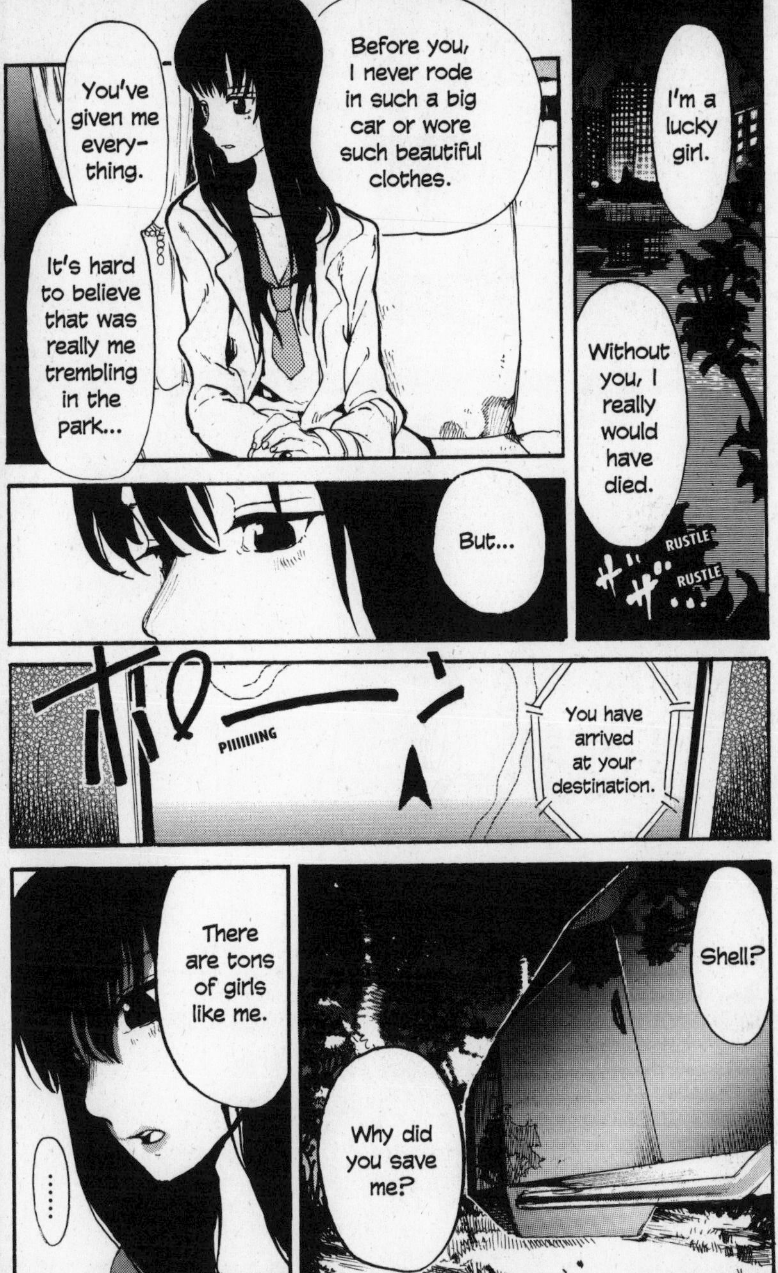
I'm a lucky girl.
Without you, I really would have died.
RUSTLE
RUSTLE
Before you, I never rode in such a big car or wore such beautiful clothes.
You've given me every-thing.
It's hard to believe that was really me trembling in the park...
But...
You have arrived at your destination.
PIIIIIING
Shell?
Why did you save me?
There are tons of girls like me.
......

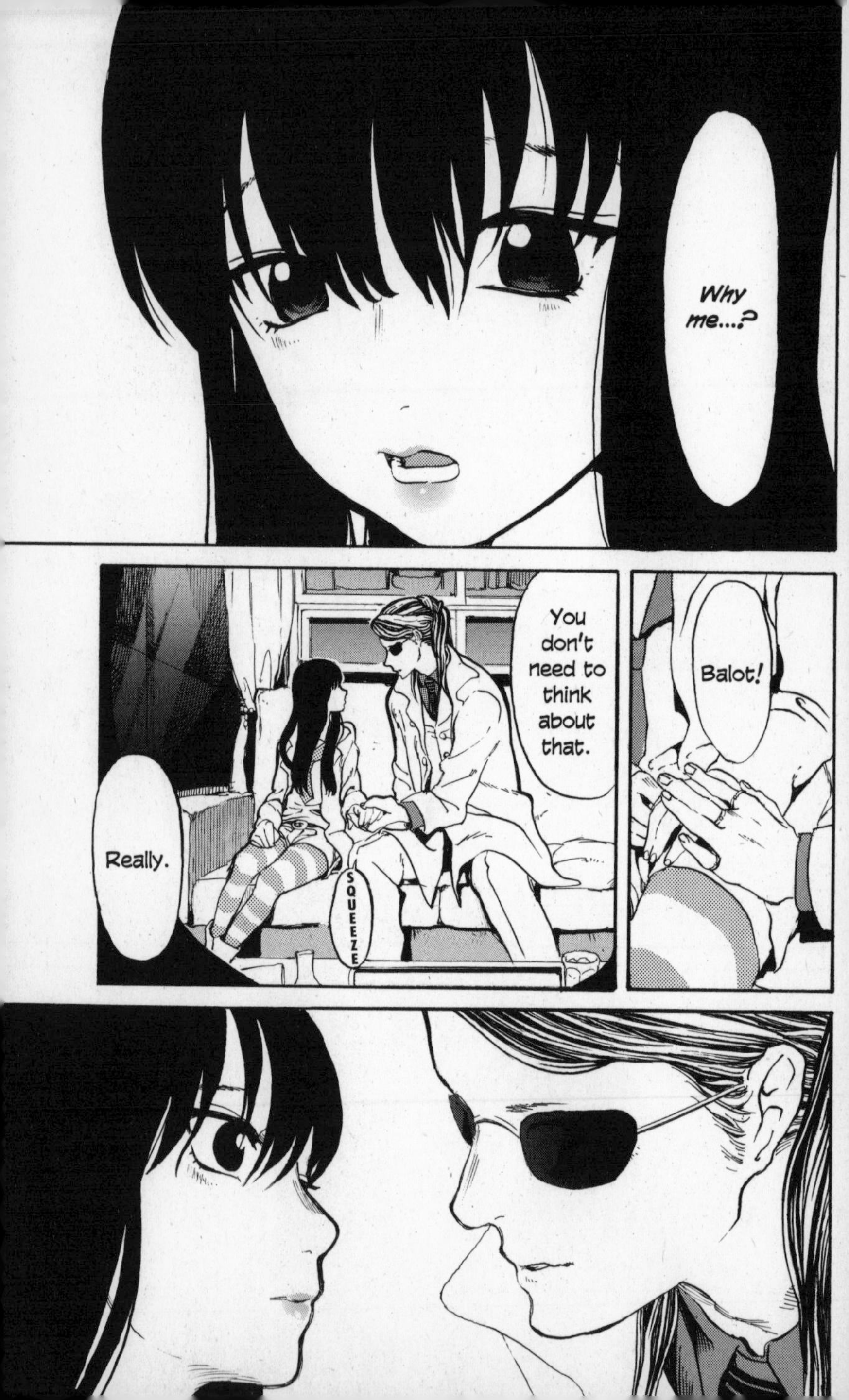
Why me...?
Balot!
You don't need to think about that.
SQUEEZE
Really.

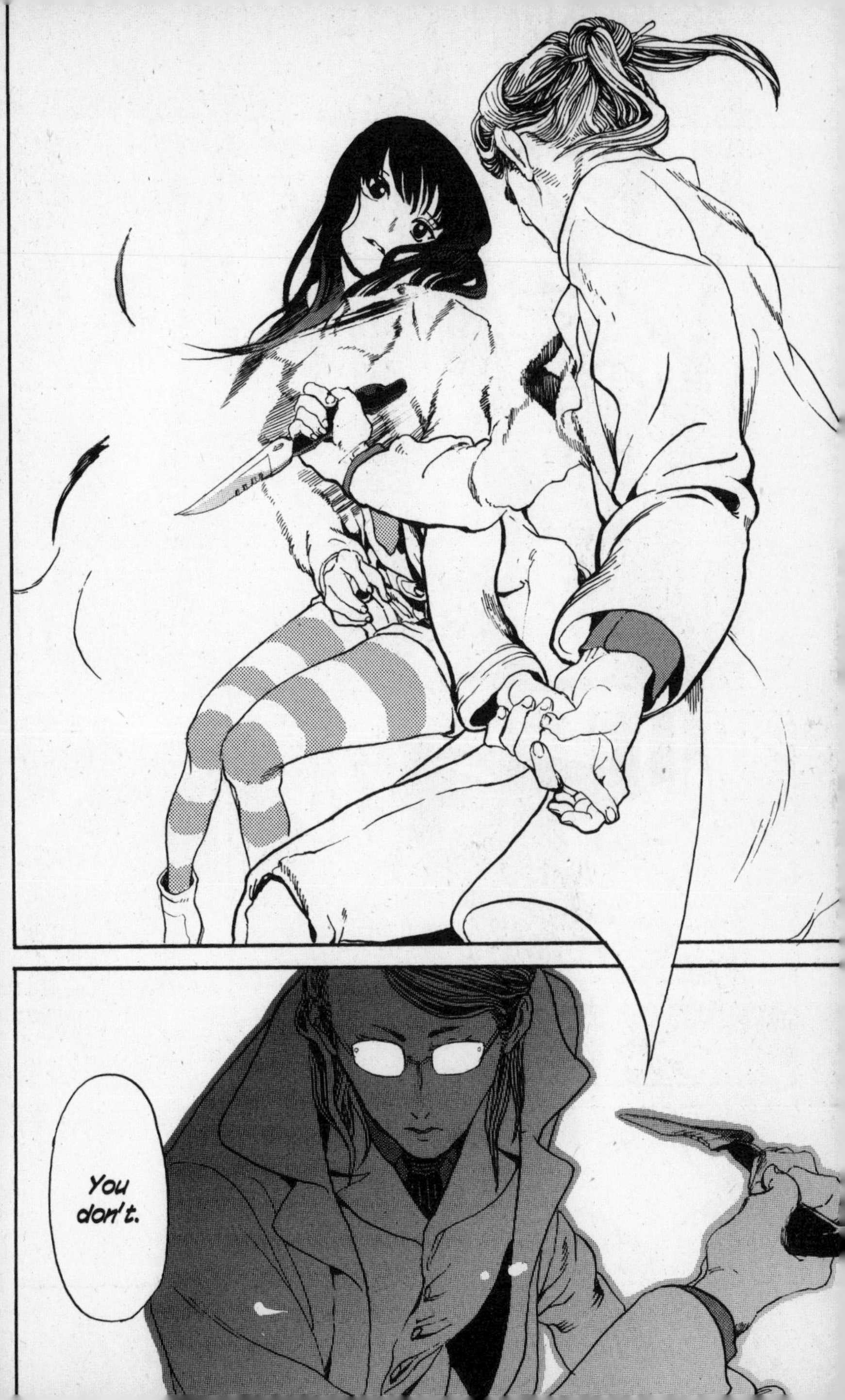
You don't.

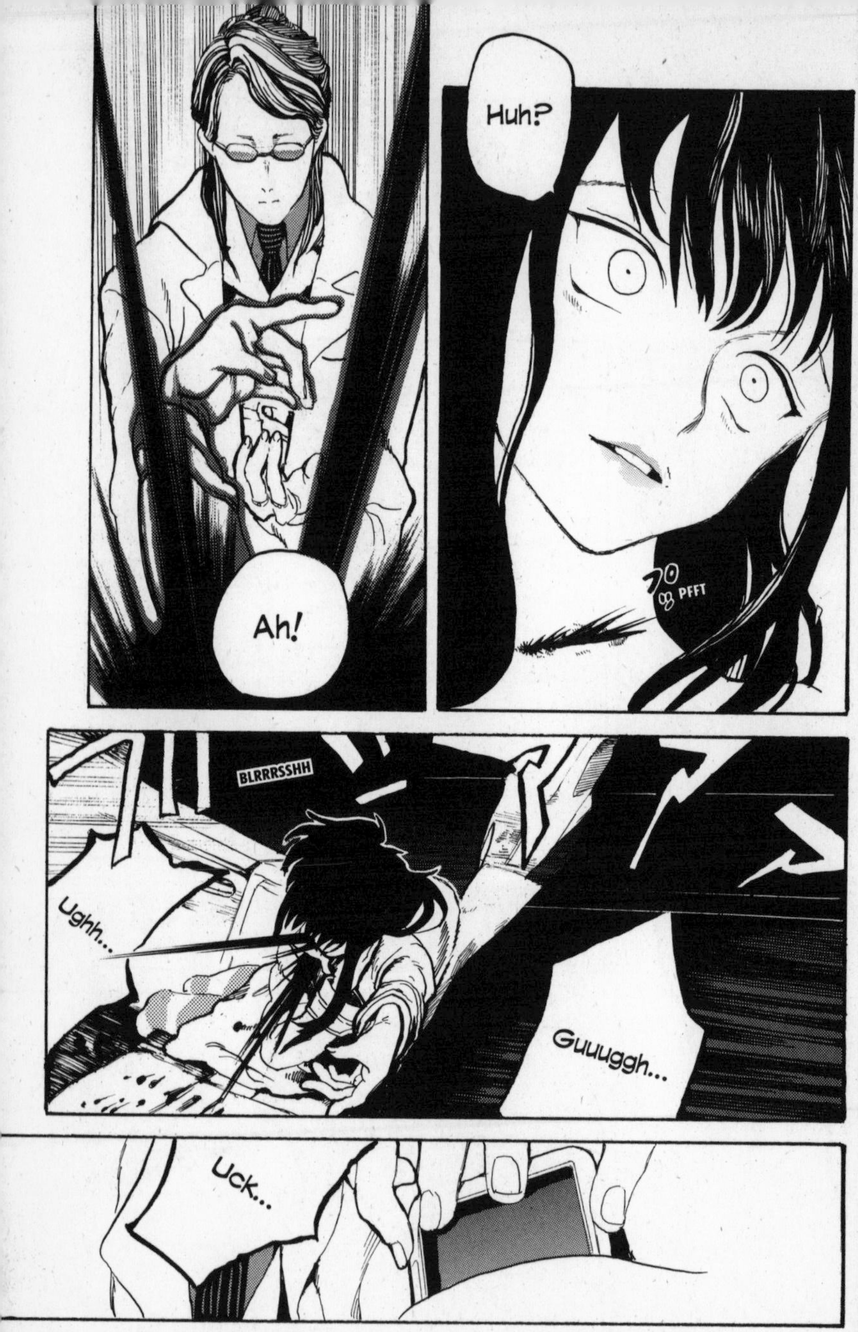
Huh?
PFFT
Ah!
BLRRRSSHH
Ughh...
Guuuggh...
Uck...

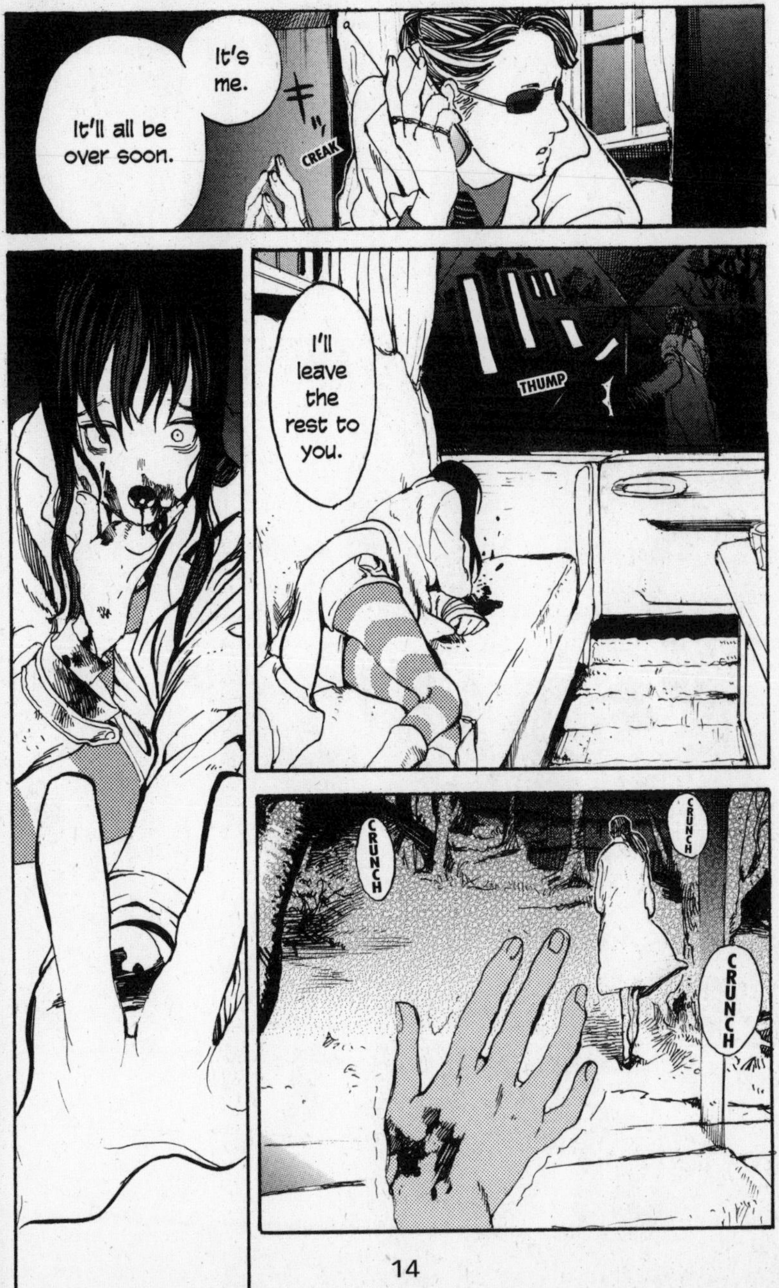
It's me.
It'll all be over soon.
CREAK
I'll leave the rest to you.
THUMP
CRUNCH
CRUNCH
CRUNCH

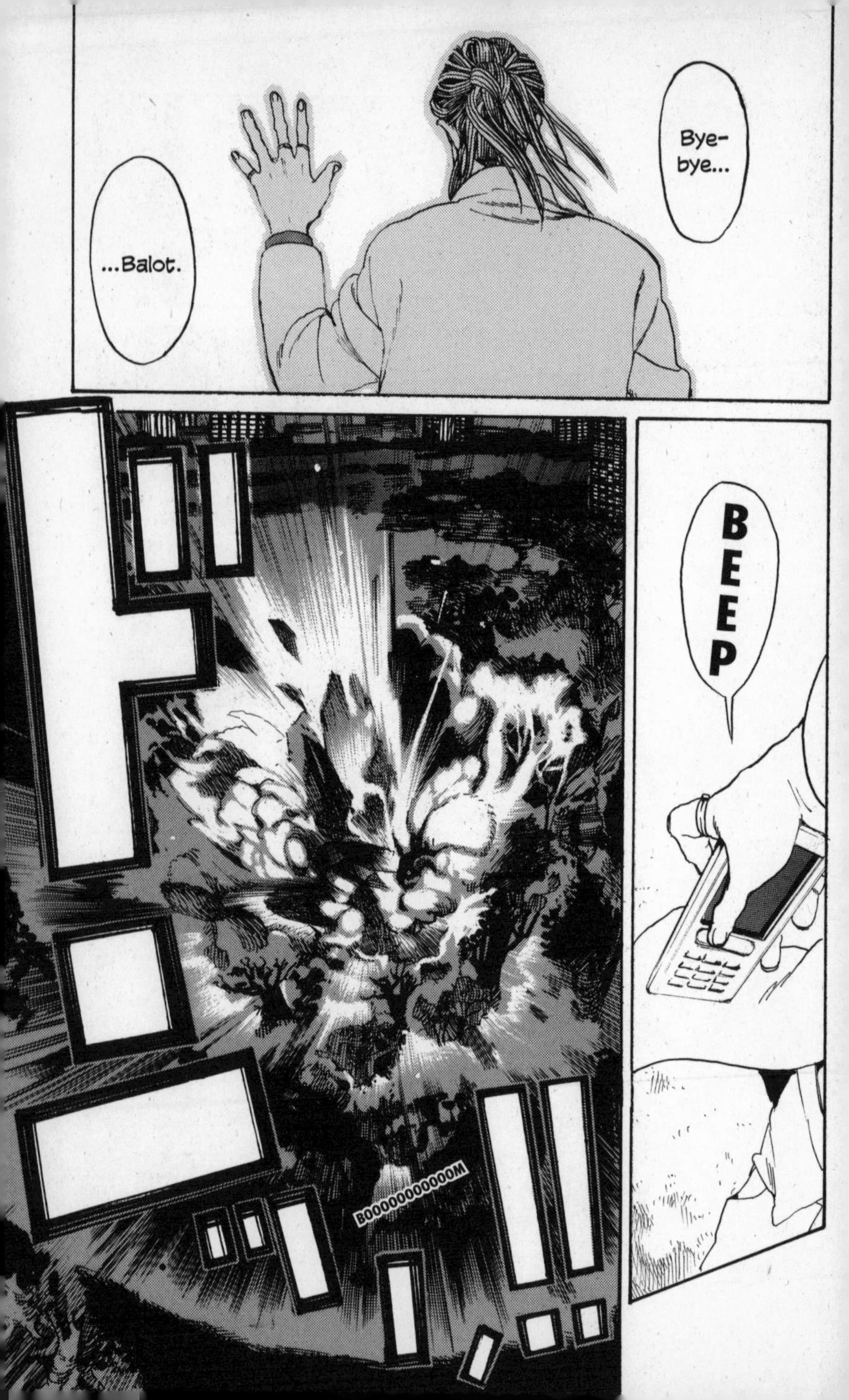
Bye-bye...
...Balot.
BEEP
BOOOOOOOOOOOM

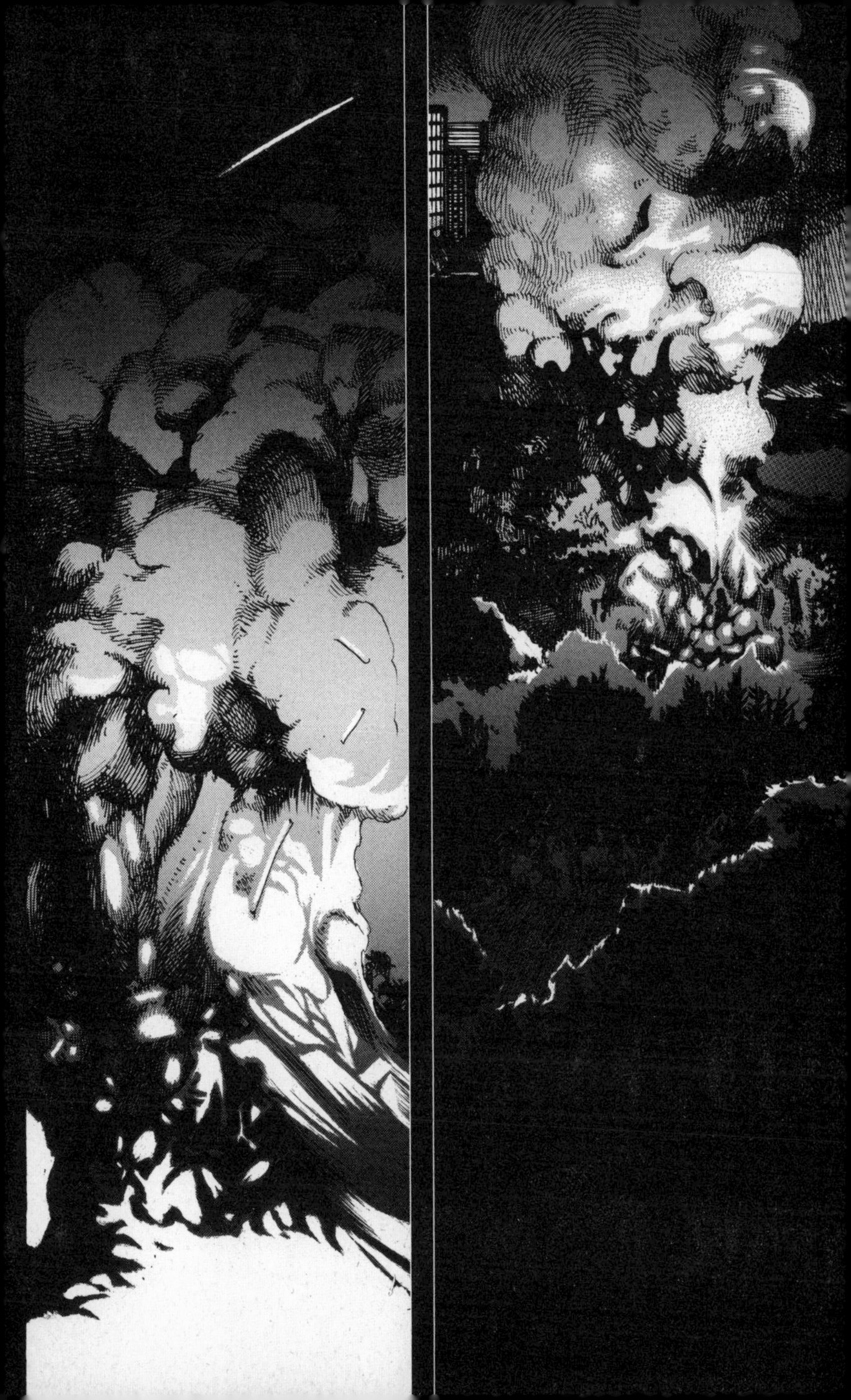

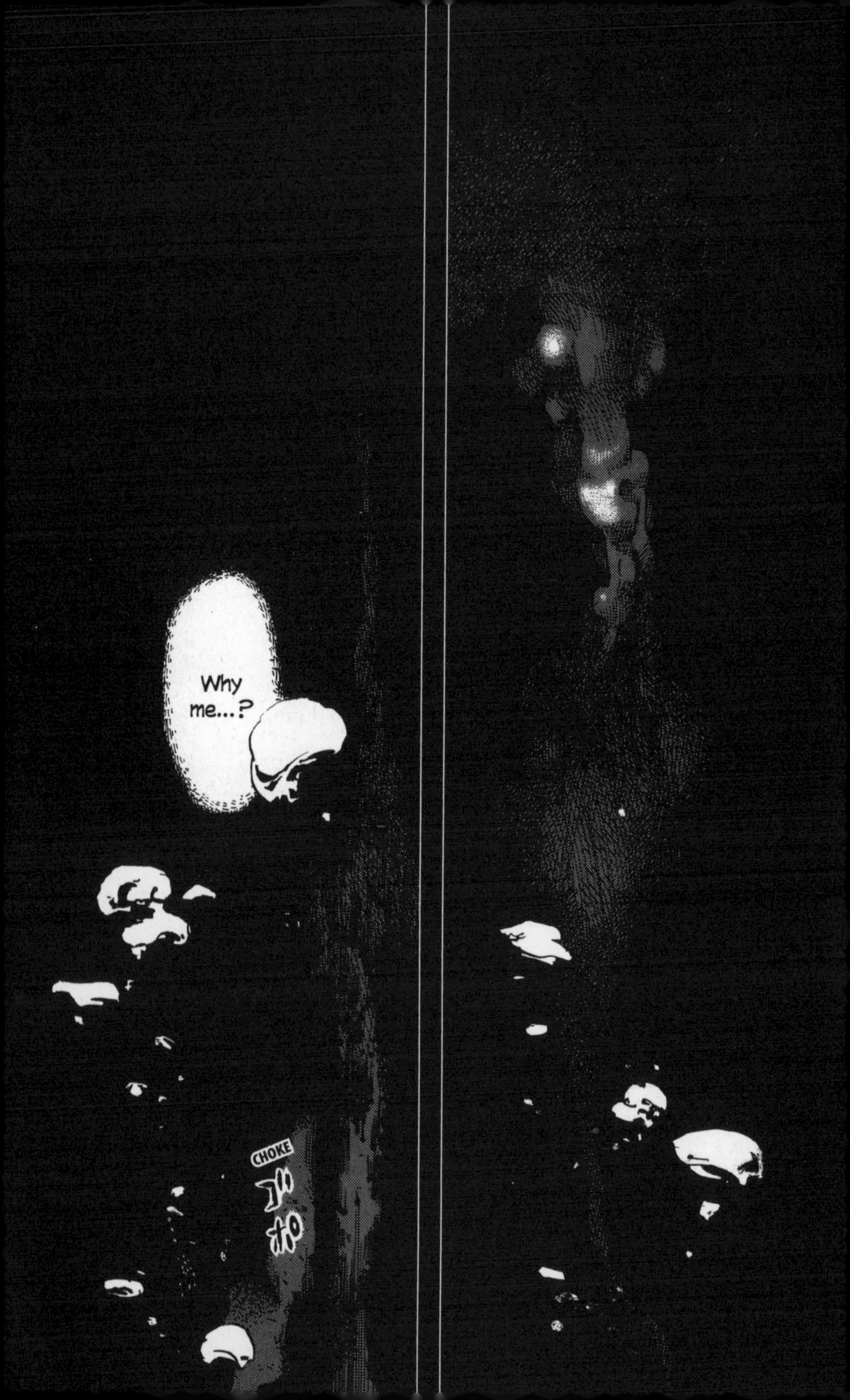
Why me...?
CHOKE

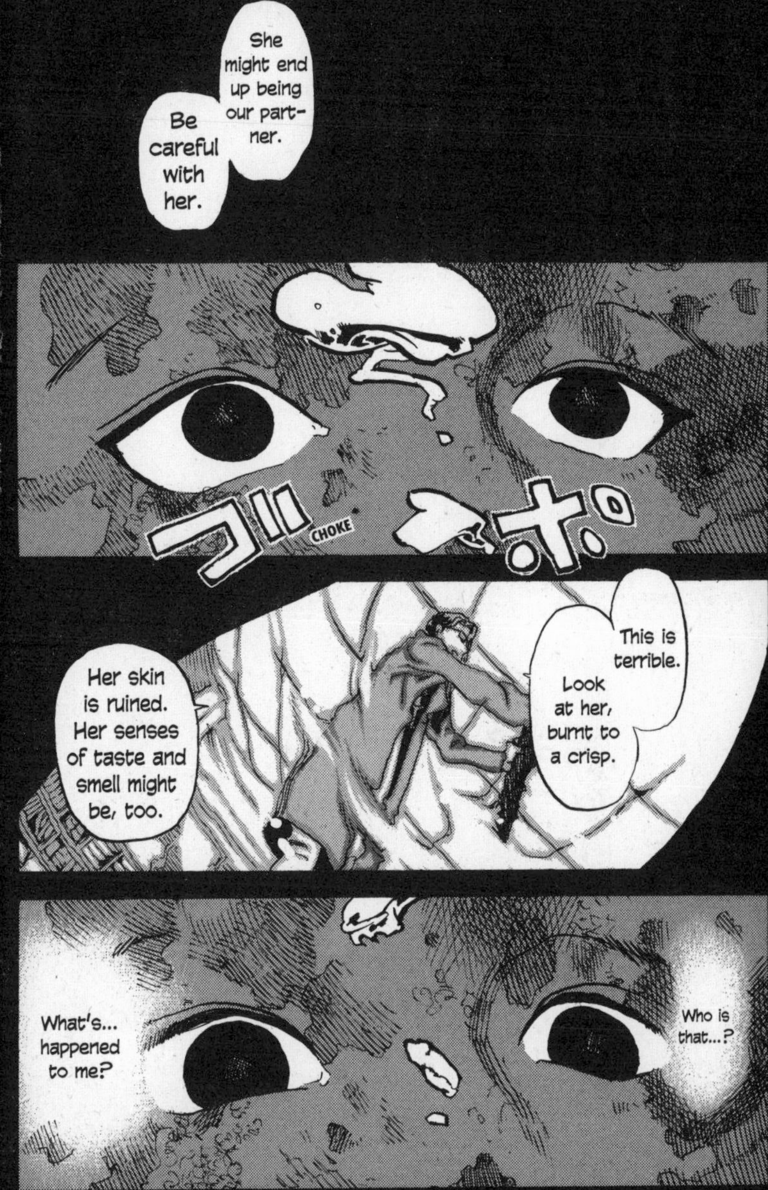
She might end up being our partner.
Be careful with her.
CHOKE
This is terrible. Look at her, burnt to a crisp.
Her skin is ruined. Her senses of taste and smell might be, too.
Who is that...?
What's... happened to me?

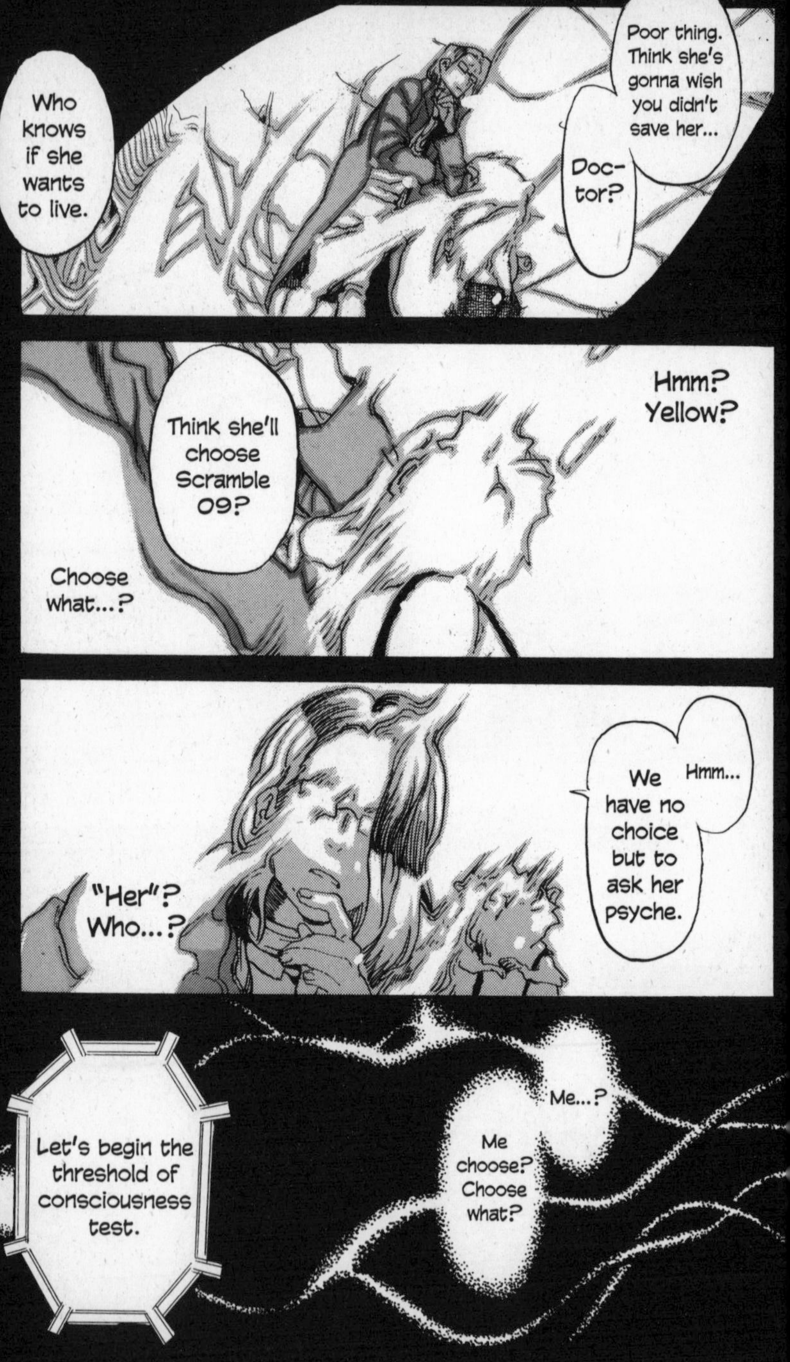
Poor thing. Think she's gonna wish you didn't save her...
Doc-tor?
Who knows if she wants to live.
Hmm? Yellow?
Think she'll choose Scramble 09?
Choose what...?
Hmm...
We have no choice but to ask her psyche.
"Her"? Who...?
Me...?
Me choose? Choose what?
Let's begin the threshold of consciousness test.

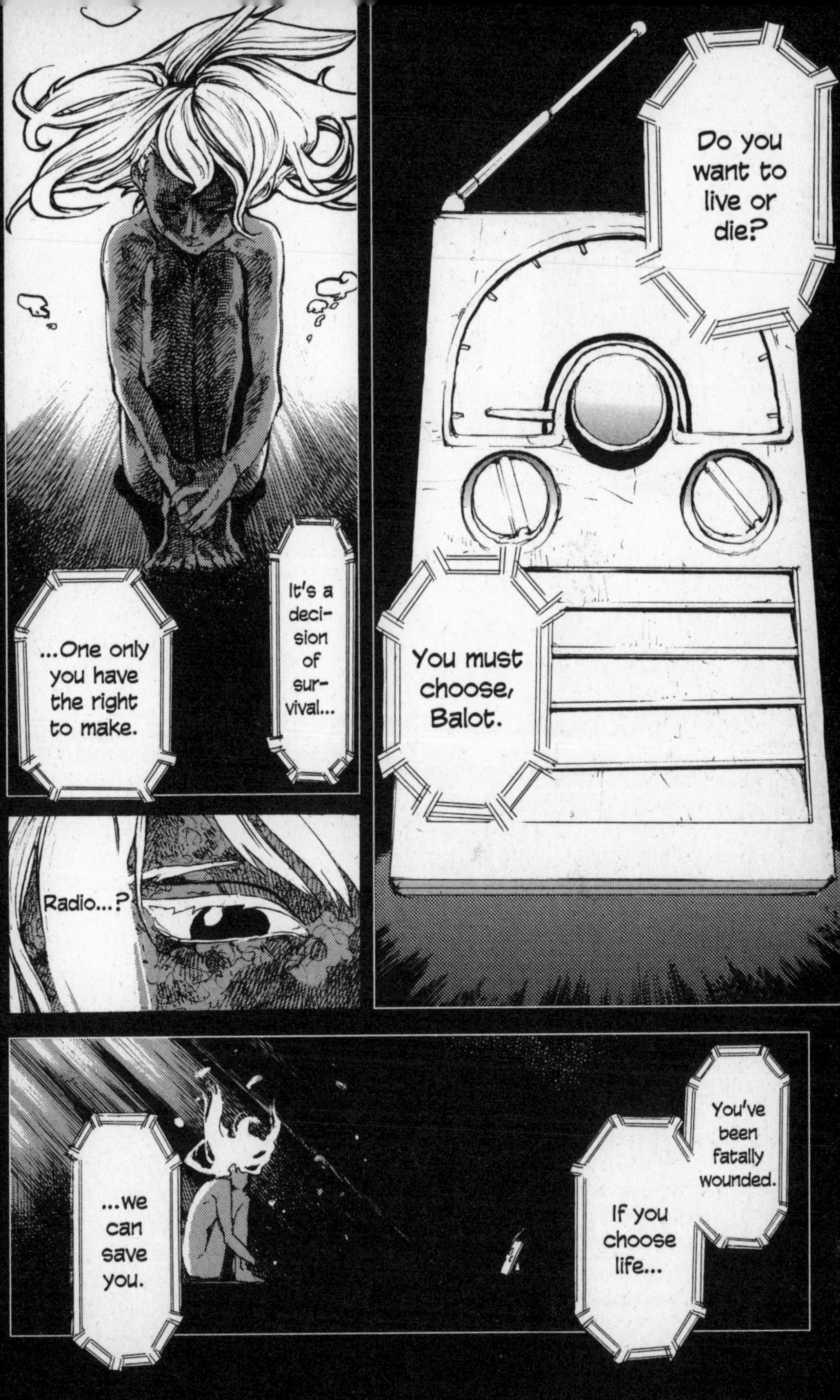
Do you want to live or die?
You must choose, Balot.
It's a decision of survival...
...One only you have the right to make.
Radio...?
You've been fatally wounded.
If you choose life...
...we can save you.

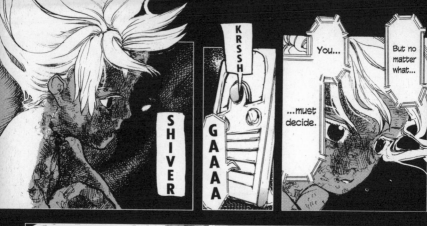

KRSSH

SHIVER

GAAAA

You... ...must decide.

But no matter what...

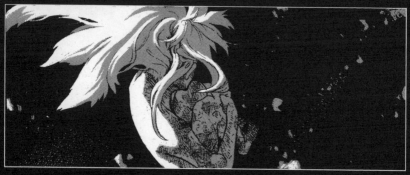

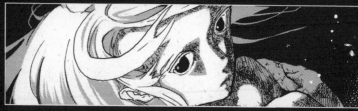

Will you live? Or will you die?

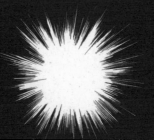

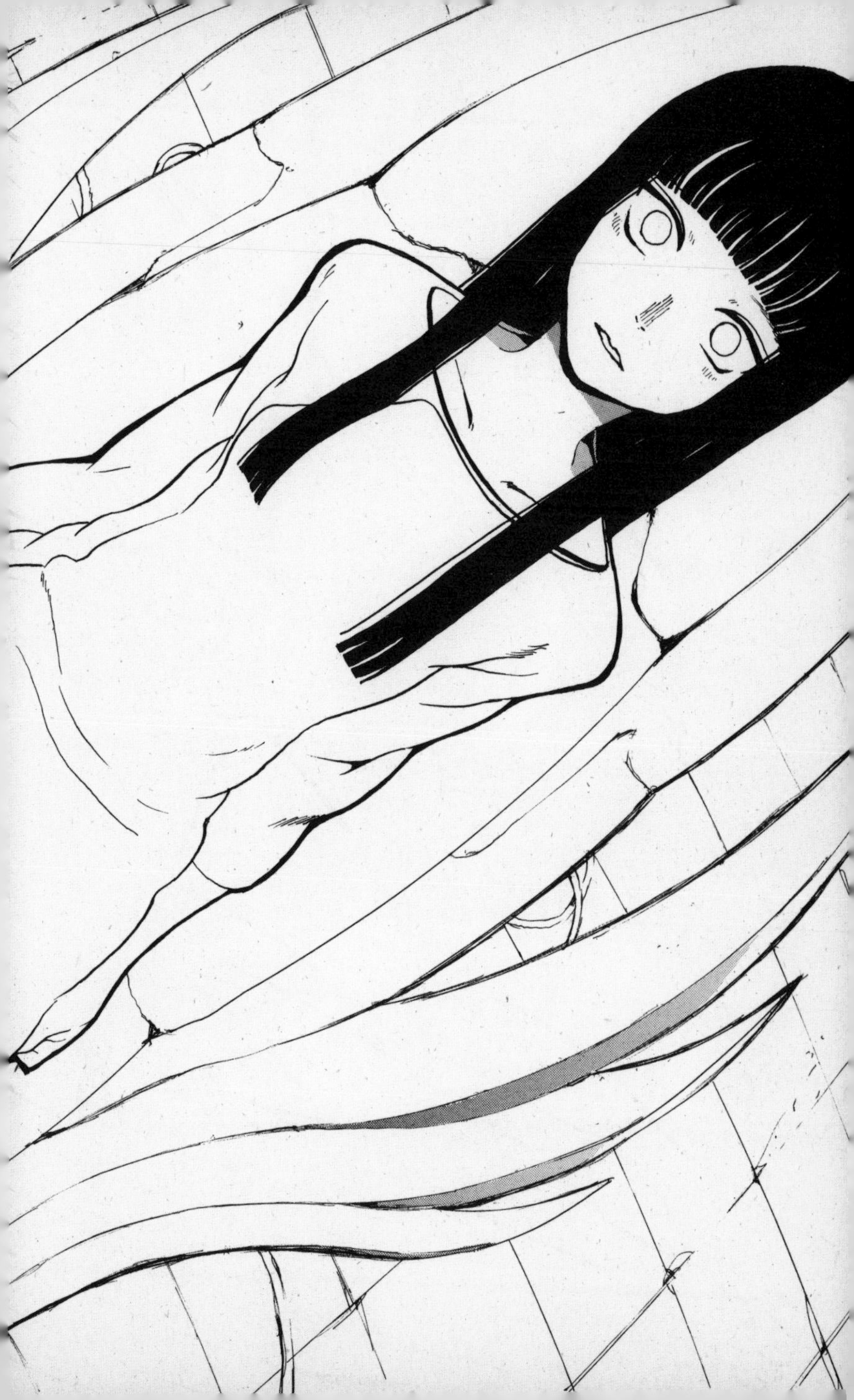

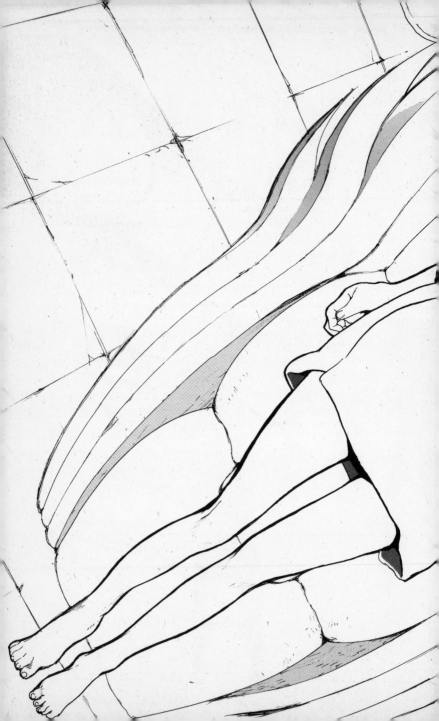

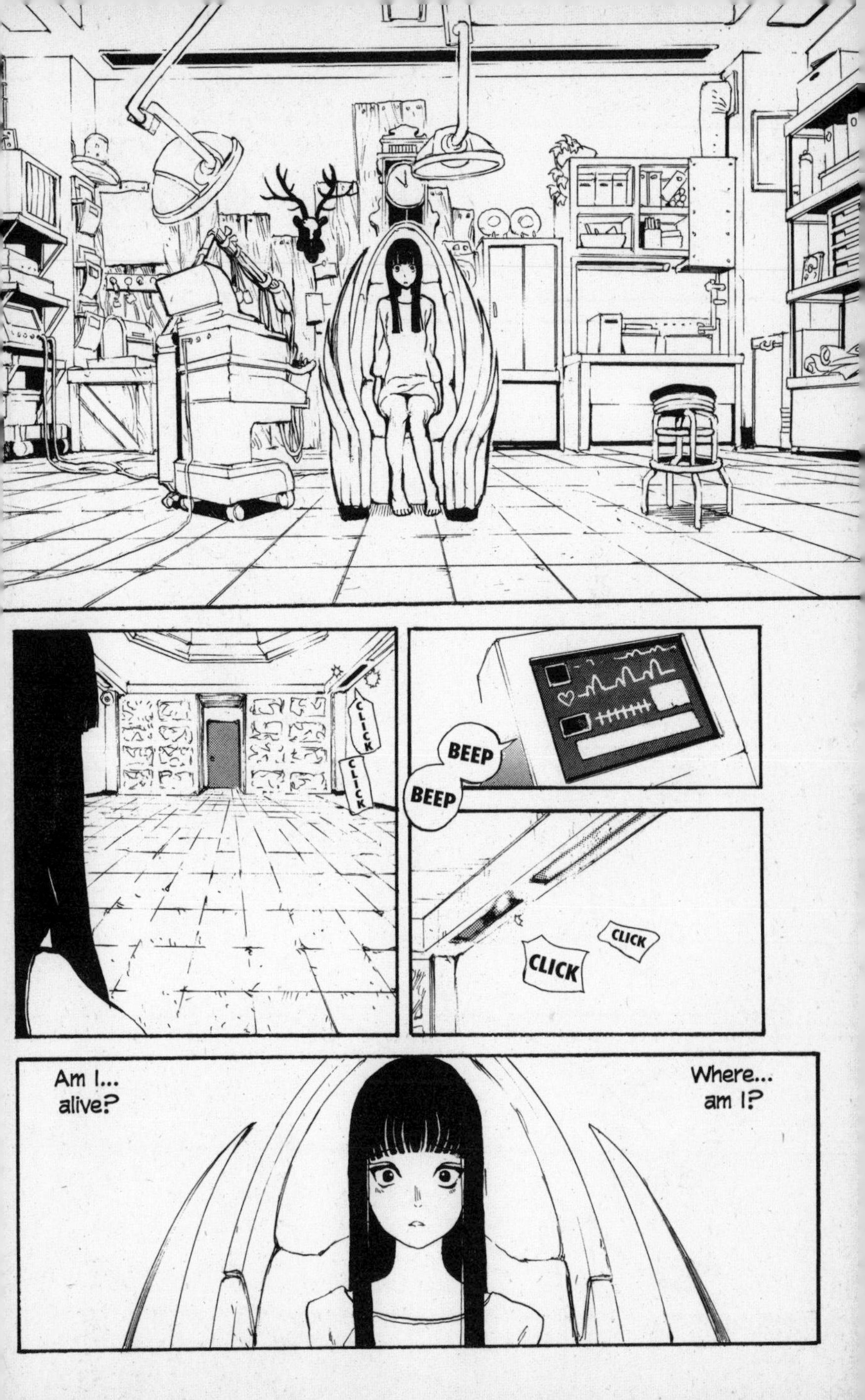
BEEP
BEEP
CLICK
CLICK
CLICK
CLICK
Where... am I?
Am I... alive?

ぺた
POKE
I'm alive?
GRAB
むに
What time is it?
10 o'clock?
At night? Or in the morning?
....

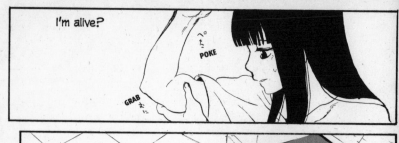

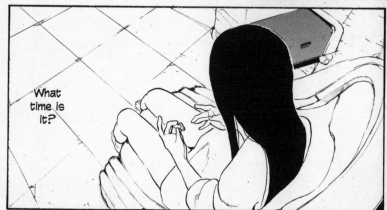

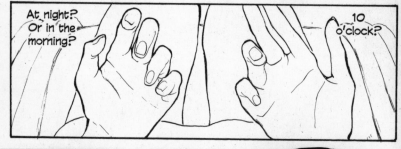

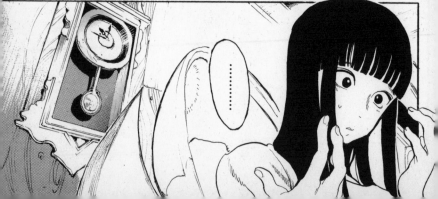

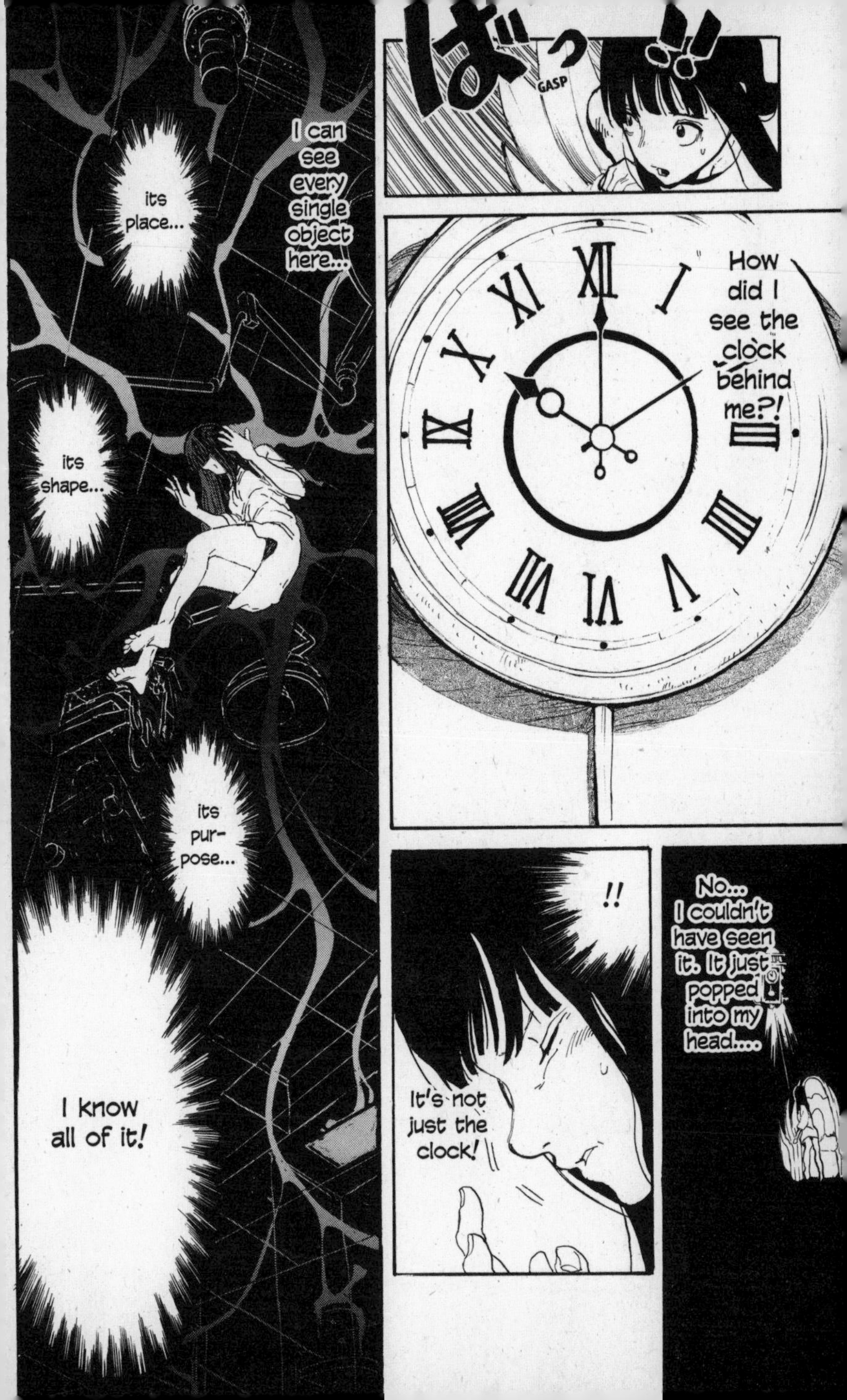
ばっ
GASP
How did I see the clock behind me?!
No... I couldn't have seen it. It just popped into my head....
!!
It's not just the clock!
I can see every single object here...
its place...
its shape...
its purpose...
I know all of it!

What...
What is this feeling?
TWINGE
!
Hm?
What is this?
Thread?
Connected to every-thing...
Is this why?
It's even connected to the light...?
What is it?
......
PULL

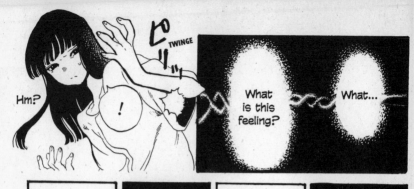

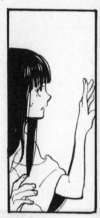

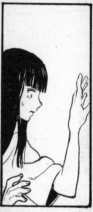

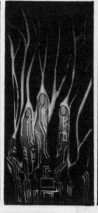

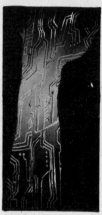

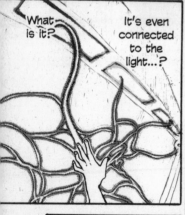

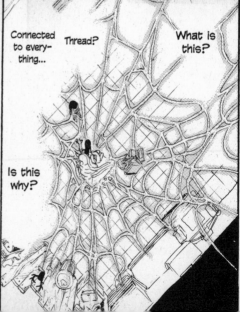

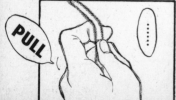

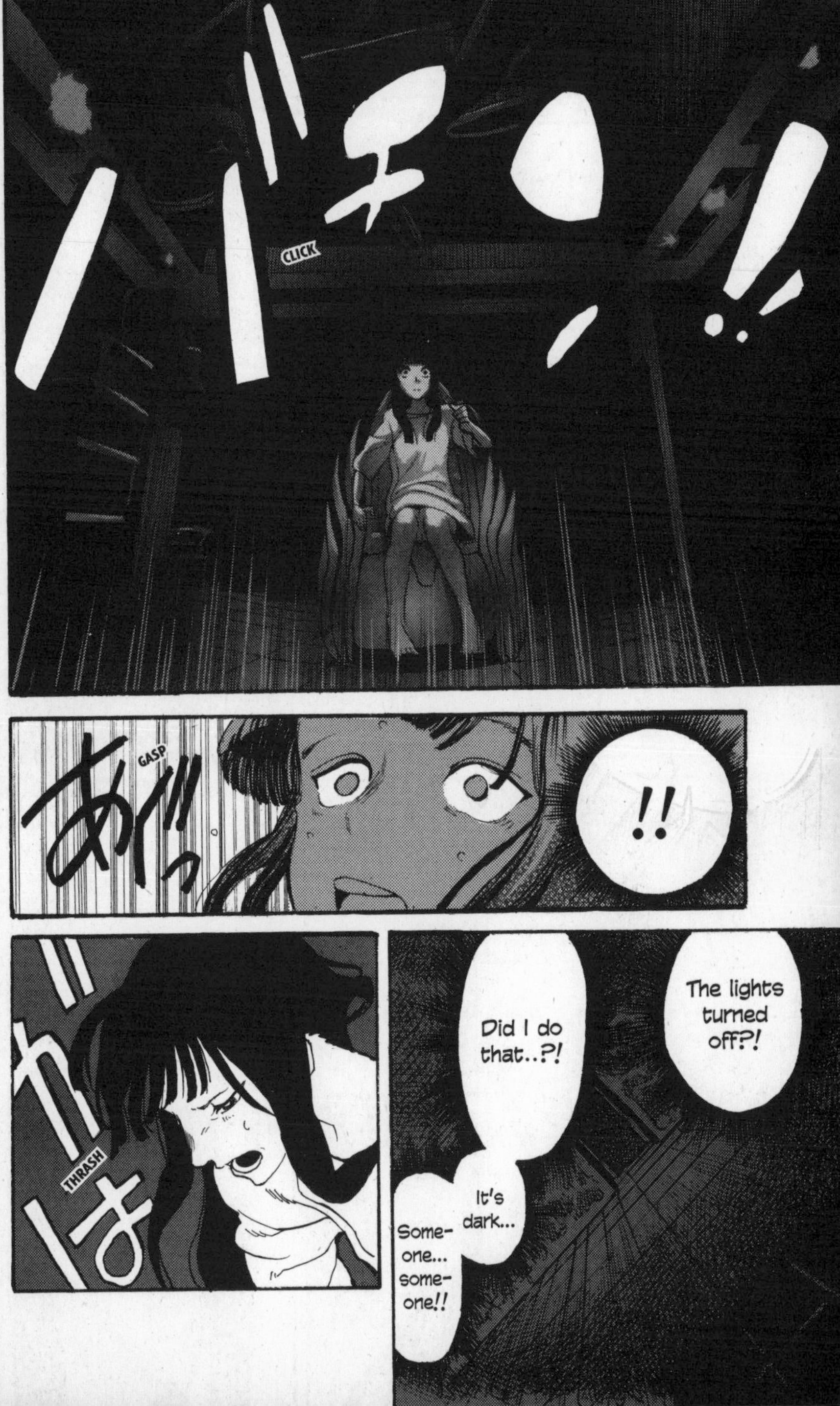
CLICK
GASP
!!
The lights turned off?!
Did I do that..?!
It's dark...
Some-one... some-one!!
THRASH

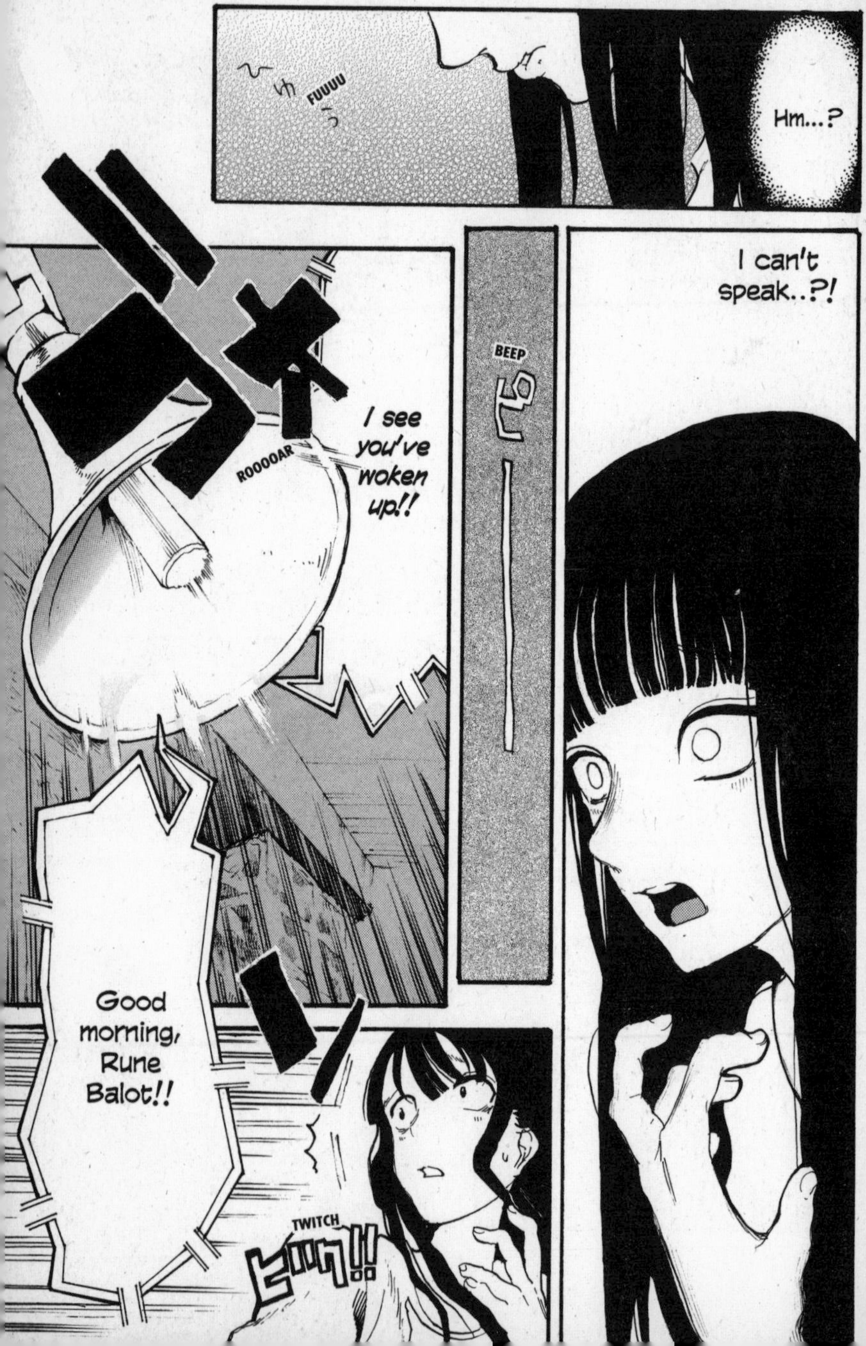
Hm...?
FUUUU
I can't speak..?!
BEEP
ROOOOAR
I see you've woken up!!
Good morning, Rune Balot!!
TWITCH

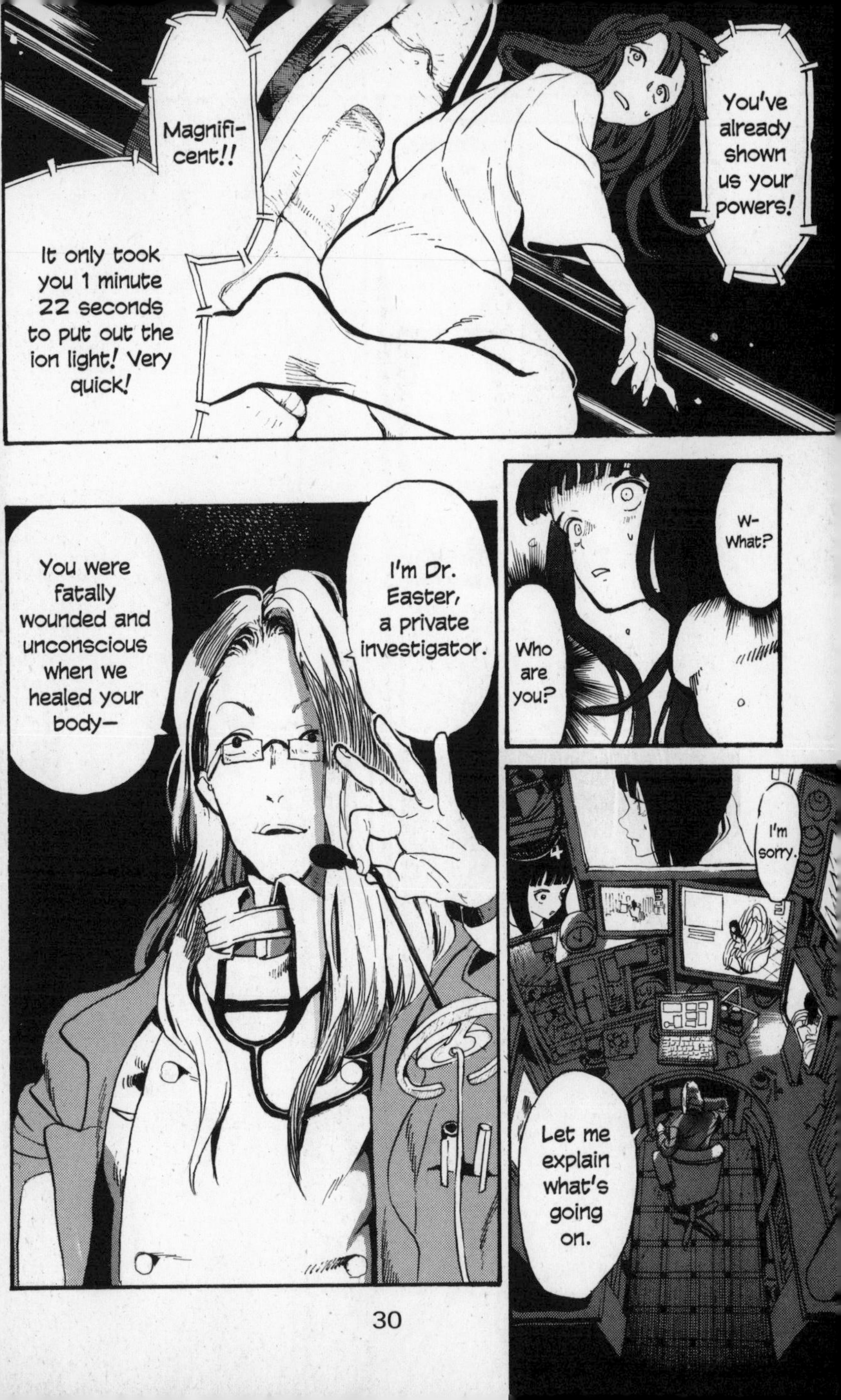
You've already shown us your powers!
Magnifi-cent!!
It only took you 1 minute 22 seconds to put out the ion light! Very quick!
W-What?
Who are you?
I'm sorry.
Let me explain what's going on.
I'm Dr. Easter, a private investigator.
You were fatally wounded and unconscious when we healed your body—

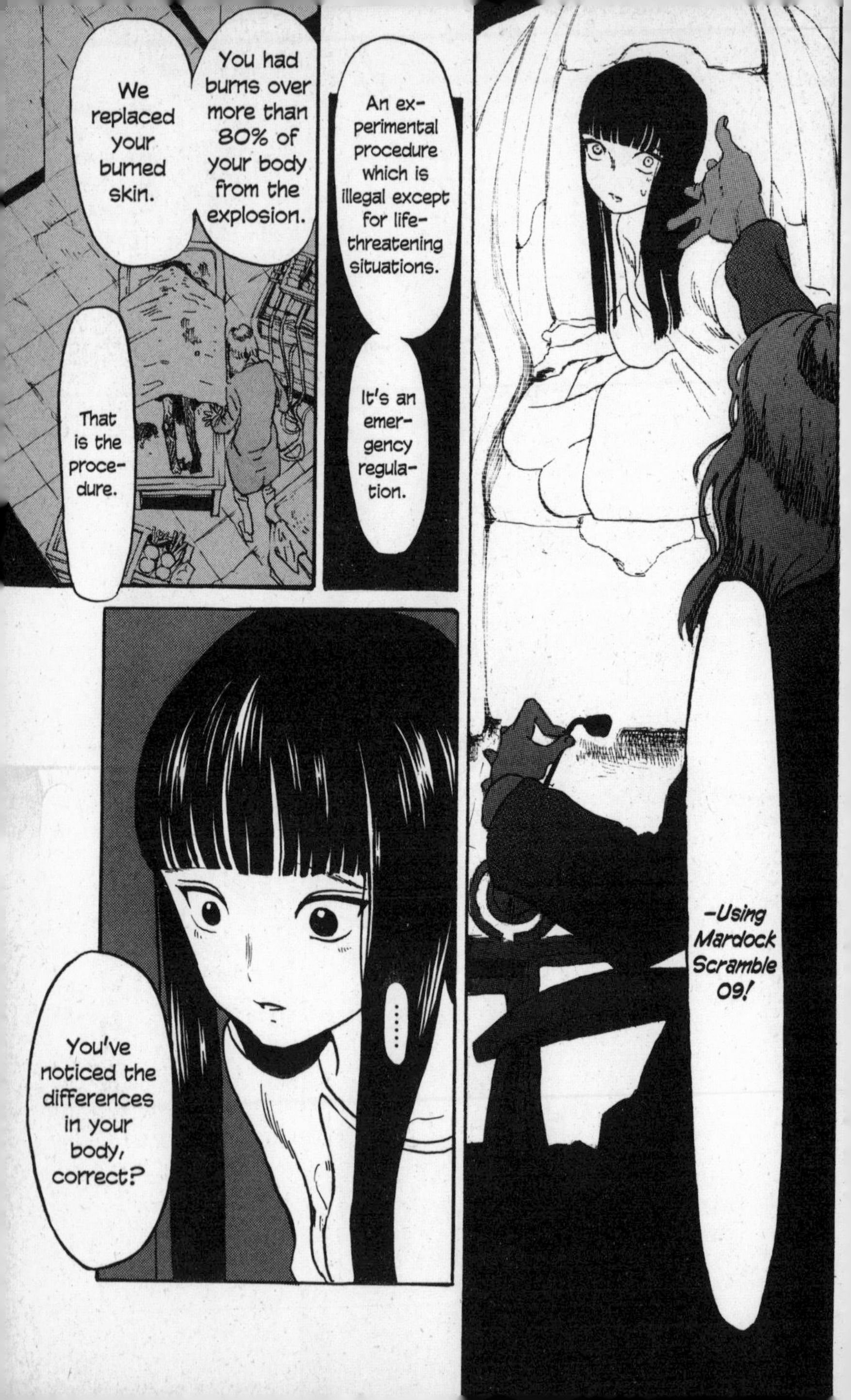
–Using Mardock Scramble 09!
An experimental procedure which is illegal except for life-threatening situations.
It's an emergency regulation.
You had burns over more than 80% of your body from the explosion.
We replaced your burned skin.
That is the procedure.
......
You've noticed the differences in your body, correct?

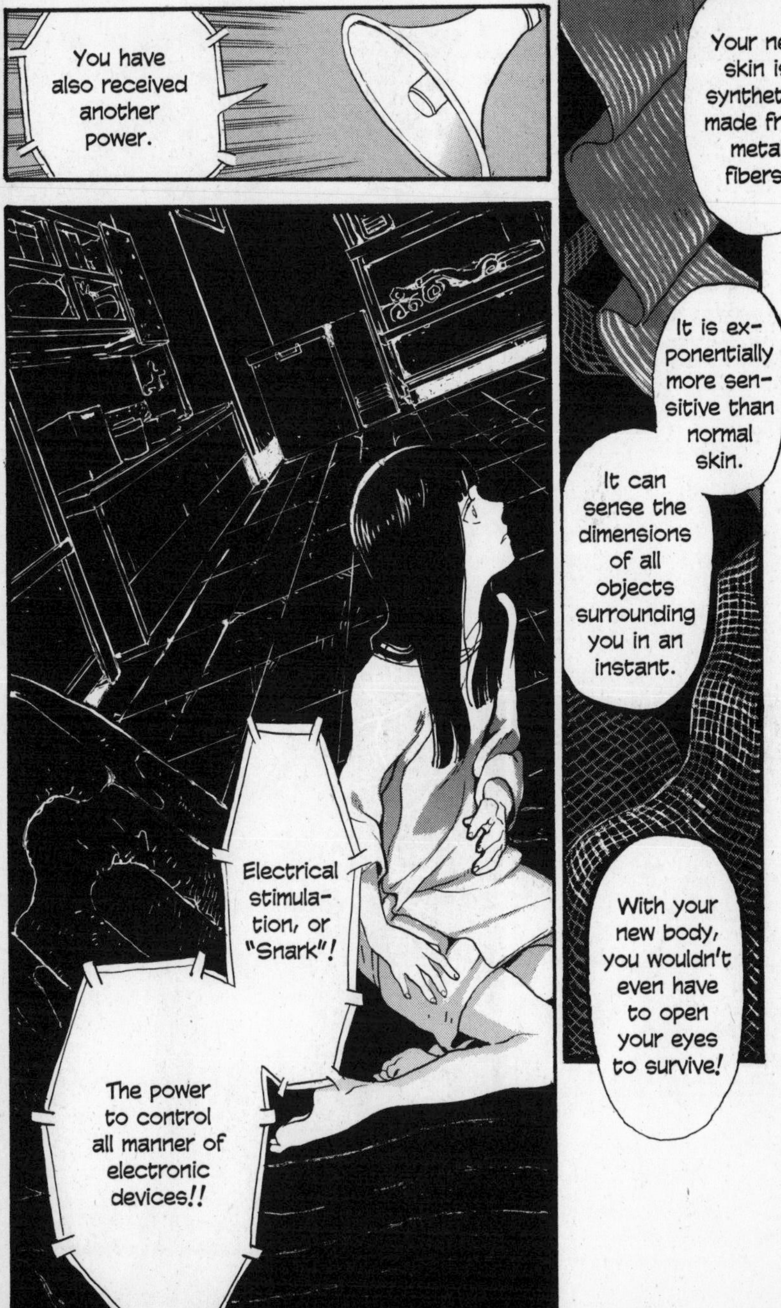
Your new skin is synthetic, made from metal fibers.
It is exponentially more sensitive than normal skin.
It can sense the dimensions of all objects surrounding you in an instant.
With your new body, you wouldn't even have to open your eyes to survive!
You have also received another power.
Electrical stimulation, or "Snark"!
The power to control all manner of electronic devices!!

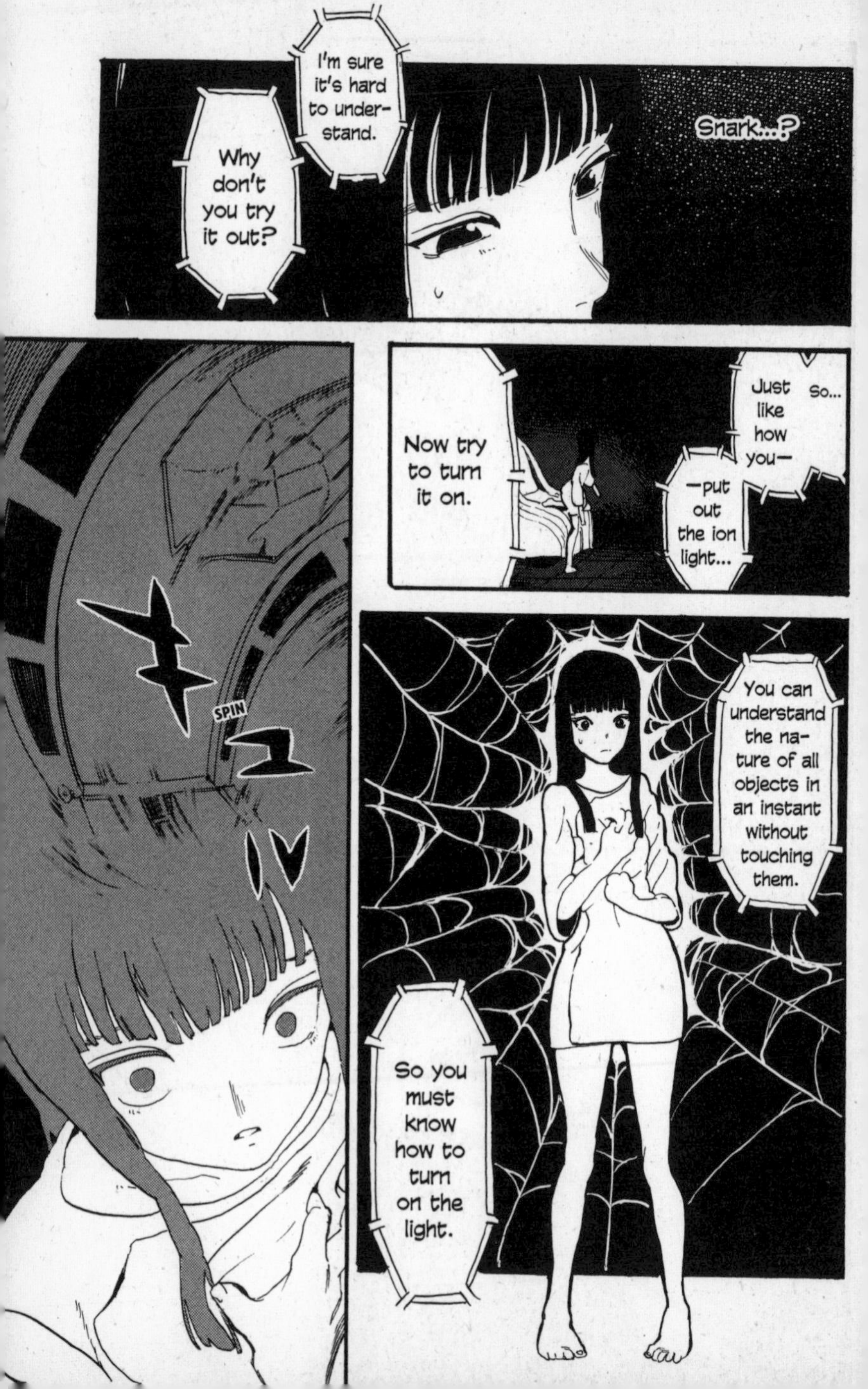
Snark...?
I'm sure it's hard to understand.
Why don't you try it out?
So...
Just like how you—
—put out the ion light...
Now try to turn it on.
You can understand the nature of all objects in an instant without touching them.
So you must know how to turn on the light.
SPIN

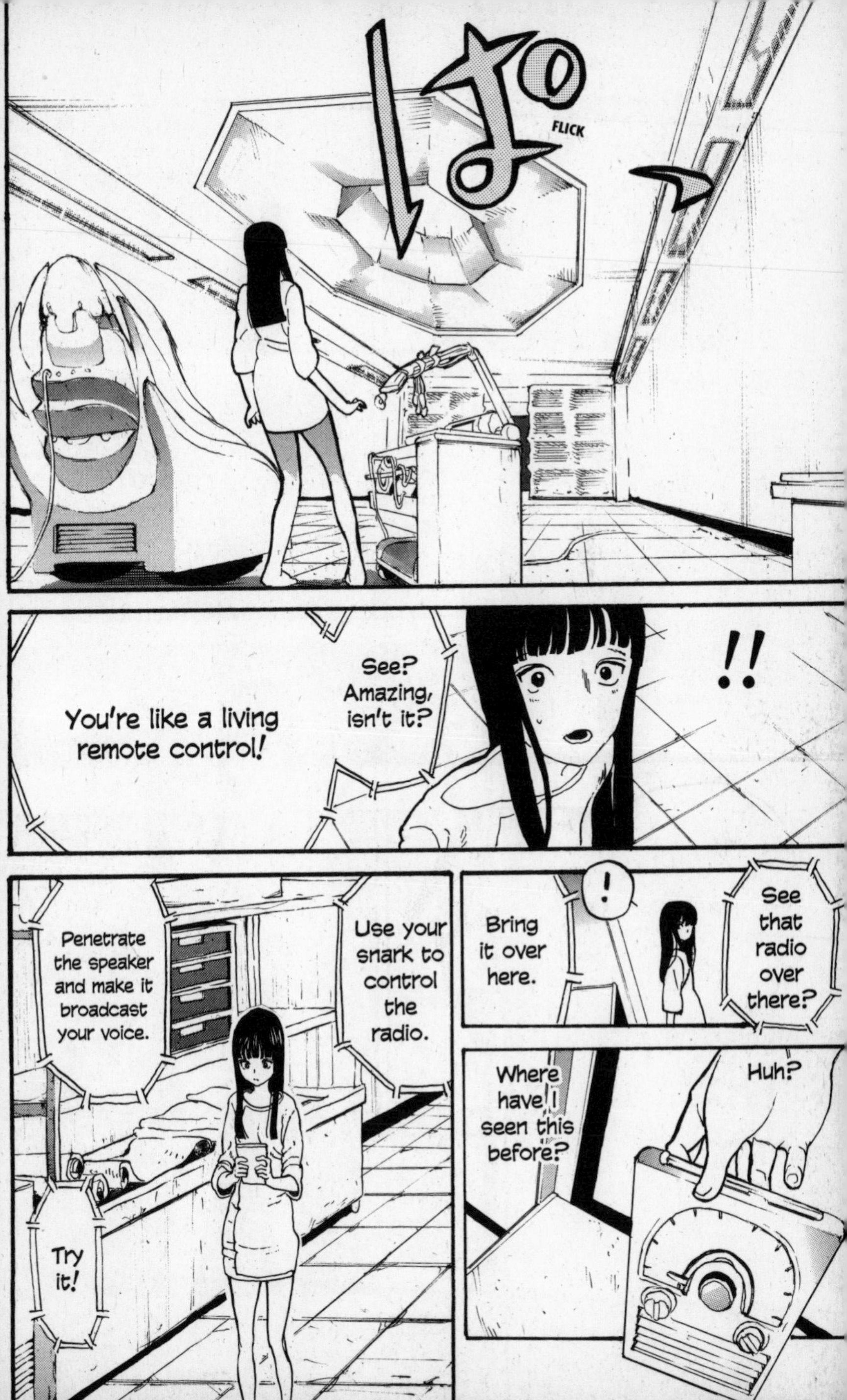
ぱ
FLICK
!!
See? Amazing, isn't it?
You're like a living remote control!
See that radio over there?
!
Bring it over here.
Huh?
Where have I seen this before?
Use your snark to control the radio.
Penetrate the speaker and make it broadcast your voice.
Try it!

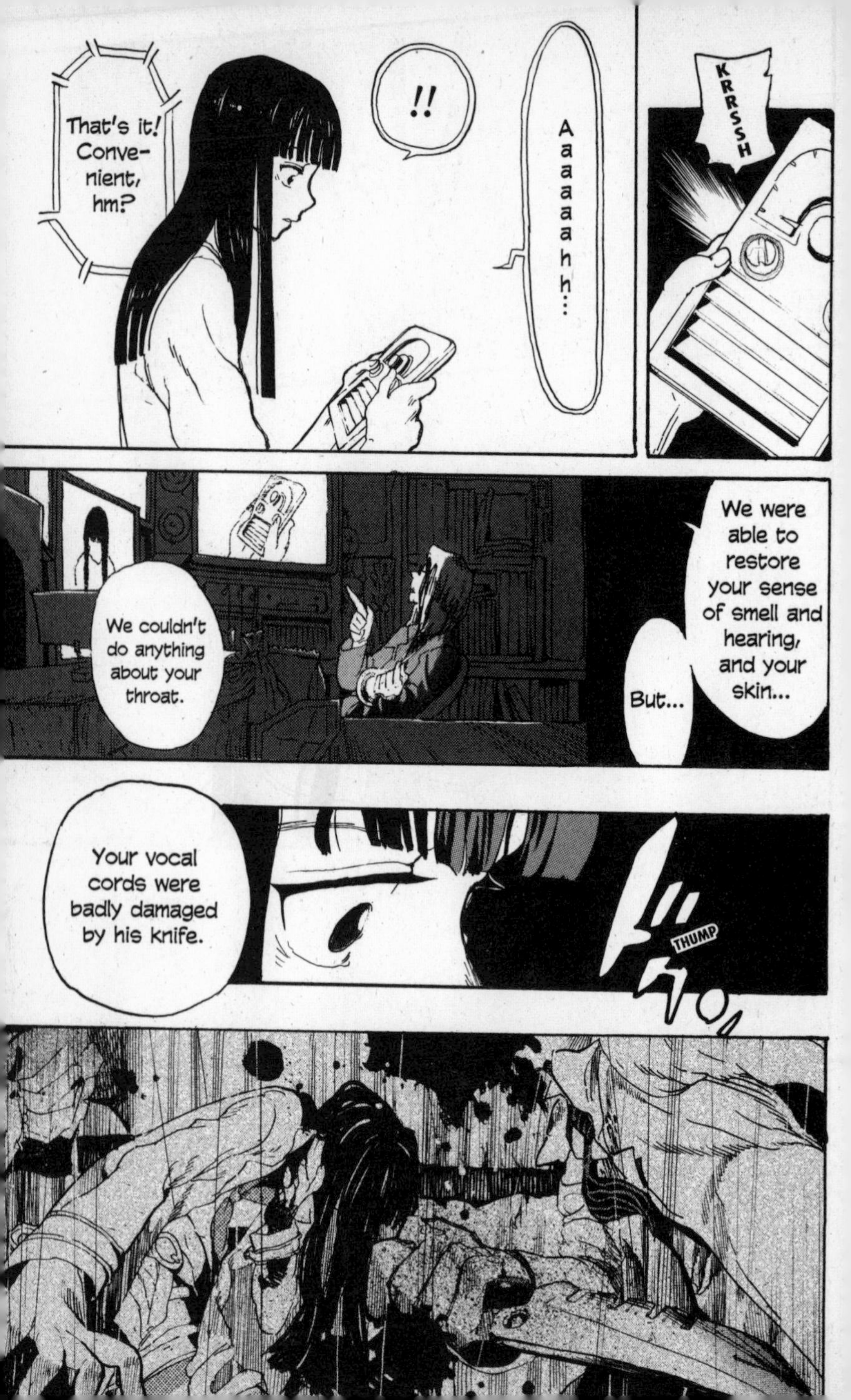
KRRSSH
Aaaaaahh...
!!
That's it! Conve-nient, hm?
We were able to restore your sense of smell and hearing, and your skin...
But...
We couldn't do anything about your throat.
THUMP
Your vocal cords were badly damaged by his knife.

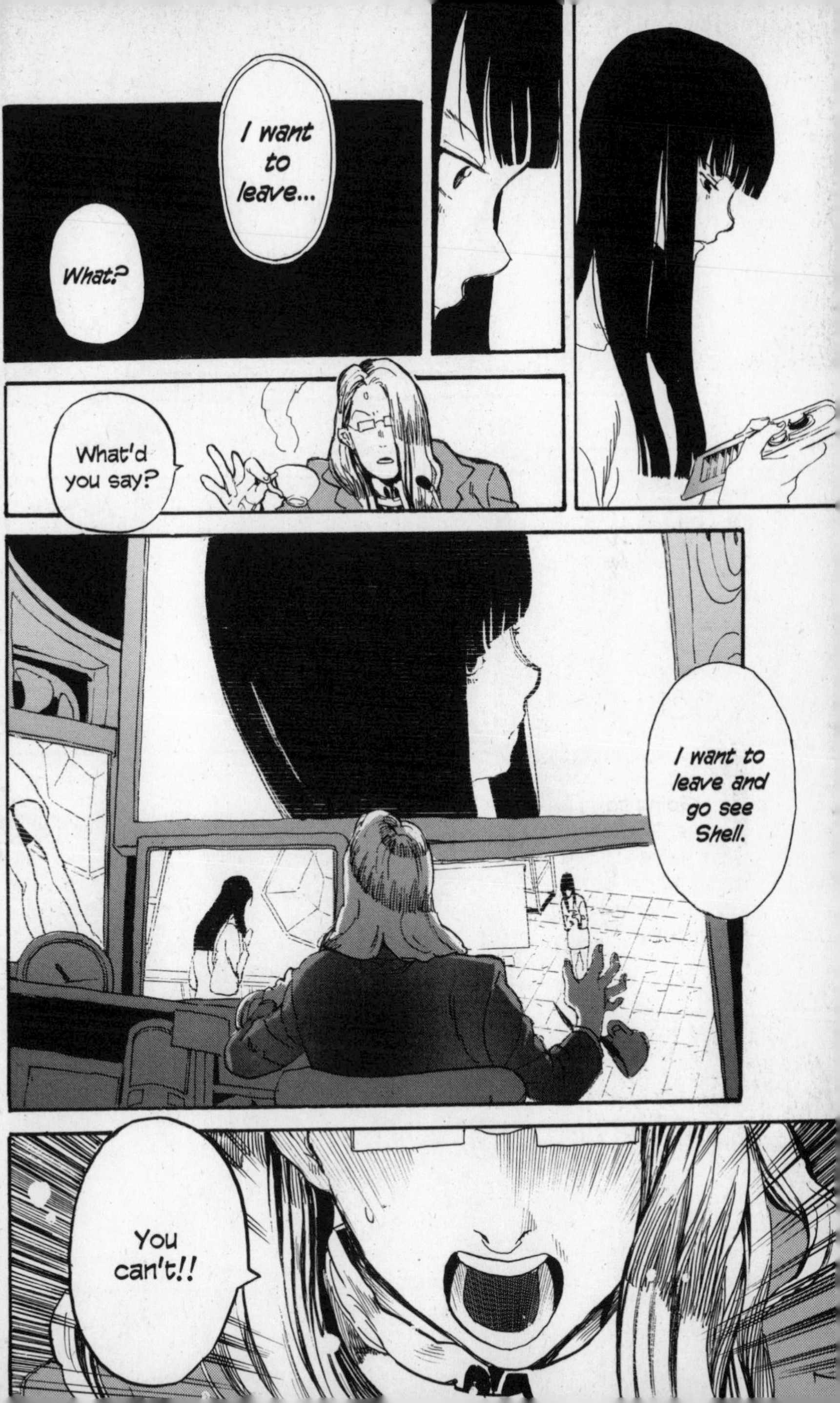
I want to leave...
What?
What'd you say?
I want to leave and go see Shell.
You can't!!

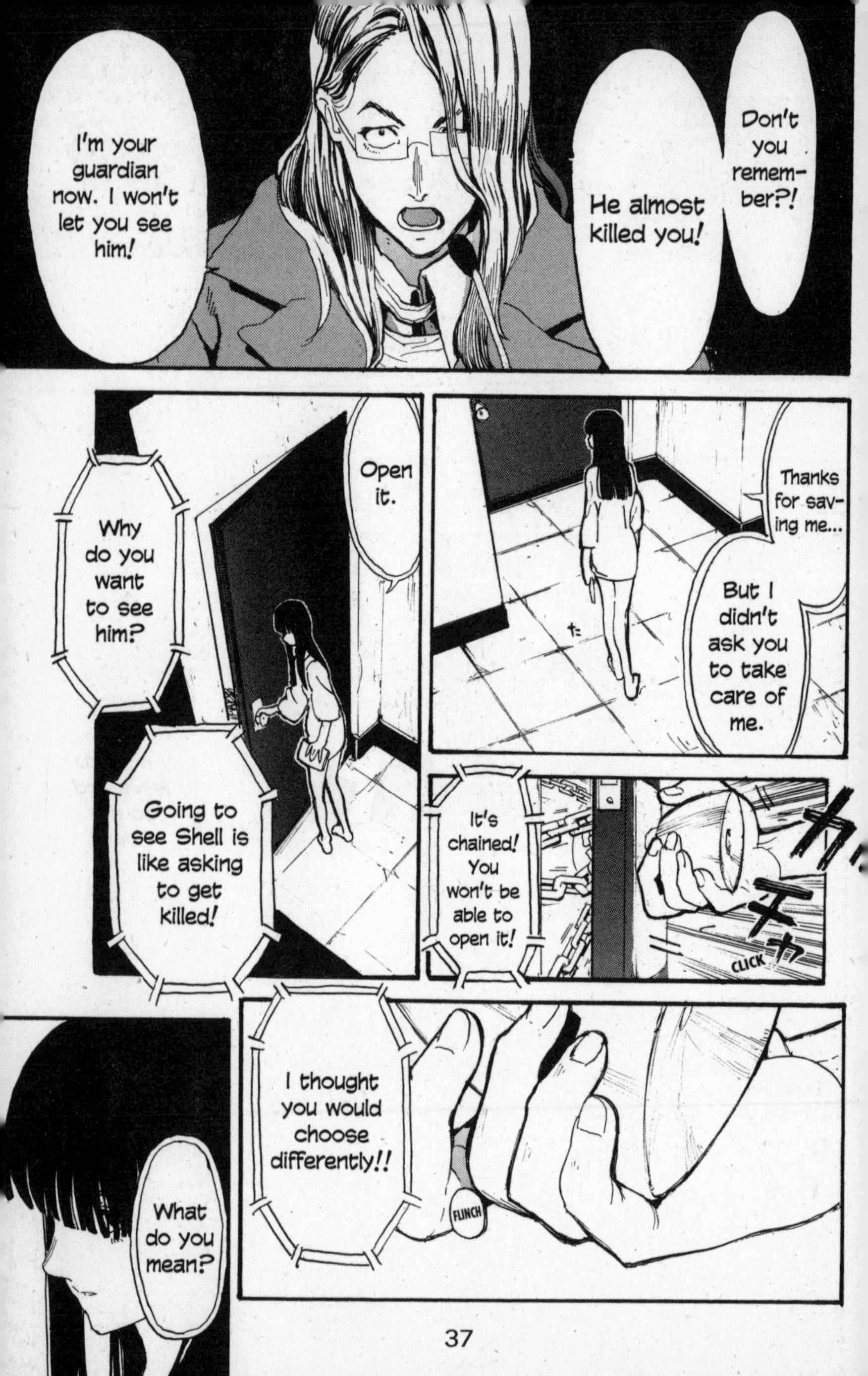
Don't you remember?!
He almost killed you!
I'm your guardian now. I won't let you see him!
Thanks for saving me...
But I didn't ask you to take care of me.
CLICK
It's chained! You won't be able to open it!
Open it.
Why do you want to see him?
Going to see Shell is like asking to get killed!
FLINCH
I thought you would choose differently!!
What do you mean?

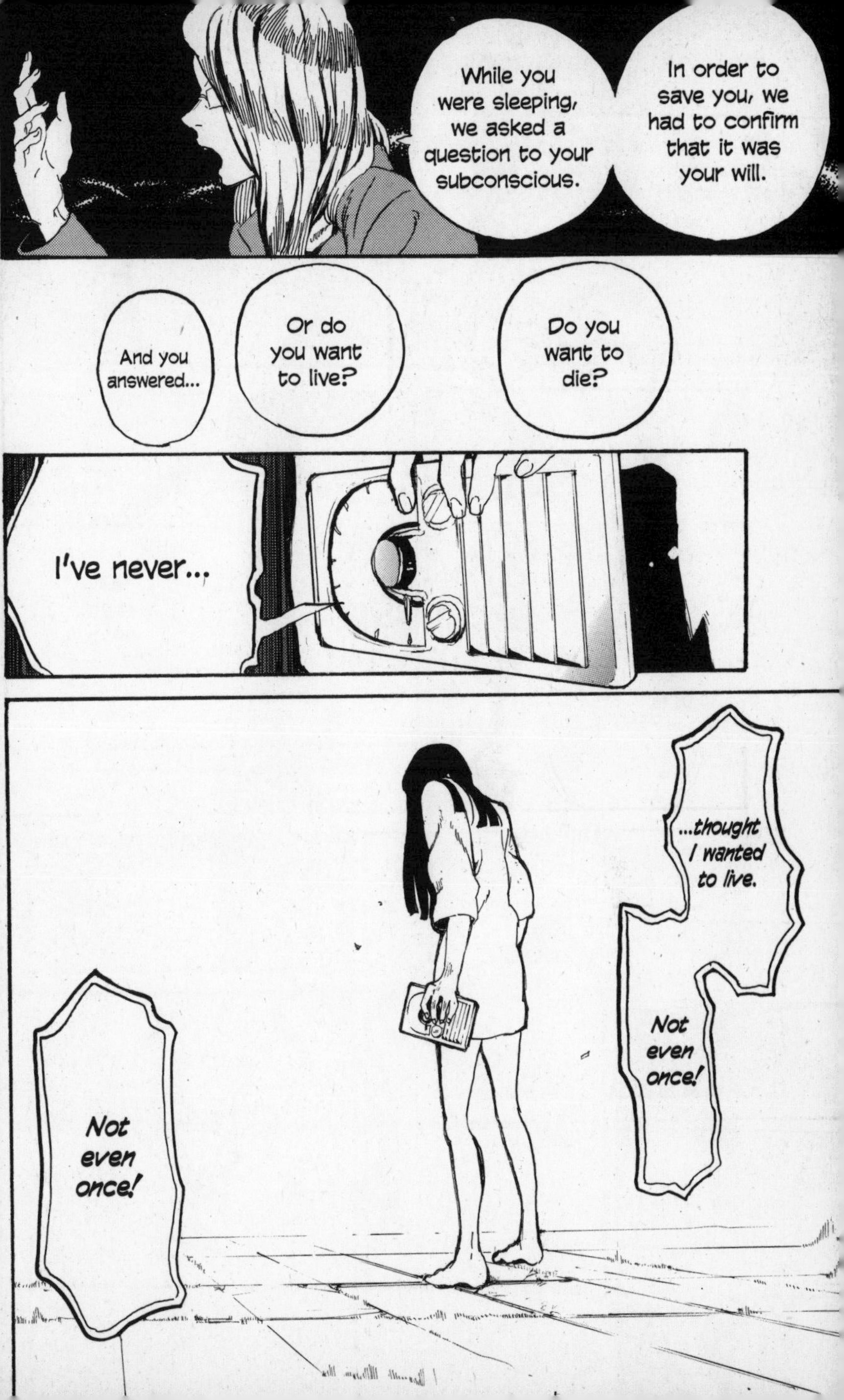
In order to save you, we had to confirm that it was your will.
While you were sleeping, we asked a question to your subconscious.
Do you want to die?
Or do you want to live?
And you answered...
I've never...
...thought I wanted to live.
Not even once!
Not even once!

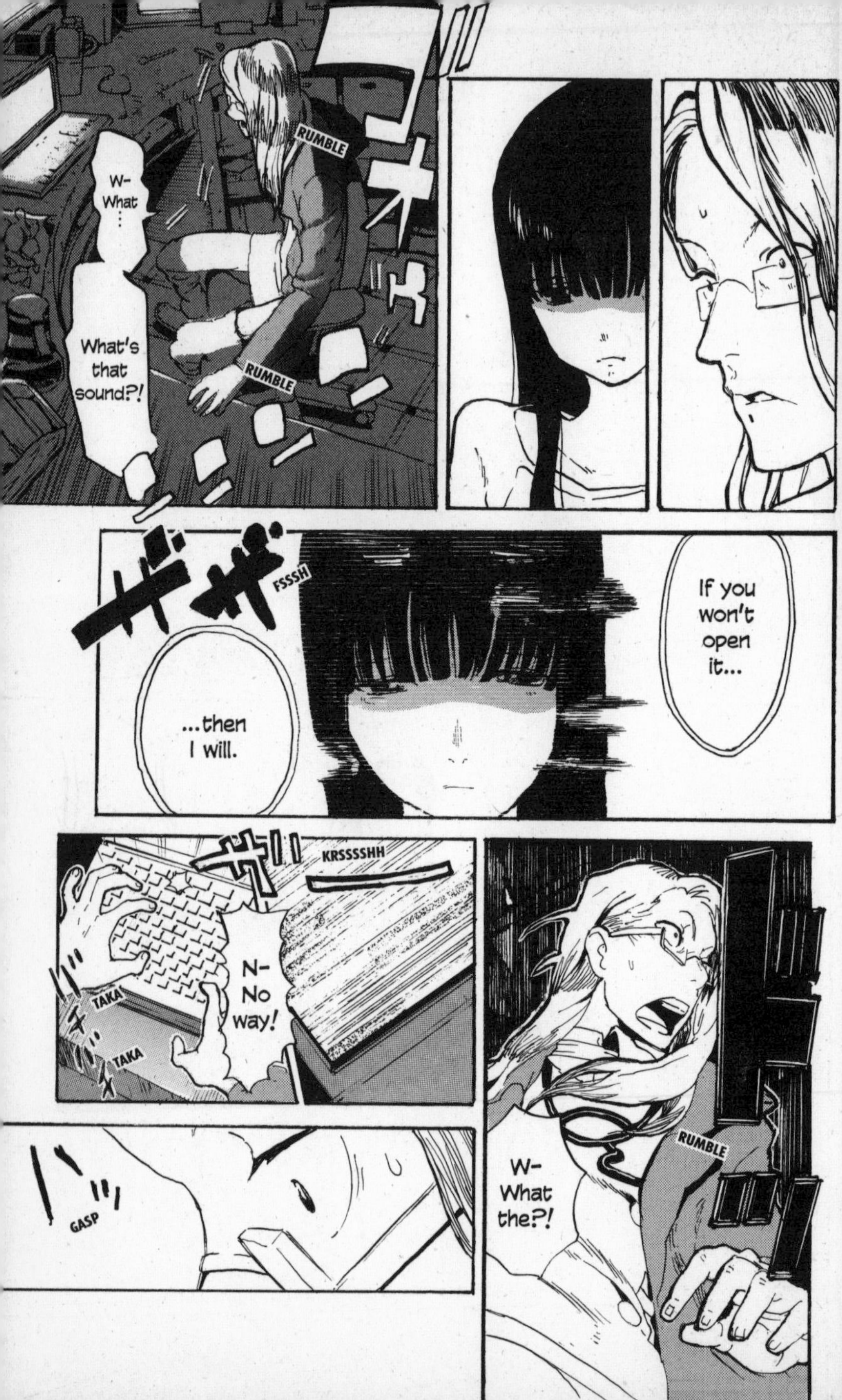
RUMBLE
W- What ...
What's that sound?!
RUMBLE
If you won't open it...
...then I will.
FSSSH
RUMBLE
W- What the?!
KRSSSSHH
N- No way!
TAKA
TAKA
GASP

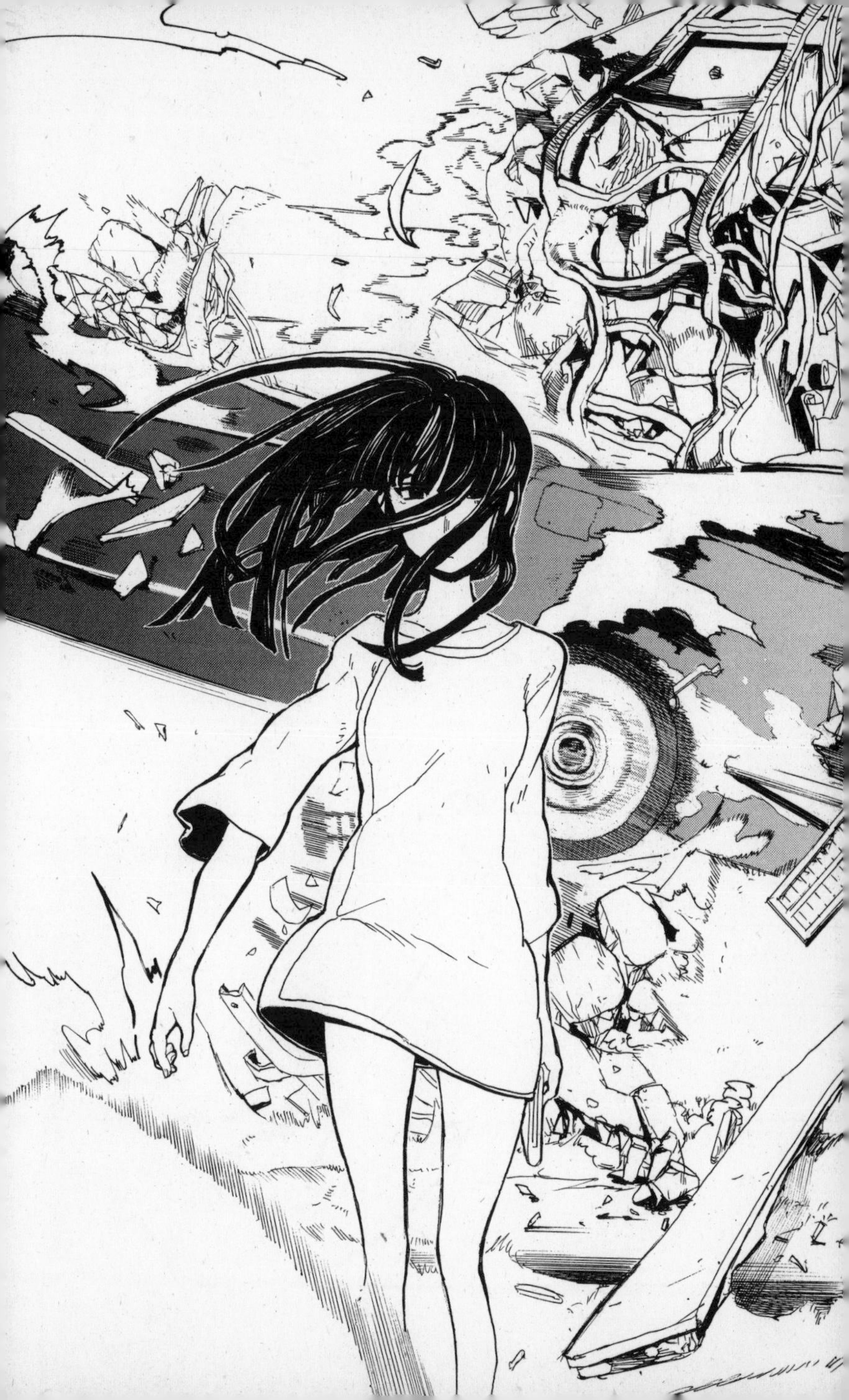

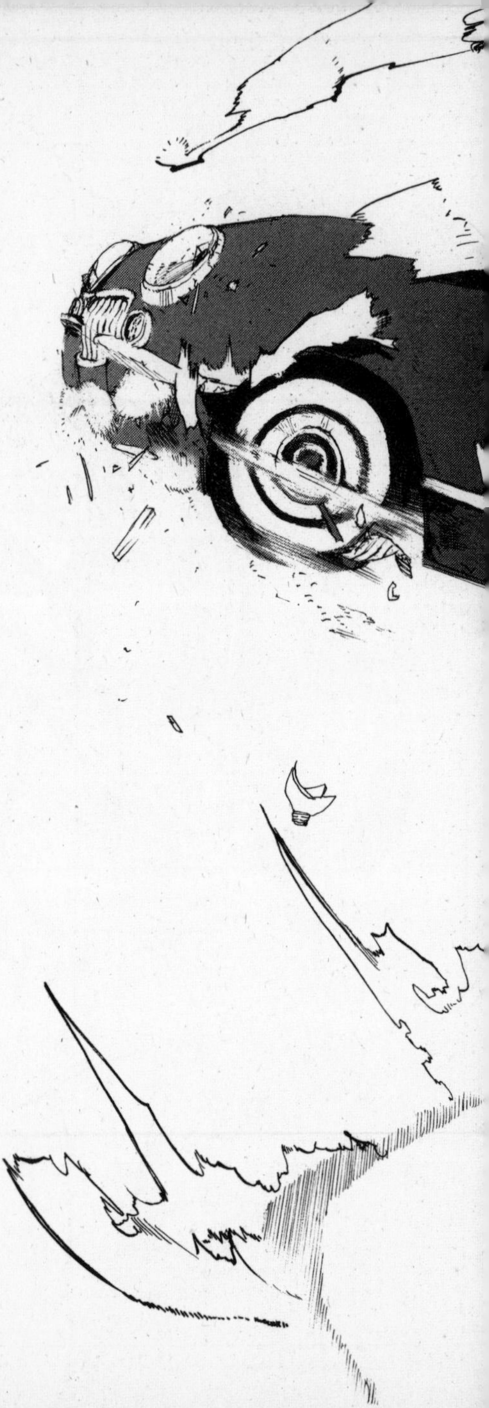

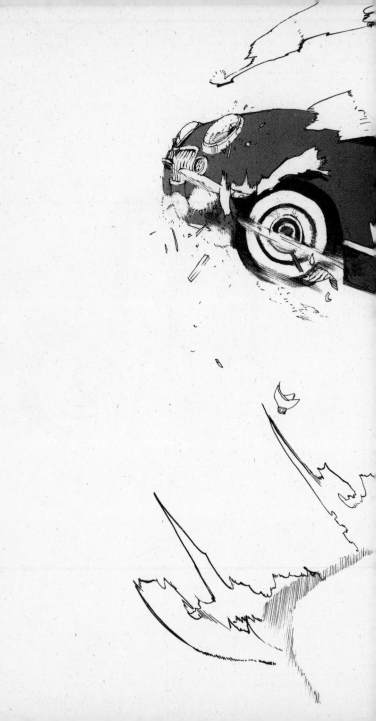

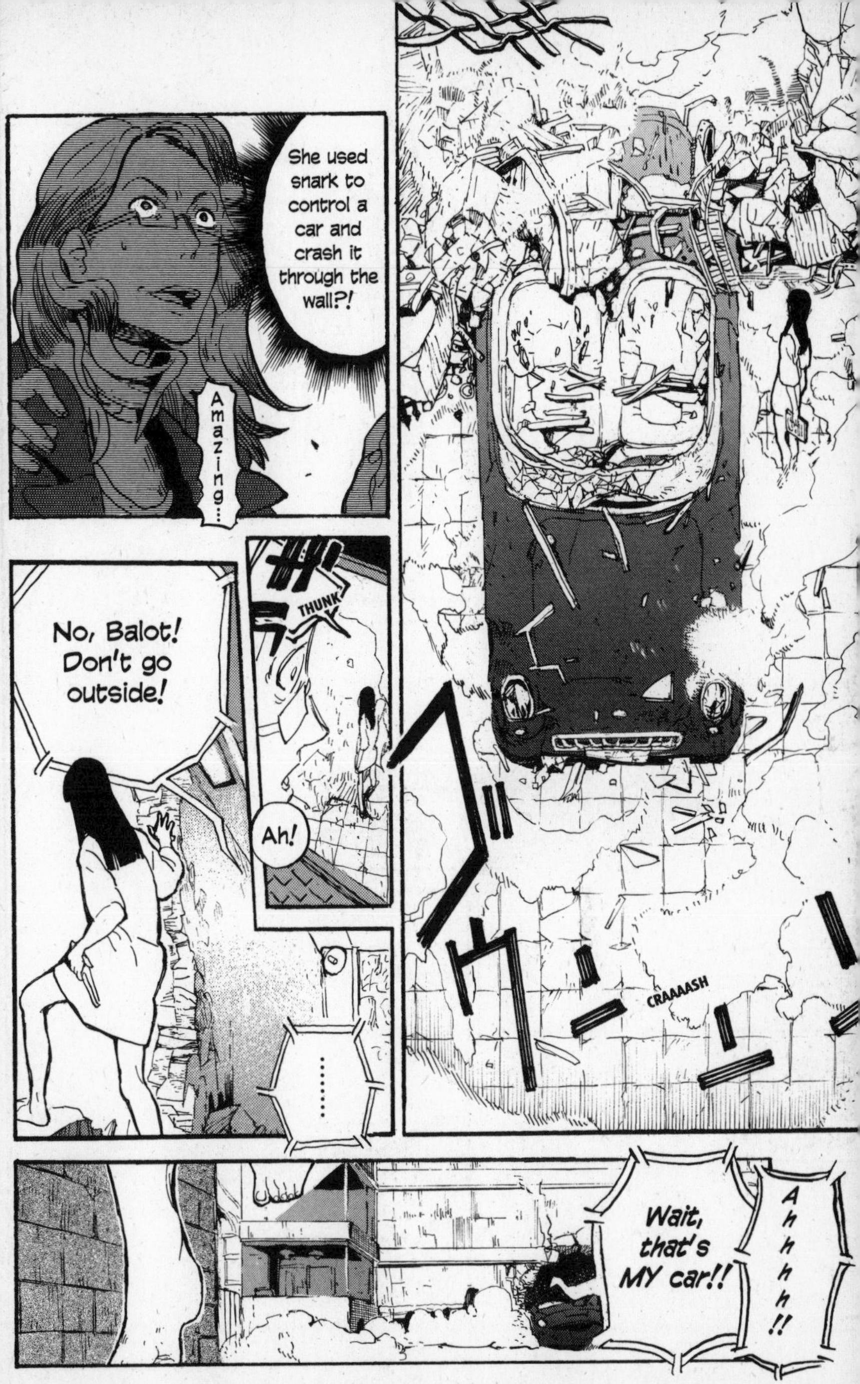
CRAAAASH
She used snark to control a car and crash it through the wall?!
Amazing...
THUNK
Ah!
No, Balot! Don't go outside!
......
Ahhhh!!
Wait, that's MY car!!

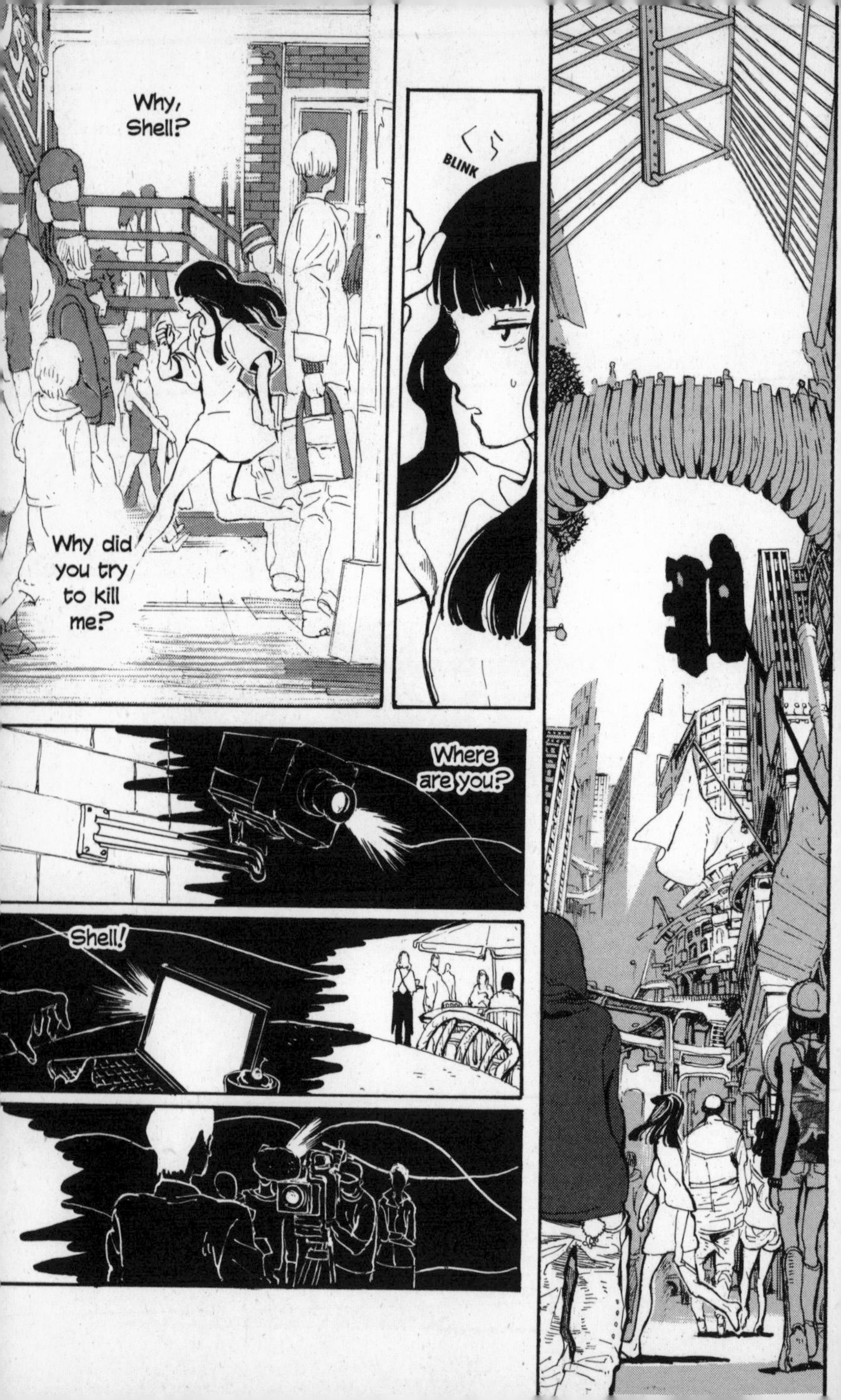
BLINK
Why, Shell?
Why did you try to kill me?
Where are you?
Shell!

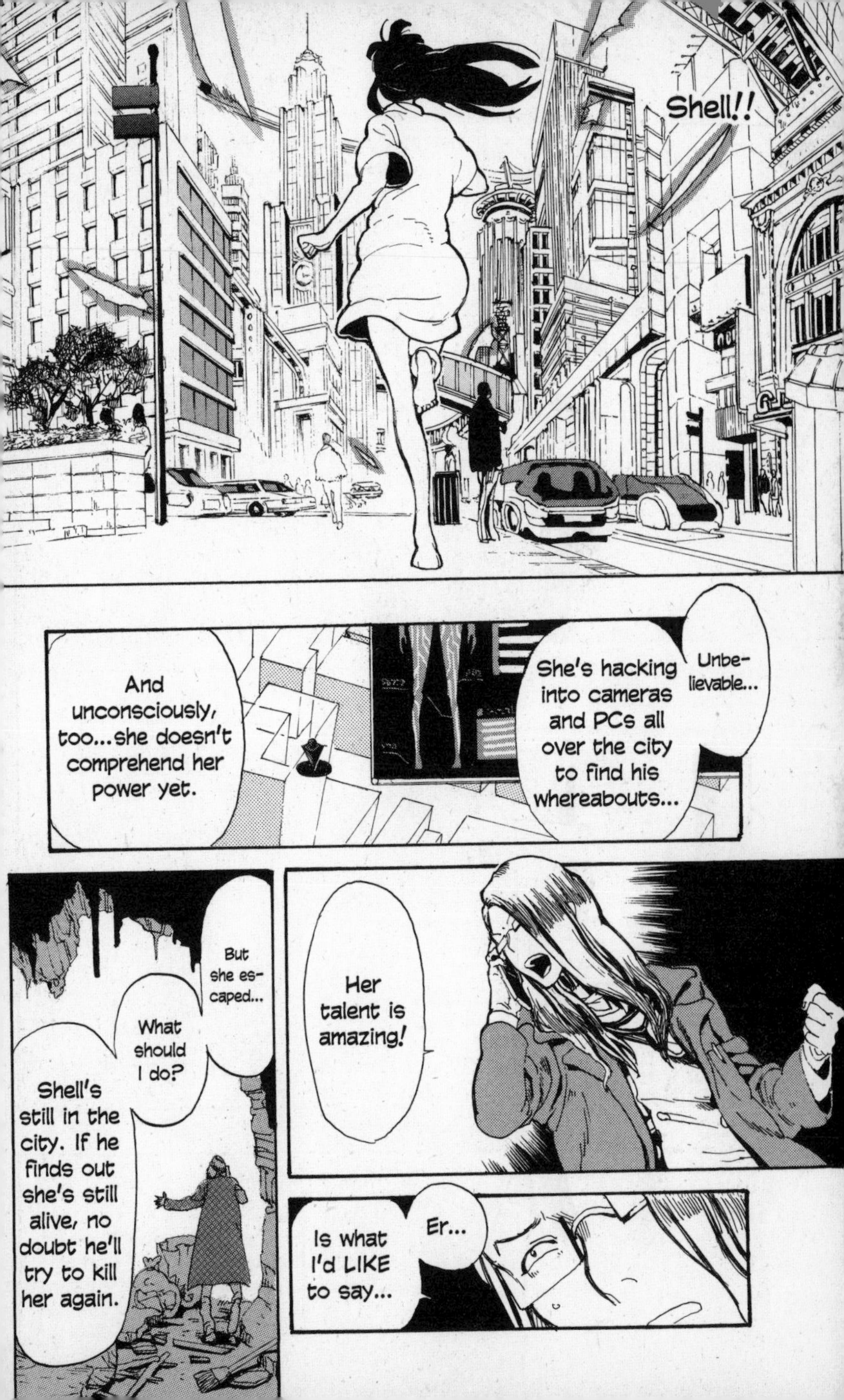
Shell!!
Unbe-lievable...
She's hacking into cameras and PCs all over the city to find his whereabouts...
And unconsciously, too...she doesn't comprehend her power yet.
Her talent is amazing!
Er...
Is what I'd LIKE to say...
But she es-caped...
What should I do?
Shell's still in the city. If he finds out she's still alive, no doubt he'll try to kill her again.

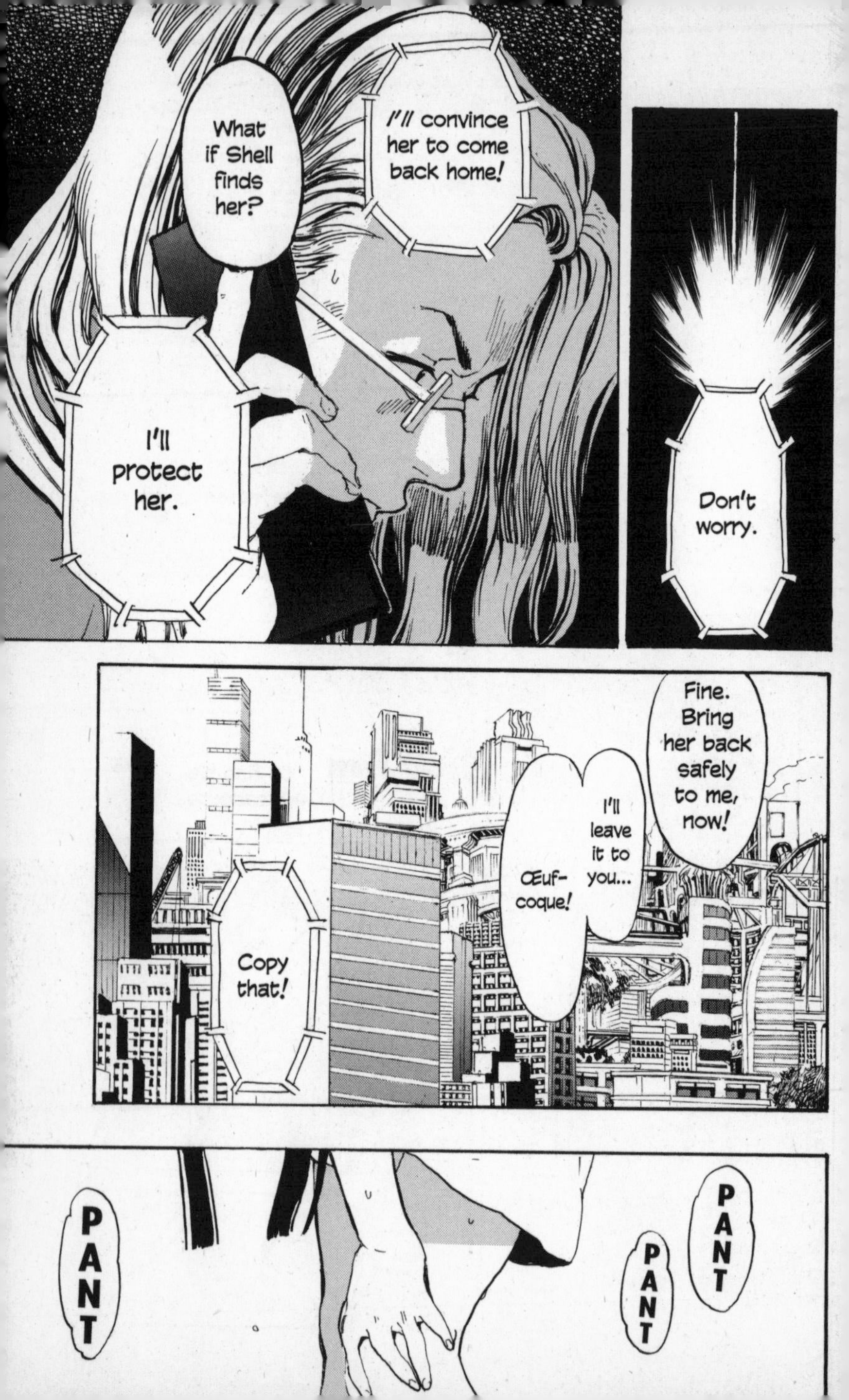
Don't worry.
I'll convince her to come back home!
What if Shell finds her?
I'll protect her.
Fine. Bring her back safely to me, now!
I'll leave it to you...
Œuf-coque!
Copy that!
PANT
PANT
PANT

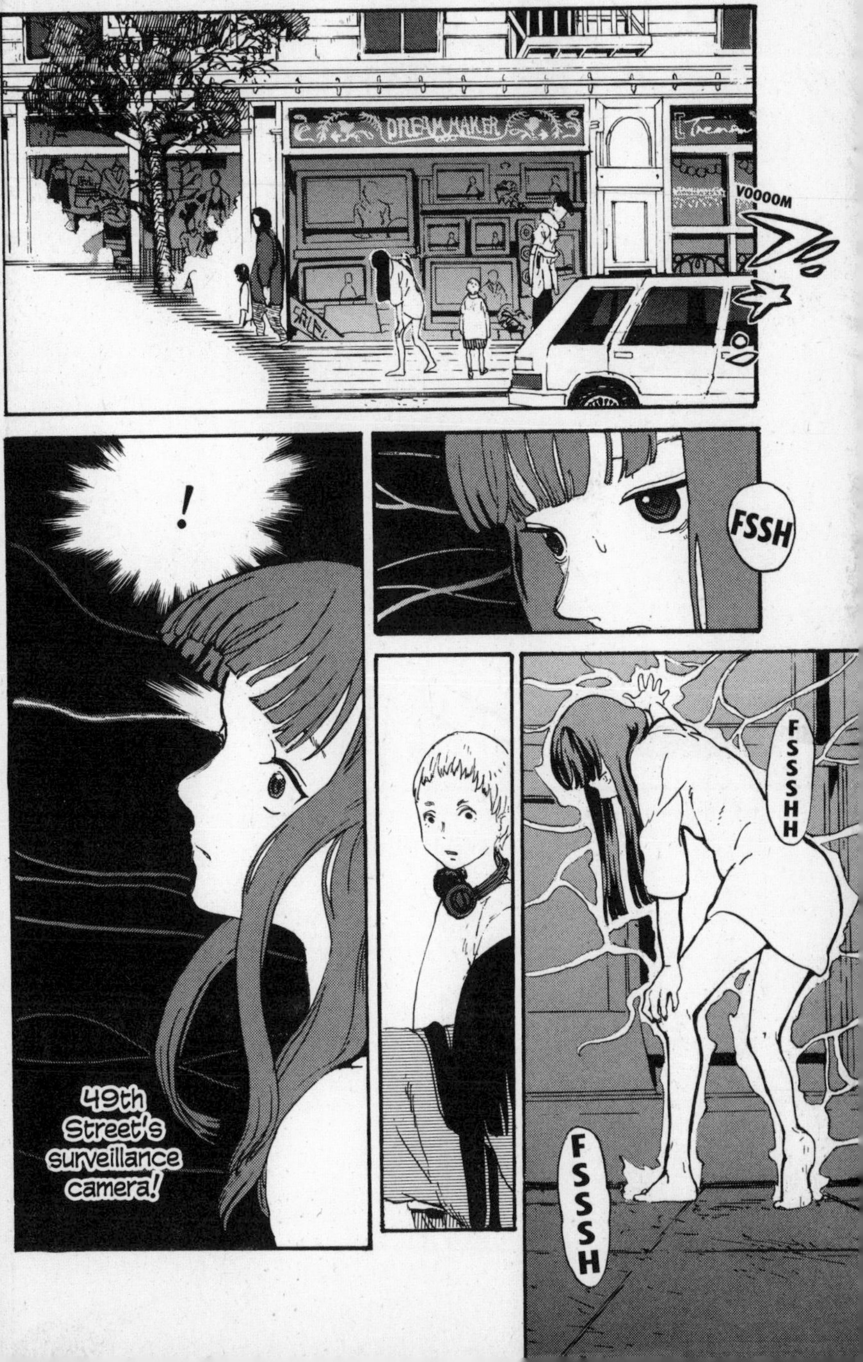
DREAMMAKER
VOOOOM
FSSH
FSSSHH
FSSSH
!
49th Street's surveillance camera!

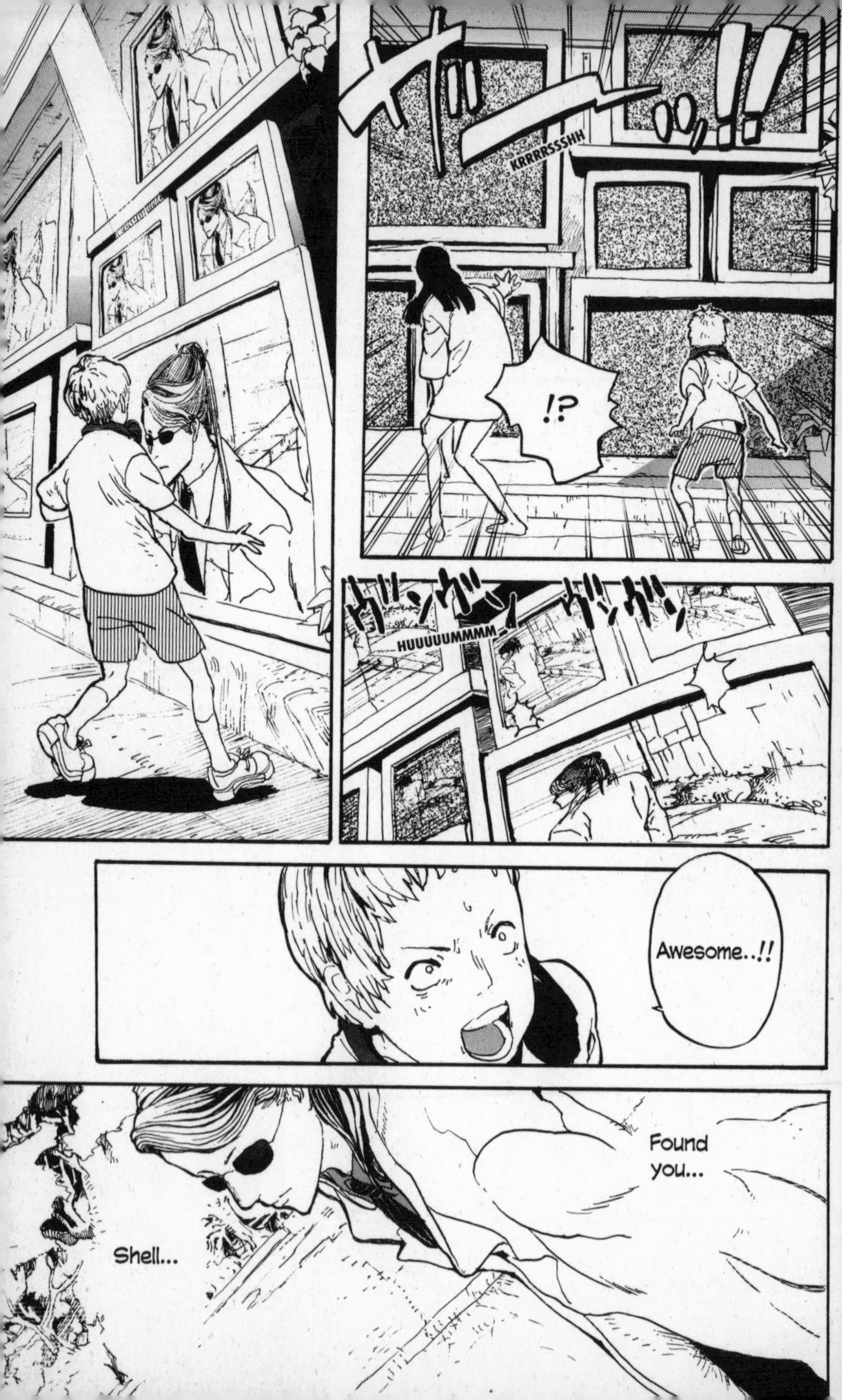
KRRRSSSHH
!?
HUUUUMMMM
Awesome..!!
Found you...
Shell...

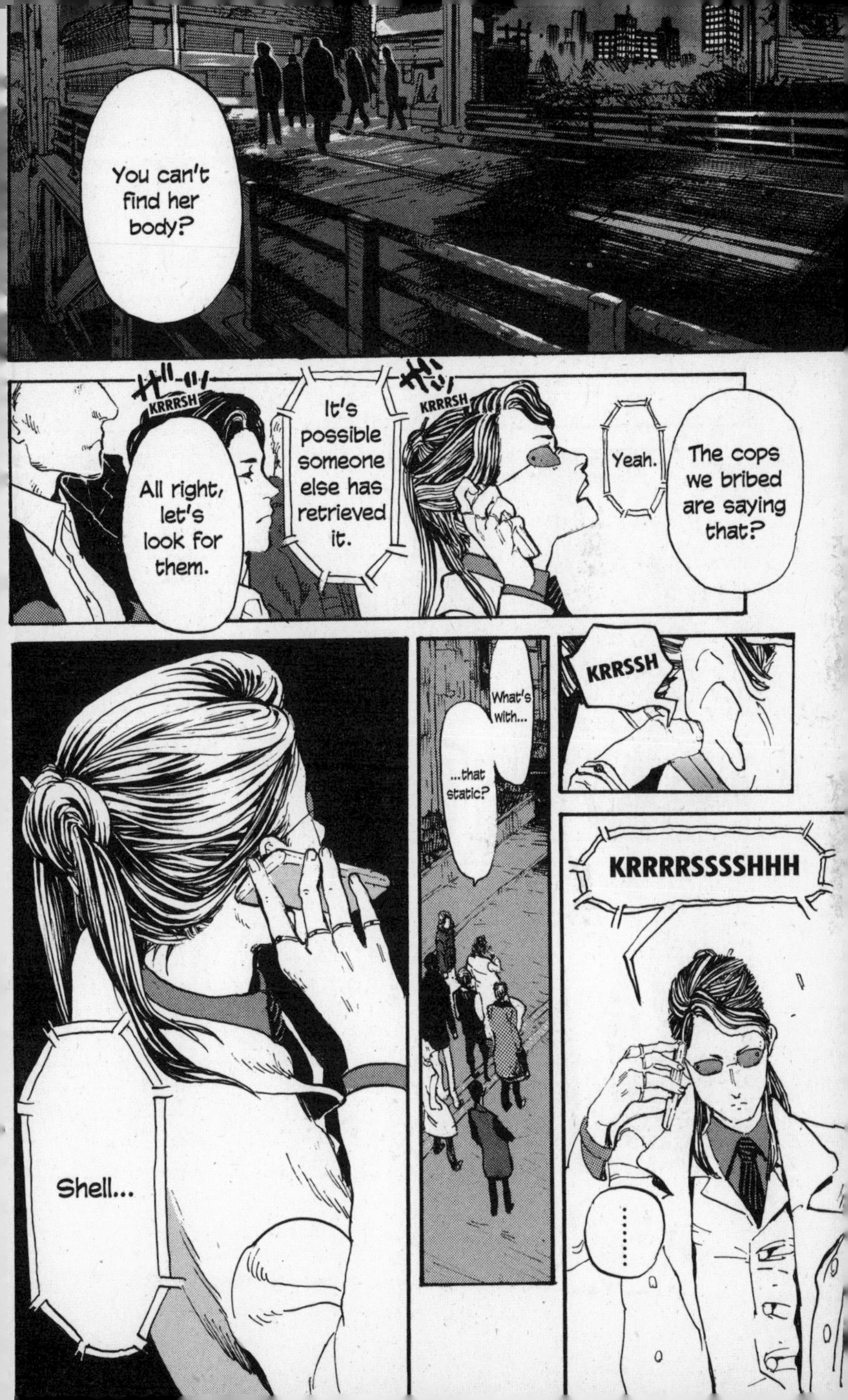
You can't find her body?
The cops we bribed are saying that?
Yeah.
KRRRSH
It's possible someone else has retrieved it.
KRRRSH
All right, let's look for them.
KRRSH
KRRRRSSSSHHH
......
What's with...
...that static?
Shell...

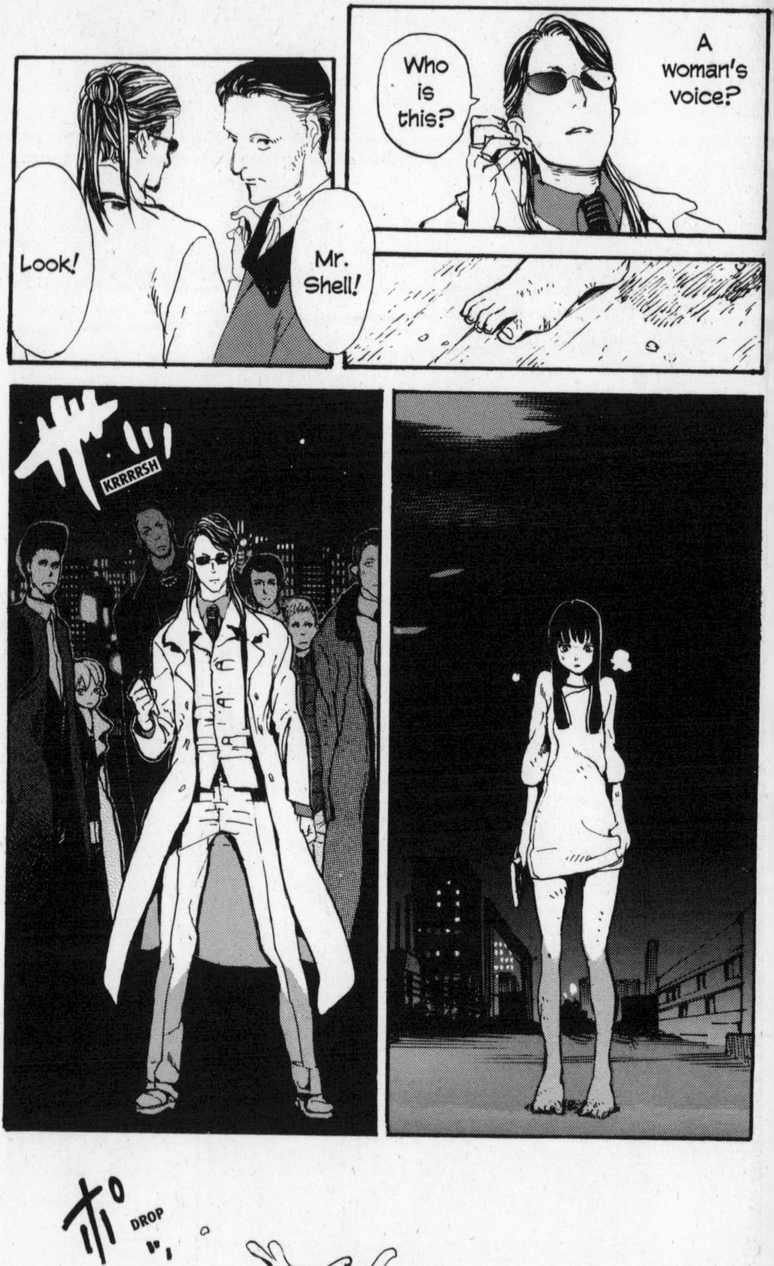
A woman's voice?
Who is this?
Mr. Shell!
Look!
KRRRRSH
DROP

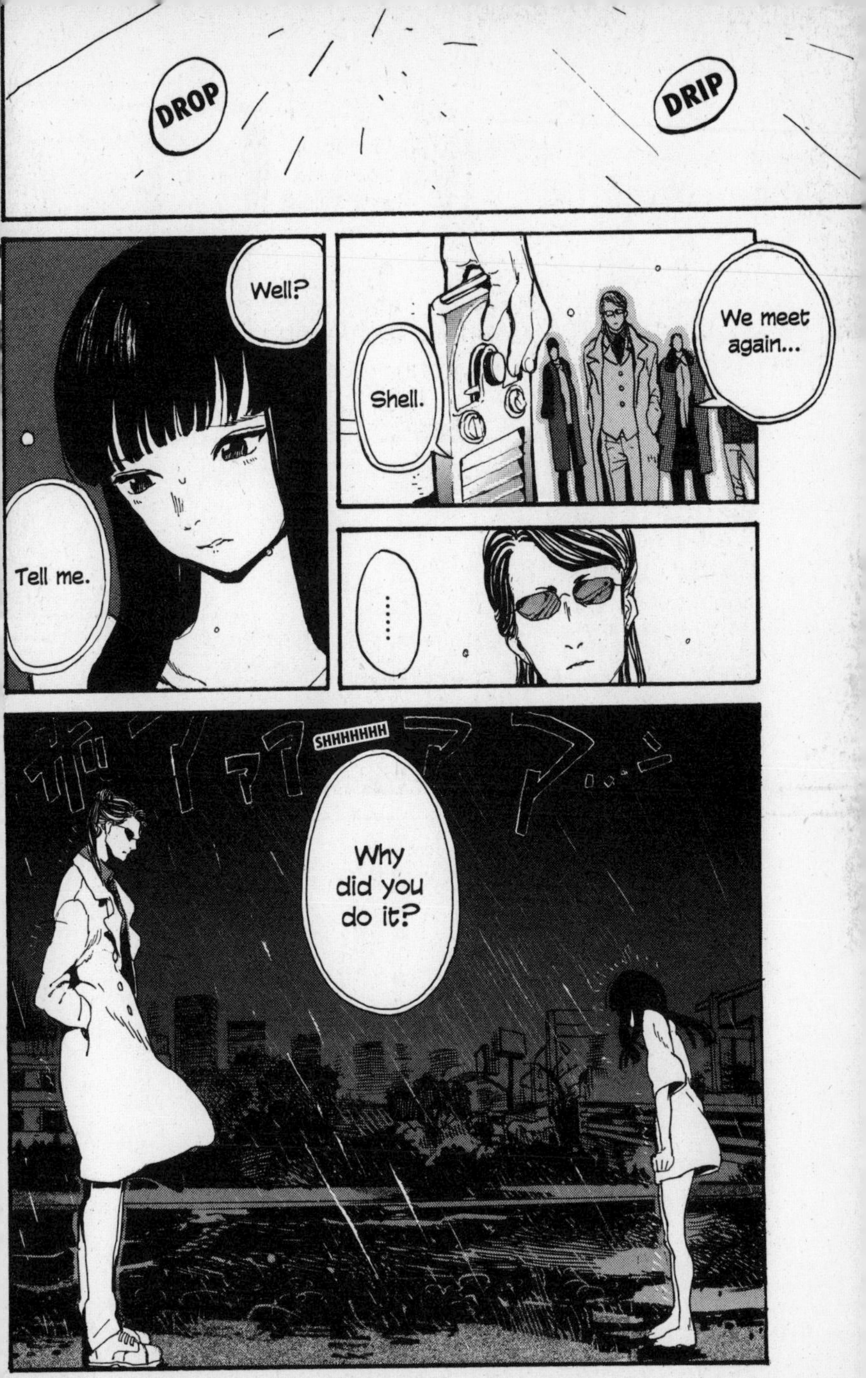
DRIP
DROP
We meet again...
Shell.
......
Well?
Tell me.
SHHHHHHH
Why did you do it?

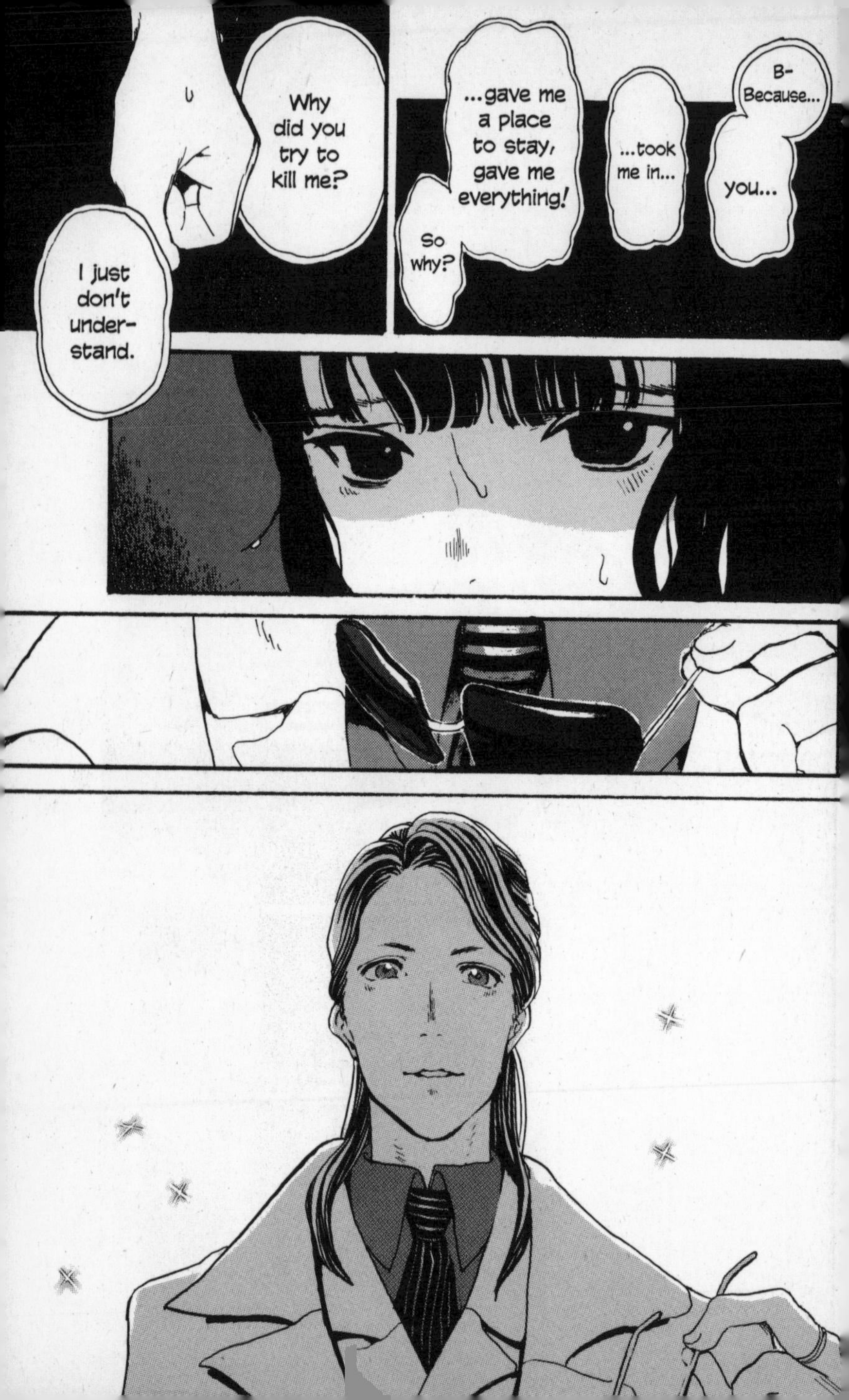
B-Because...
you...
...took me in...
...gave me a place to stay, gave me everything!
So why?
Why did you try to kill me?
I just don't under-stand.

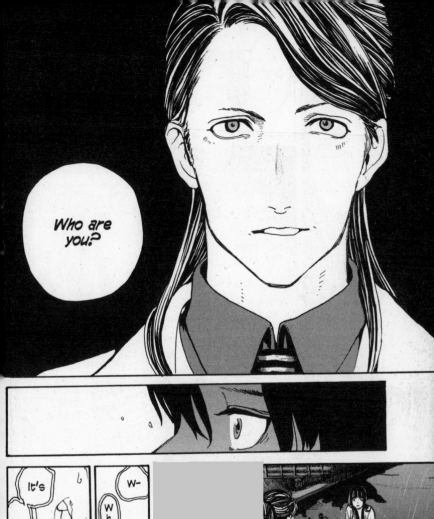

Who are you?

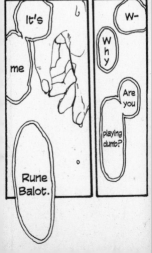

It's me

Rune Balot.

W- Why

Are you playing dumb?

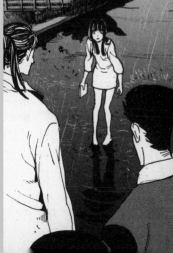

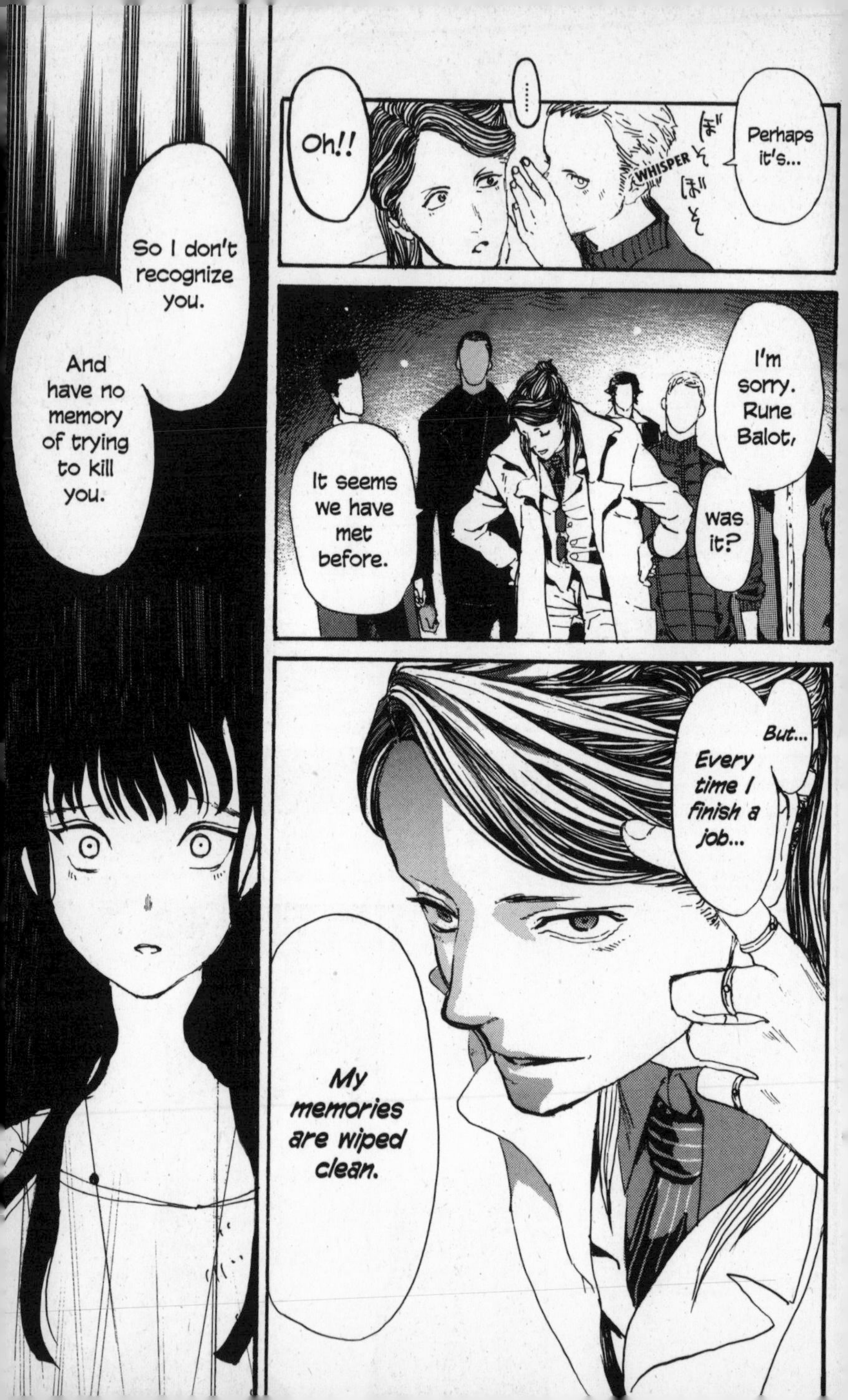
Perhaps it's...
WHISPER
ぼそぼそ
......
Oh!!
I'm sorry. Rune Balot,
was it?
It seems we have met before.
But... Every time I finish a job...
My memories are wiped clean.
So I don't recognize you.
And have no memory of trying to kill you.

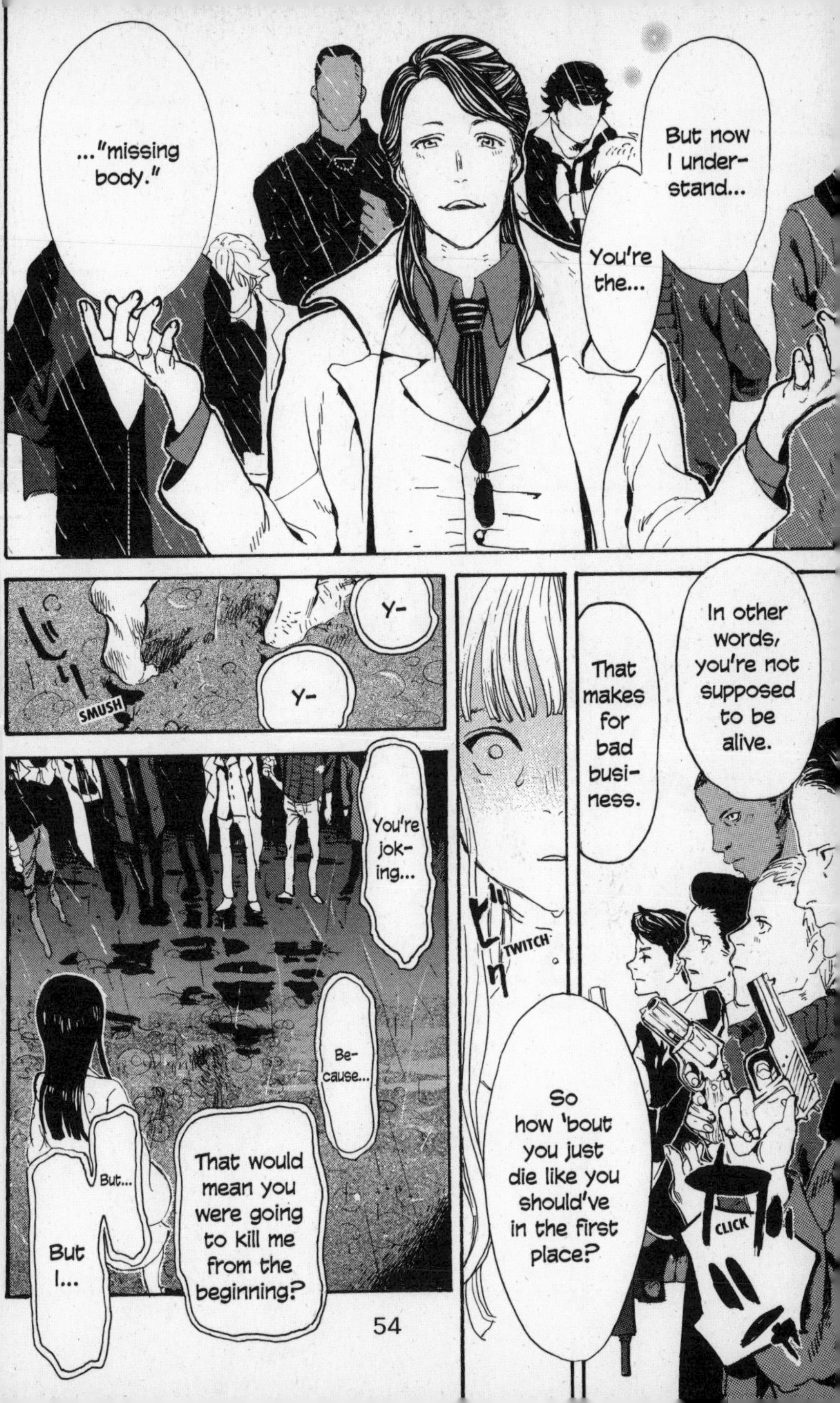
But now I under-stand...
You're the...
..."missing body."
In other words, you're not supposed to be alive.
That makes for bad busi-ness.
So how 'bout you just die like you should've in the first place?
CLICK
TWITCH
Y-
Y-
SMUSH
You're jok-ing...
Be-cause...
That would mean you were going to kill me from the beginning?
But...
But I...

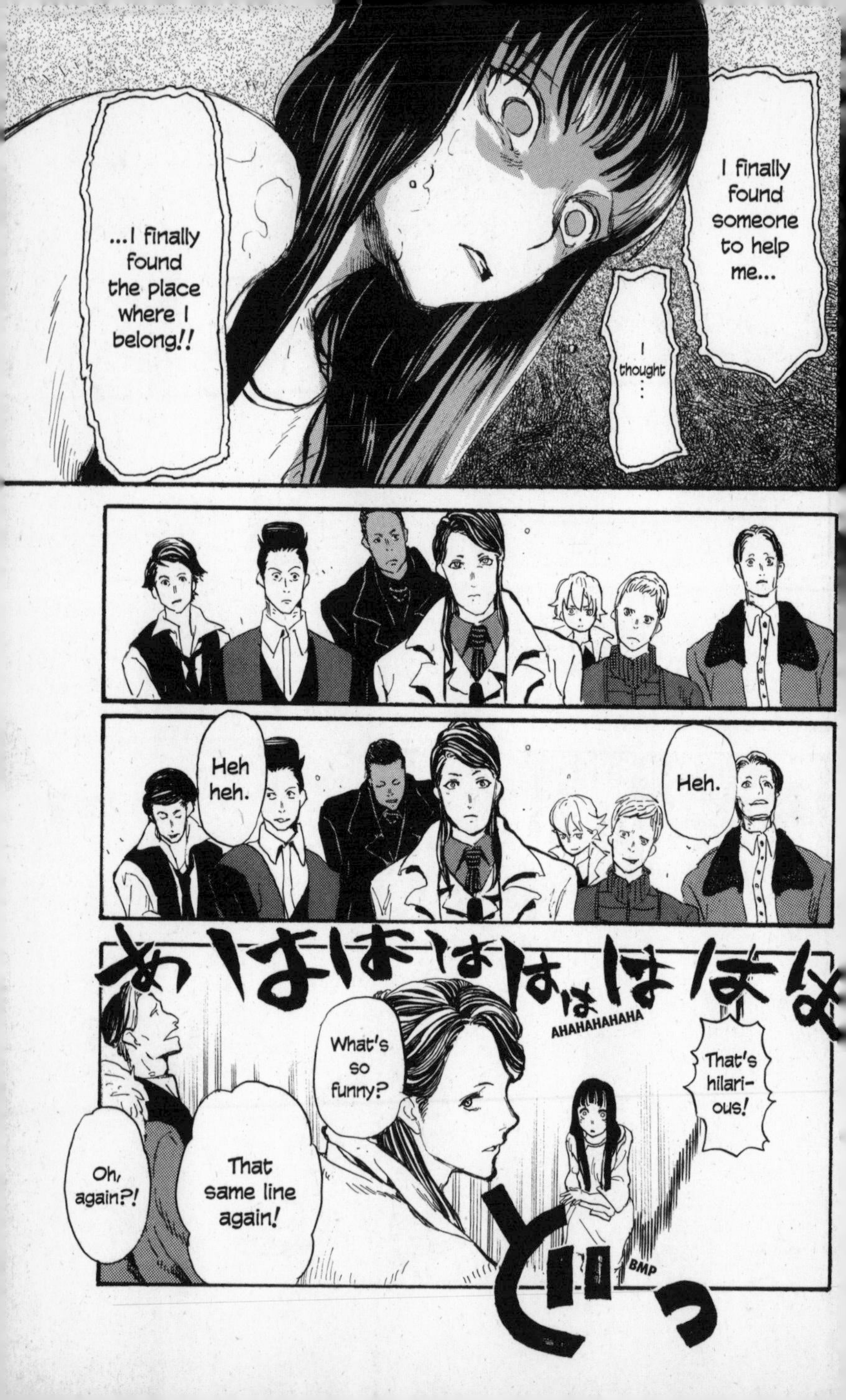
I finally found someone to help me...
I thought...
...I finally found the place where I belong!!
Heh.
Heh heh.
AHAHAHAHAHA
That's hilari-ous!
What's so funny?
That same line again!
Oh, again?!
BMP

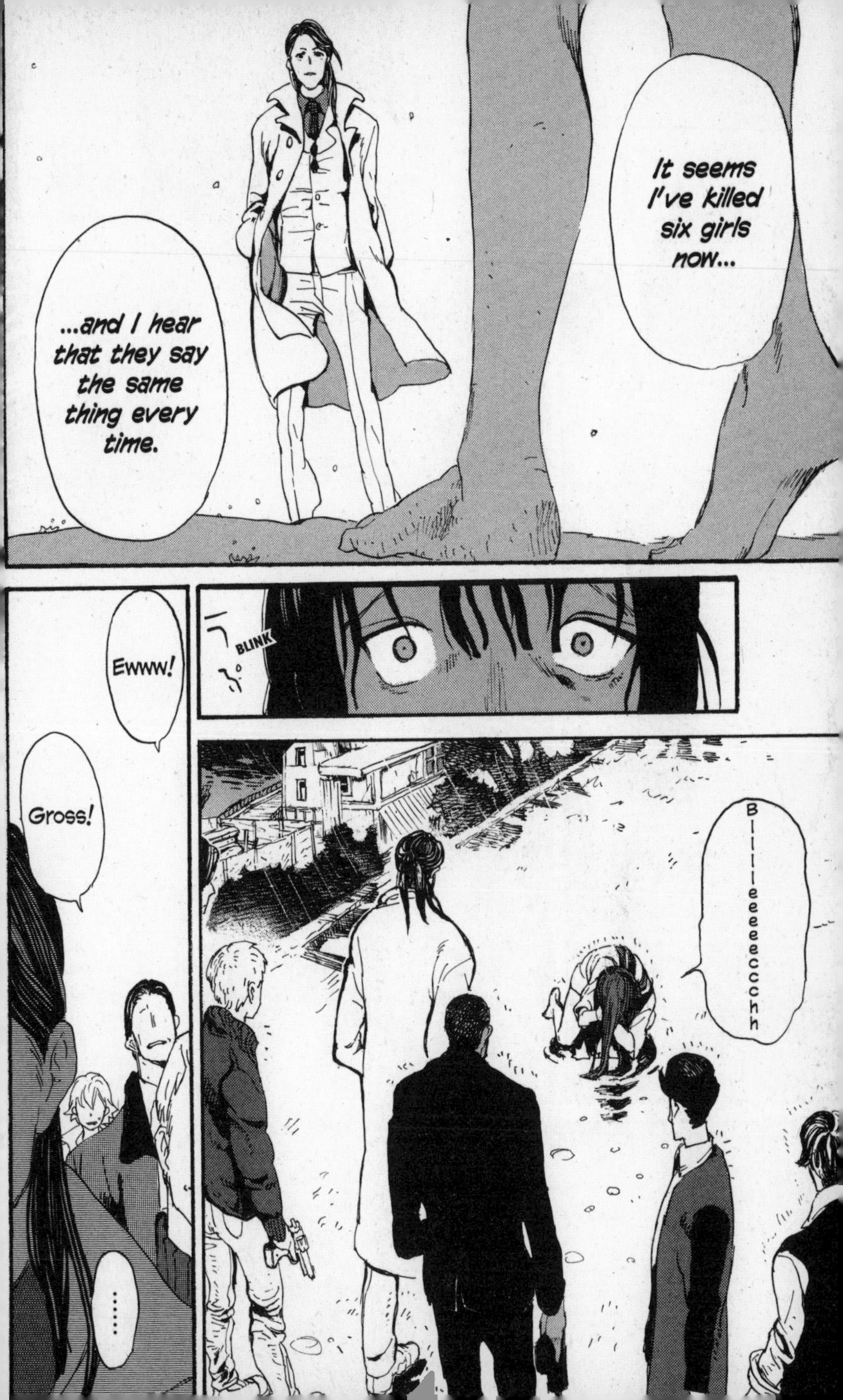

It seems I've killed six girls now...
...and I hear that they say the same thing every time.
BLINK
Bllleeeeecchh
Ewww!
Gross!
......

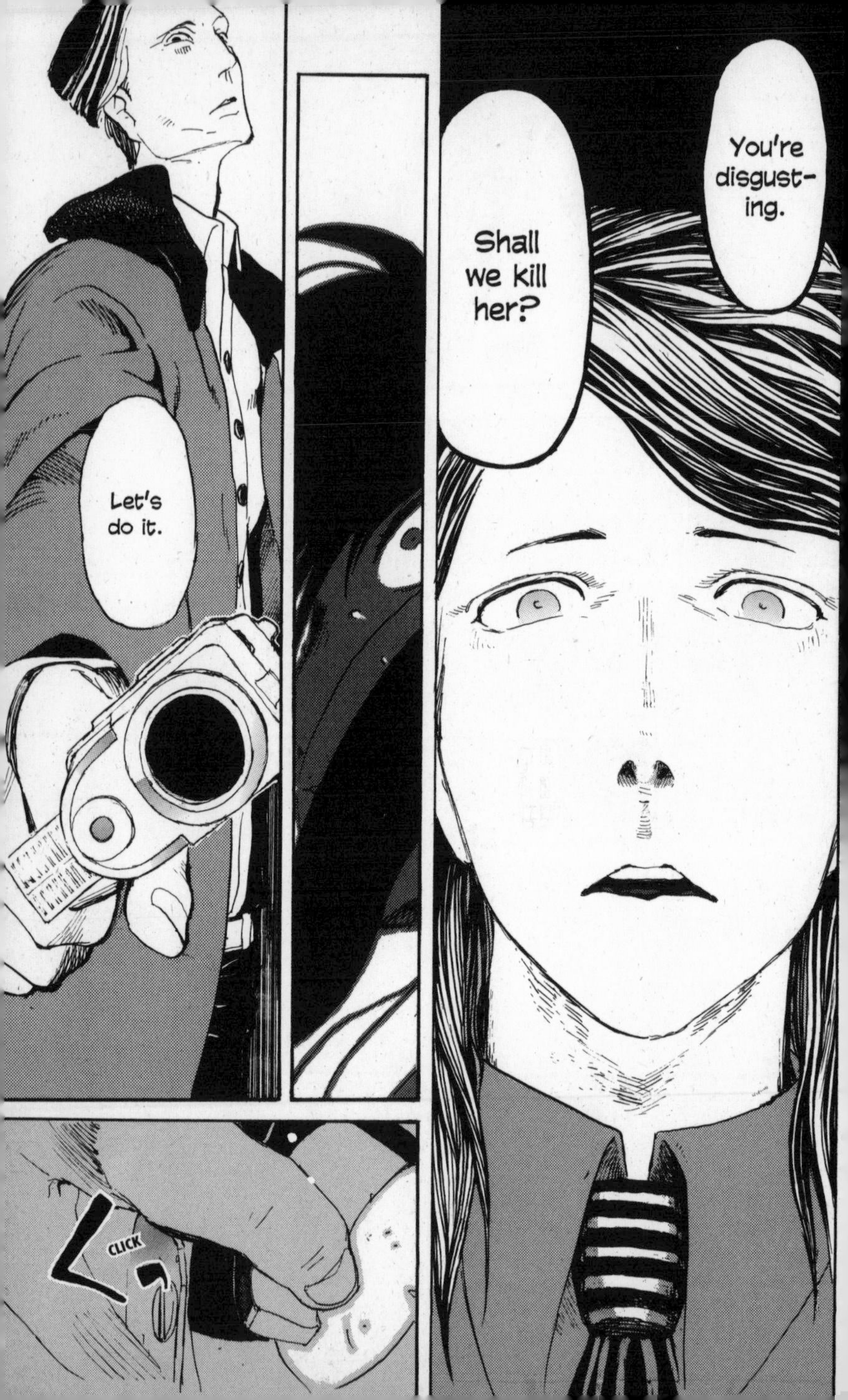
You're disgusting.
Shall we kill her?
Let's do it.
CLICK

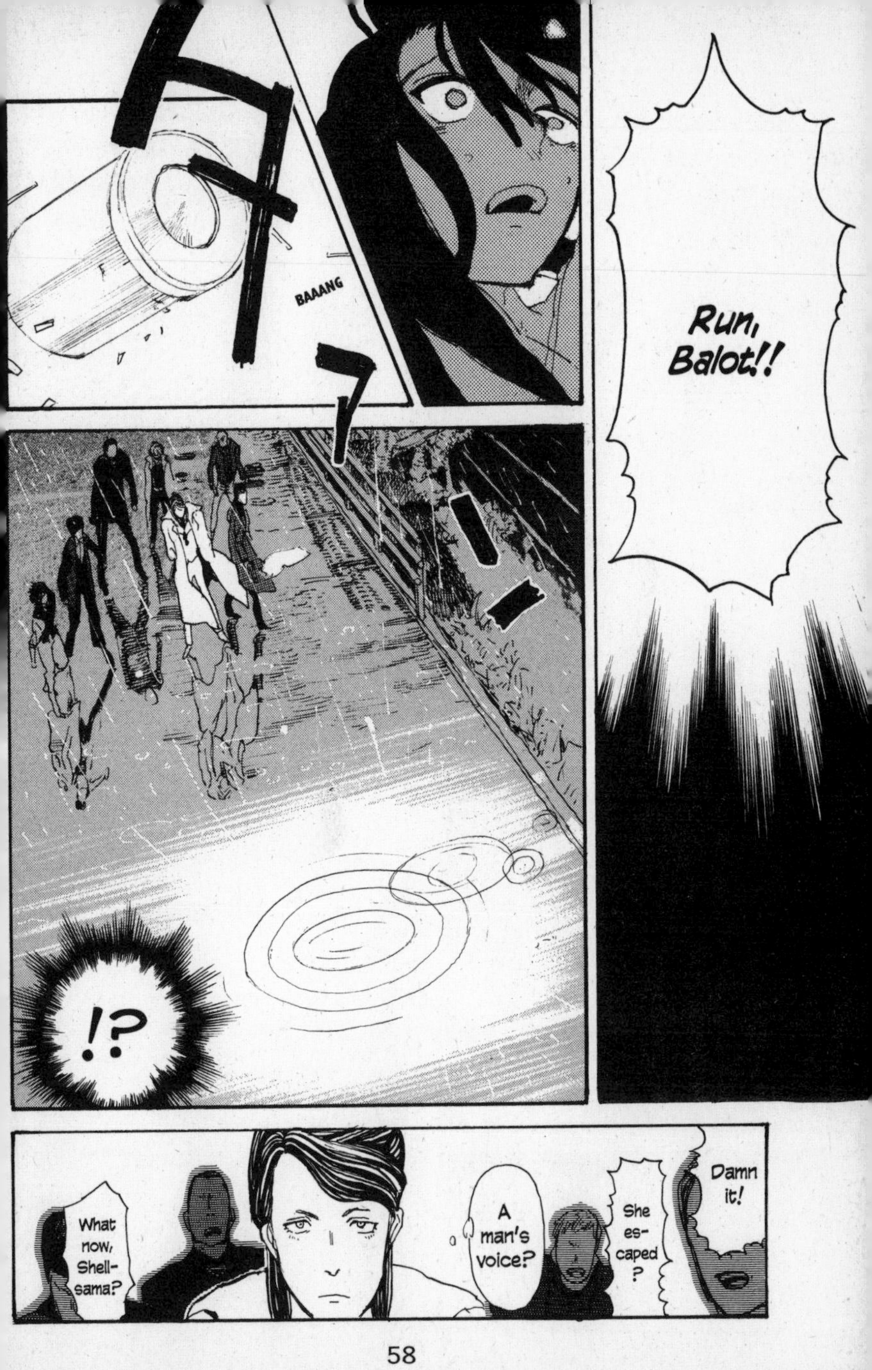
Run, Balot!!
BAAANG
!?
Damn it!
She es-caped?
A man's voice?
What now, Shell-sama?

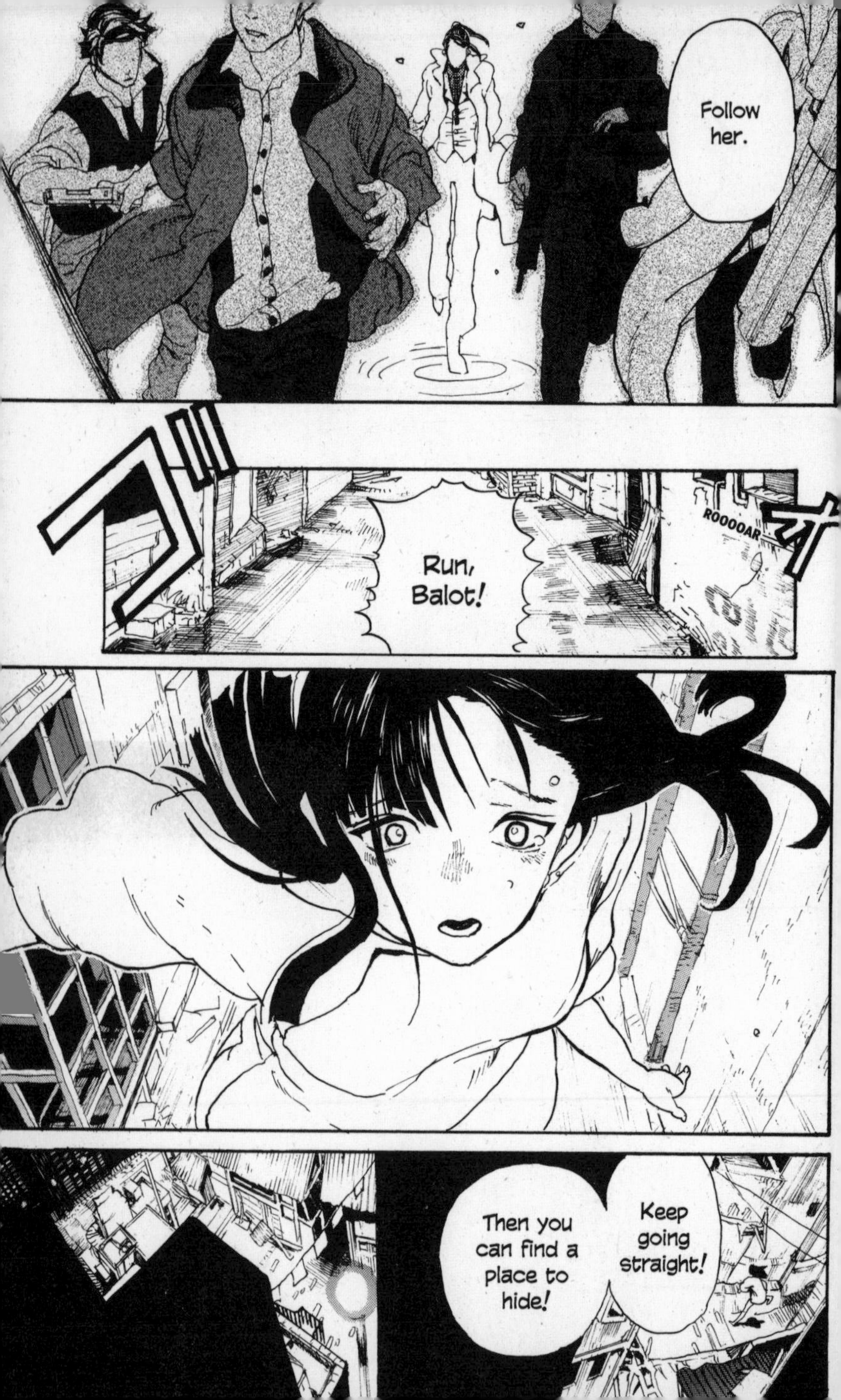
Follow her.
ROOOOAR
Run, Balot!
Keep going straight!
Then you can find a place to hide!

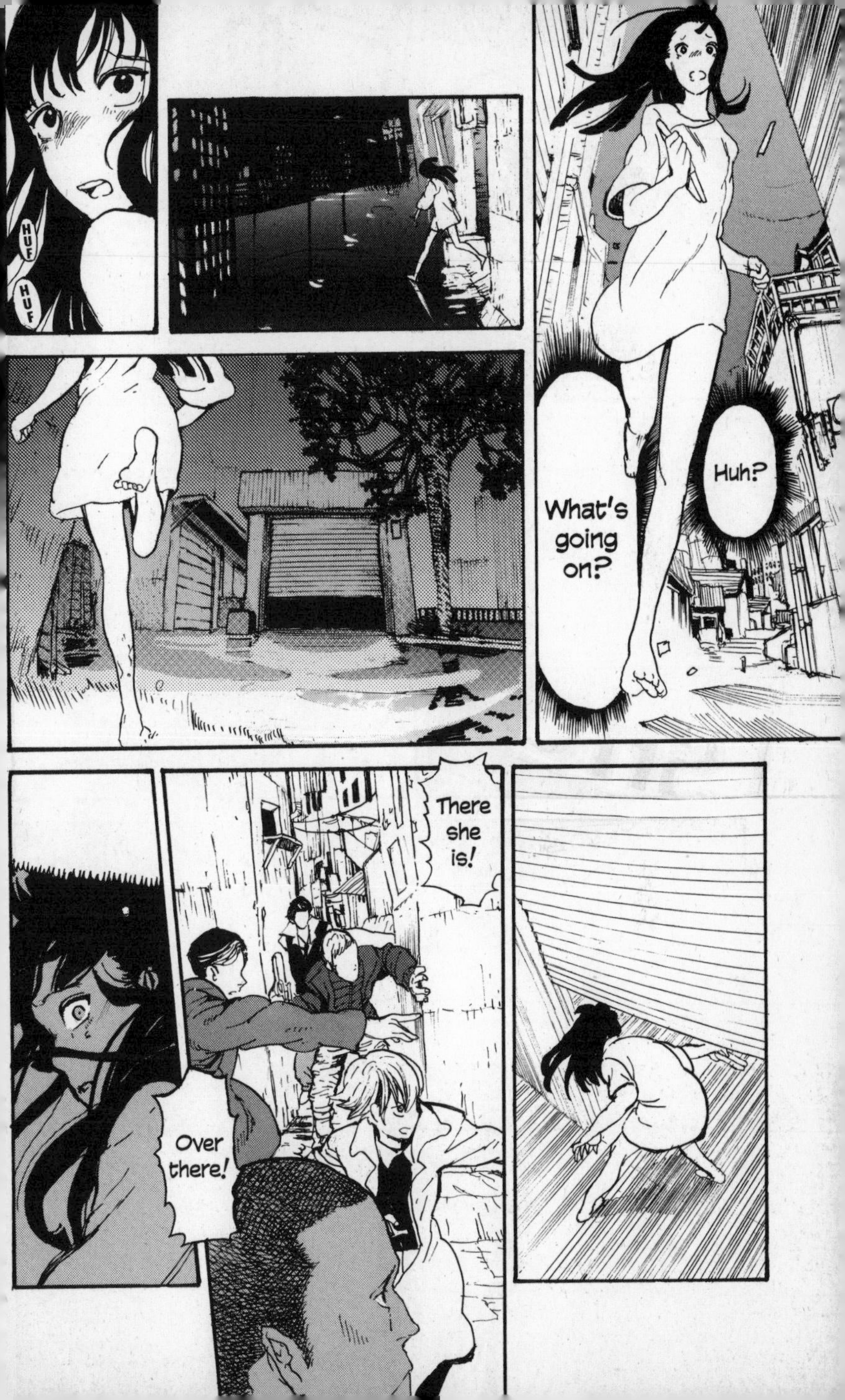
Huh?
What's going on?
HUF
HUF
There she is!
Over there!

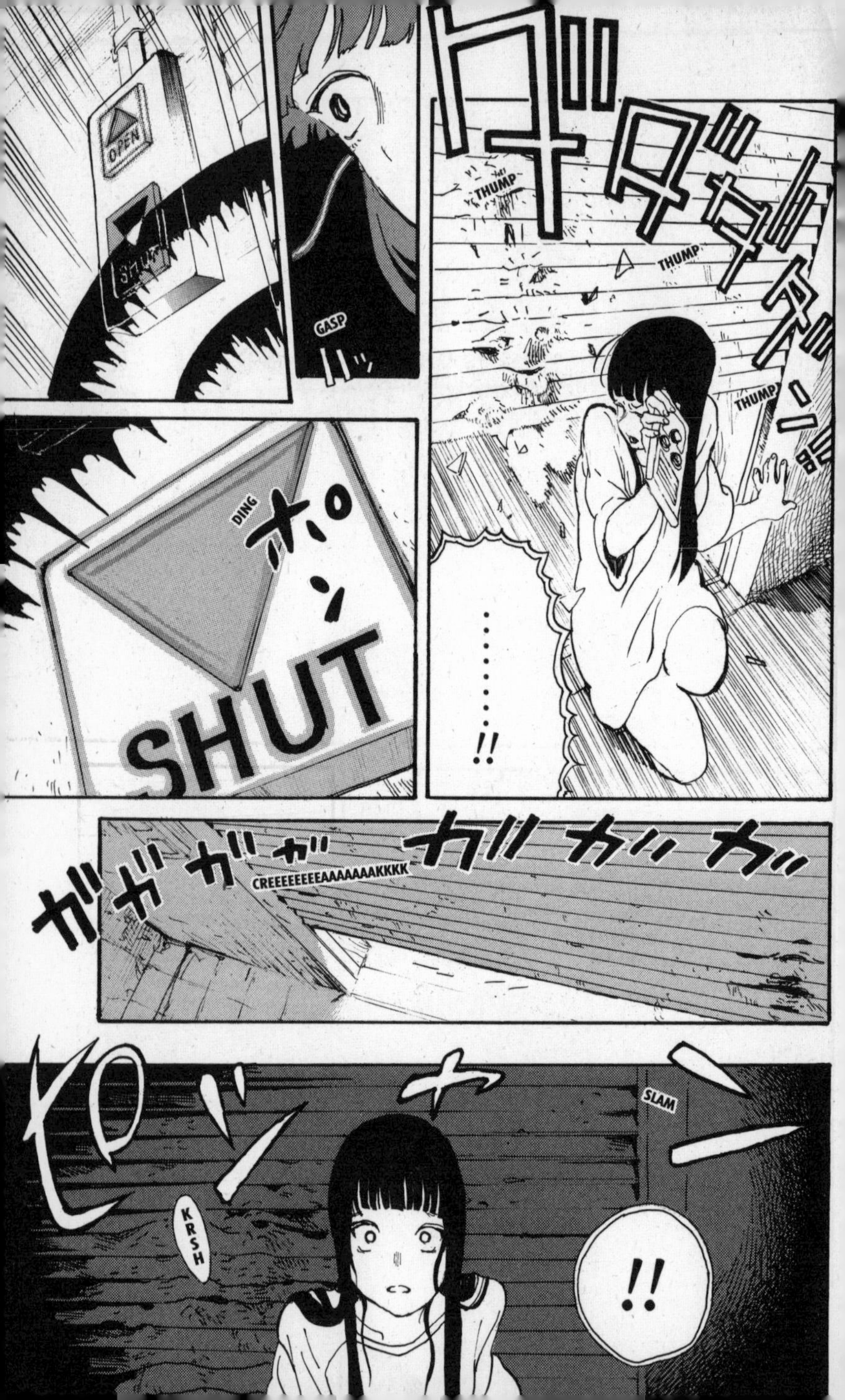
THUMP
THUMP
THUMP
......!!
GASP
OPEN
SHUT
DING
SHUT
CREEEEEEEEEAAAAAAAAKKKK
SLAM
KRSH
!!

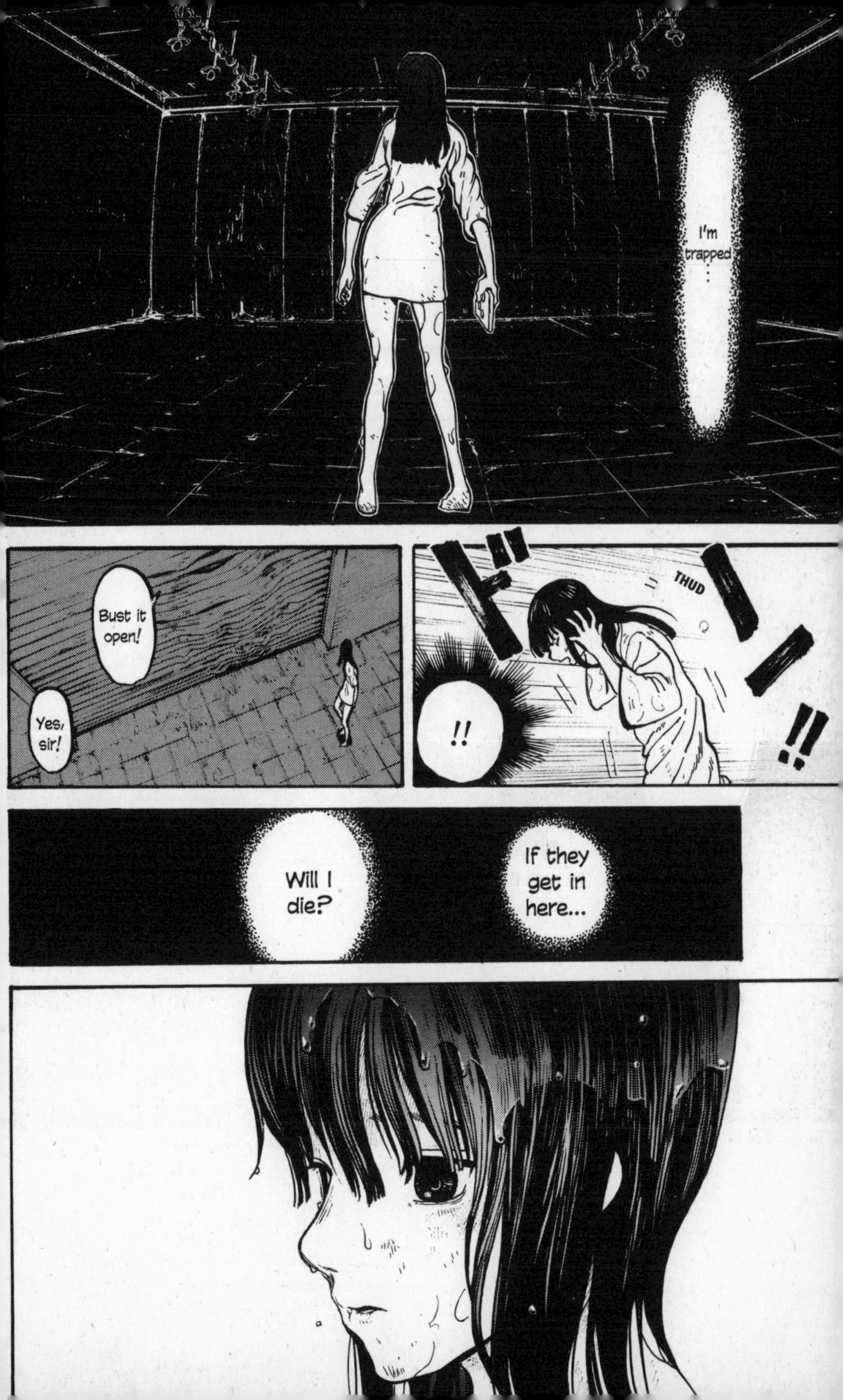
I'm trapped...
THUD
!!
!!
Bust it open!
Yes, sir!
If they get in here...
Will I die?

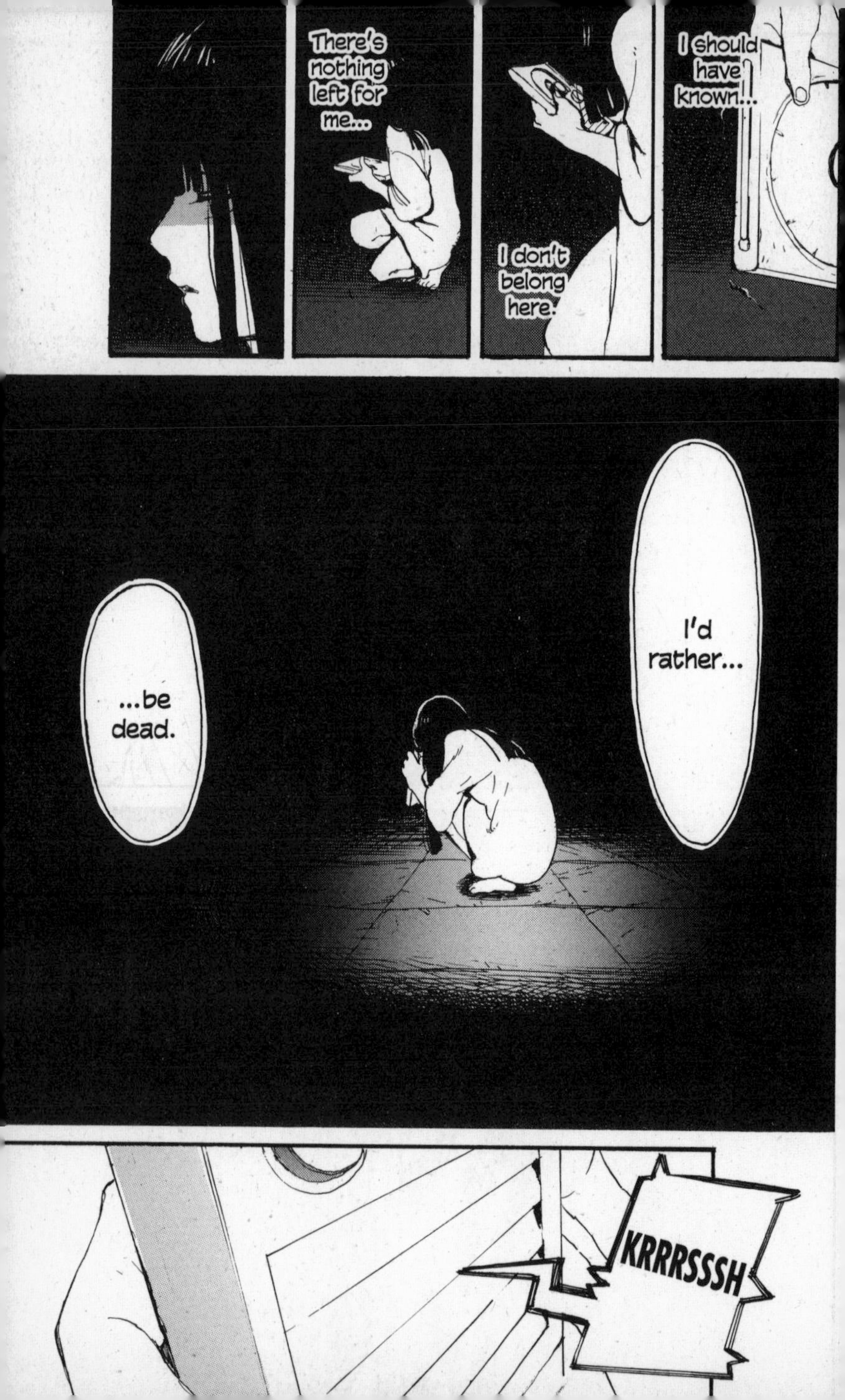

I should have known...
I don't belong here.
There's nothing left for me...
I'd rather...
...be dead.
KRRRSSSH

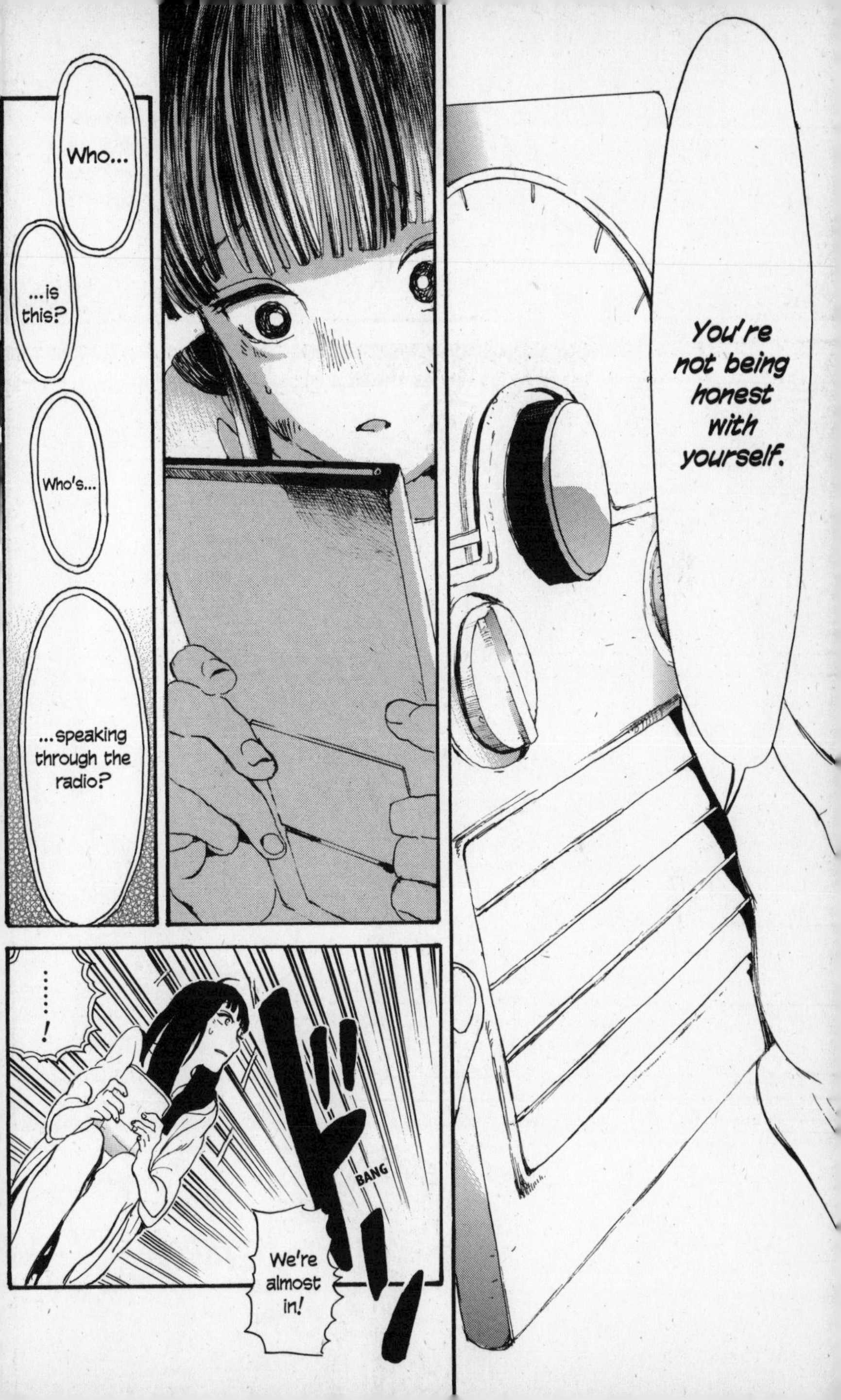
You're not being honest with yourself.
Who...
...is this?
Who's...
...speaking through the radio?
......!
BANG
We're almost in!

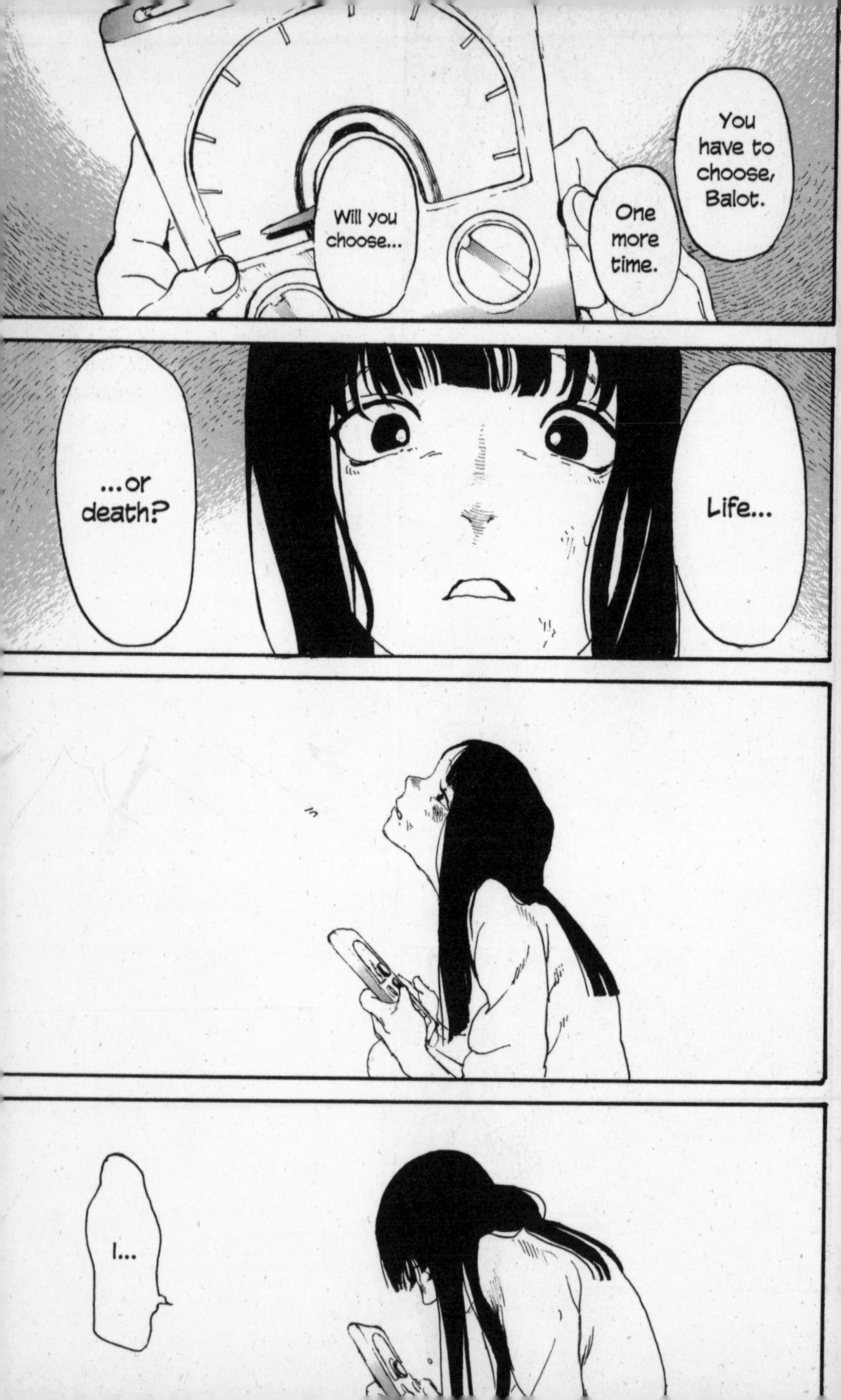
You have to choose, Balot.
One more time.
Will you choose...
Life...
...or death?
I...

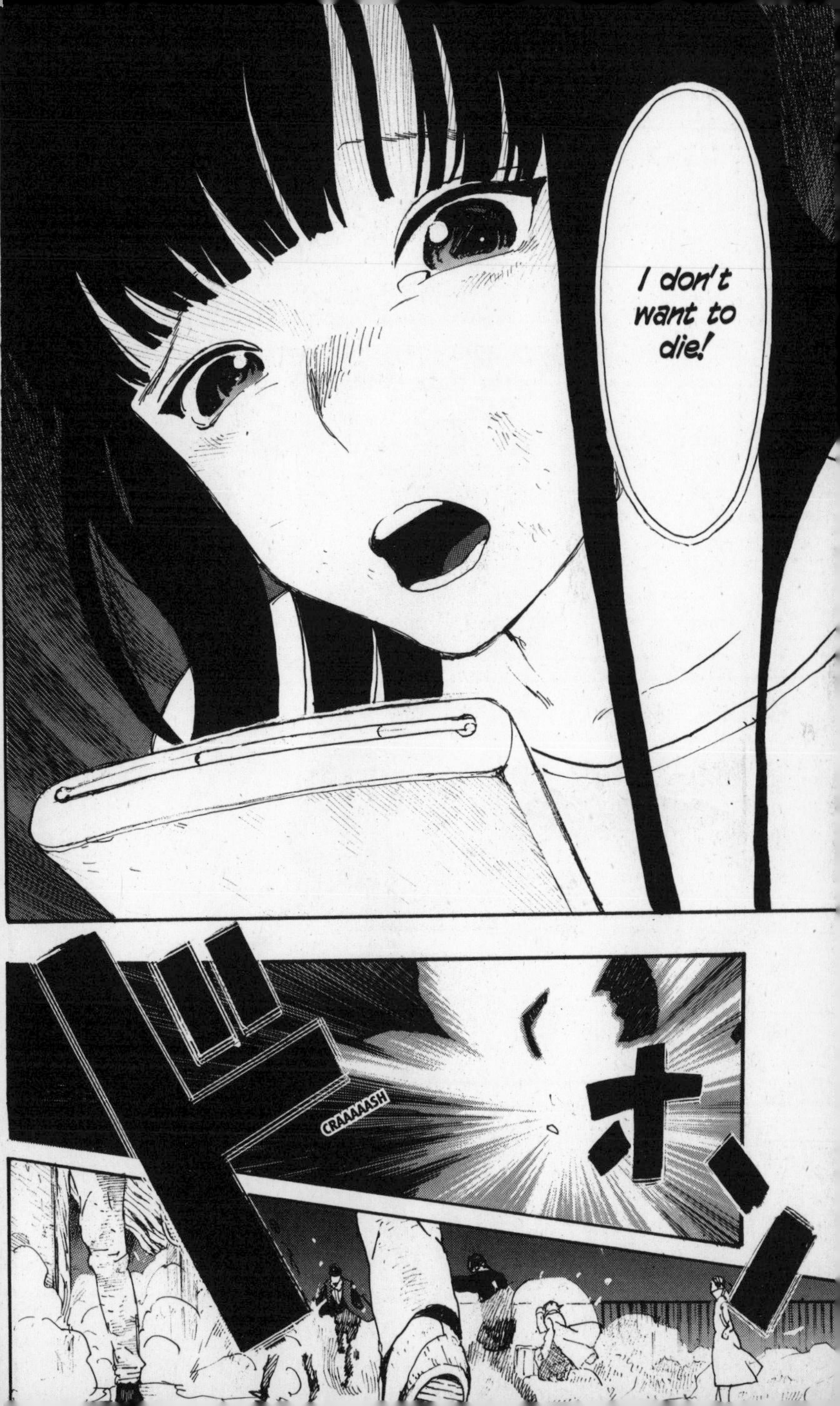
I don't want to die!
CRAAAAASH

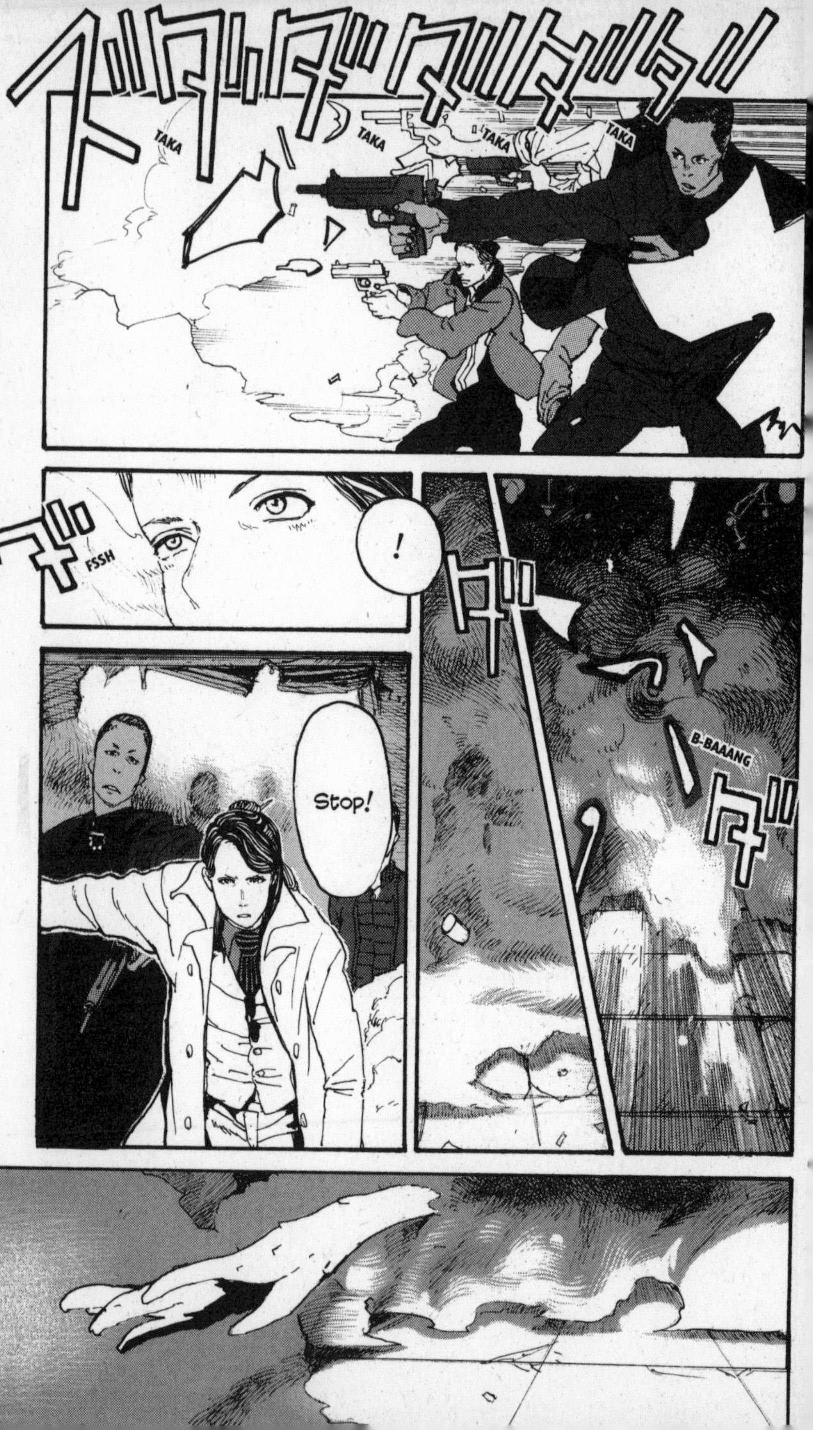
TAKA
TAKA
TAKA
TAKA
B-BAAANG
!
FSSH
Stop!

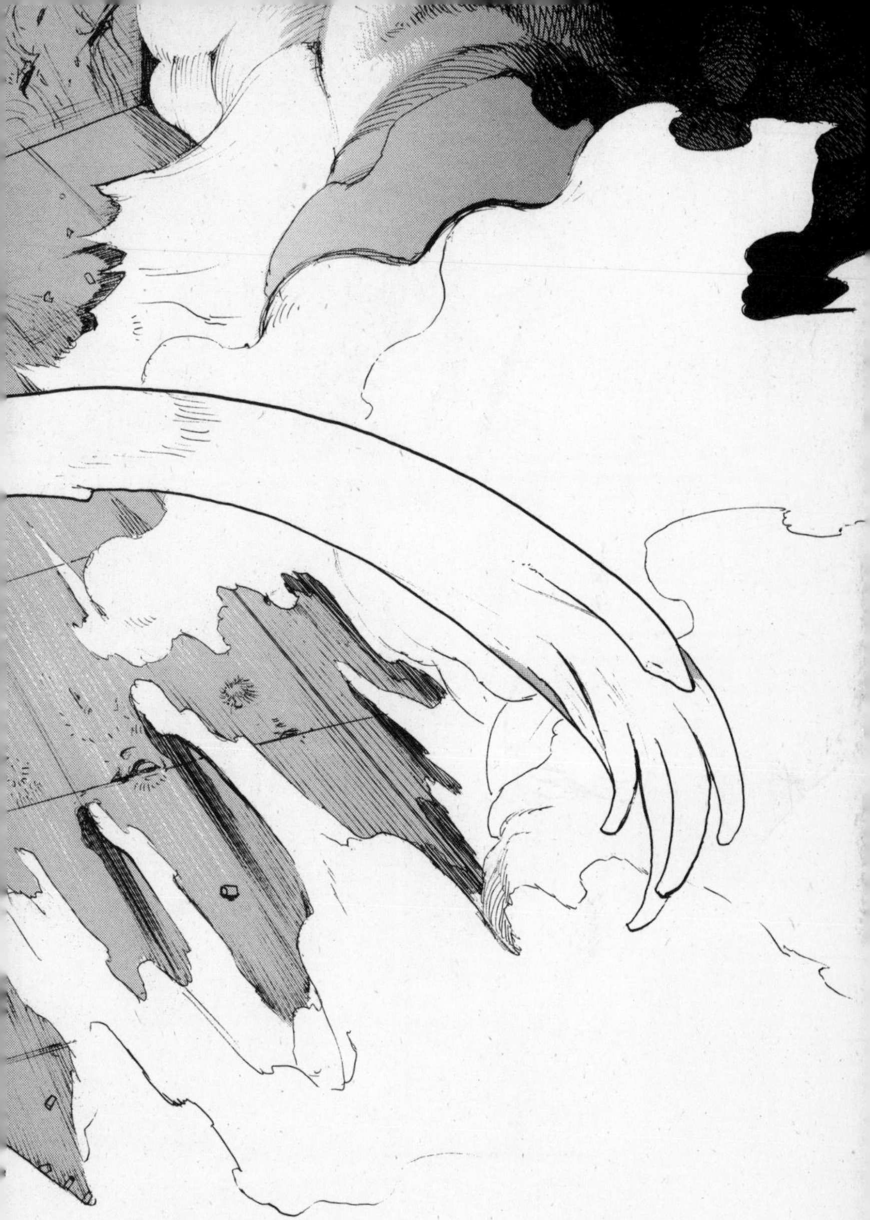

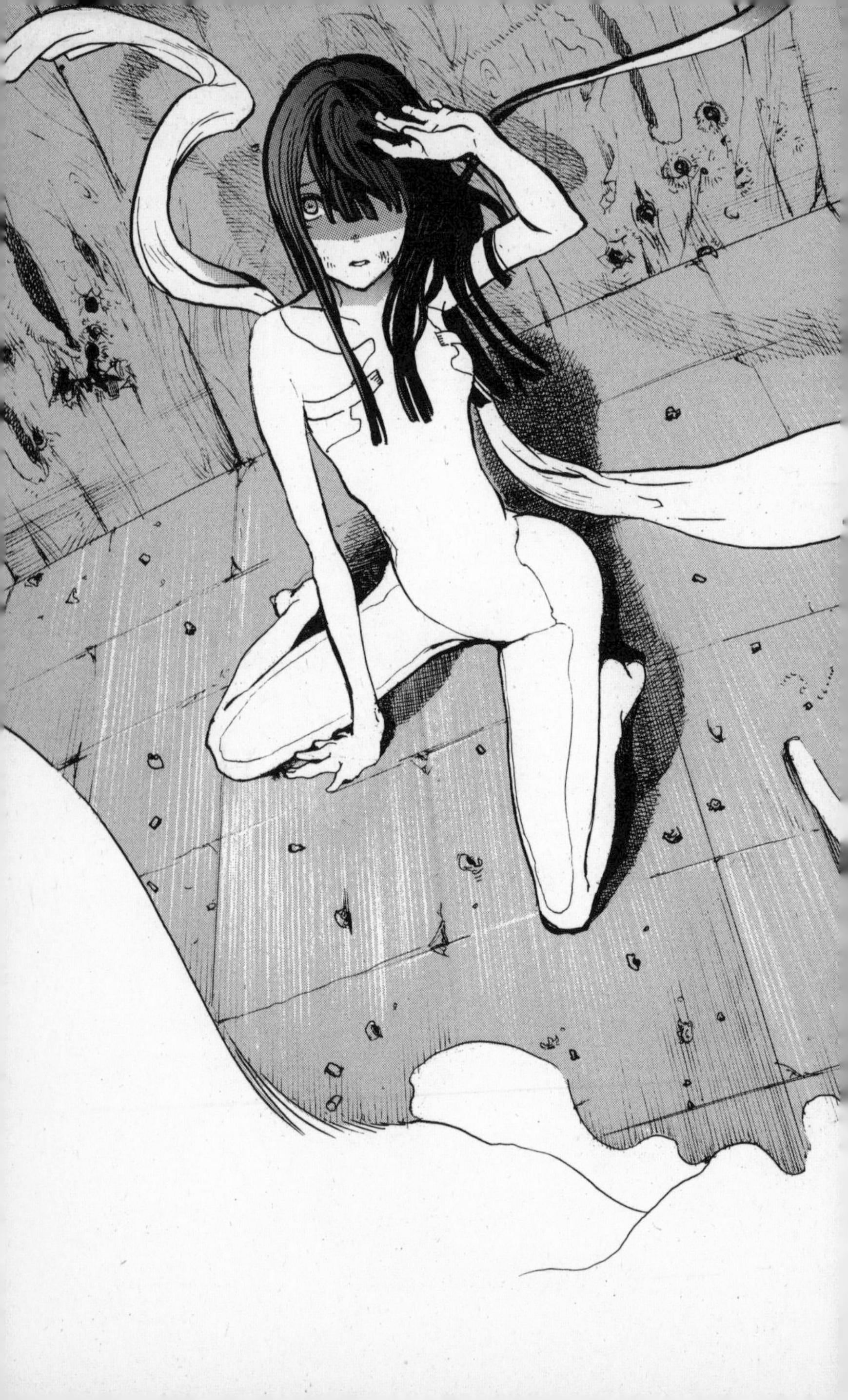

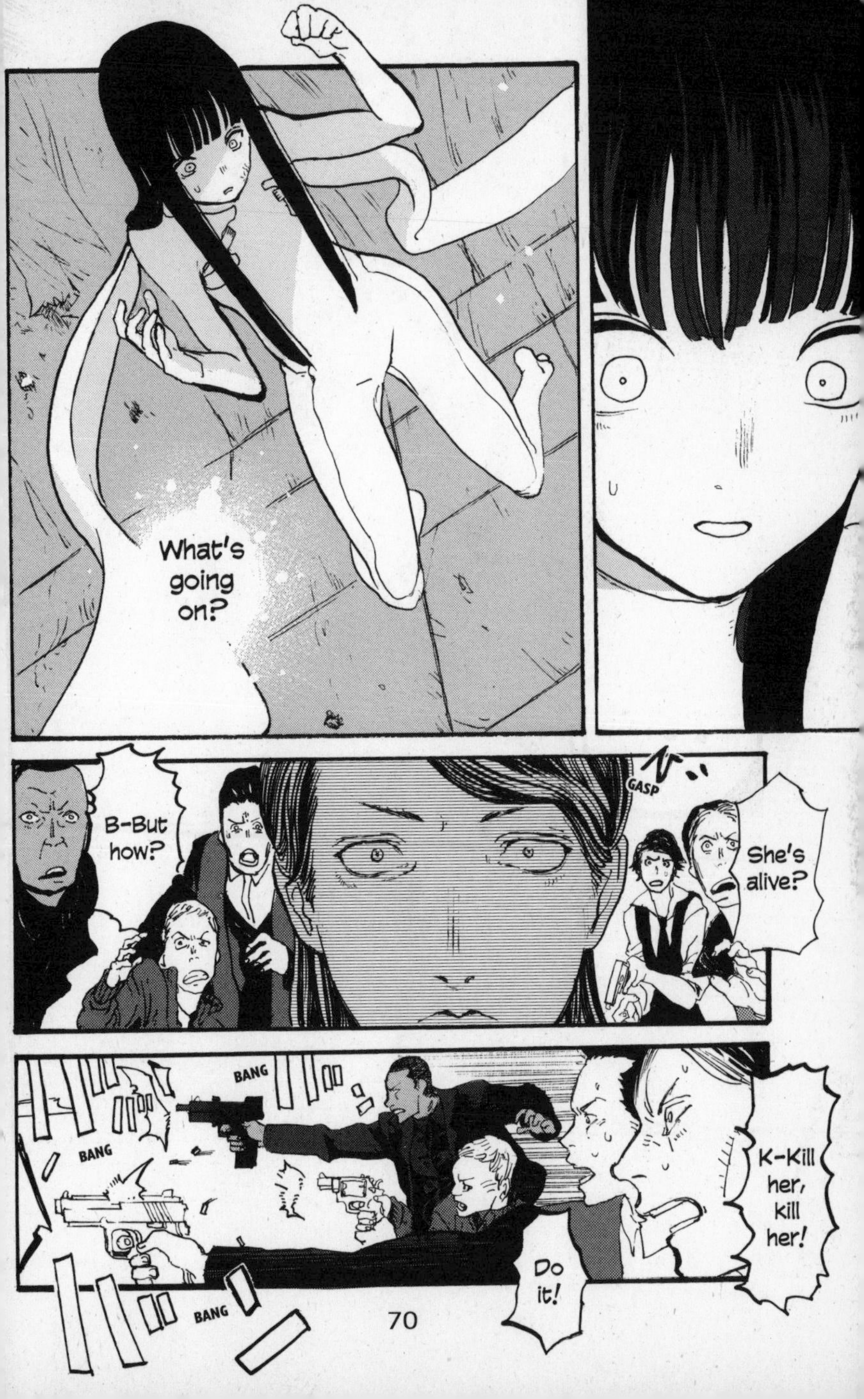
What's going on?
GASP
She's alive?
B-But how?
K-Kill her, kill her!
Do it!
BANG
BANG
BANG

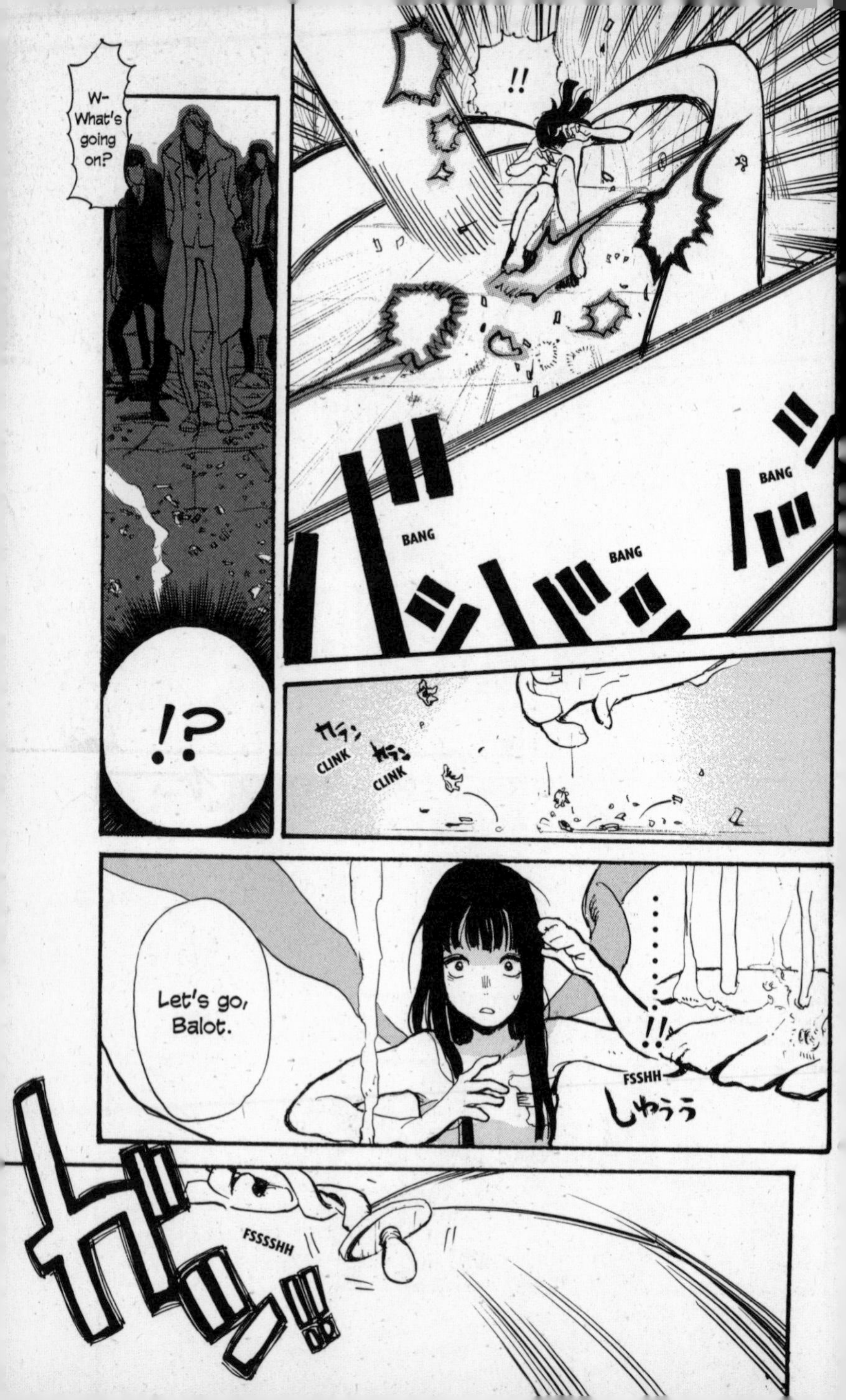
!!
BANG
BANG
BANG
CLINK
CLINK
W- What's going on?
!?
......!!
FSSHH
Let's go, Balot.
FSSSSHH

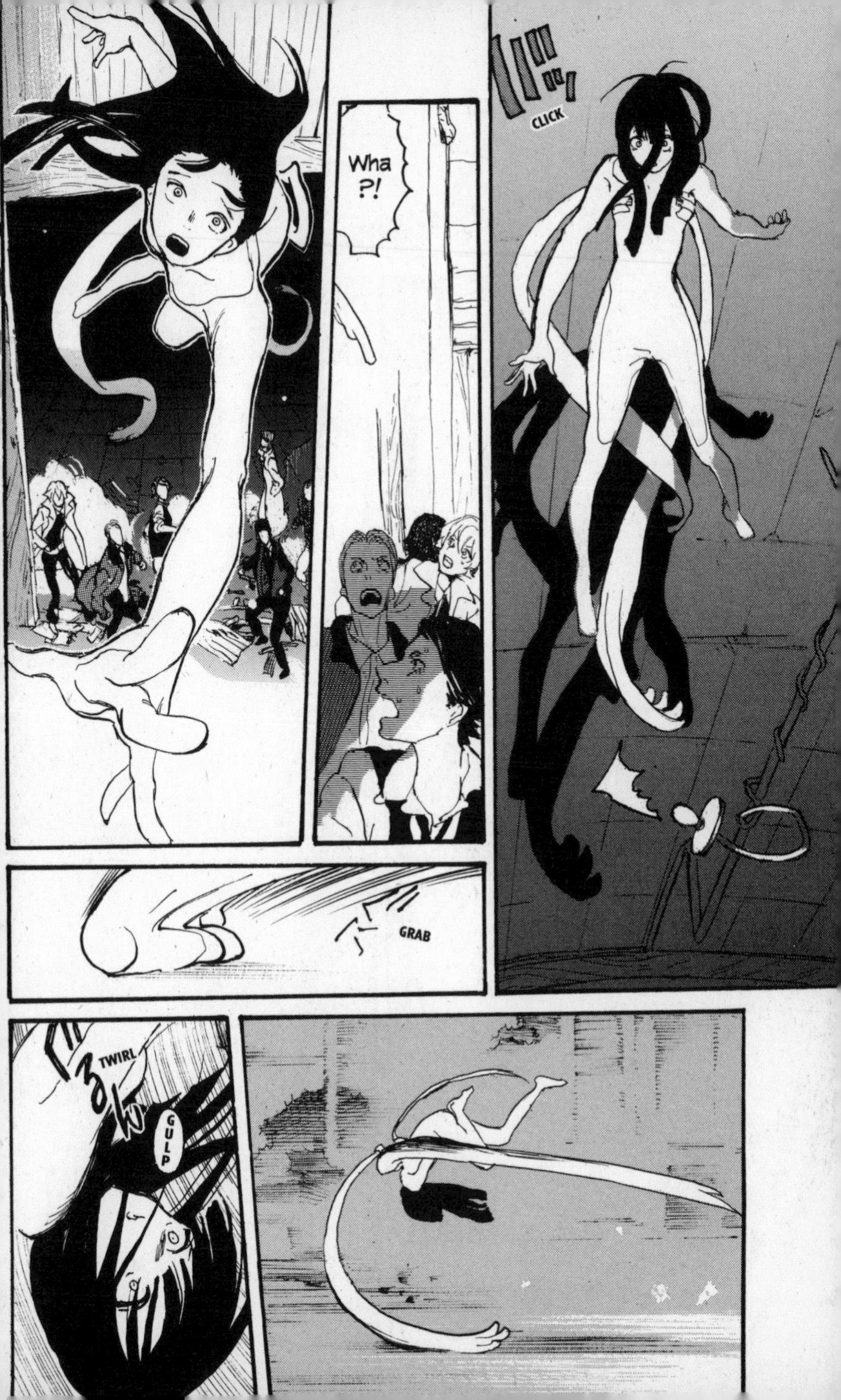
CLICK
Wha ?!
GRAB
TWIRL
GULP

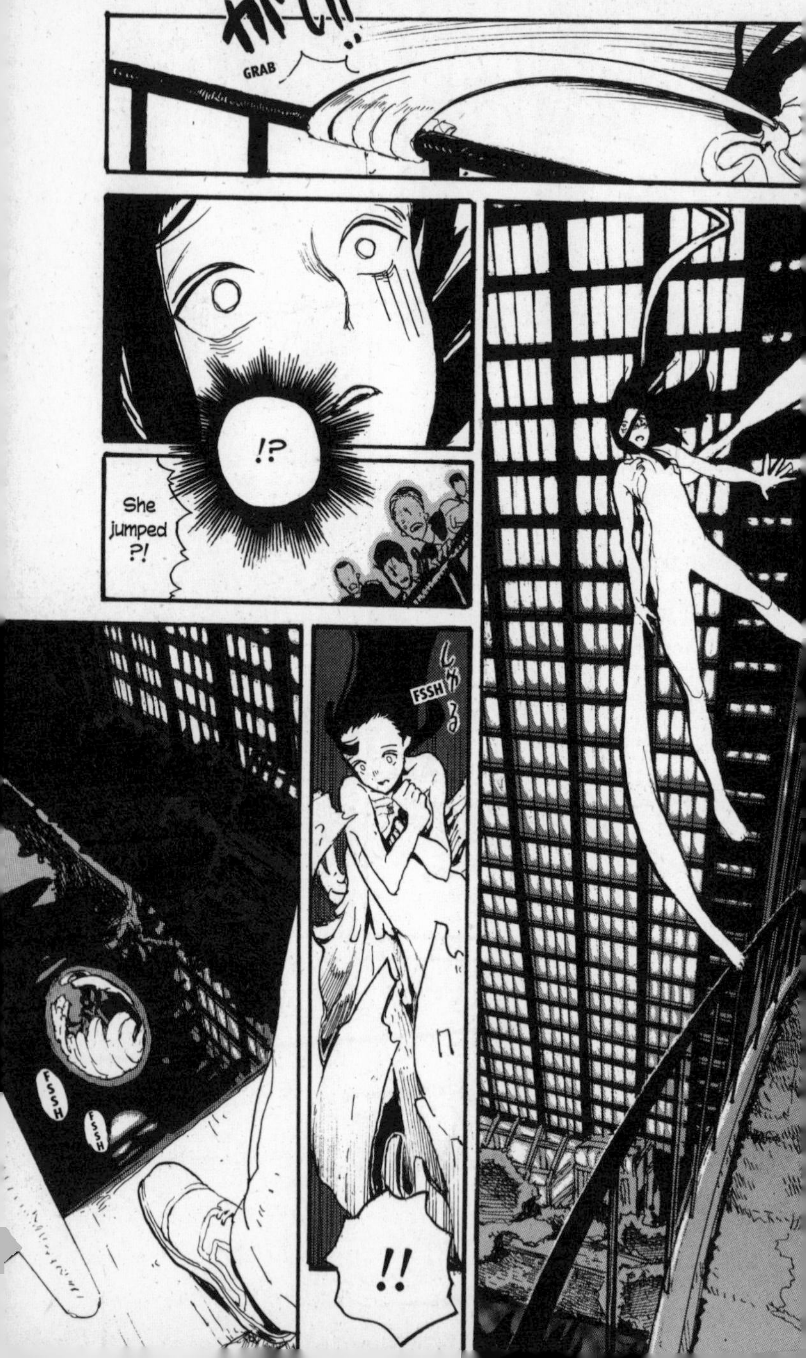
GRAB
!?
She jumped ?!
FSSH
!!
FSSH
FSSH

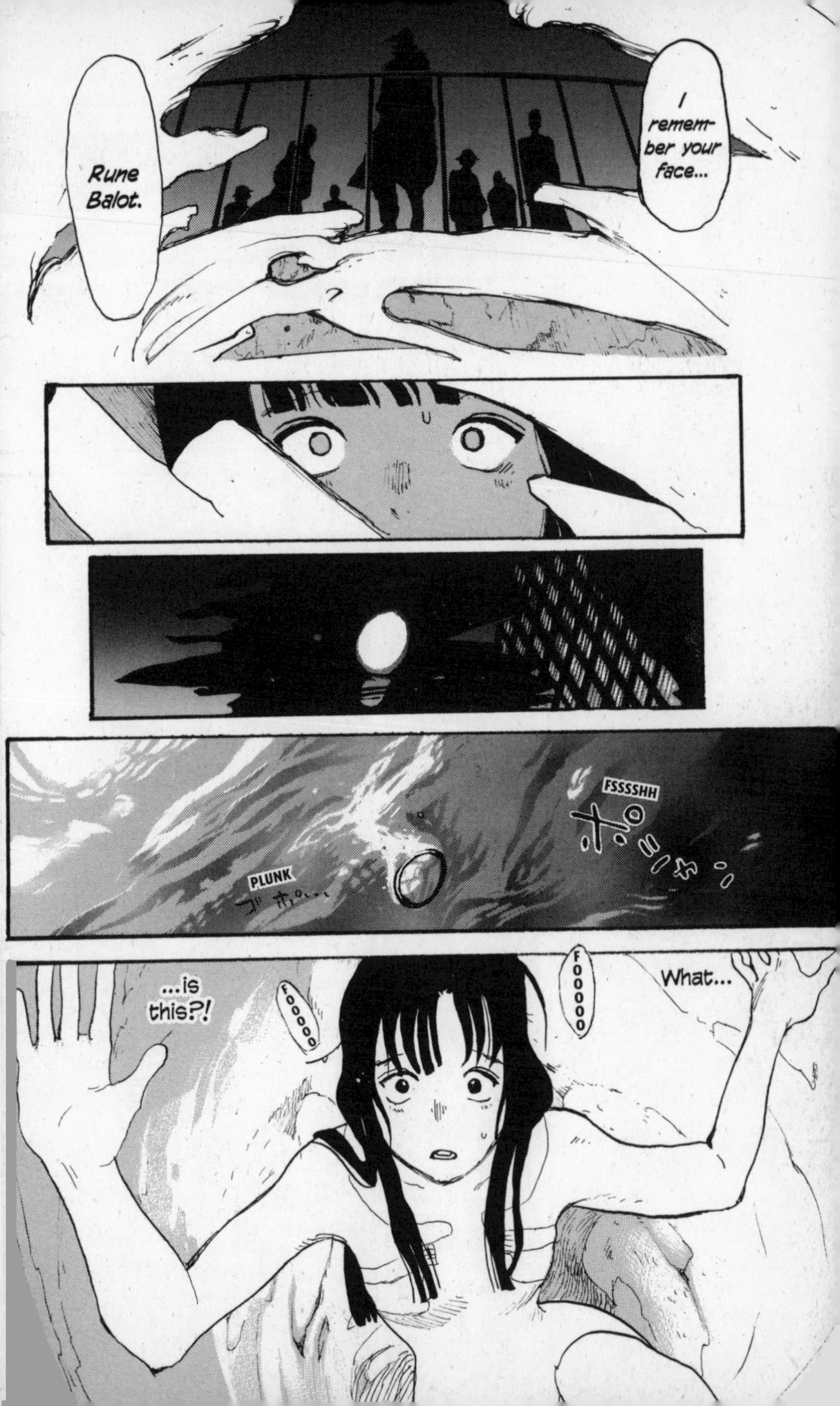

I remember your face...
Rune Balot.
FSSSSHH
PLUNK
What...
FOOOOO
FOOOOO
...is this?!

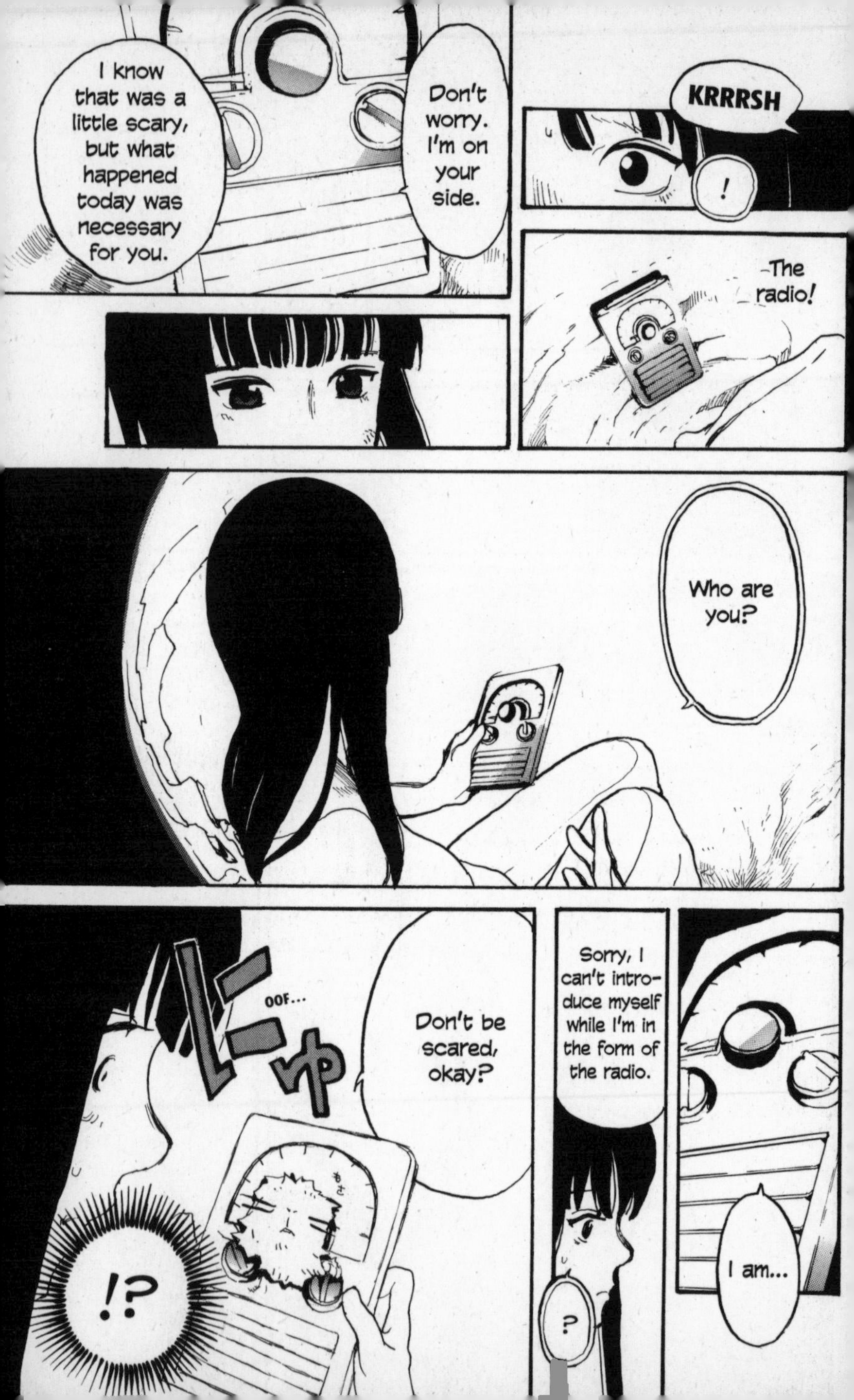
KRRRSH
!
The radio!
Don't worry. I'm on your side.
I know that was a little scary, but what happened today was necessary for you.
Who are you?
I am...
Sorry, I can't intro-duce myself while I'm in the form of the radio.
?
Don't be scared, okay?
OOF...
!?

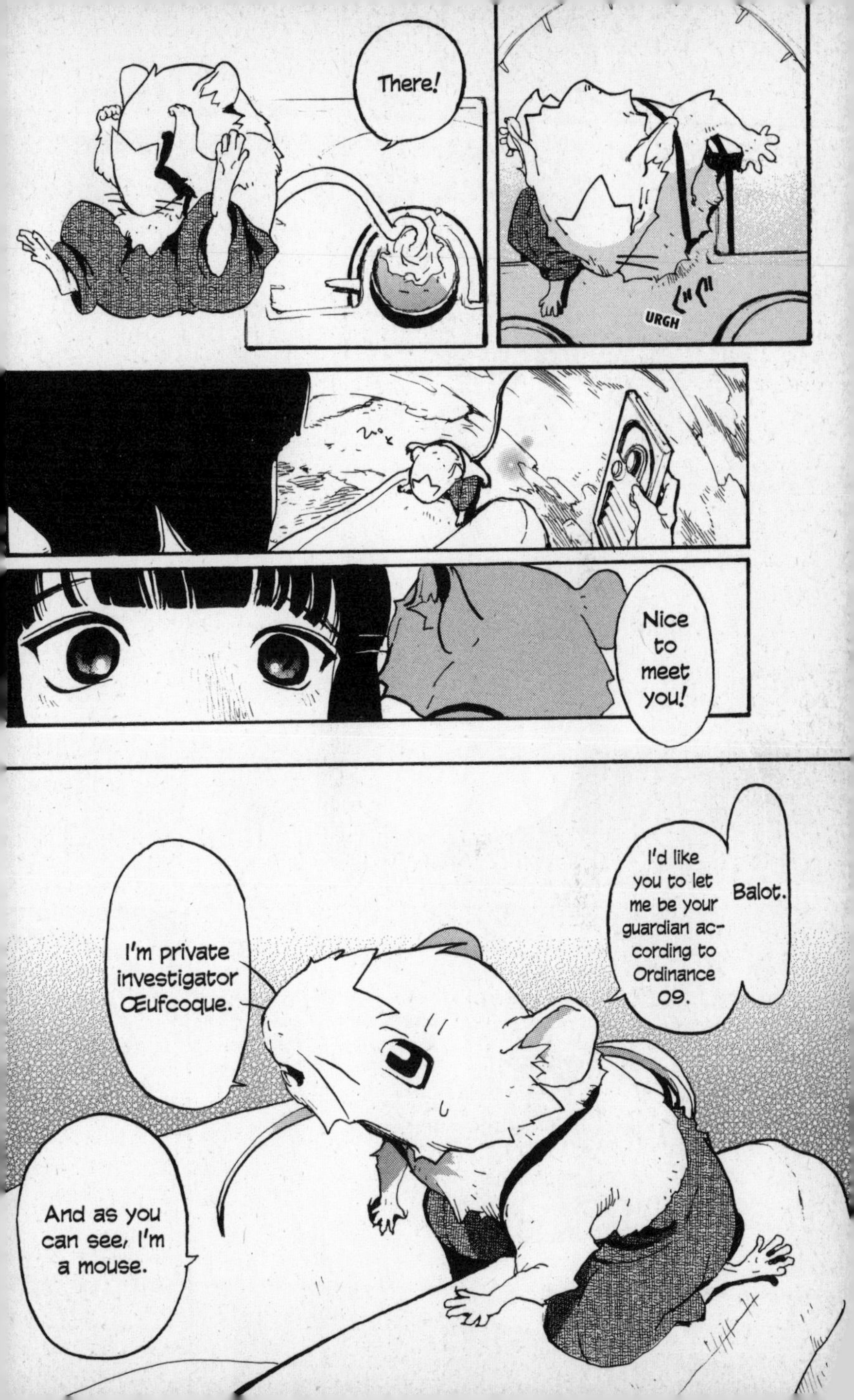
URGH
There!
Nice to meet you!
Balot.
I'd like you to let me be your guardian according to Ordinance 09.
I'm private investigator Œufcoque.
And as you can see, I'm a mouse.

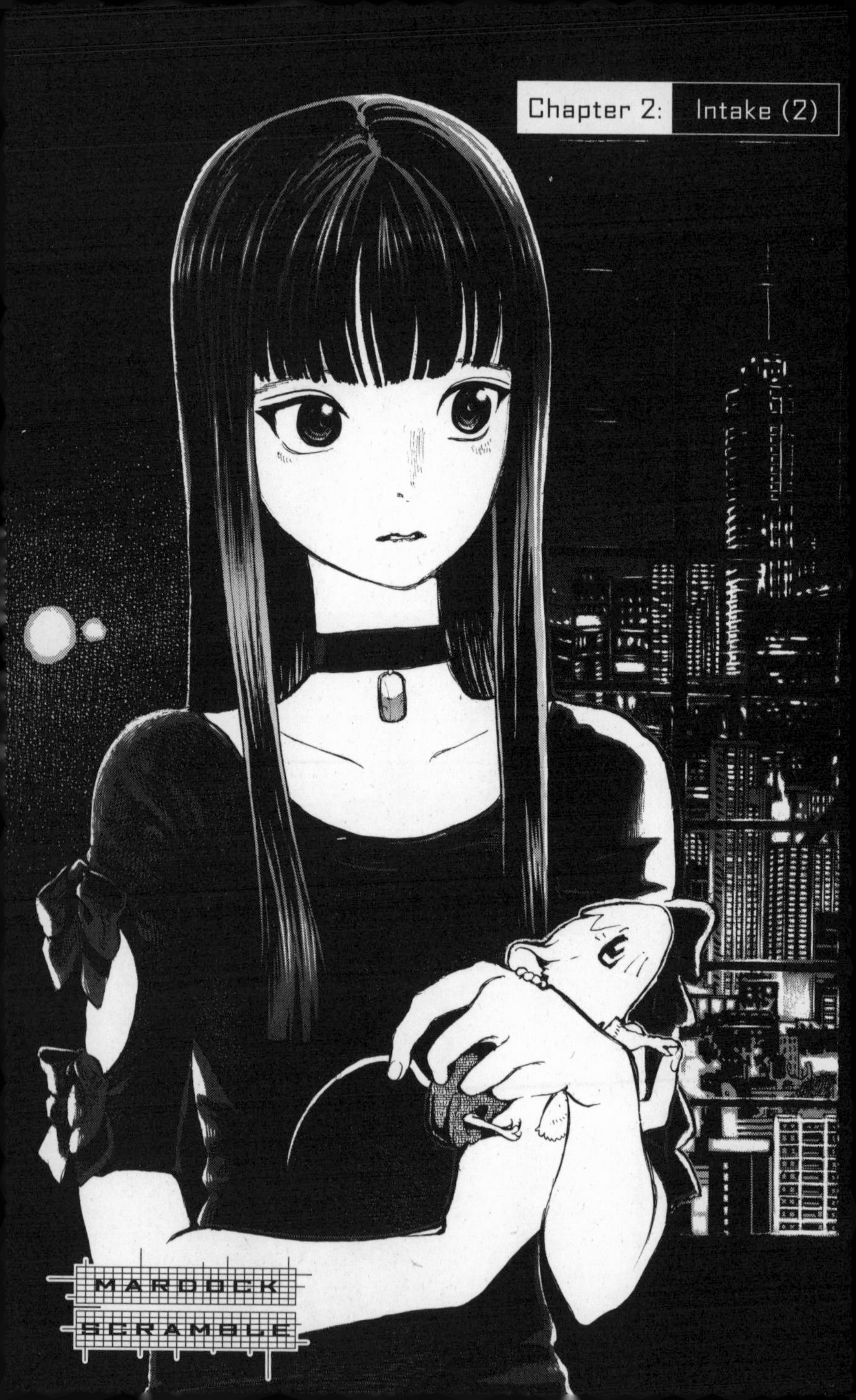
Chapter 2: Intake (2)
MARDOCK
SCRAMBLE

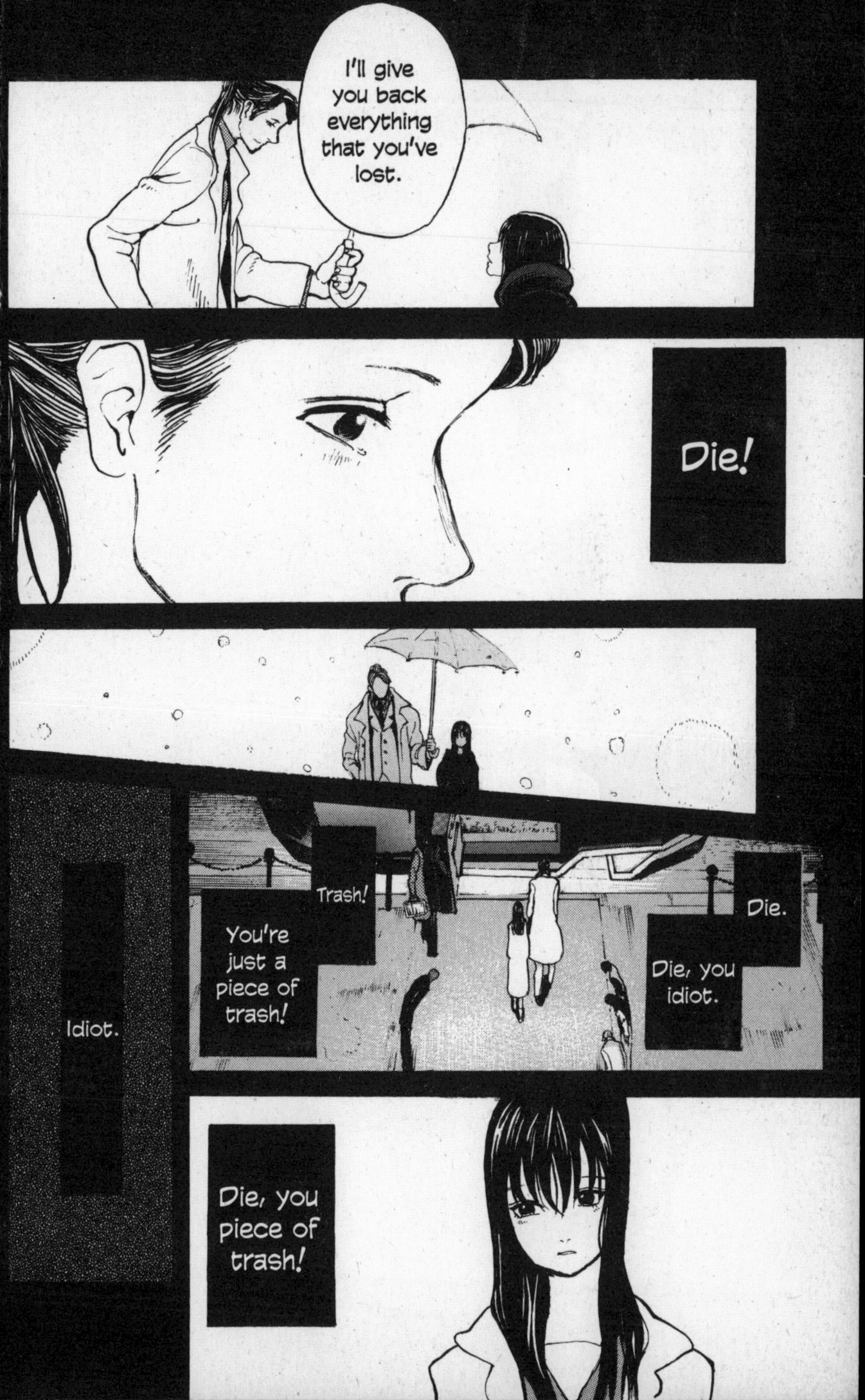
I'll give you back everything that you've lost.
Die!
Die.
Die, you idiot.
Trash!
You're just a piece of trash!
Die, you piece of trash!
Idiot.

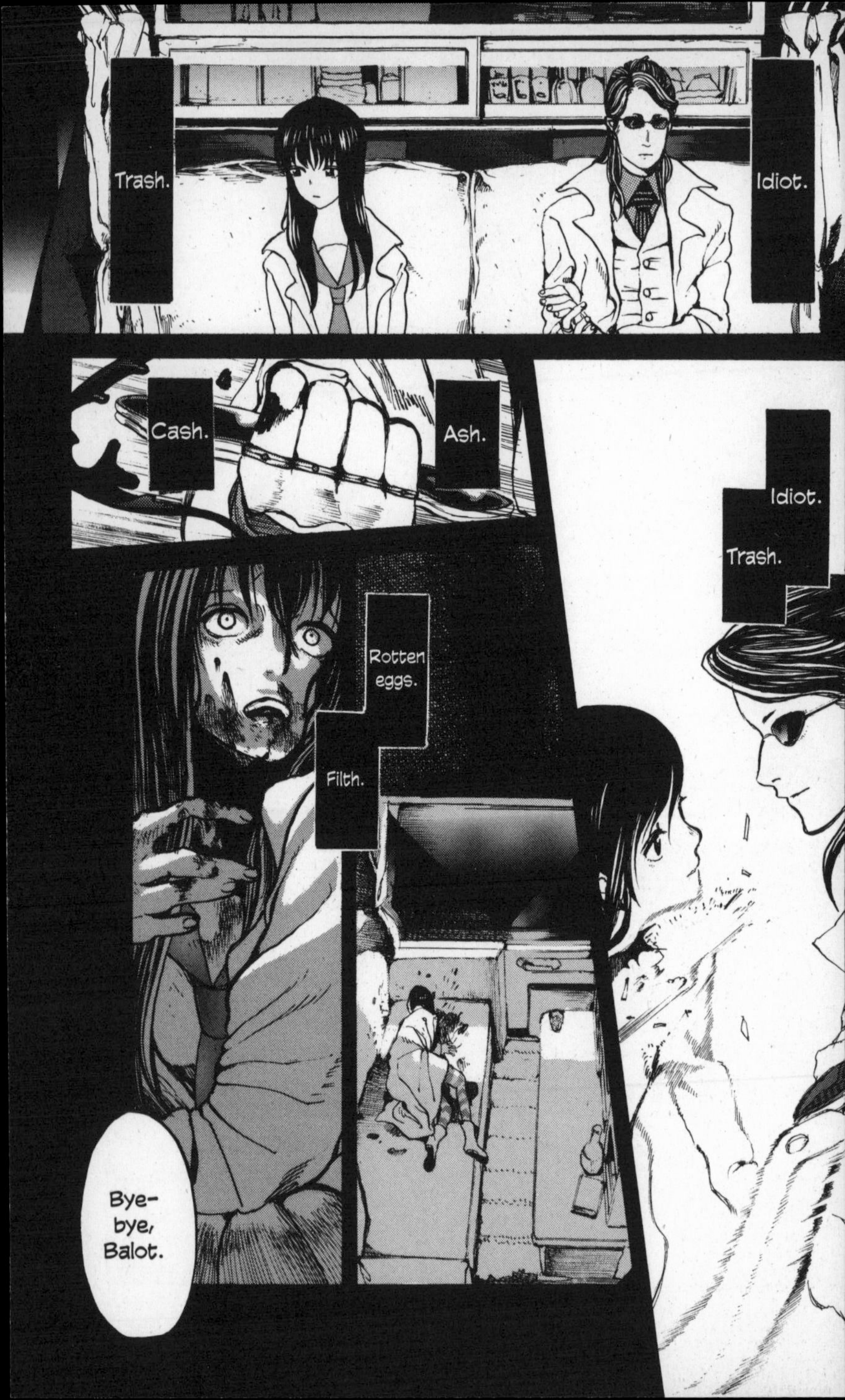
Idiot.
Trash.
Idiot.
Trash.
Ash.
Cash.
Rotten eggs.
Filth.
Bye-bye, Balot.

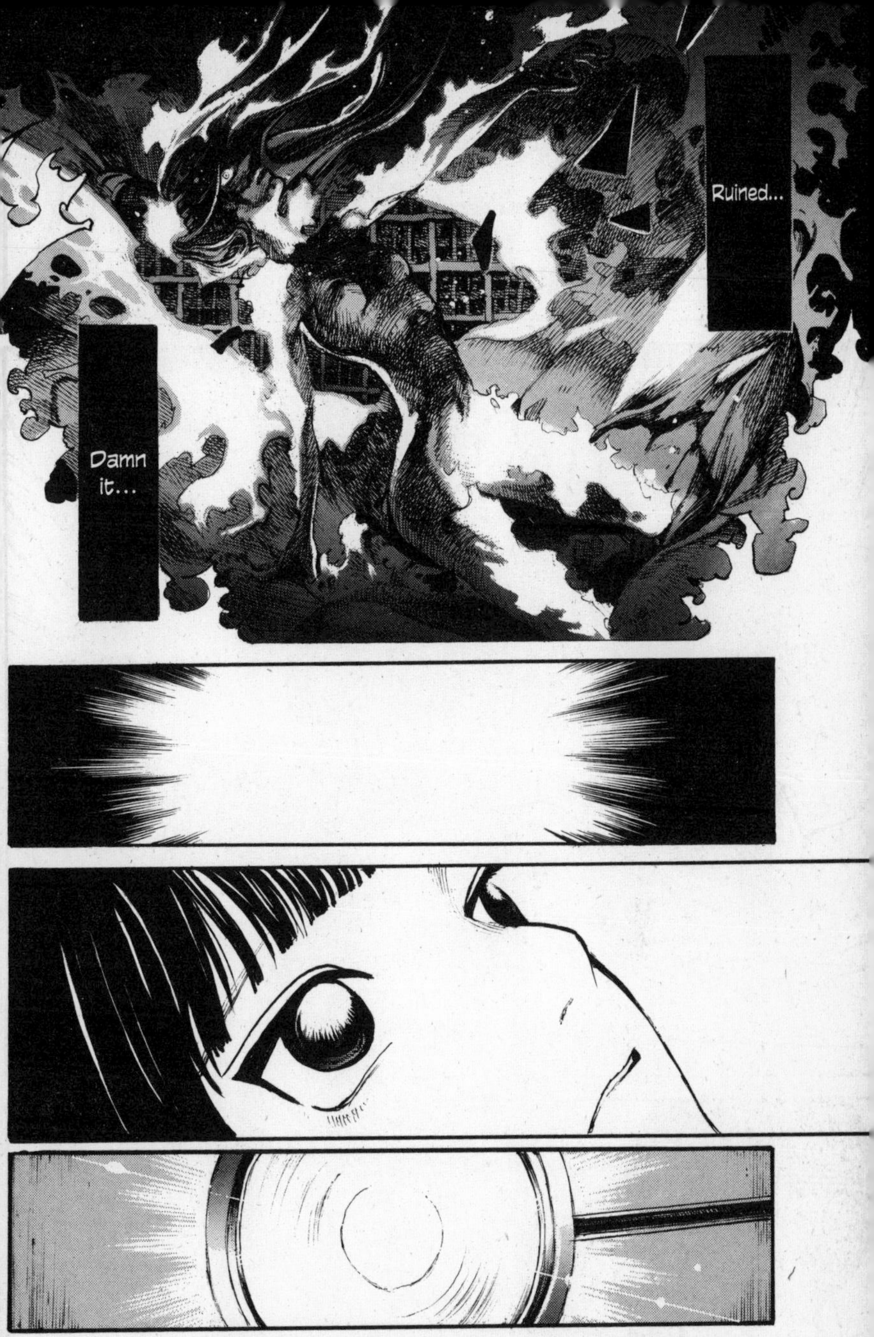
Ruined...
Damn it...

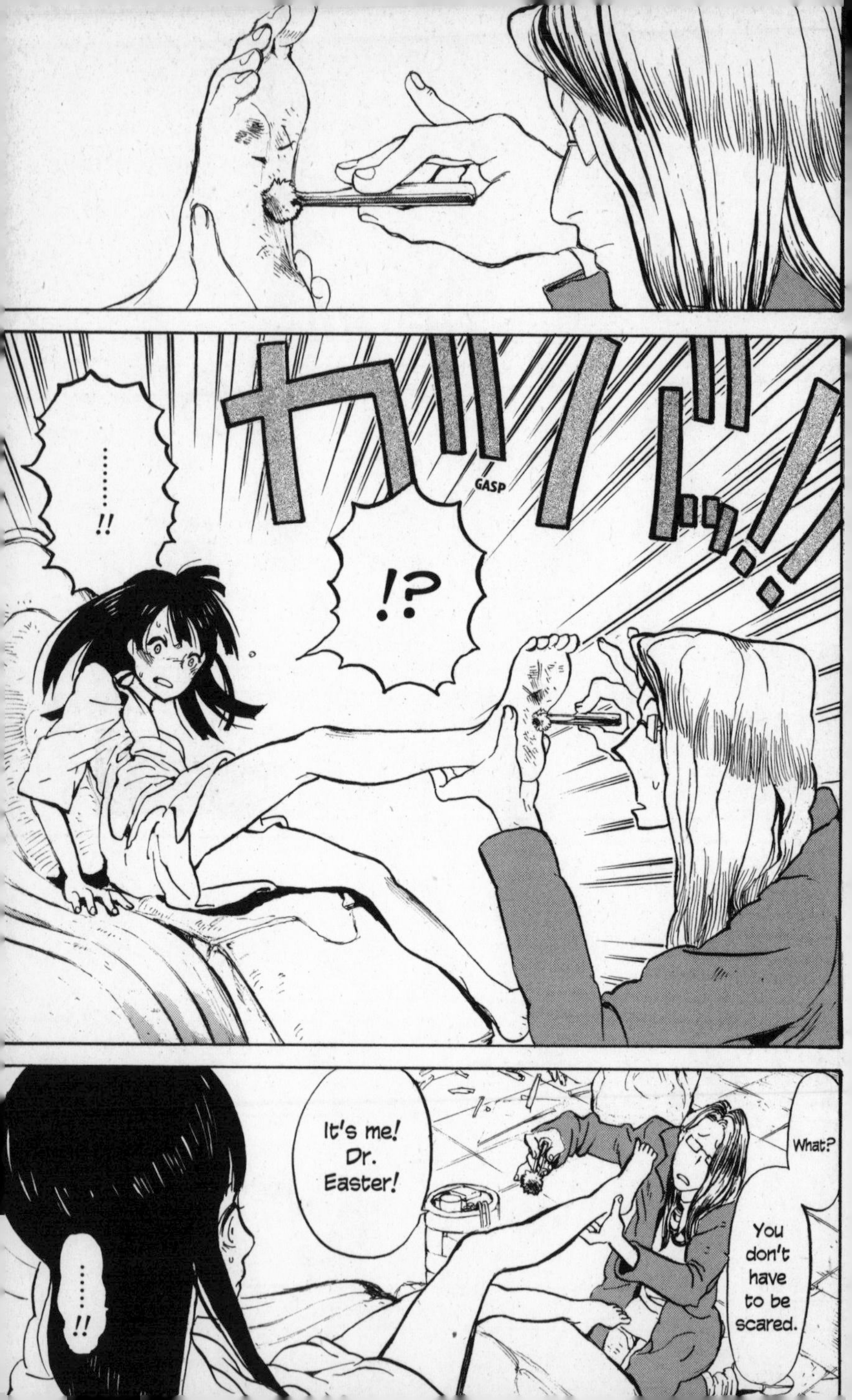
GASP
!?
......!!
What?
You don't have to be scared.
It's me! Dr. Easter!
......!!

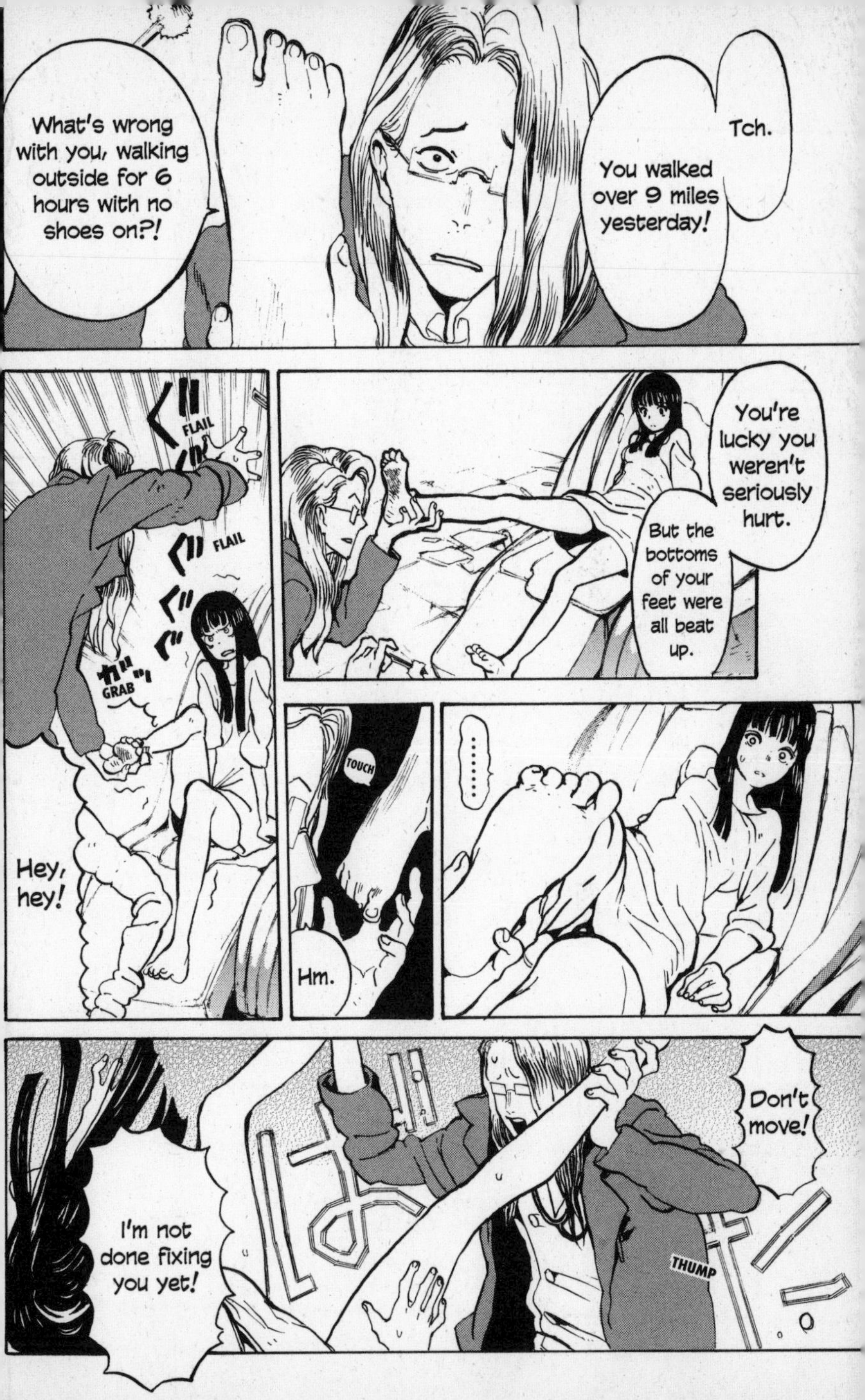
Tch.
You walked over 9 miles yesterday!
What's wrong with you, walking outside for 6 hours with no shoes on?!
You're lucky you weren't seriously hurt.
But the bottoms of your feet were all beat up.
......
TOUCH
Hm.
FLAIL
FLAIL
GRAB
Hey, hey!
Don't move!
THUMP
I'm not done fixing you yet!

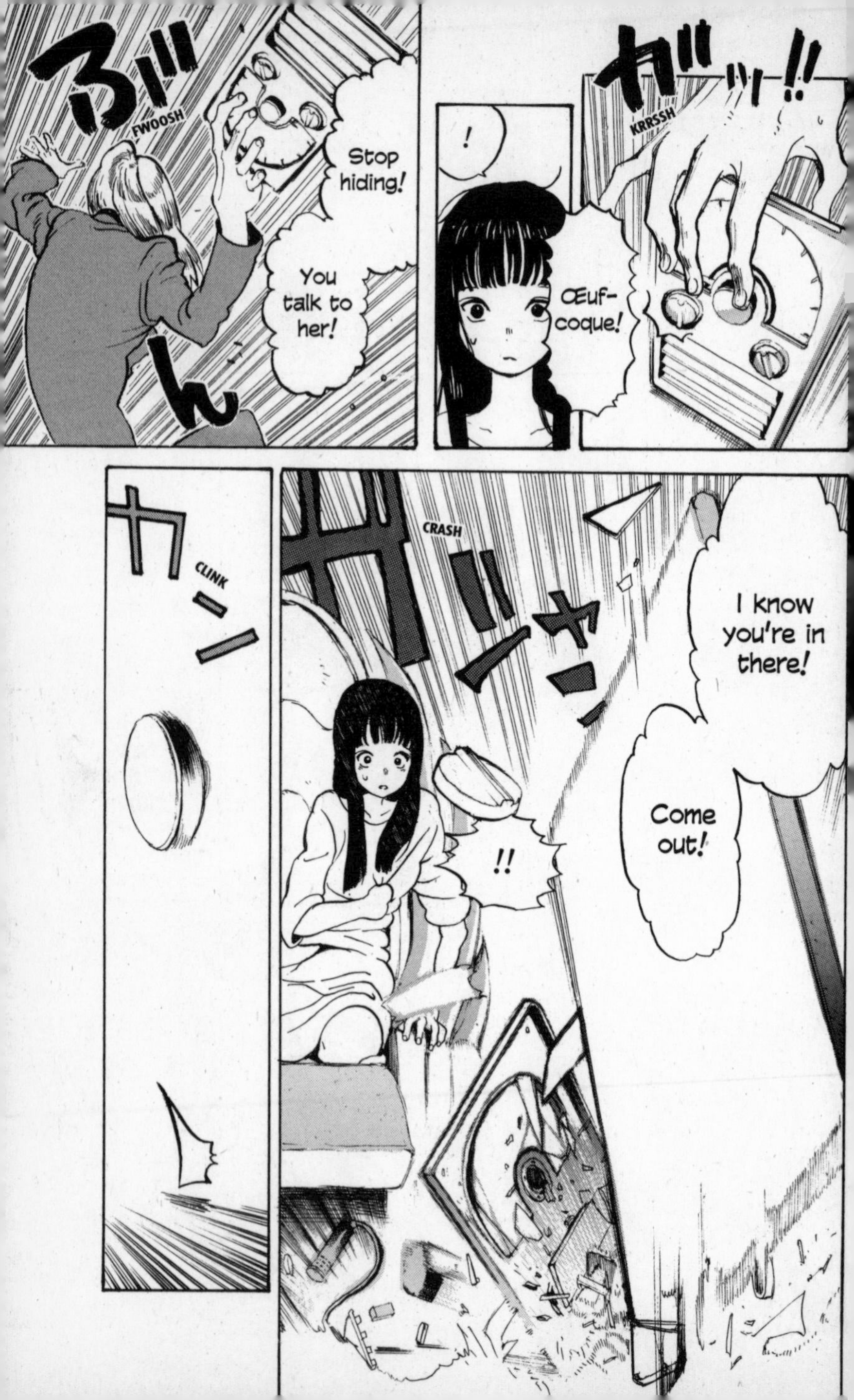
KRRSSH
!
Œuf-coque!
FWOOSH
Stop hiding!
You talk to her!
CRASH
I know you're in there!
Come out!
!!
CLINK

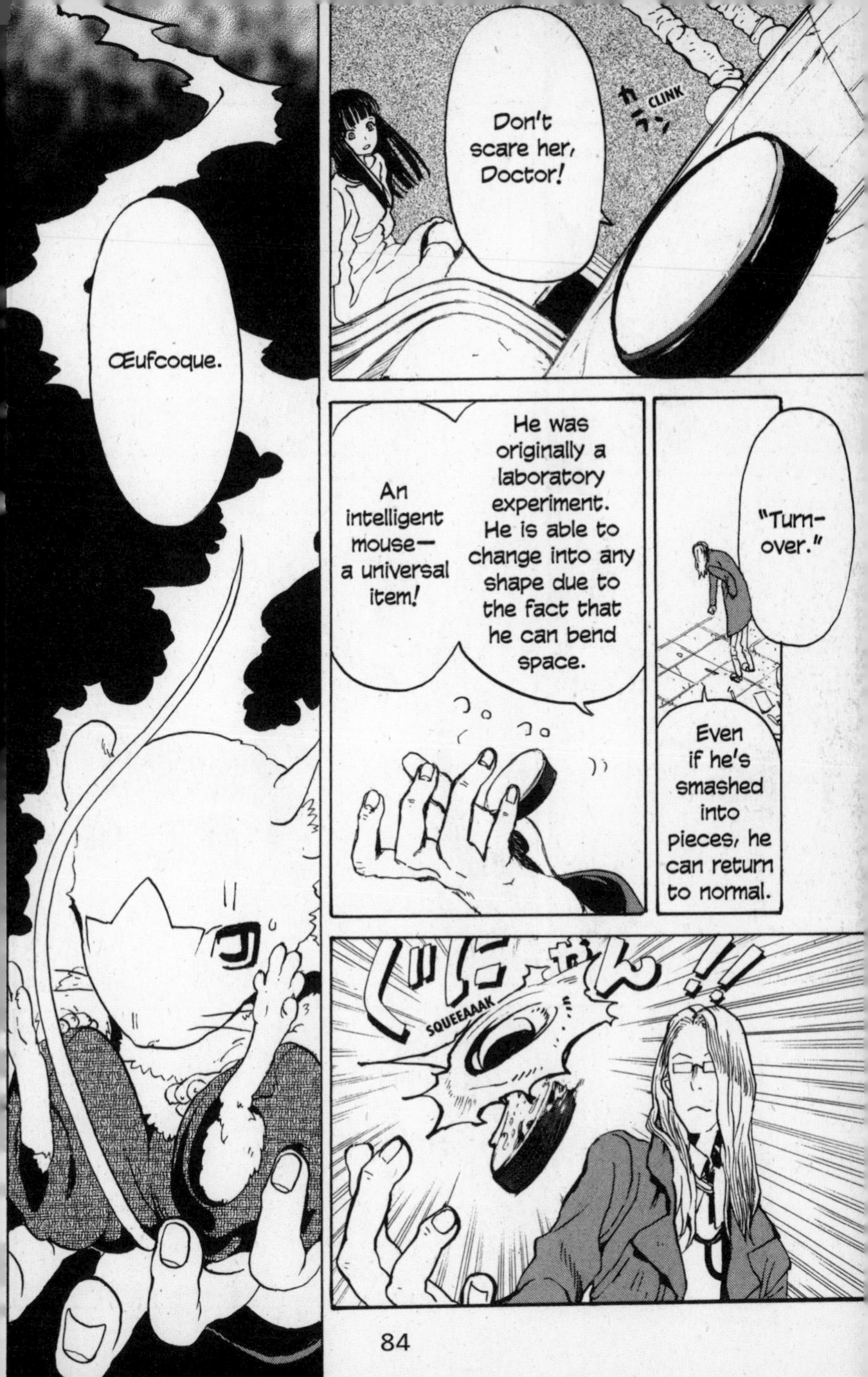
CLINK
Don't scare her, Doctor!
"Turn-over."
Even if he's smashed into pieces, he can return to normal.
He was originally a laboratory experiment. He is able to change into any shape due to the fact that he can bend space.
An intelligent mouse—a universal item!
SQUEEAAAK
Œufcoque.

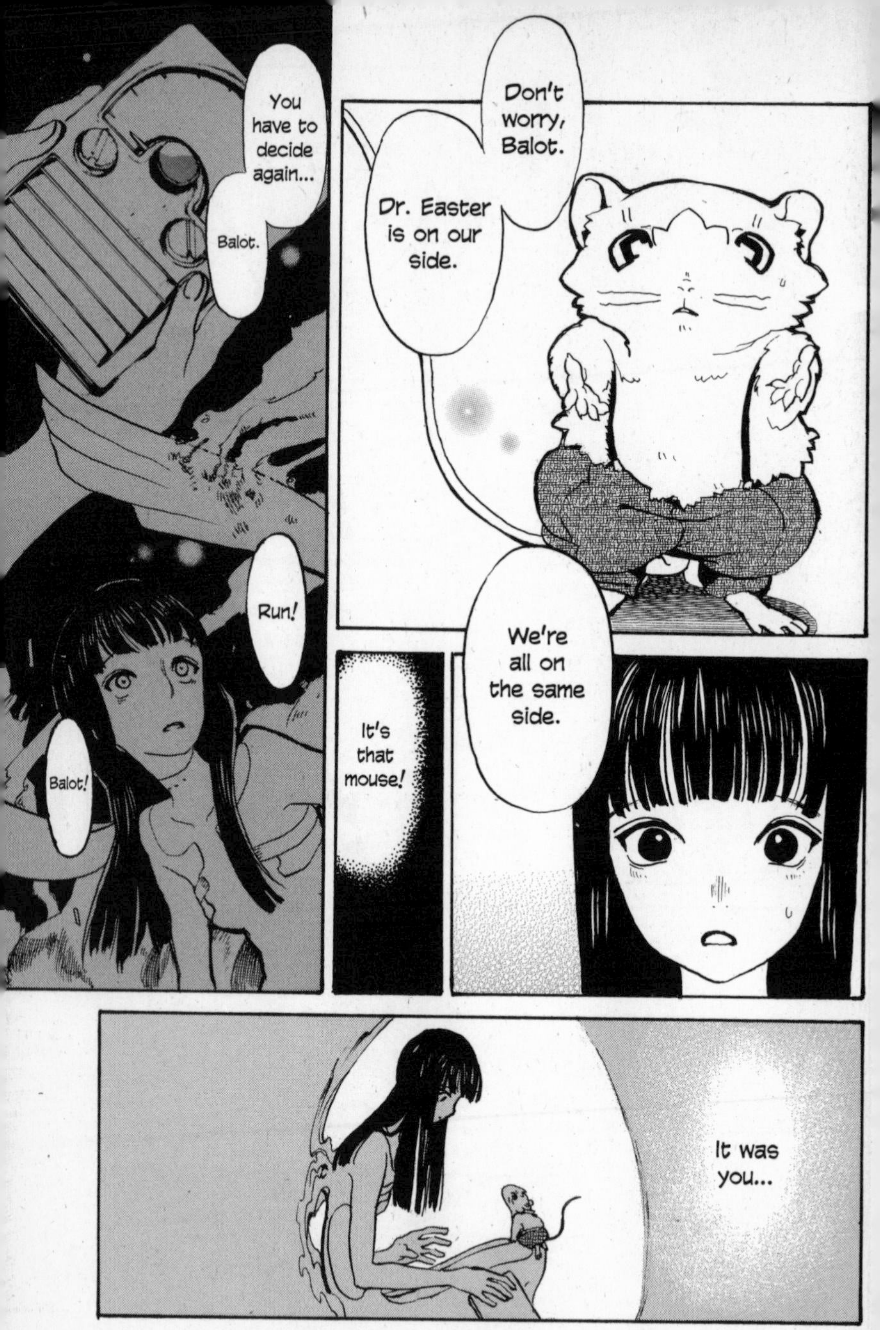
Don't worry, Balot.
Dr. Easter is on our side.
We're all on the same side.
It's that mouse!
You have to decide again...
Balot.
Run!
Balot!
It was you...

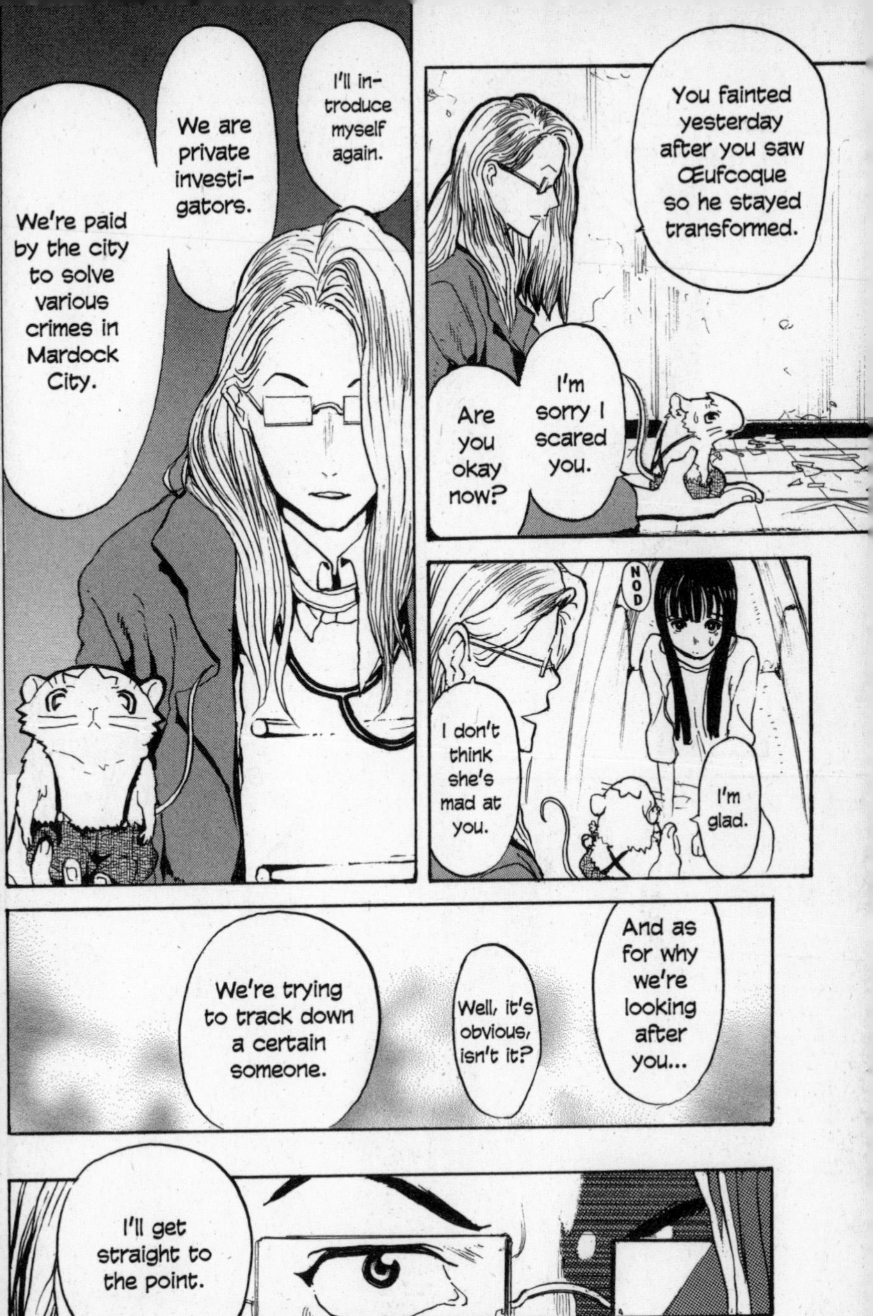
You fainted yesterday after you saw Œufcoque so he stayed transformed.
I'm sorry I scared you.
Are you okay now?
NOD
I'm glad.
I don't think she's mad at you.
I'll in-troduce myself again.
We are private investi-gators.
We're paid by the city to solve various crimes in Mardock City.
And as for why we're looking after you...
Well, it's obvious, isn't it?
We're trying to track down a certain someone.
I'll get straight to the point.

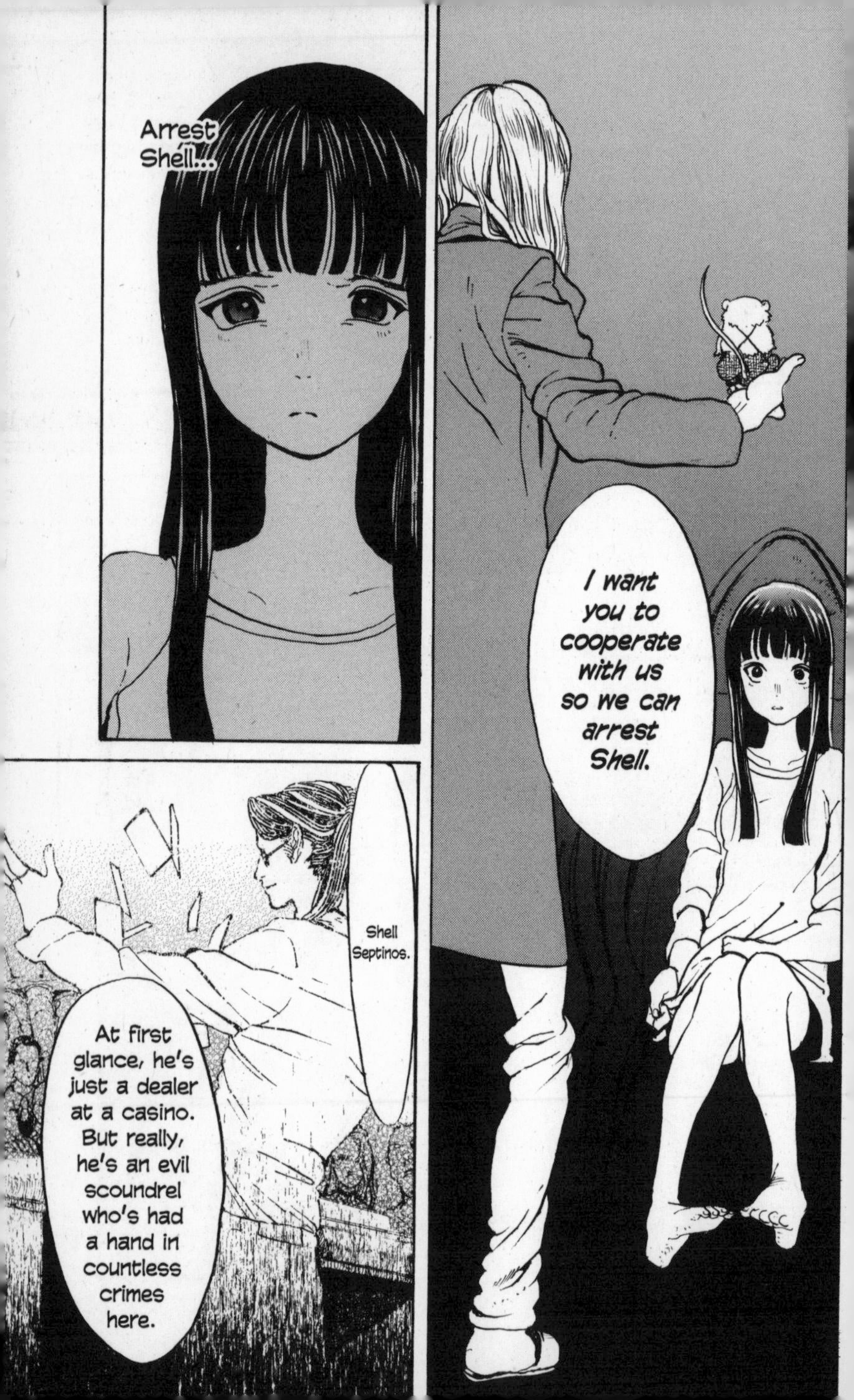
I want you to cooperate with us so we can arrest Shell.
Arrest Shell...
Shell Septinos.
At first glance, he's just a dealer at a casino. But really, he's an evil scoundrel who's had a hand in countless crimes here.

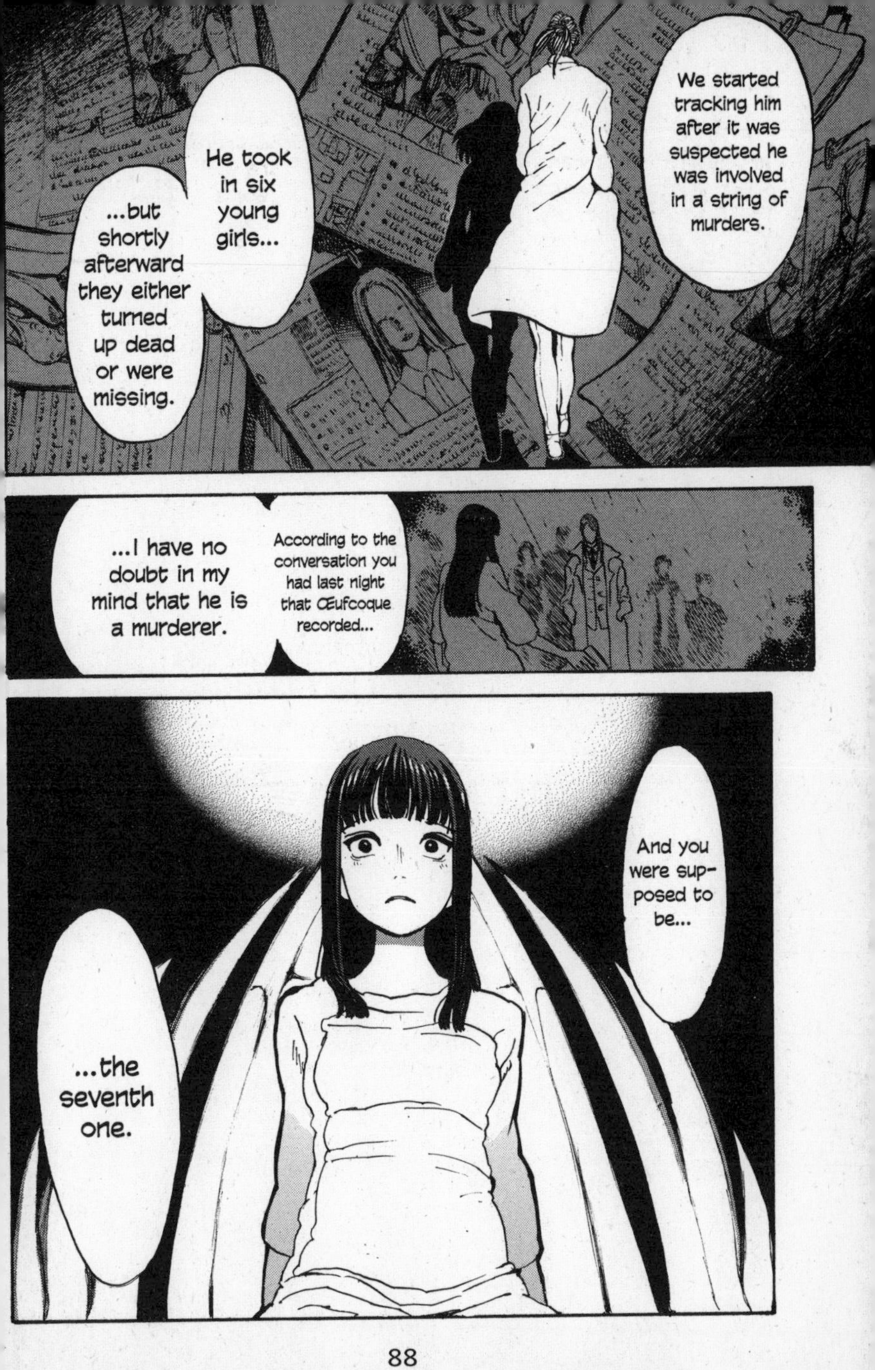
We started tracking him after it was suspected he was involved in a string of murders.
He took in six young girls...
...but shortly afterward they either turned up dead or were missing.
According to the conversation you had last night that Œufcoque recorded...
...I have no doubt in my mind that he is a murderer.
And you were sup-posed to be...
...the seventh one.

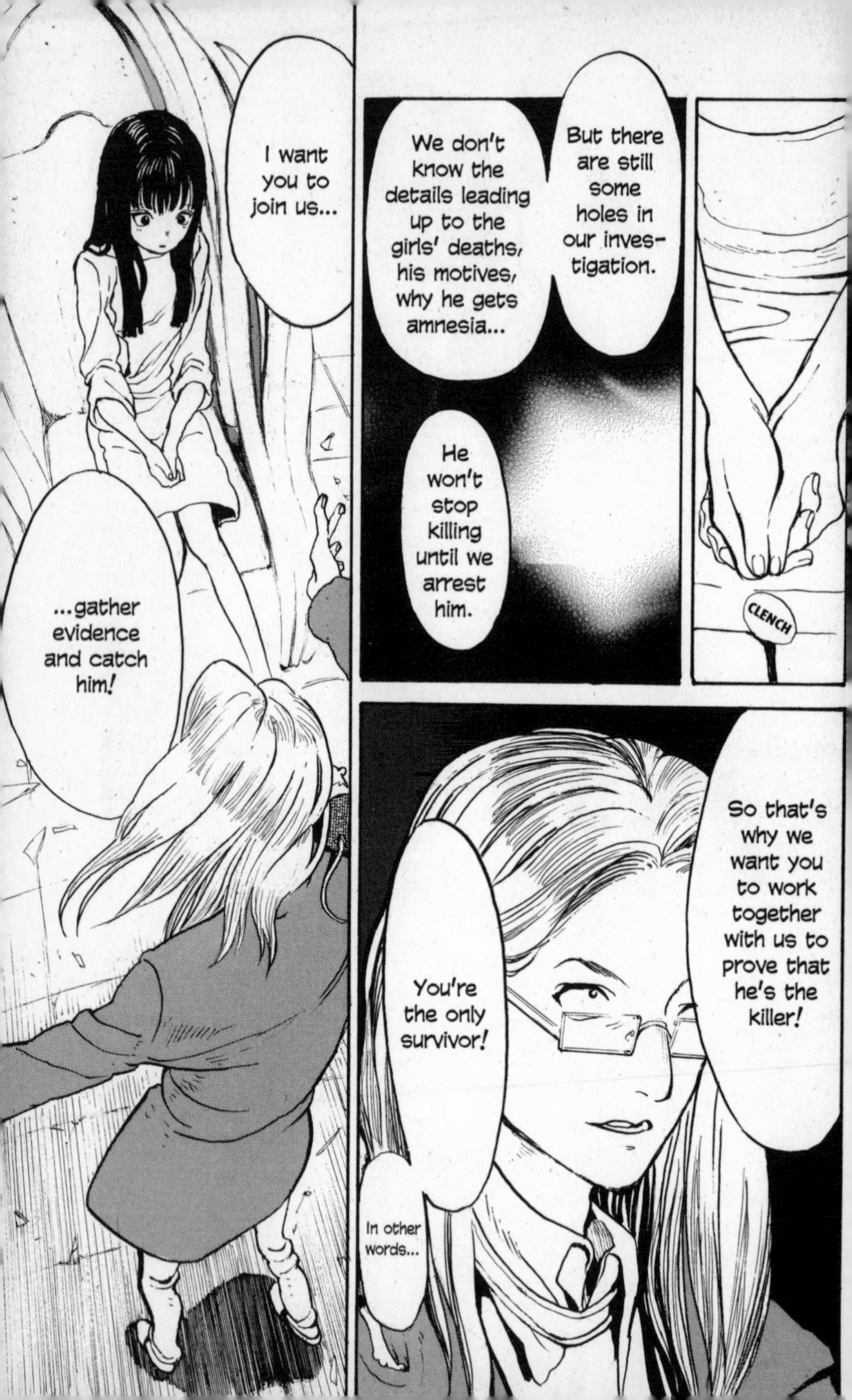
CLENCH
But there are still some holes in our investigation.
We don't know the details leading up to the girls' deaths, his motives, why he gets amnesia...
He won't stop killing until we arrest him.
So that's why we want you to work together with us to prove that he's the killer!
You're the only survivor!
In other words...
I want you to join us...
...gather evidence and catch him!

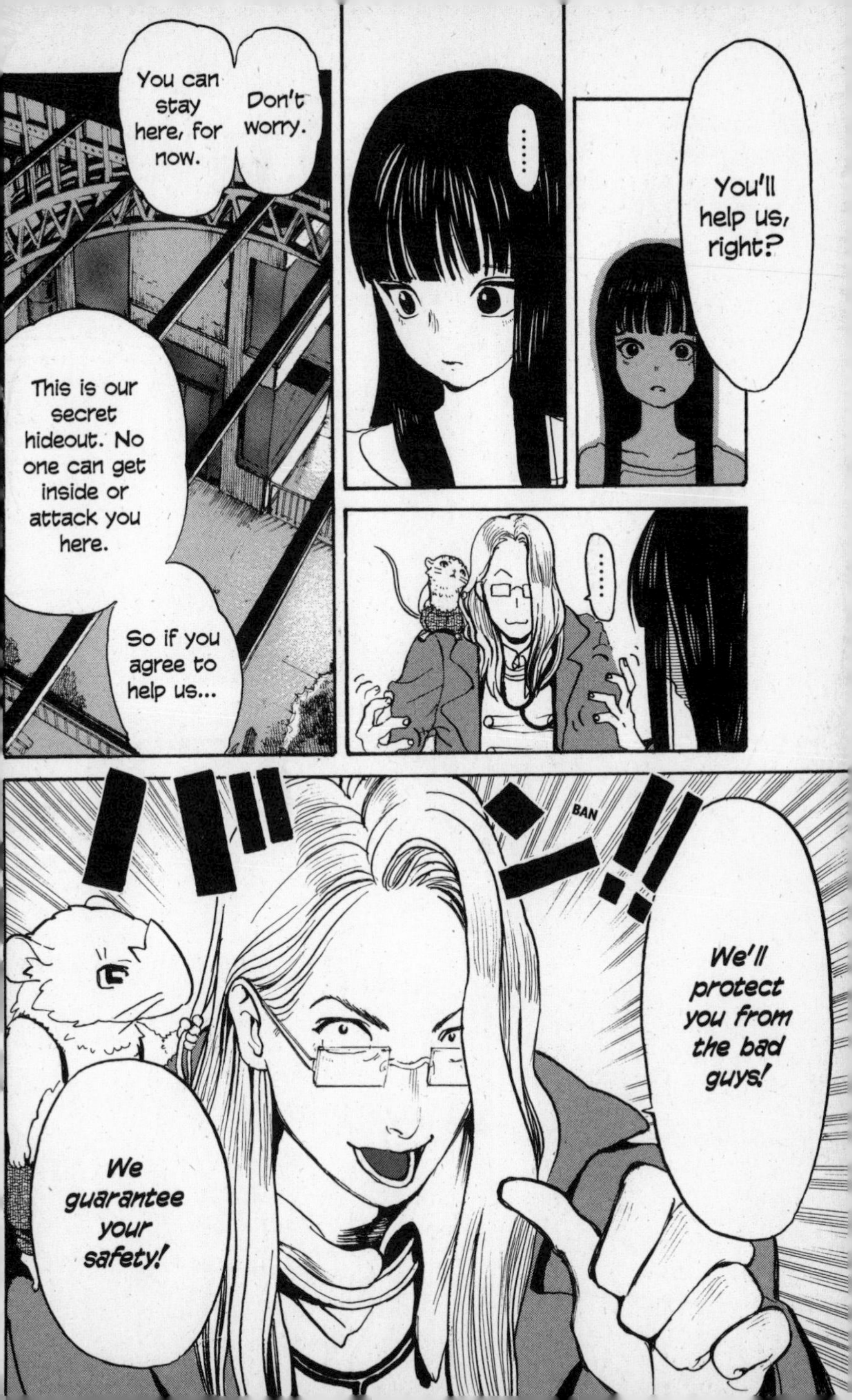
You'll help us, right?
......
......
Don't worry.
You can stay here, for now.
This is our secret hideout. No one can get inside or attack you here.
So if you agree to help us...
BAN
We'll protect you from the bad guys!
We guarantee your safety!

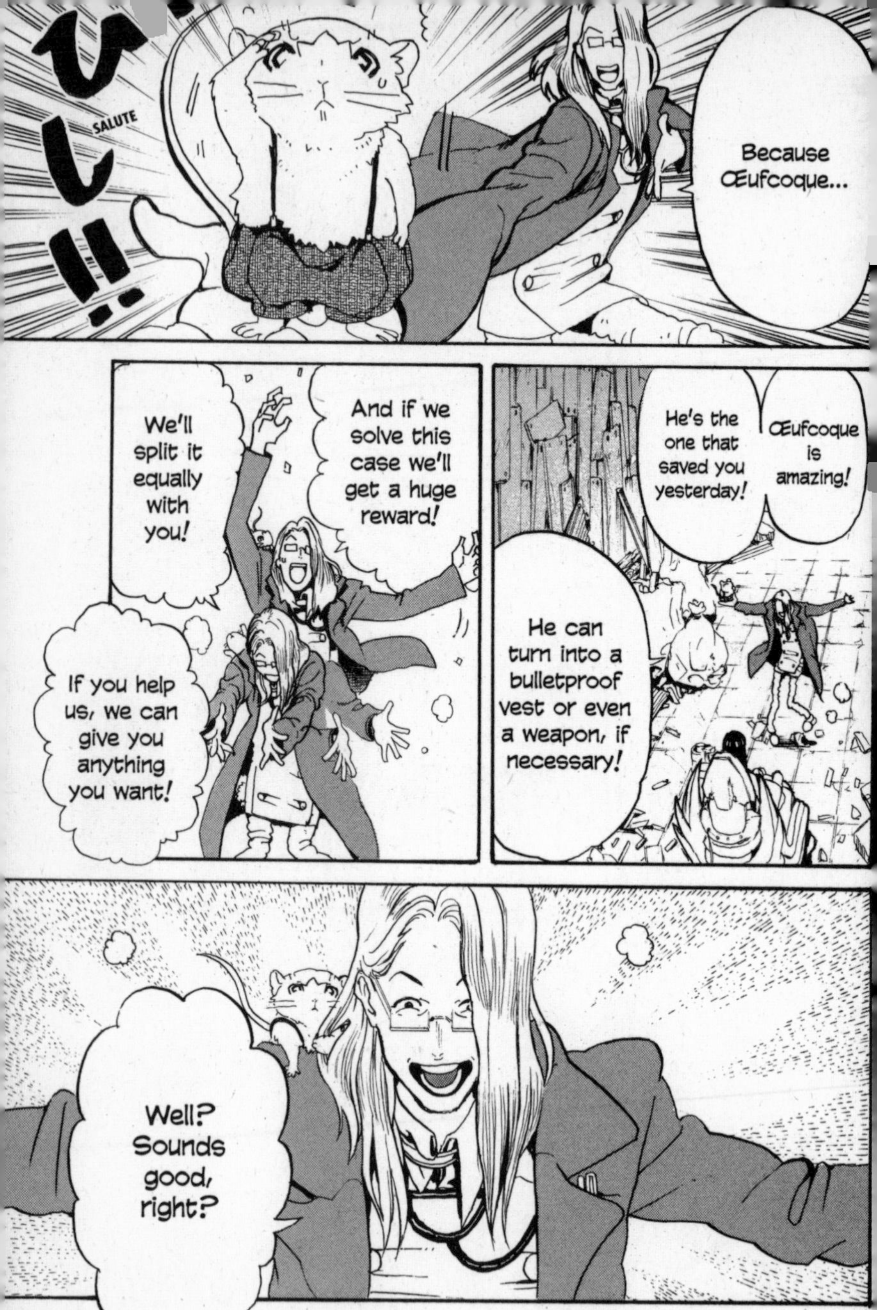
Because Œufcoque...
SALUTE
Œufcoque is amazing!
He's the one that saved you yesterday!
He can turn into a bulletproof vest or even a weapon, if necessary!
And if we solve this case we'll get a huge reward!
We'll split it equally with you!
If you help us, we can give you anything you want!
Well? Sounds good, right?

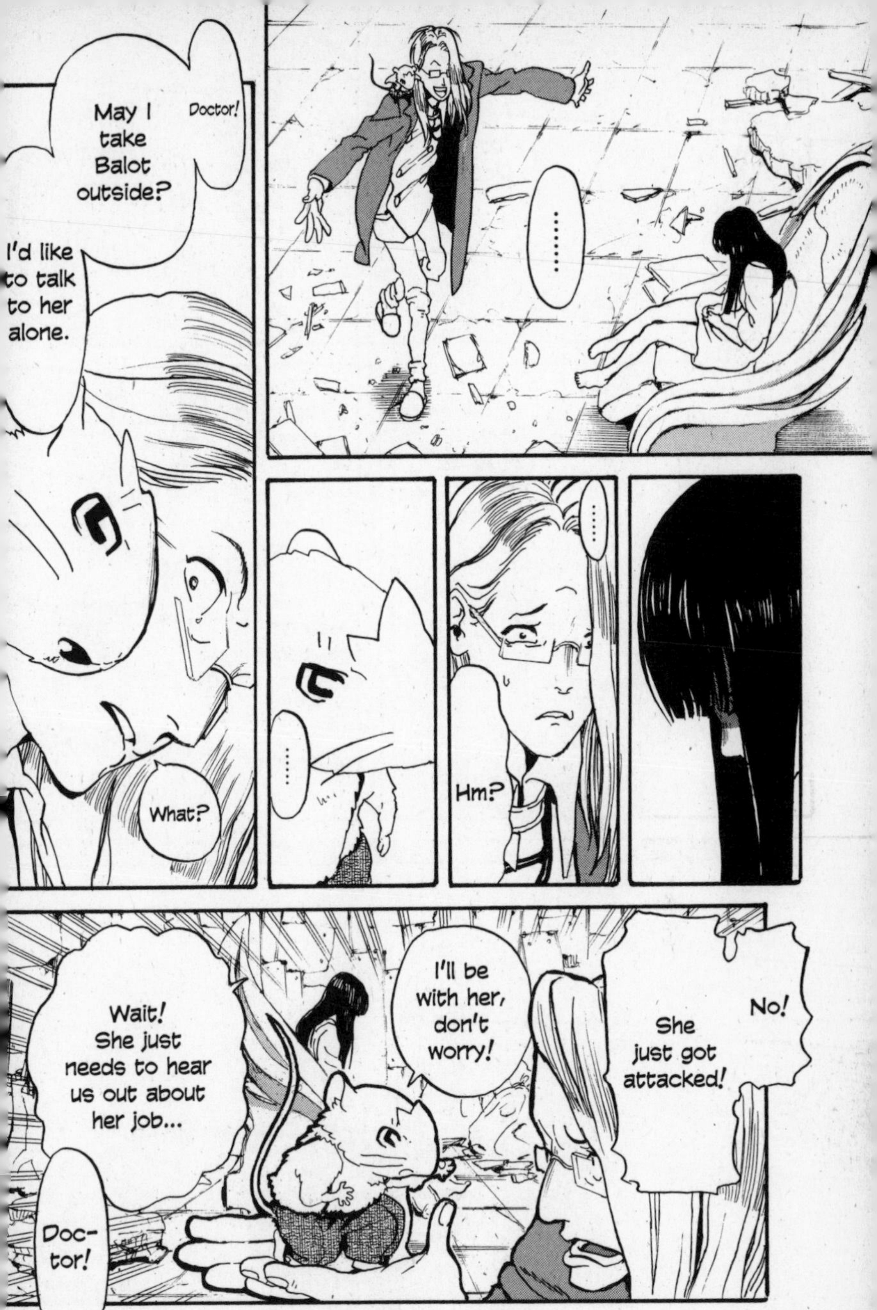
……
……
Hm?
……
Doctor!
May I take Balot outside?
I'd like to talk to her alone.
What?
No!
She just got attacked!
I'll be with her, don't worry!
Wait! She just needs to hear us out about her job...
Doc-tor!

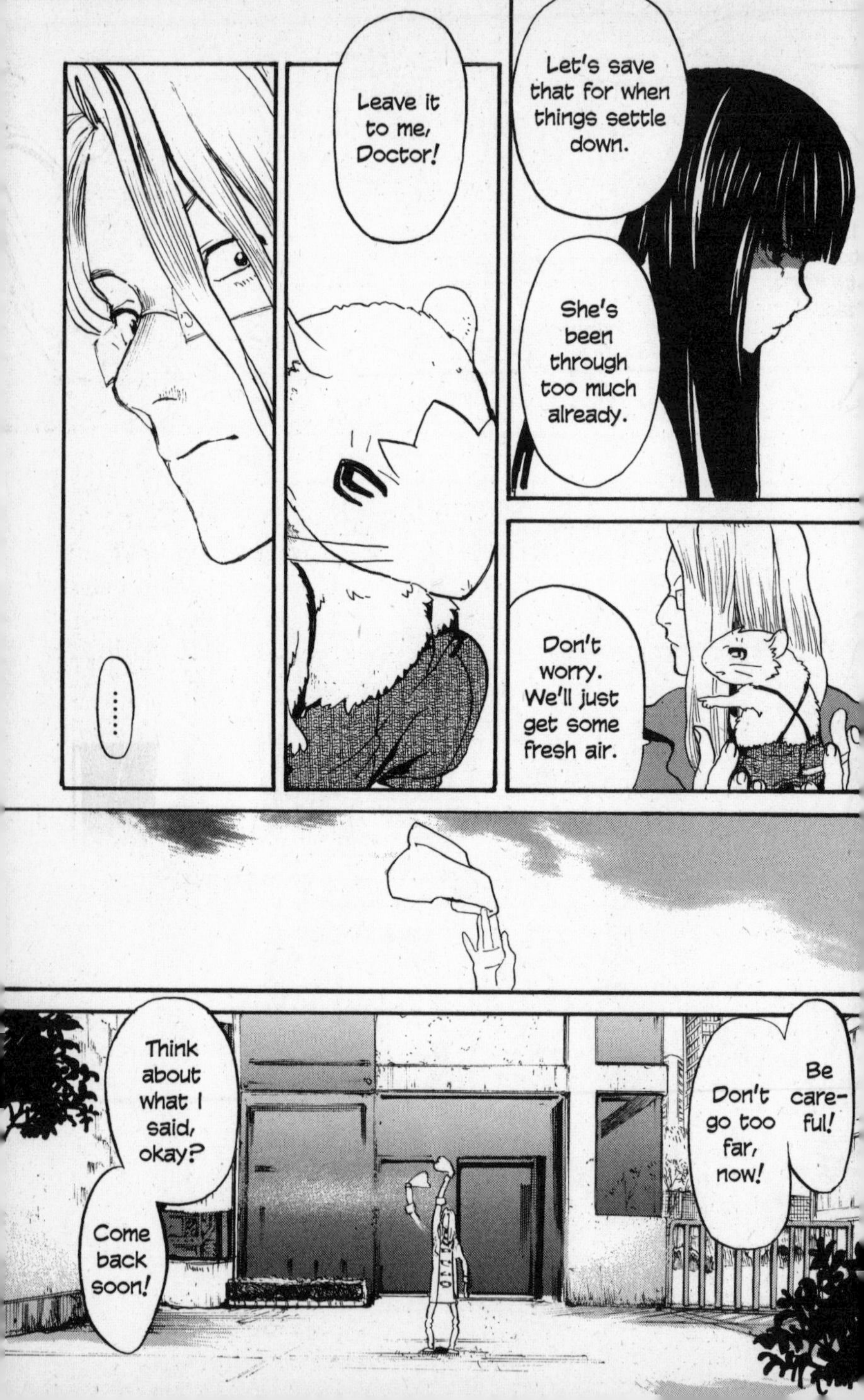
Let's save that for when things settle down.
She's been through too much already.
Don't worry. We'll just get some fresh air.
Leave it to me, Doctor!
......
Be care-ful!
Don't go too far, now!
Think about what I said, okay?
Come back soon!

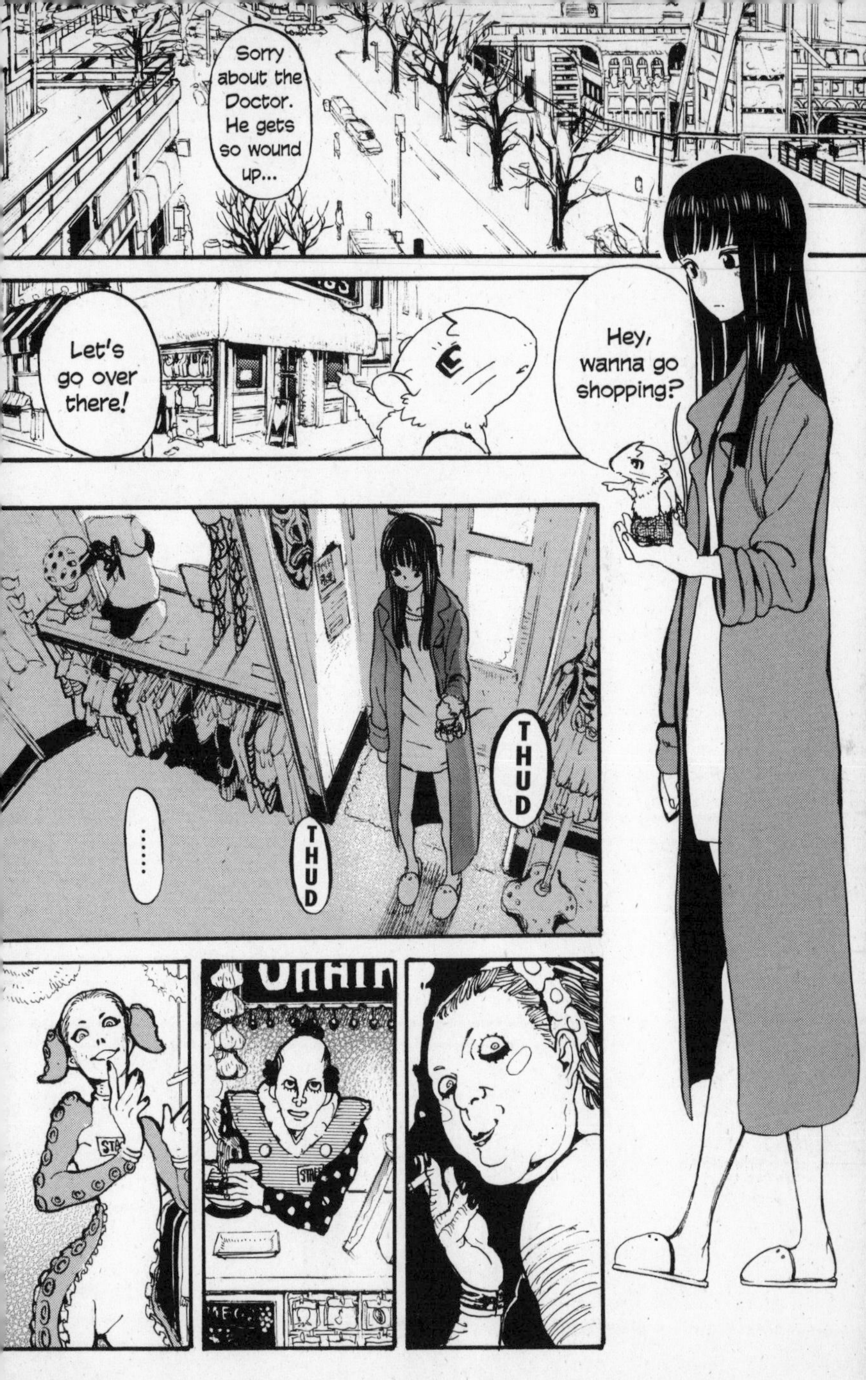
Sorry about the Doctor. He gets so wound up...
Hey, wanna go shopping?
Let's go over there!
THUD
THUD
......

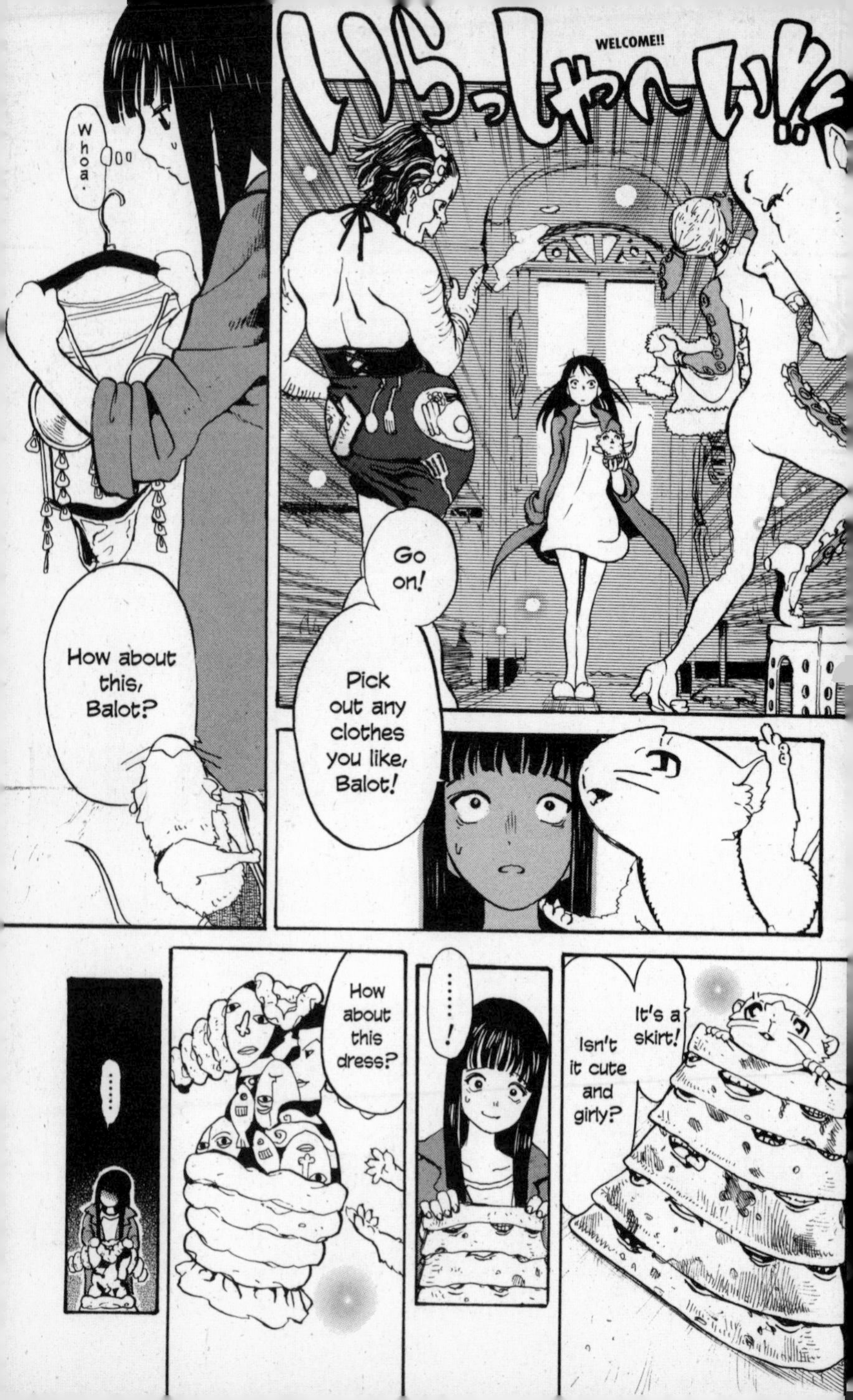
いらっしゃ〜い!!
WELCOME!!
Go on!
Pick out any clothes you like, Balot!
Whoa.
How about this, Balot?
It's a skirt!
Isn't it cute and girly?
......!
How about this dress?
......

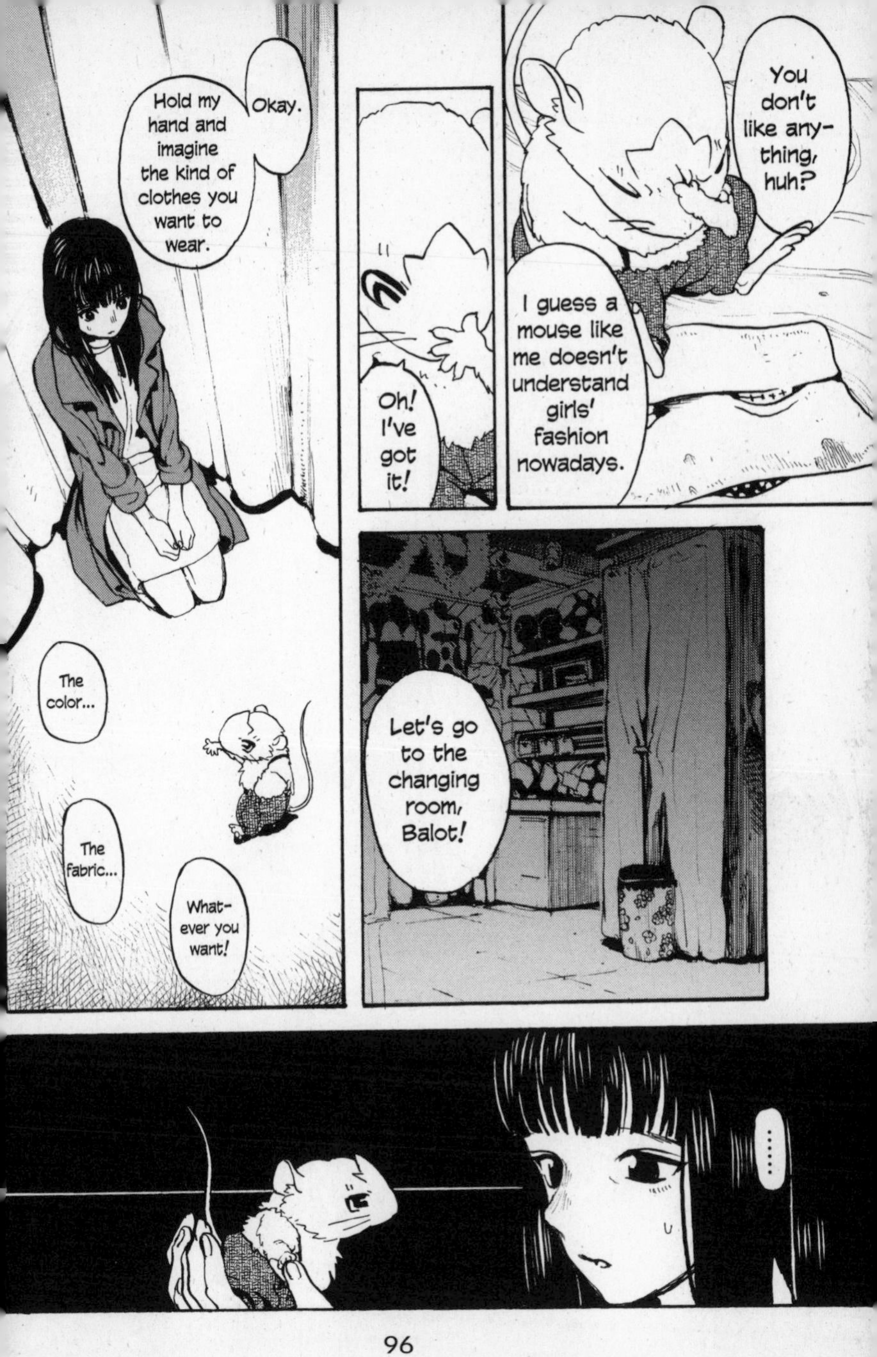
You don't like anything, huh?
I guess a mouse like me doesn't understand girls' fashion nowadays.
Oh! I've got it!
Let's go to the changing room, Balot!
Okay.
Hold my hand and imagine the kind of clothes you want to wear.
The color...
The fabric...
Whatever you want!
......

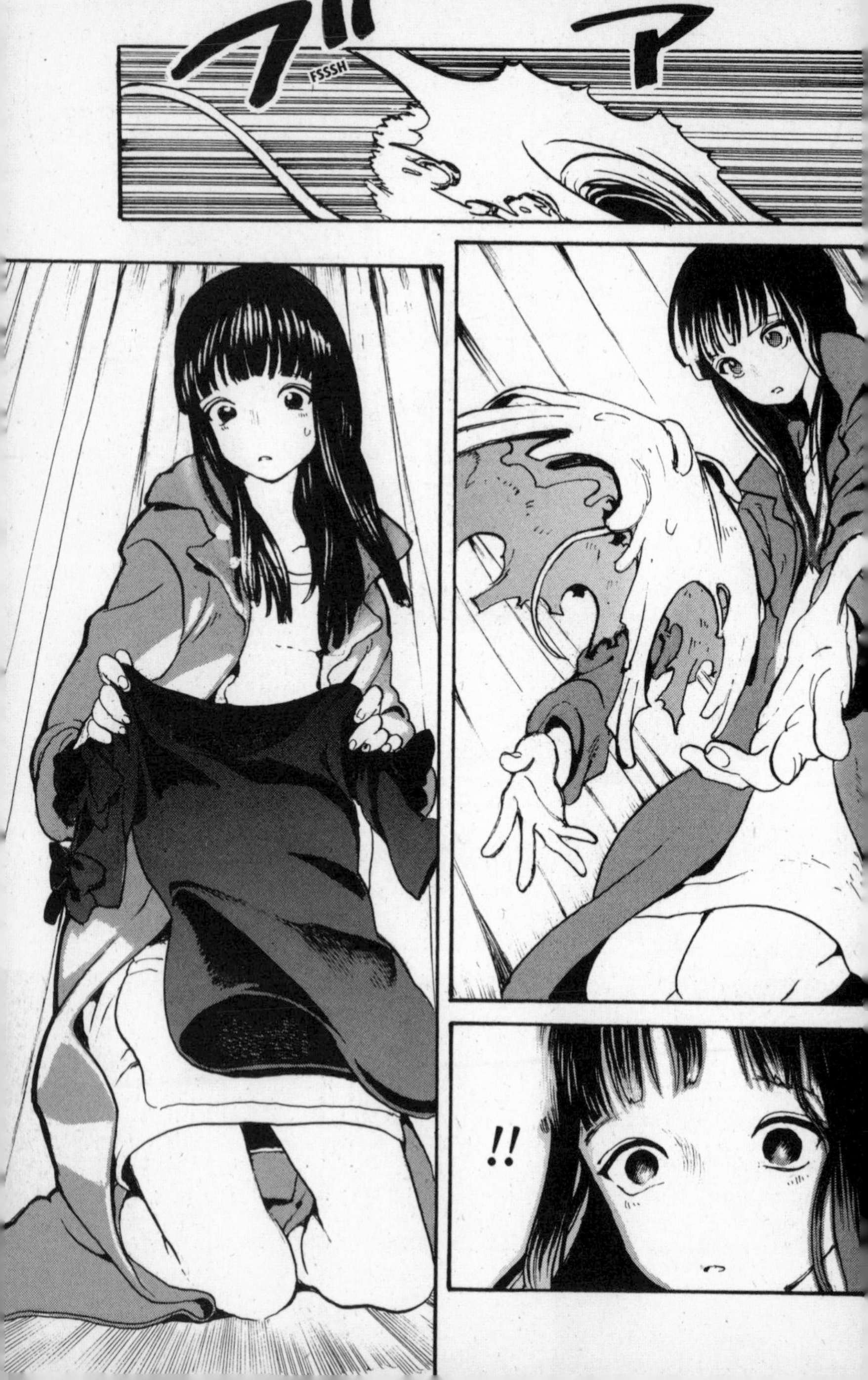
ブ
FSSSH
ア
!!

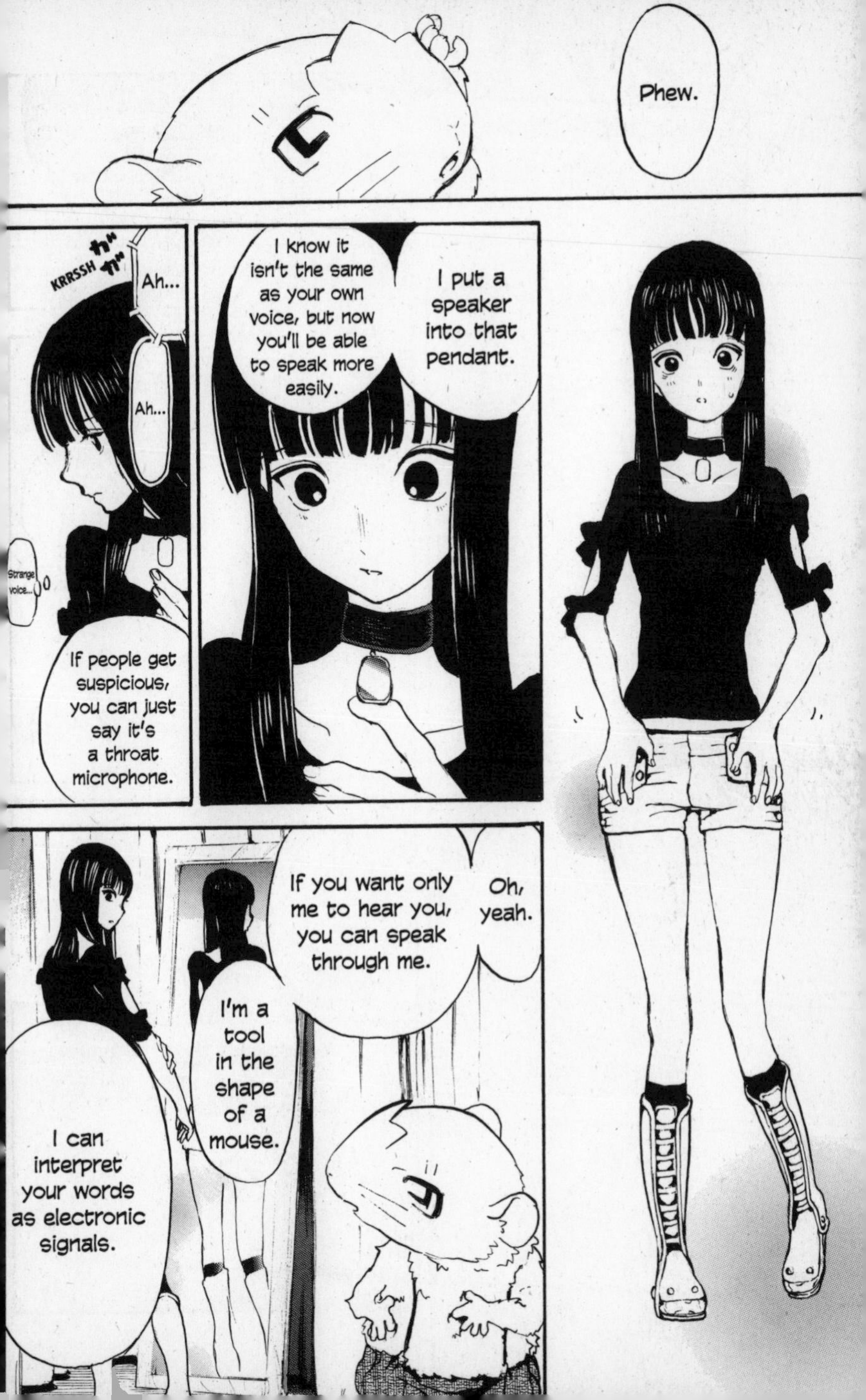
Phew.
I put a speaker into that pendant.
I know it isn't the same as your own voice, but now you'll be able to speak more easily.
KRRSSH
Ah...
Ah...
Strange voice...
If people get suspicious, you can just say it's a throat microphone.
Oh, yeah.
If you want only me to hear you, you can speak through me.
I'm a tool in the shape of a mouse.
I can interpret your words as electronic signals.

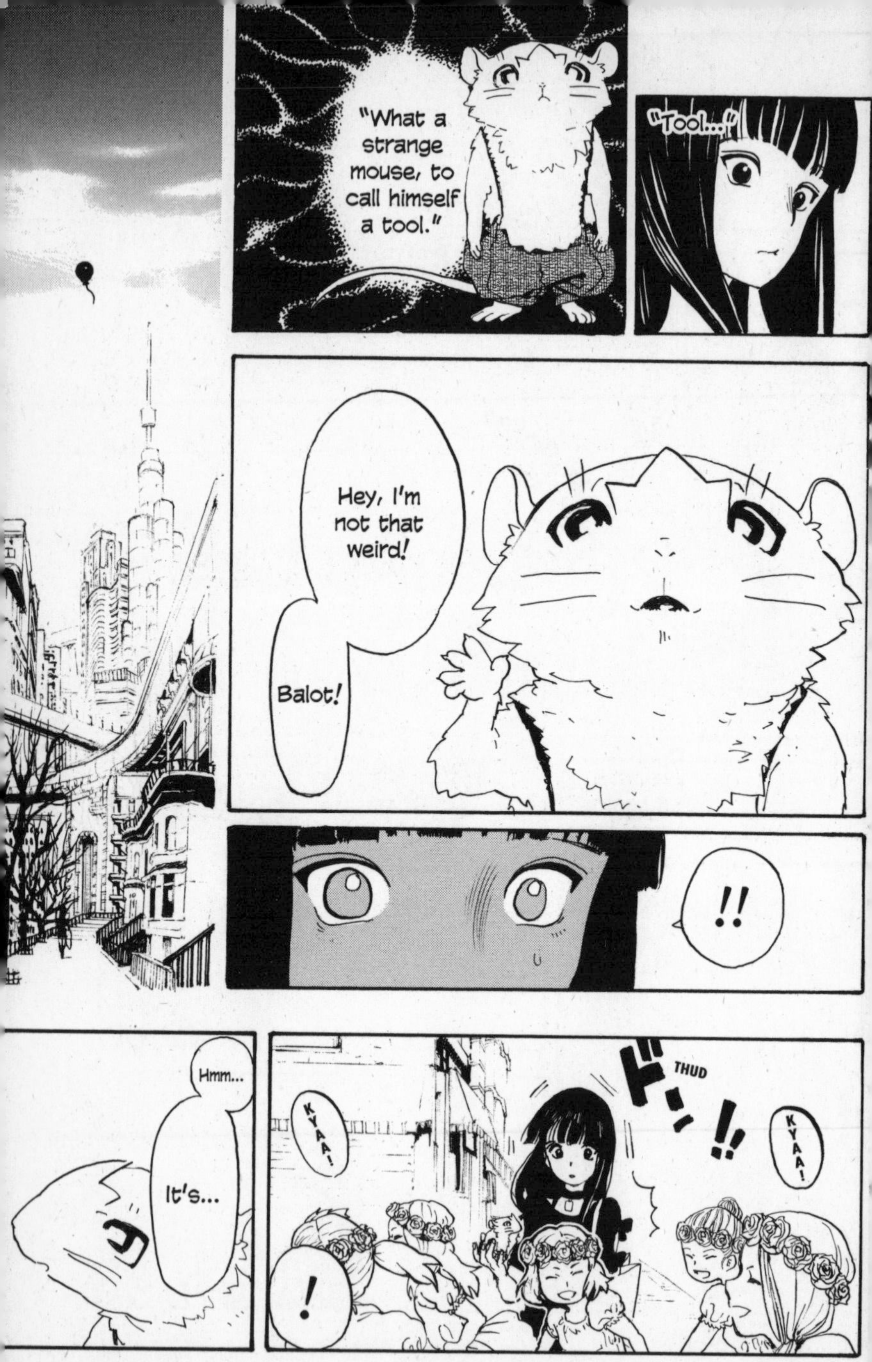
"Tool..."
"What a strange mouse, to call himself a tool."
Hey, I'm not that weird!
Balot!
!!
THUD
!!
KYAA!
KYAA!
!
Hmm...
It's...

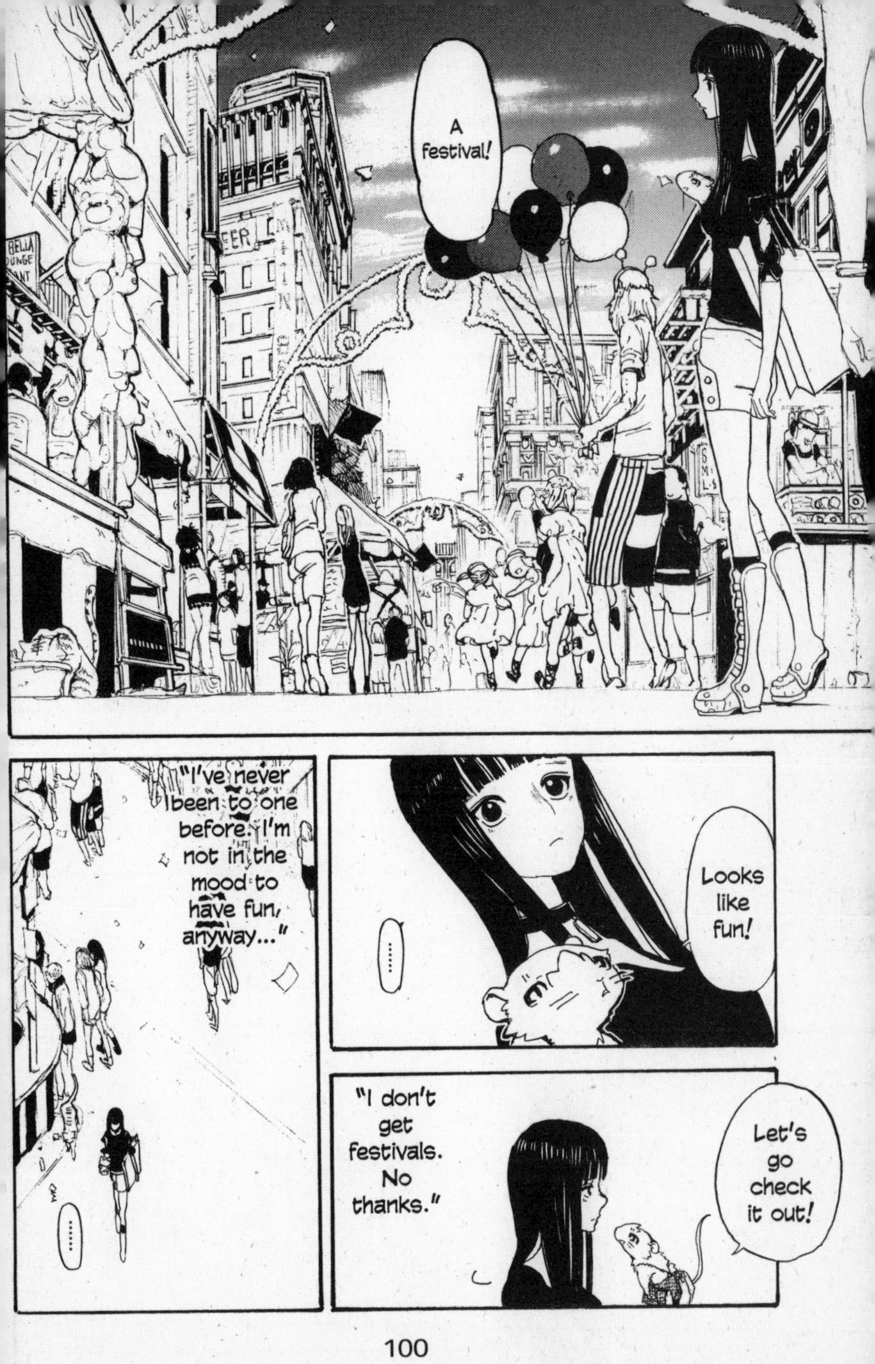
A festival!
Looks like fun!
......
Let's go check it out!
"I don't get festivals. No thanks."
"I've never been to one before. I'm not in the mood to have fun, anyway..."
......

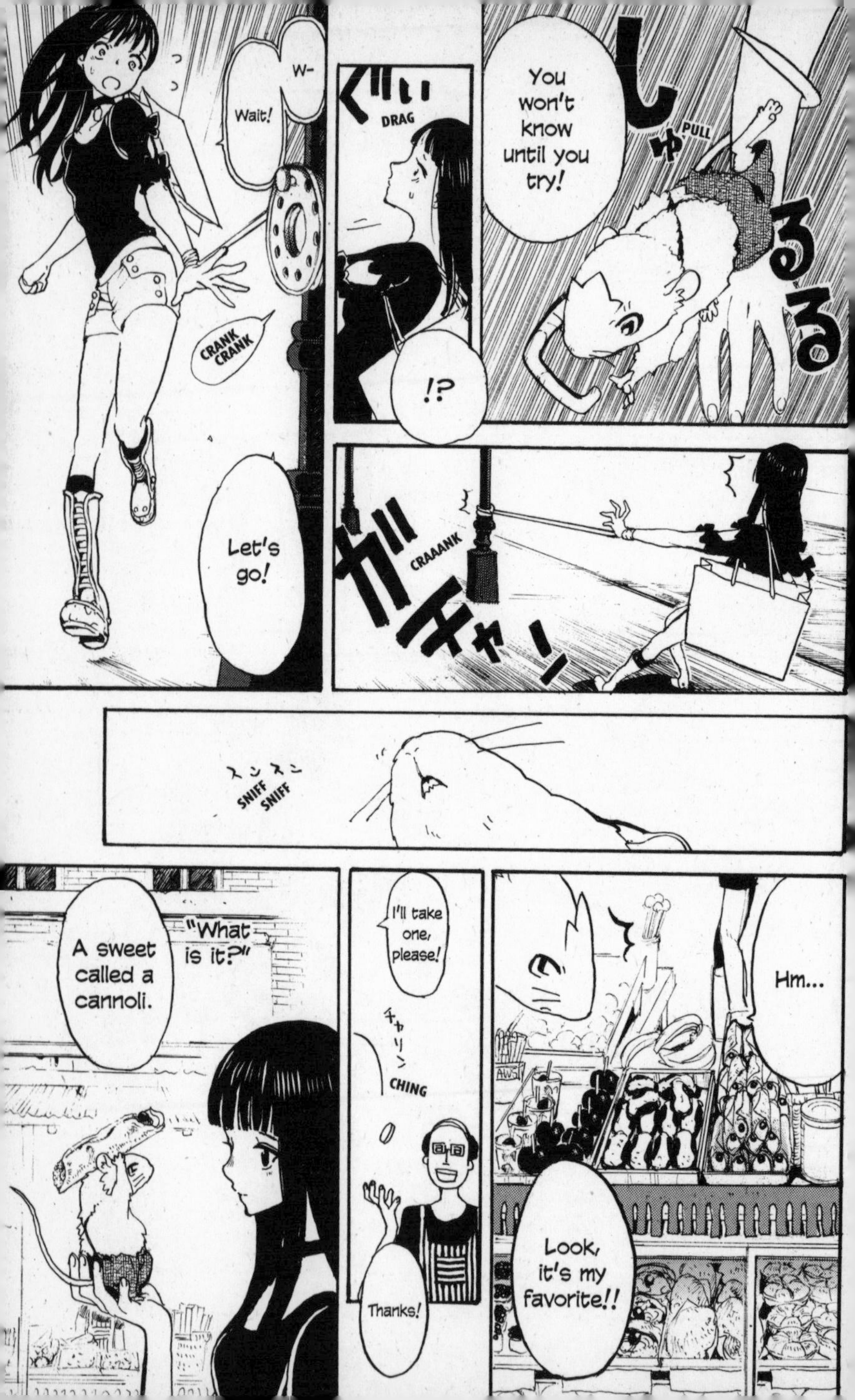

You won't know until you try!
しゅるる
PULL
くいっ
DRAG
!?
ガチャン
CRAAANK
W-
Wait!
CRANK CRANK
Let's go!
スンスン
SNIFF SNIFF
Hm...
Look, it's my favorite!!
I'll take one, please!
チャリン
CHING
Thanks!
"What is it?"
A sweet called a cannoli.

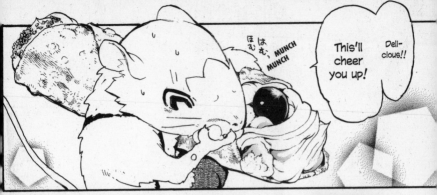

This'll cheer you up!

Deli-cious!!

はむ, ほむ, MUNCH MUNCH

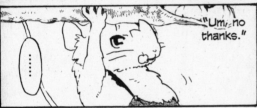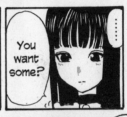

"Um, no thanks."

You want some?

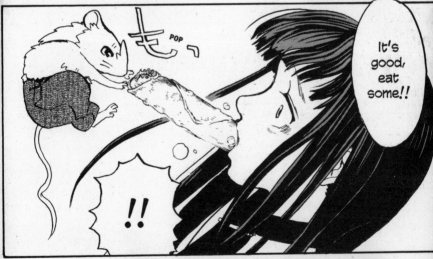

POP

It's good, eat some!!

!!

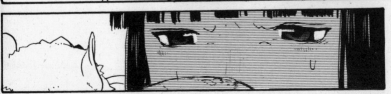

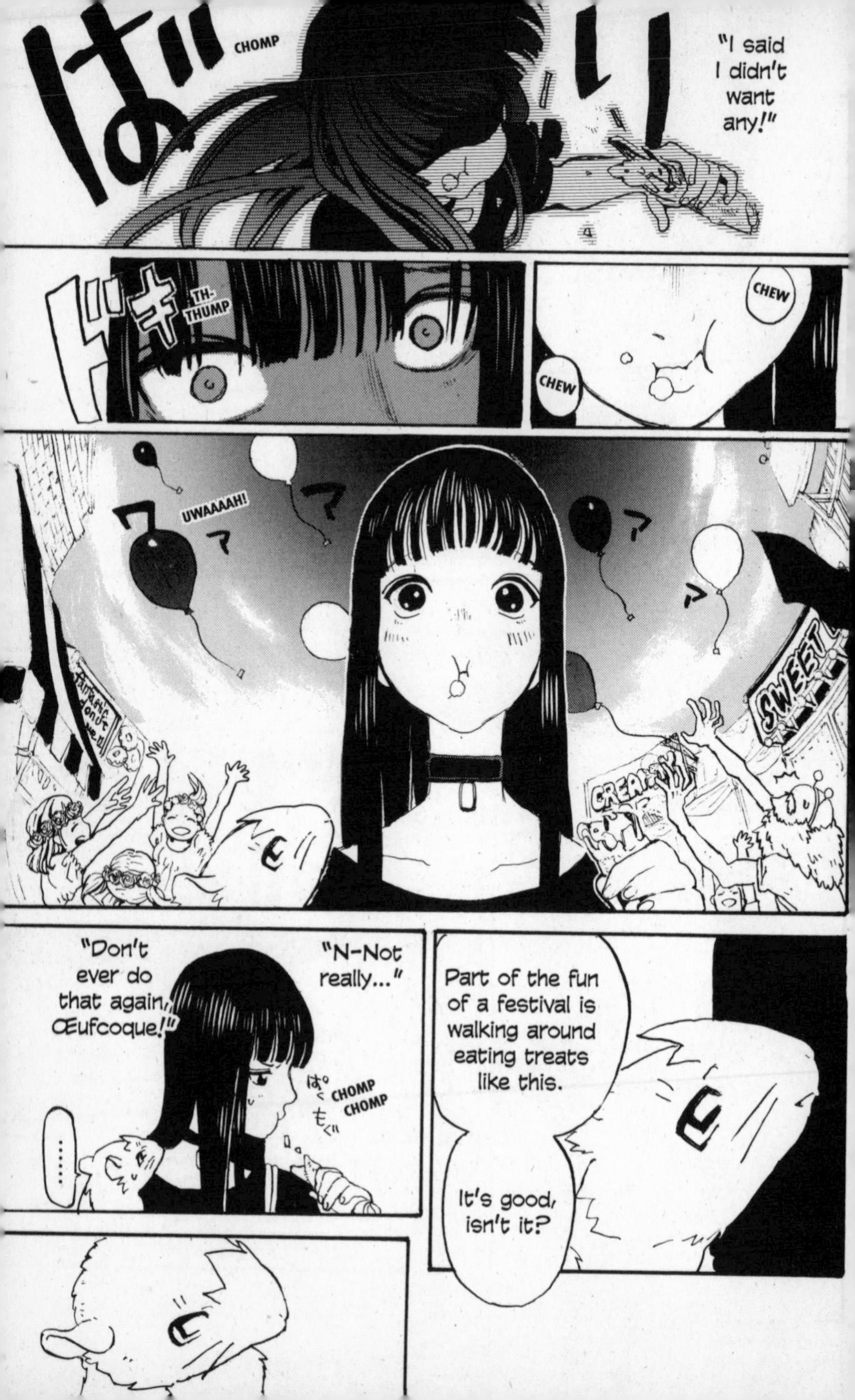
"I said I didn't want any!"
CHOMP
CHEW
CHEW
TH-THUMP
UWAAAAH!
SWEET
Part of the fun of a festival is walking around eating treats like this.
It's good, isn't it?
"N-Not really..."
"Don't ever do that again, Œufcoque!"
CHOMP CHOMP
......

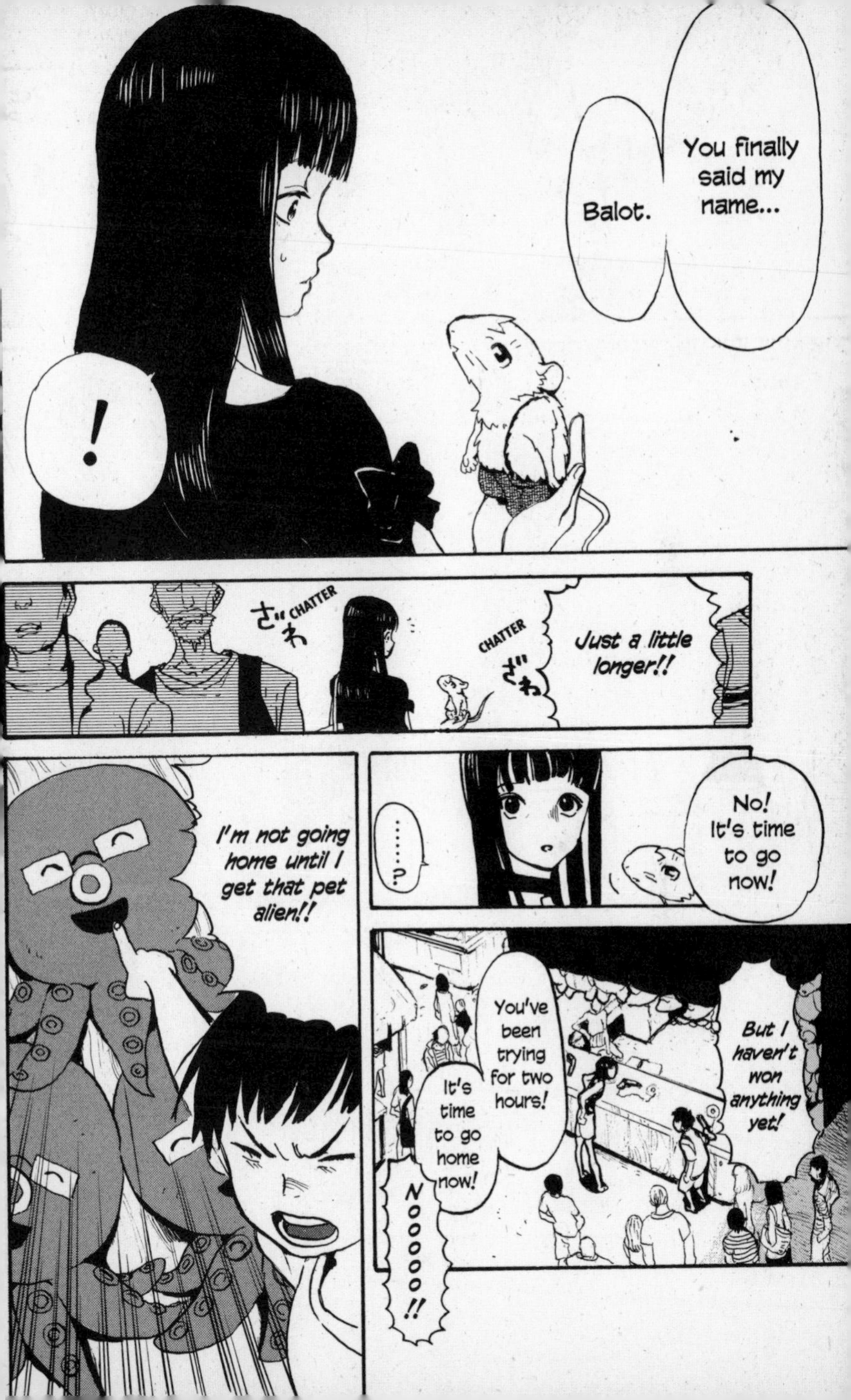
You finally said my name...
Balot.
!
Just a little longer!!
CHATTER ざわ
ざわ CHATTER
No! It's time to go now!
......?
But I haven't won anything yet!
You've been trying for two hours!
It's time to go home now!
Noooooo!!
I'm not going home until I get that pet alien!!

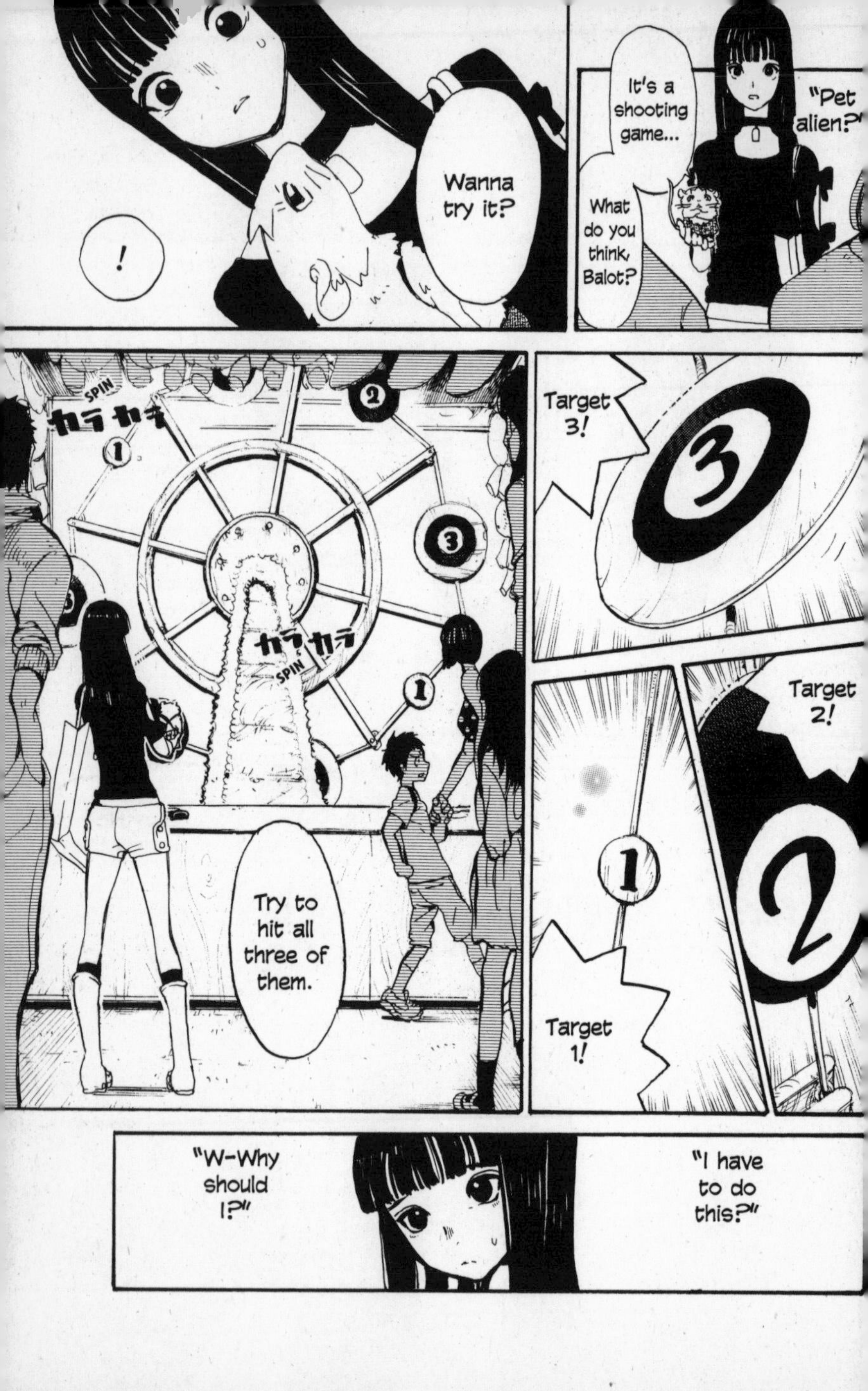
"Pet alien?"
It's a shooting game...
What do you think, Balot?
Wanna try it?
!
Target 3!
Target 2!
Target 1!
SPIN
カラカラ
カラカラ
SPIN
Try to hit all three of them.
"I have to do this?"
"W-Why should I?"

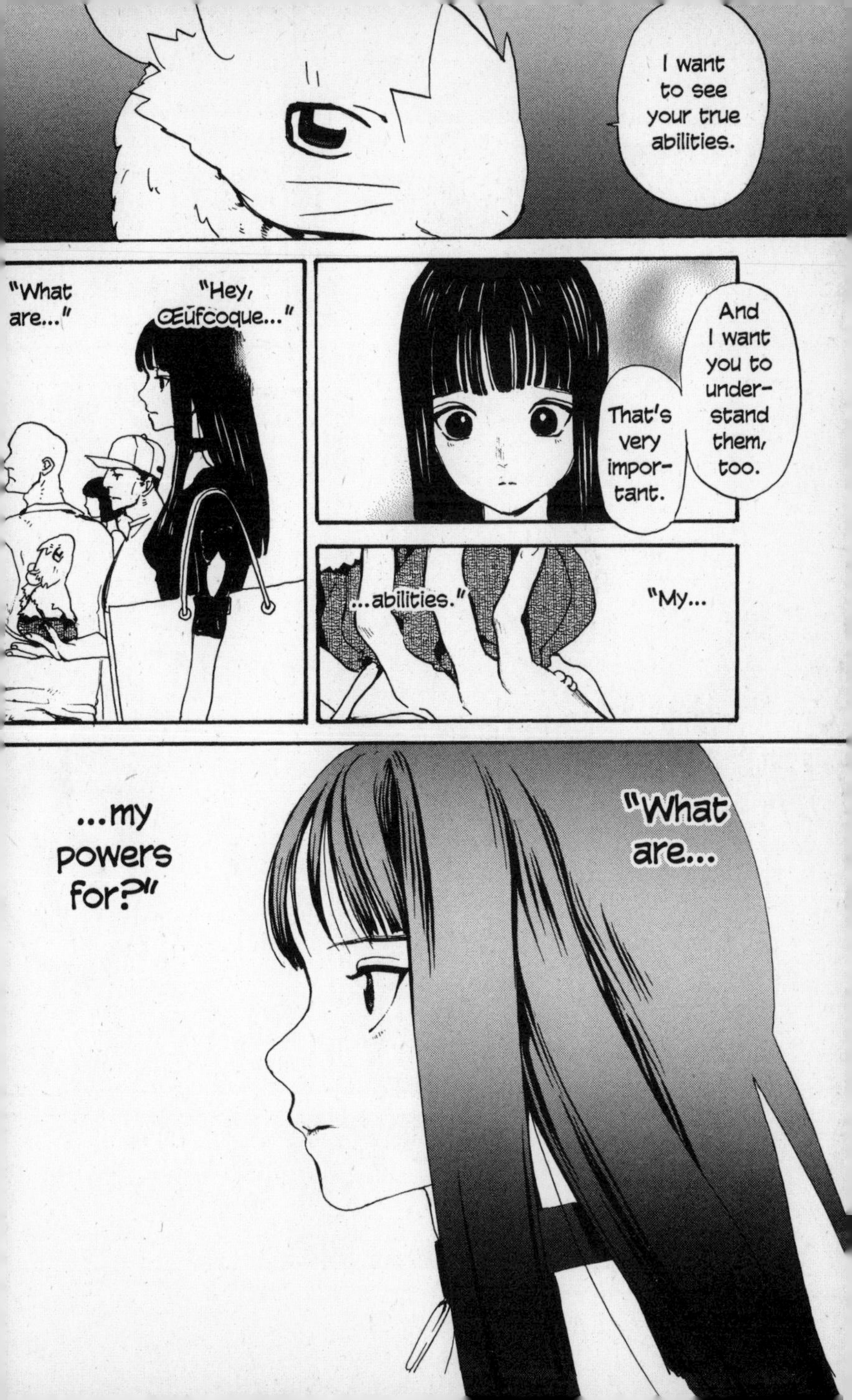
I want to see your true abilities.
And I want you to understand them, too.
That's very important.
"My...
...abilities."
"Hey, Œufcoque..."
"What are..."
"What are...
...my powers for?"

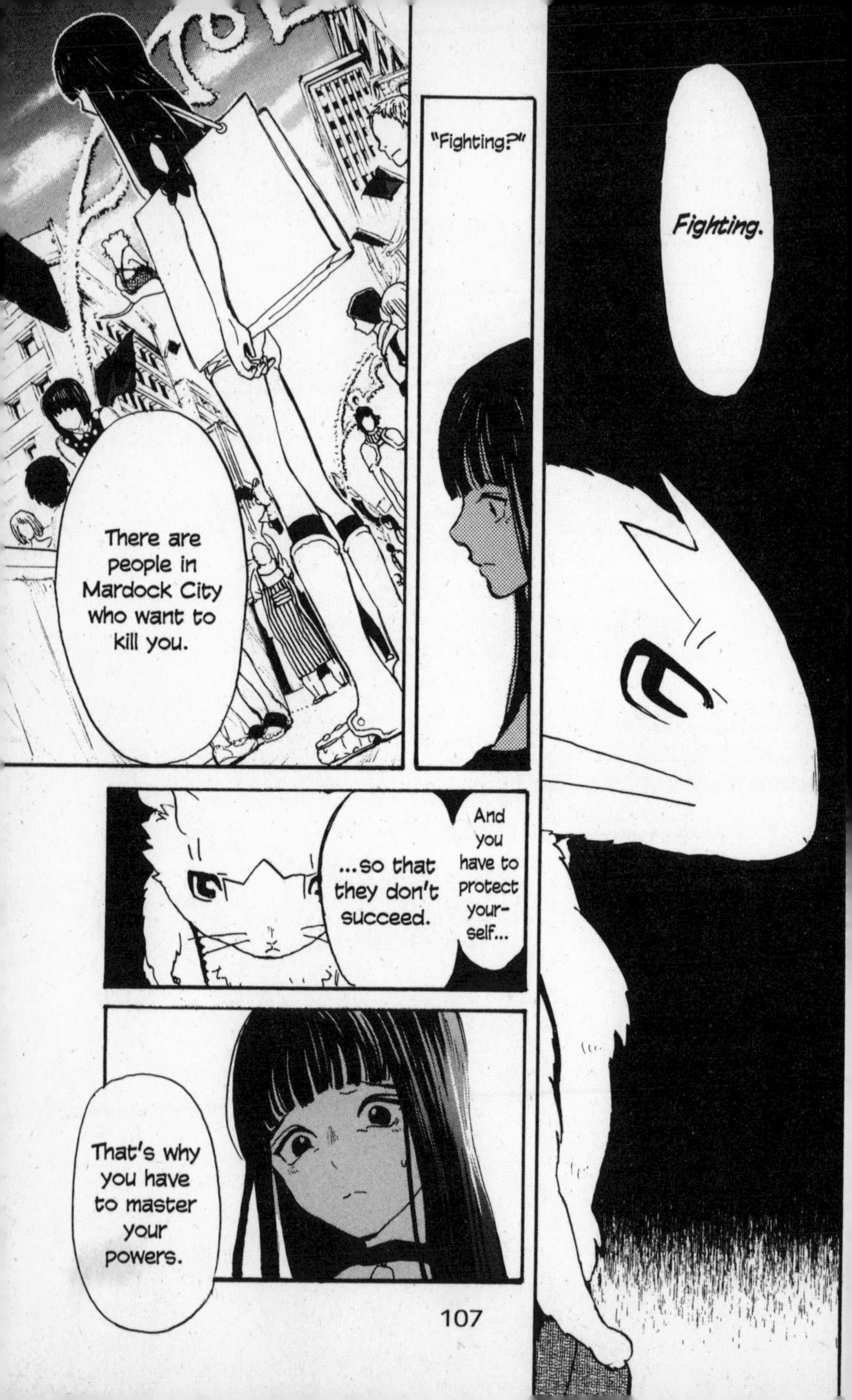
Fighting.
"Fighting?"
There are people in Mardock City who want to kill you.
And you have to protect your-self...
...so that they don't succeed.
That's why you have to master your powers.

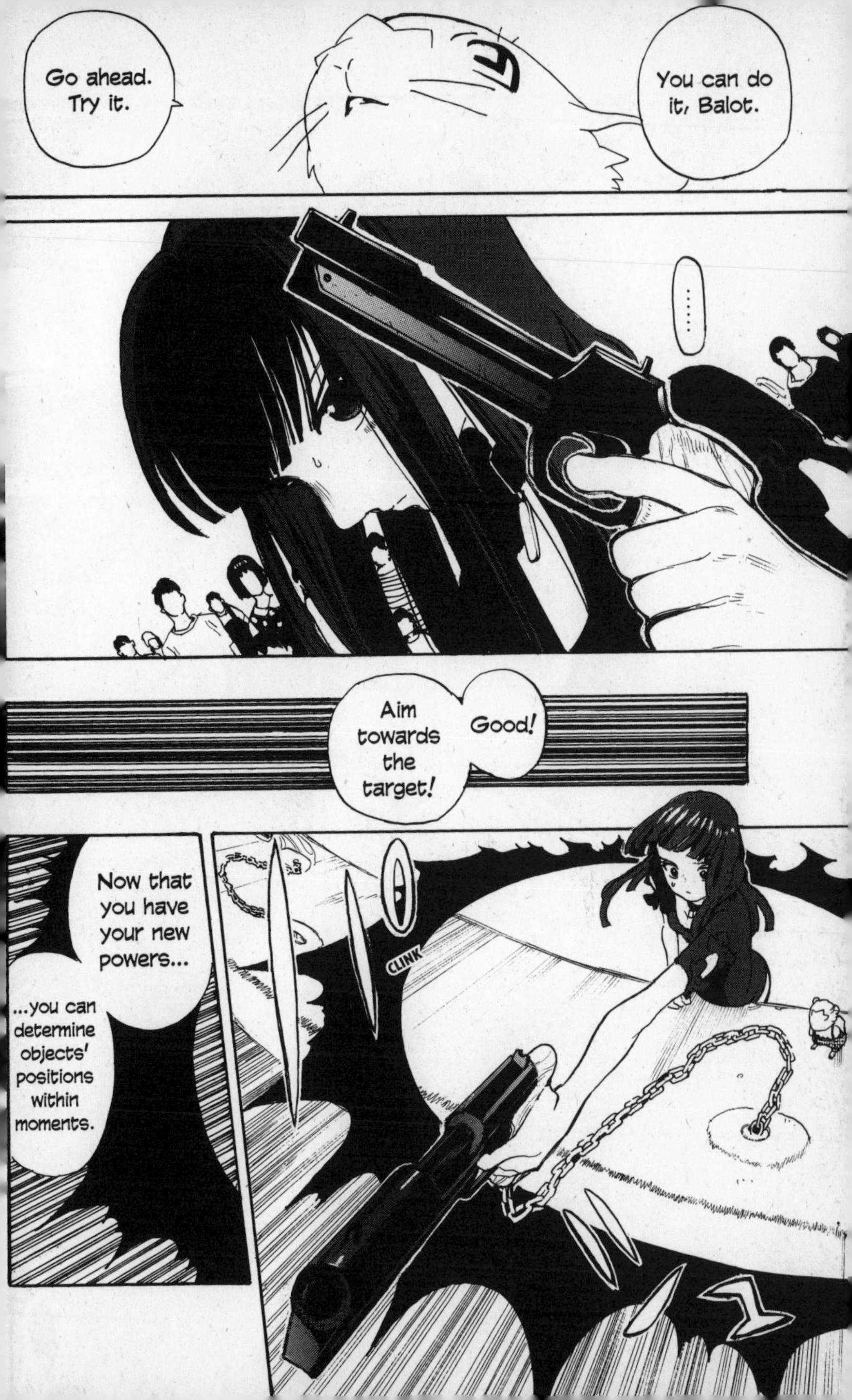

You can do it, Balot.
Go ahead. Try it.
......
Good!
Aim towards the target!
CLINK
Now that you have your new powers...
...you can determine objects' positions within moments.

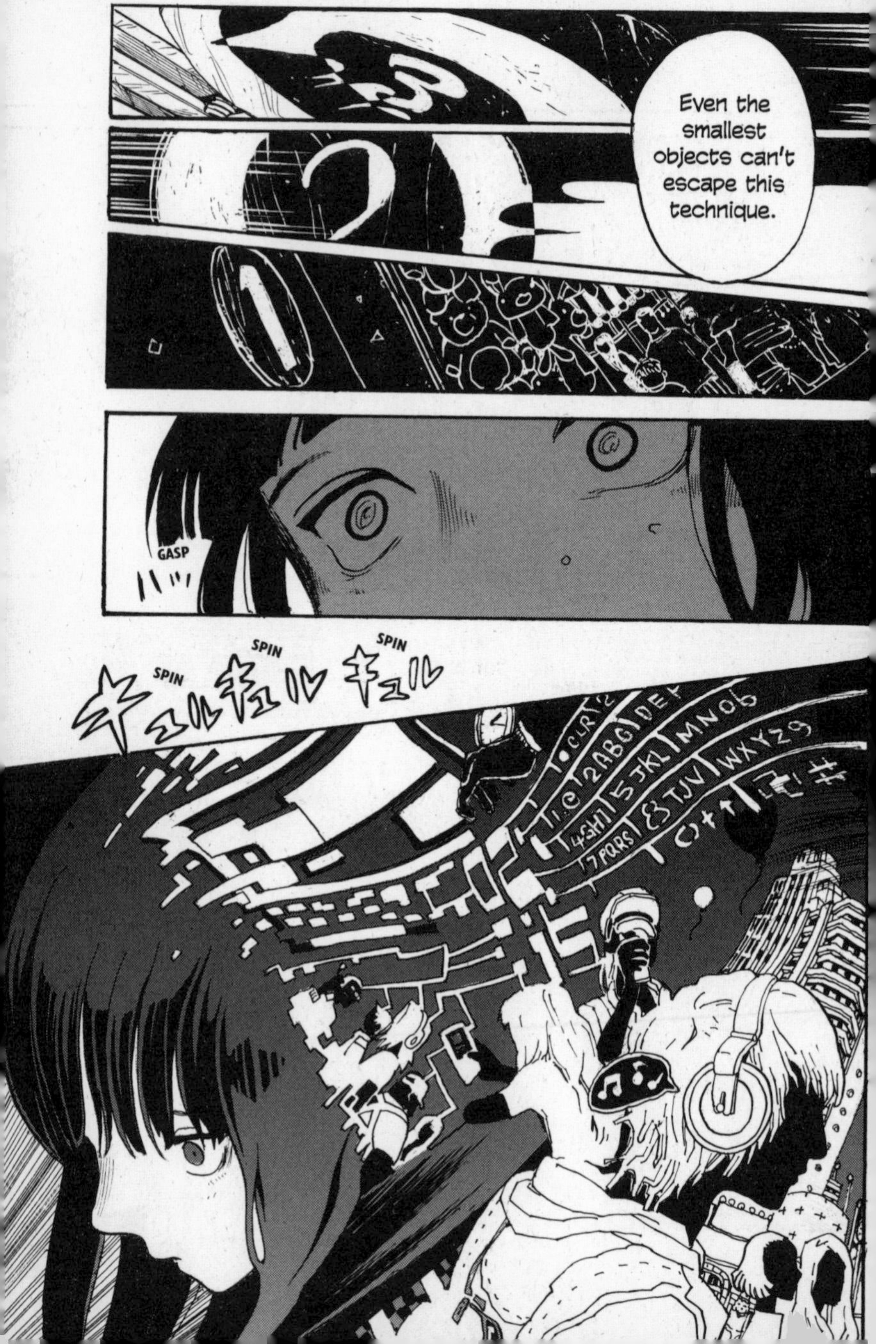
Even the smallest objects can't escape this technique.
GASP
SPIN
SPIN
SPIN

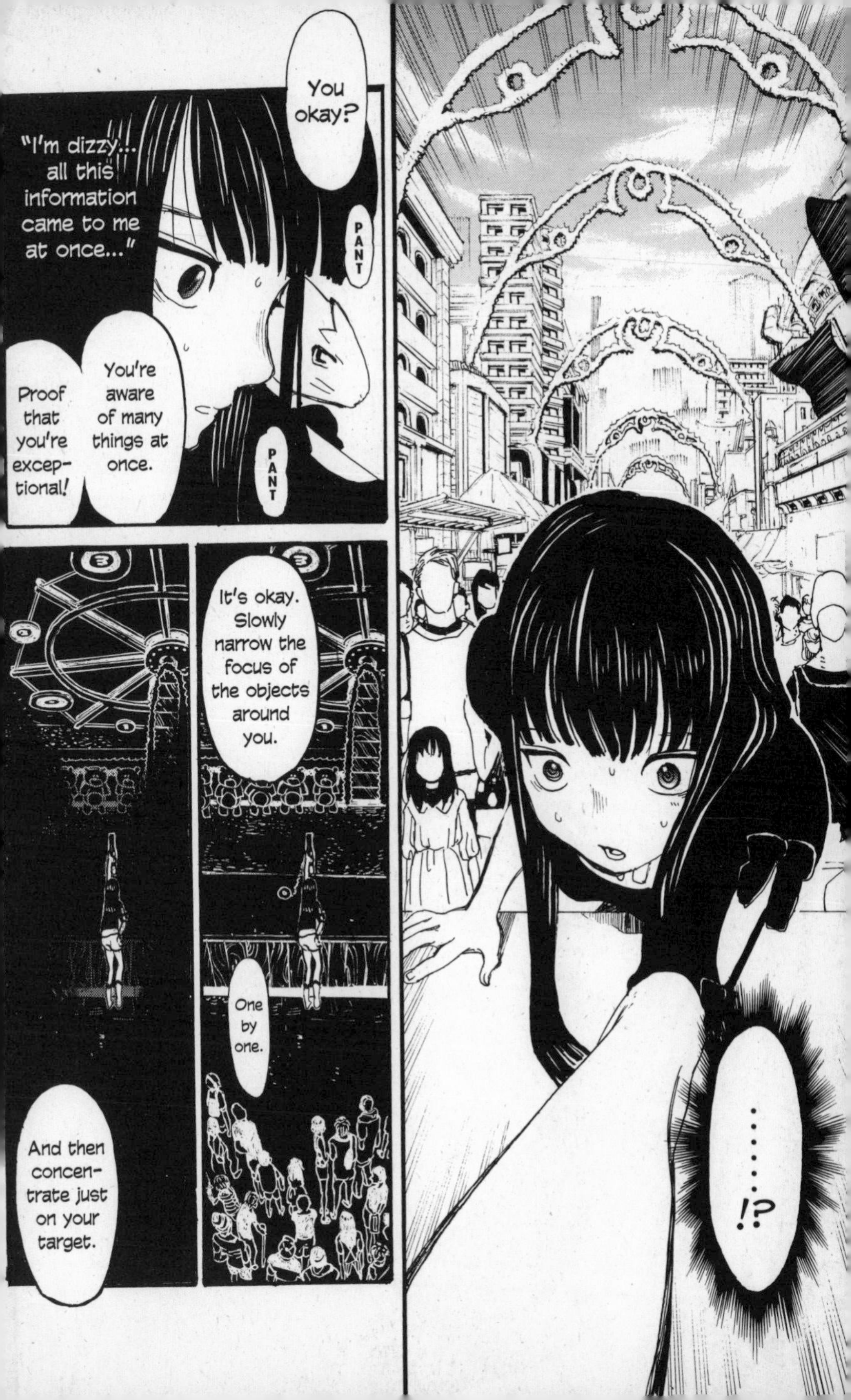
......!?
You okay?
PANT
"I'm dizzy... all this information came to me at once..."
You're aware of many things at once.
Proof that you're exceptional!
PANT
It's okay. Slowly narrow the focus of the objects around you.
One by one.
And then concentrate just on your target.

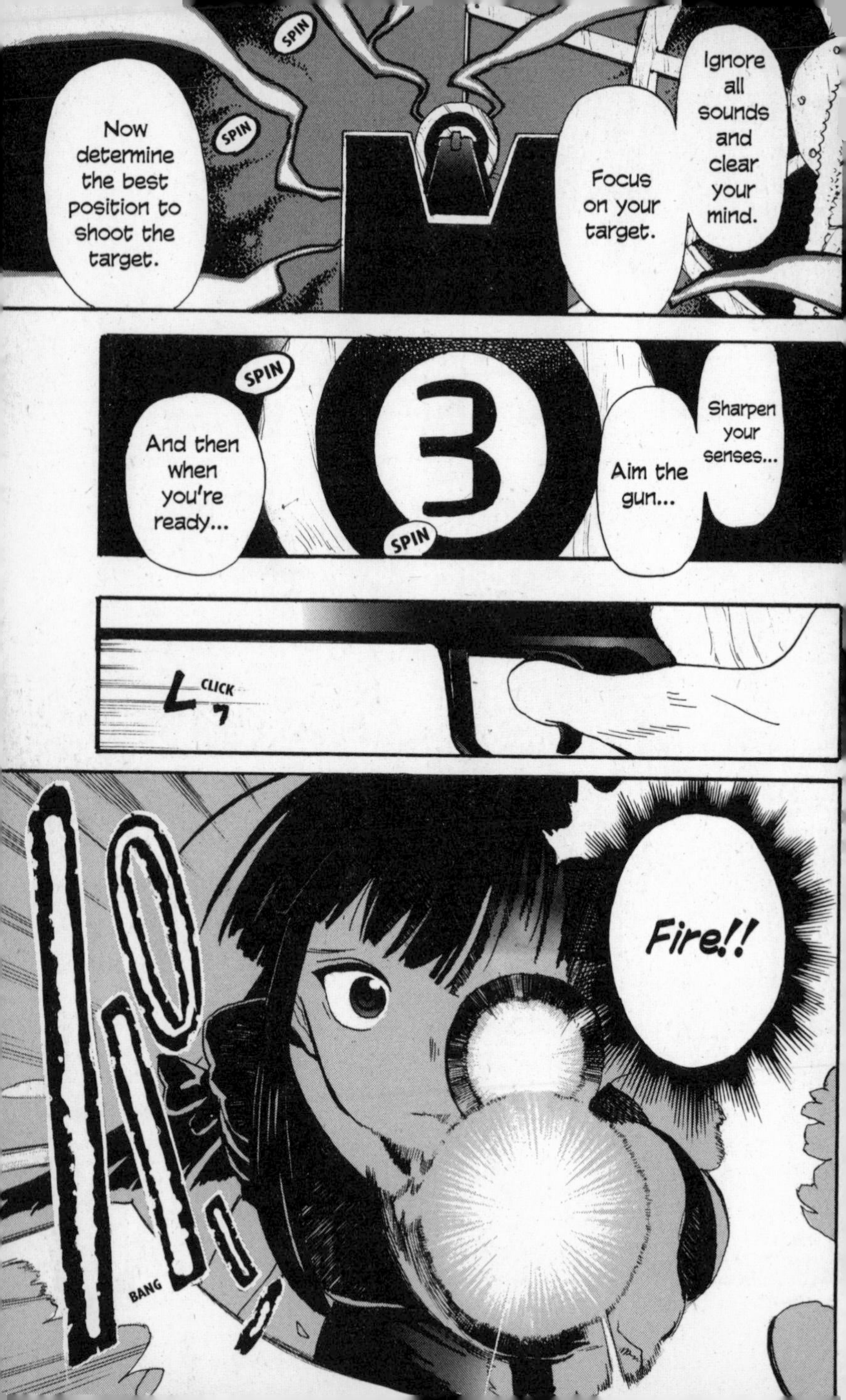
SPIN
SPIN
Ignore all sounds and clear your mind.
Focus on your target.
Now determine the best position to shoot the target.
Sharpen your senses...
Aim the gun...
3
SPIN
SPIN
And then when you're ready...
CLICK
Fire!!
BANG

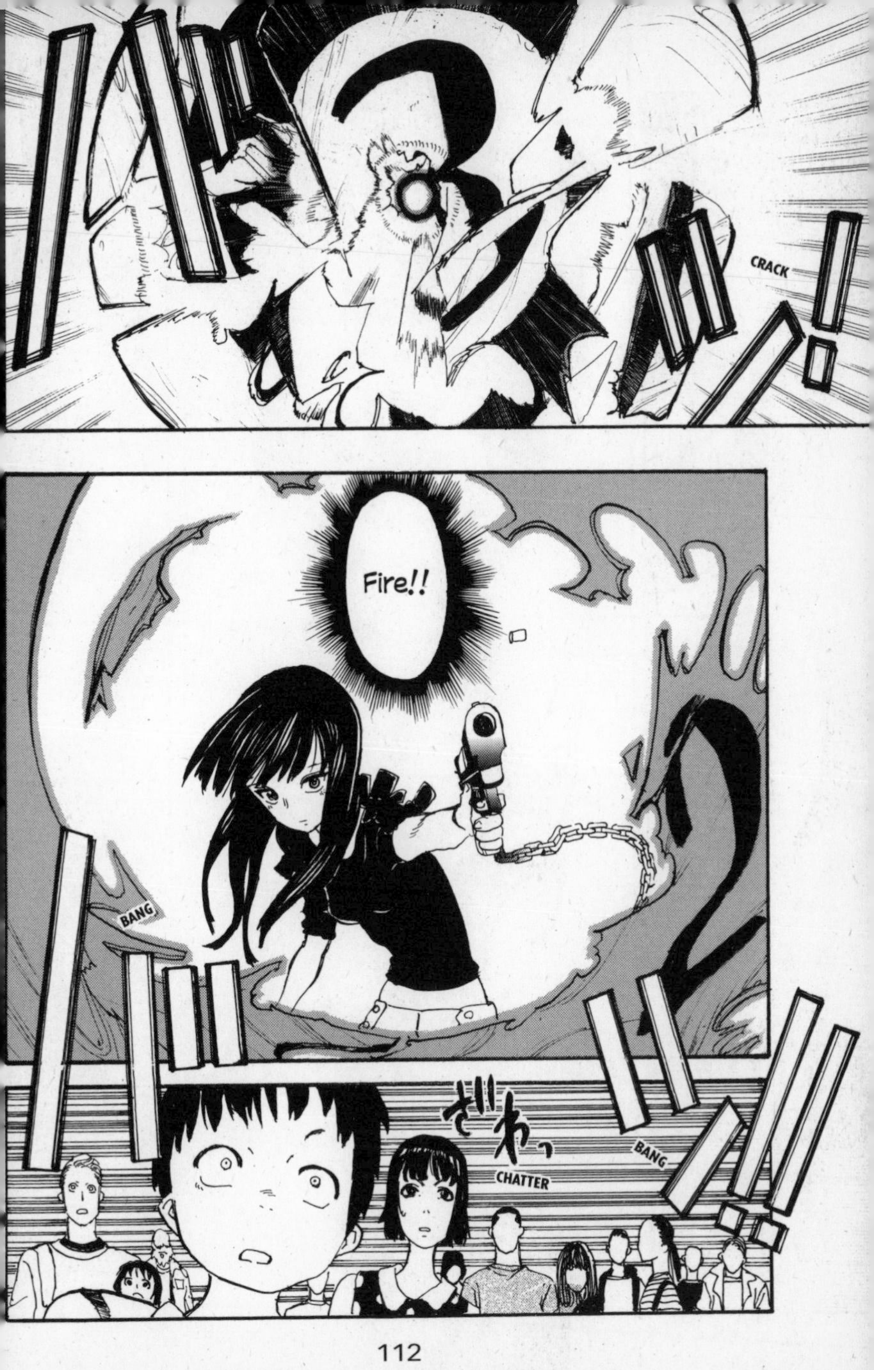
CRACK
Fire!!
BANG
BANG
ざわっ
CHATTER

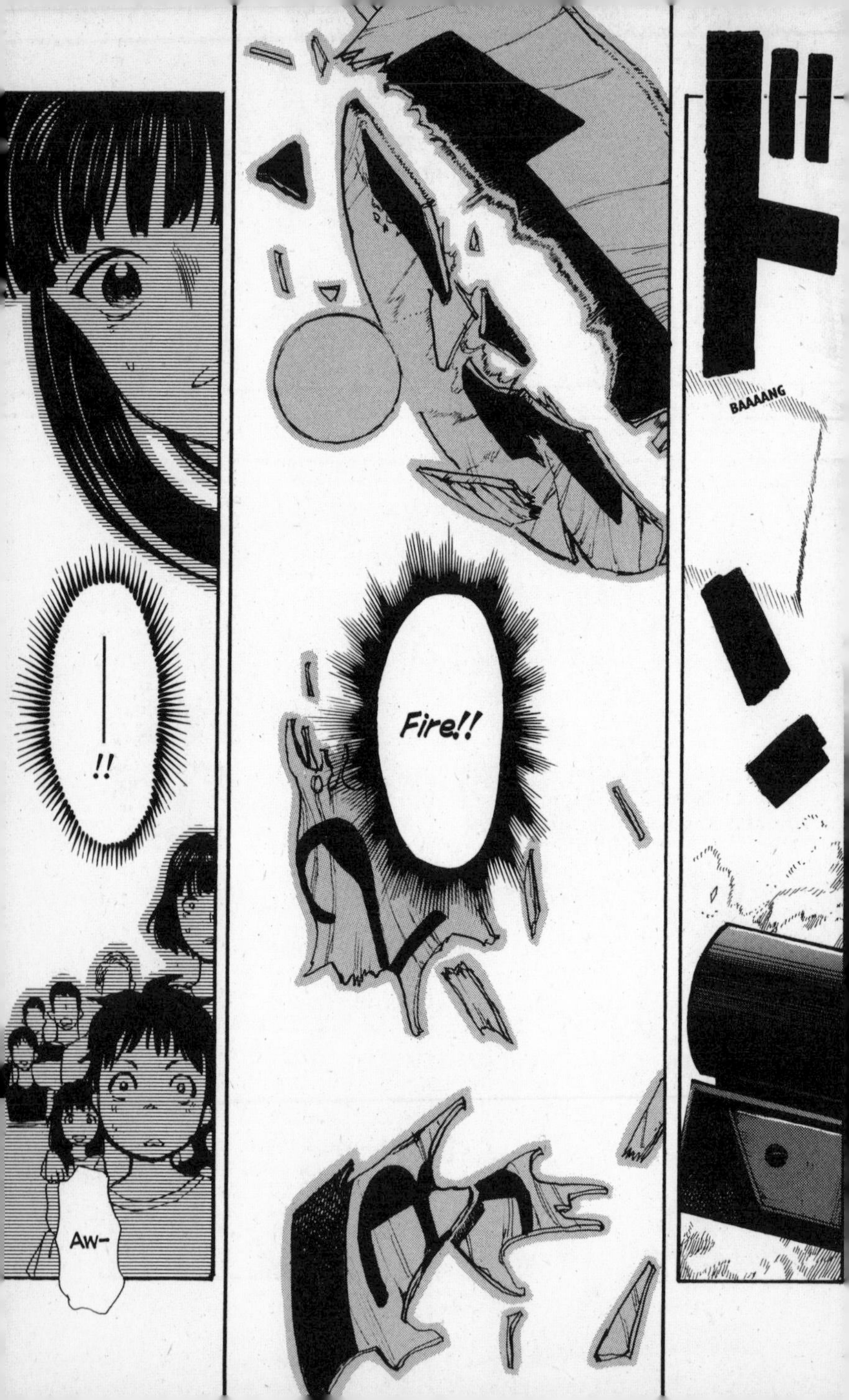
BAAAANG
Fire!!
—!!
Aw-

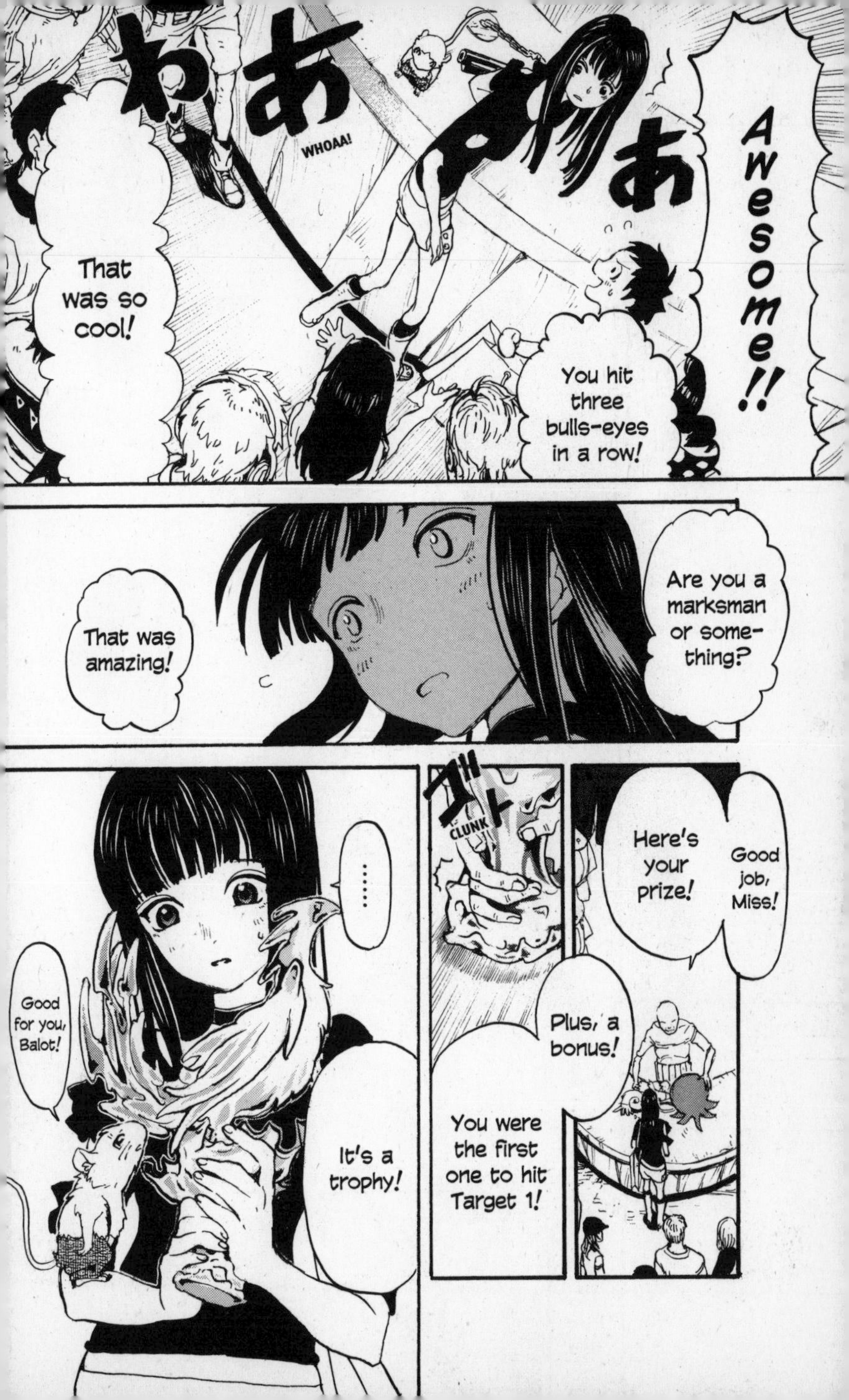

Awesome!!
わああ
WHOAA!
You hit three bulls-eyes in a row!
That was so cool!
Are you a marksman or some-thing?
That was amazing!
Good job, Miss!
Here's your prize!
Plus, a bonus!
You were the first one to hit Target 1!
CLUNK
......
It's a trophy!
Good for you, Balot!

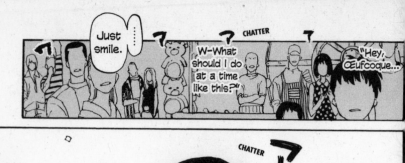

CHATTER

Just smile. ……

W-What should I do at a time like this?"

"Hey, Œufcoque…"

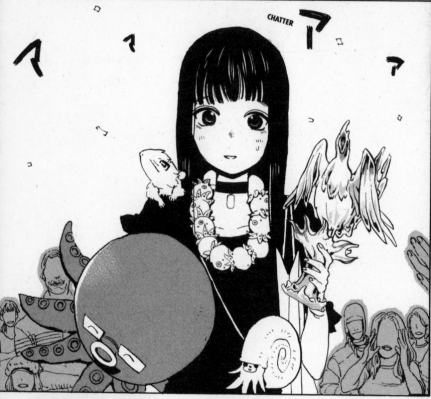

CHATTER

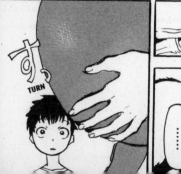

TURN

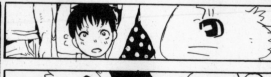

Why don't you give the pet alien to the little boy?

Balot…

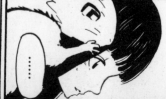

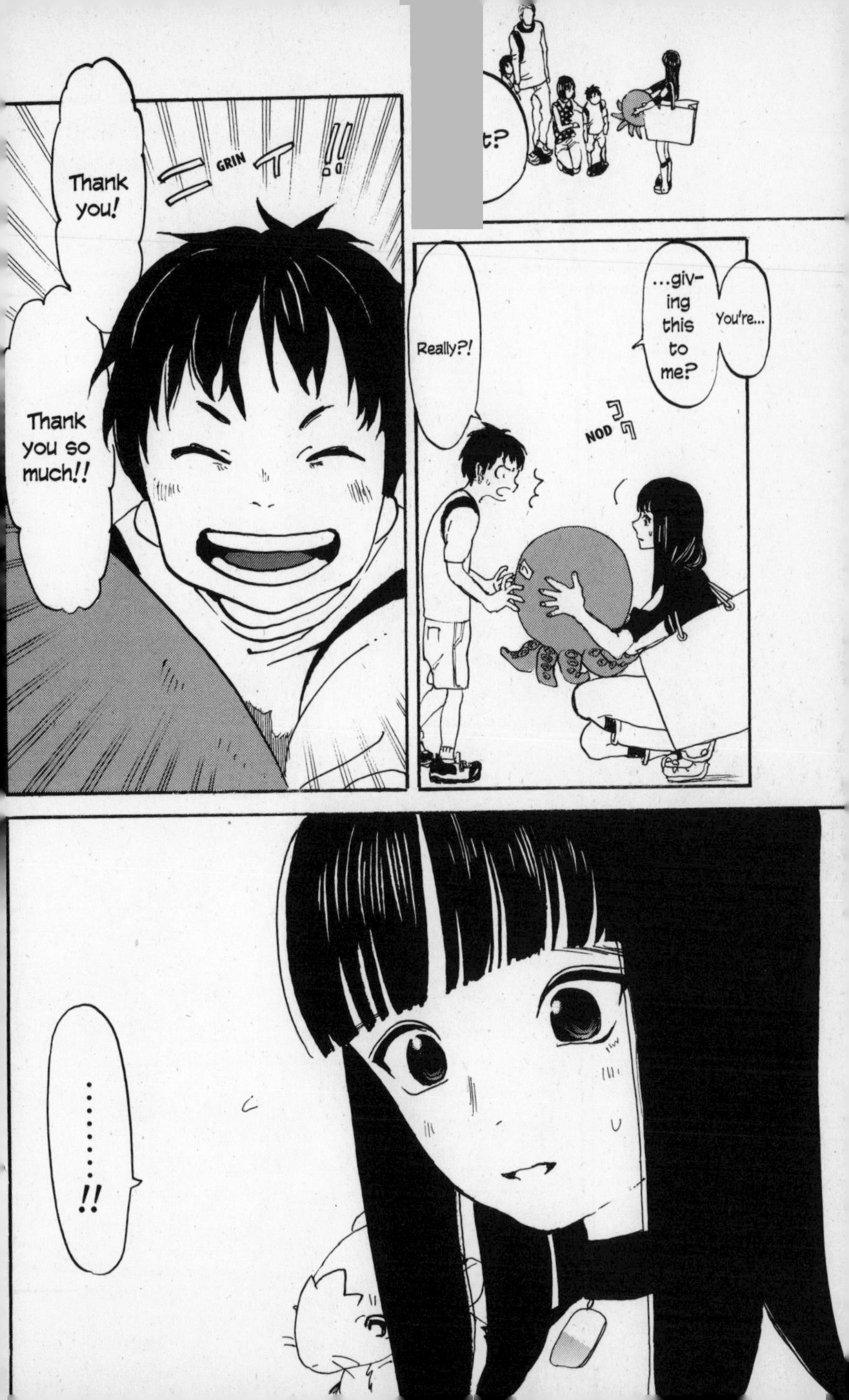
You're...
...giv-ing this to me?
NOD
Really?!
GRIN !!
Thank you!
Thank you so much!!
........!!

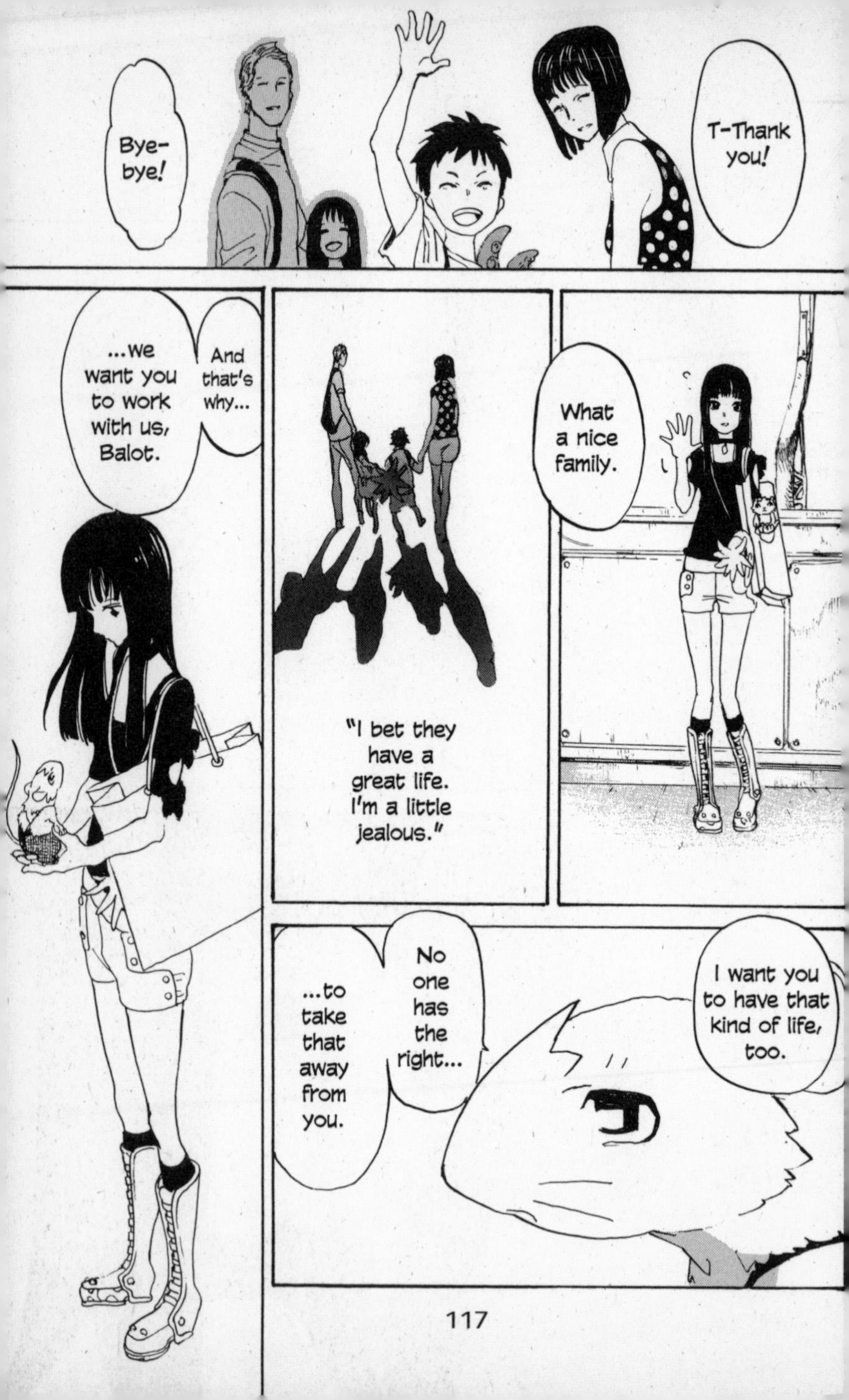
T-Thank you!
Bye-bye!
What a nice family.
"I bet they have a great life. I'm a little jealous."
I want you to have that kind of life, too.
No one has the right...
...to take that away from you.
And that's why...
...we want you to work with us, Balot.

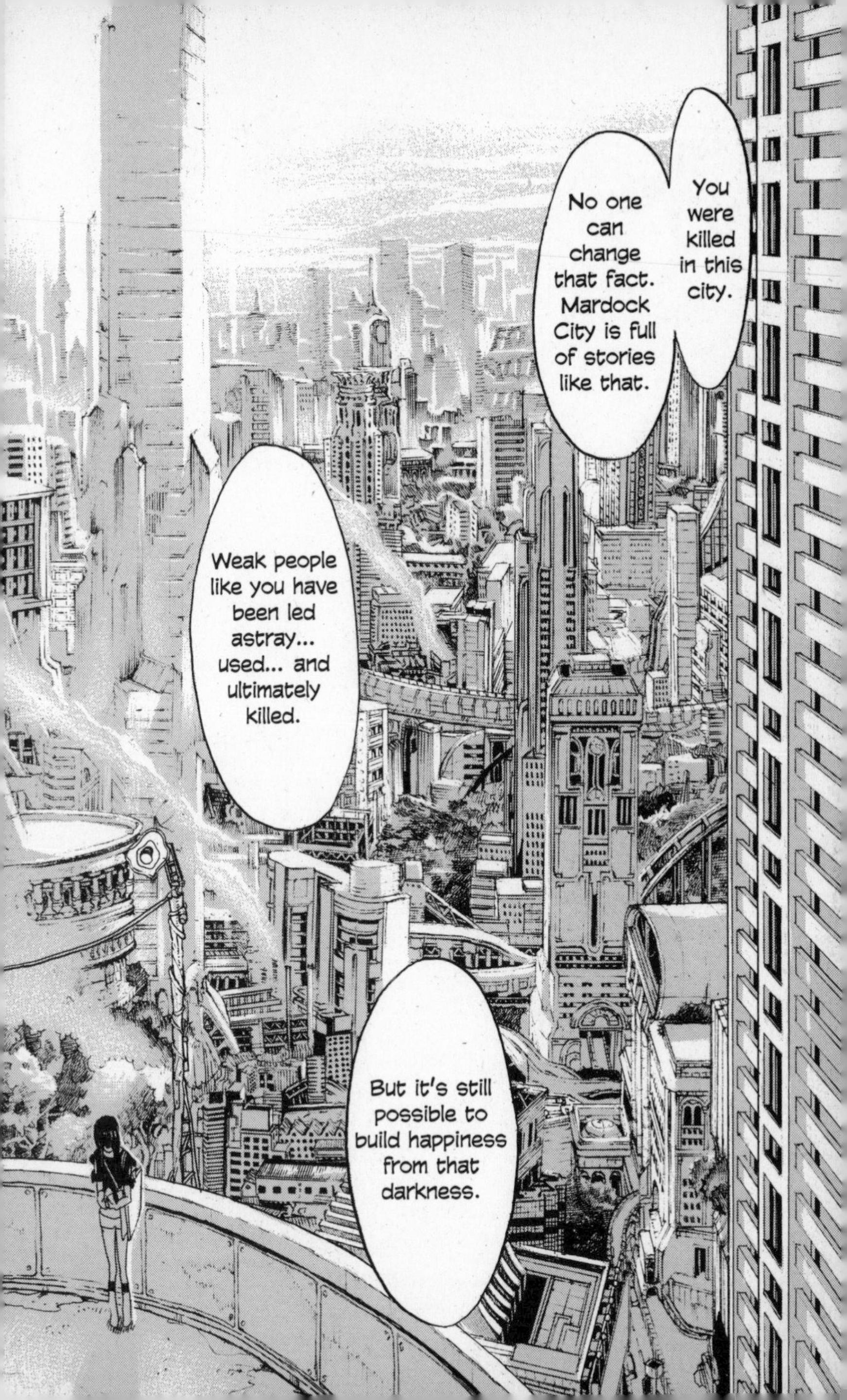
You were killed in this city.
No one can change that fact. Mardock City is full of stories like that.
Weak people like you have been led astray... used... and ultimately killed.
But it's still possible to build happiness from that darkness.

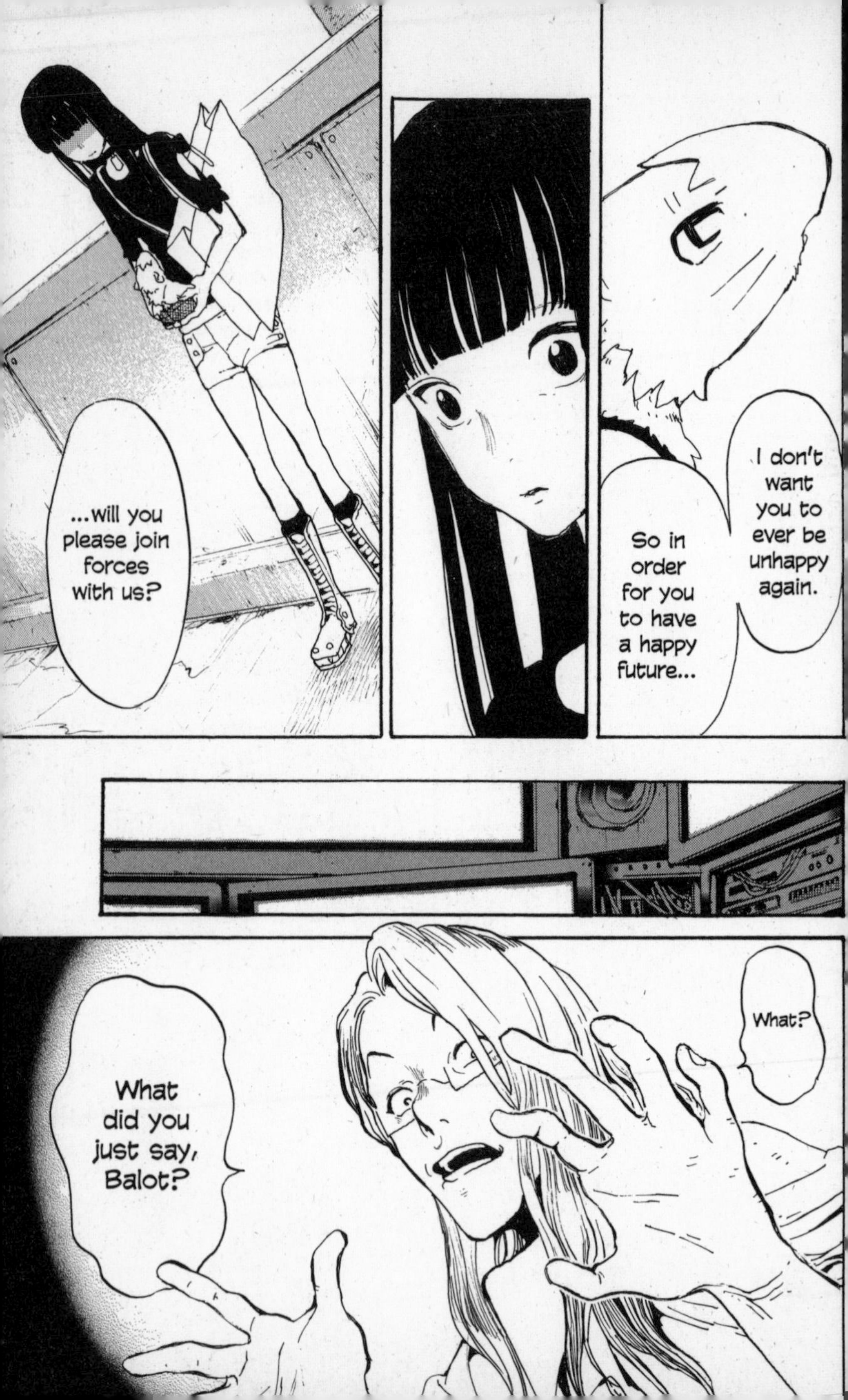
I don't want you to ever be unhappy again.
So in order for you to have a happy future...
...will you please join forces with us?
What?
What did you just say, Balot?

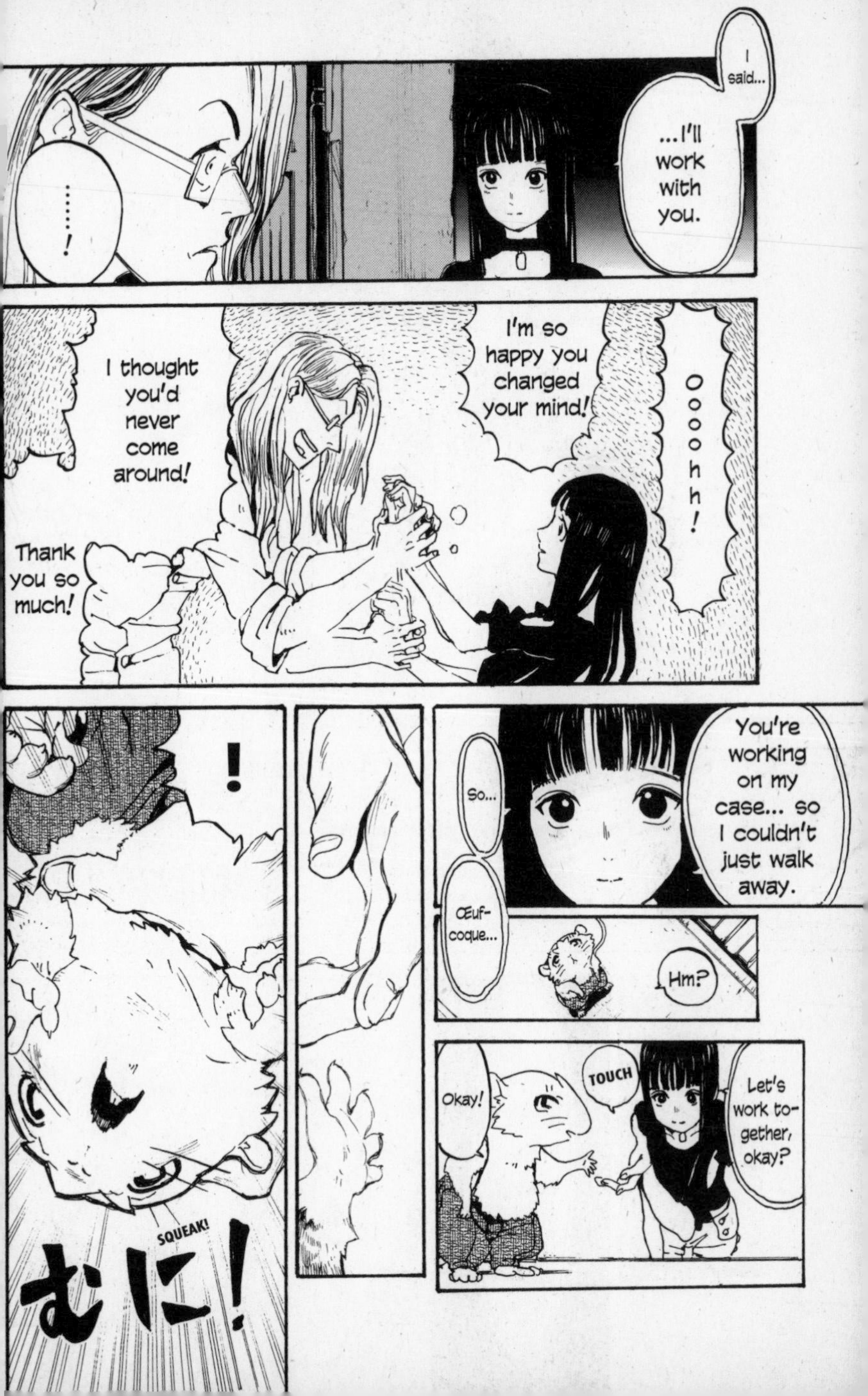
I said...
...I'll work with you.
......!
Ooooohh!
I'm so happy you changed your mind!
I thought you'd never come around!
Thank you so much!
You're working on my case... so I couldn't just walk away.
So...
Œuf-coque...
Hm?
Let's work together, okay?
TOUCH
Okay!
!
SQUEAK!
むに!

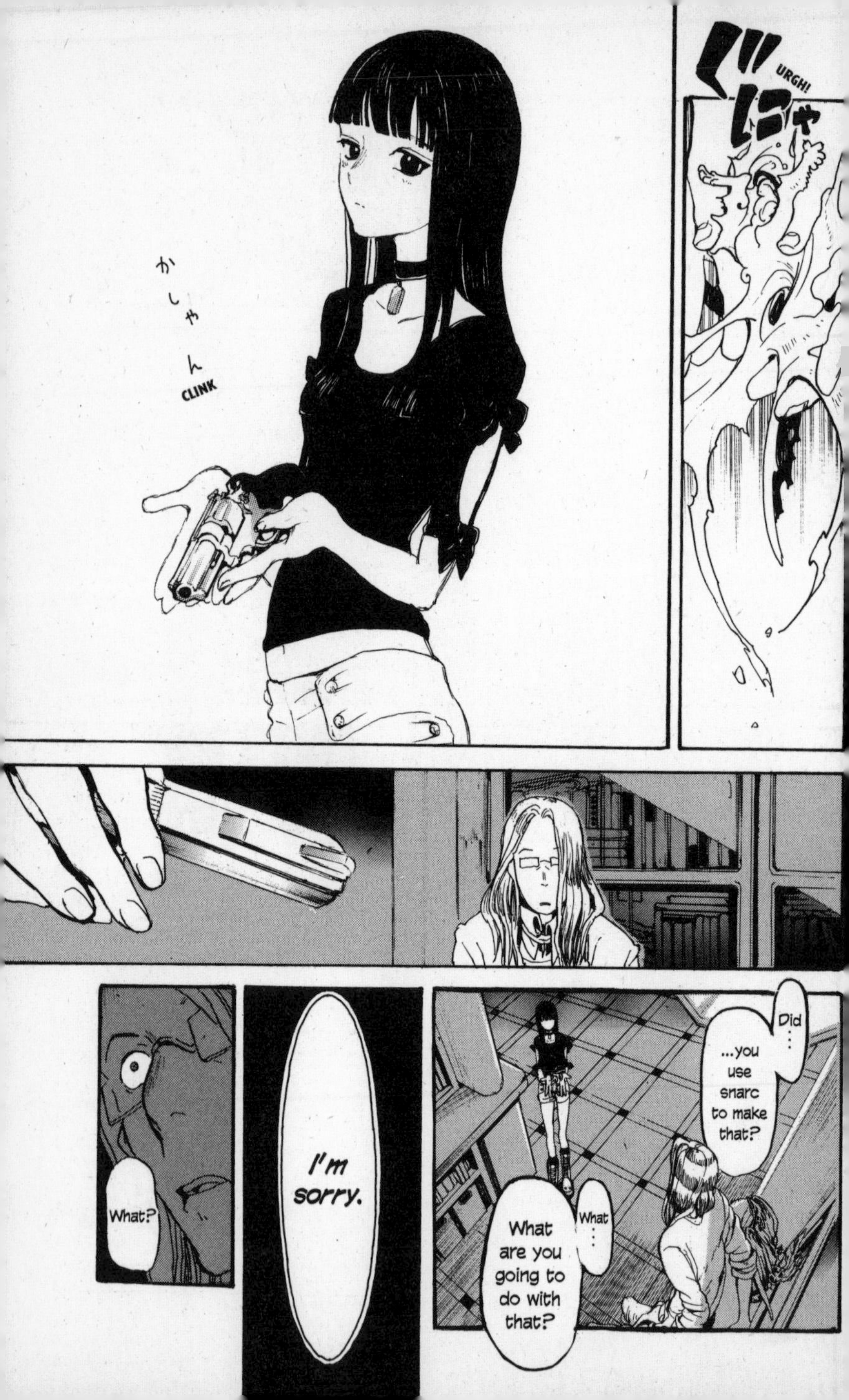

URGH!
かしゃん
CLINK
Did...
...you use snarc to make that?
What...
What are you going to do with that?
I'm sorry.
What?

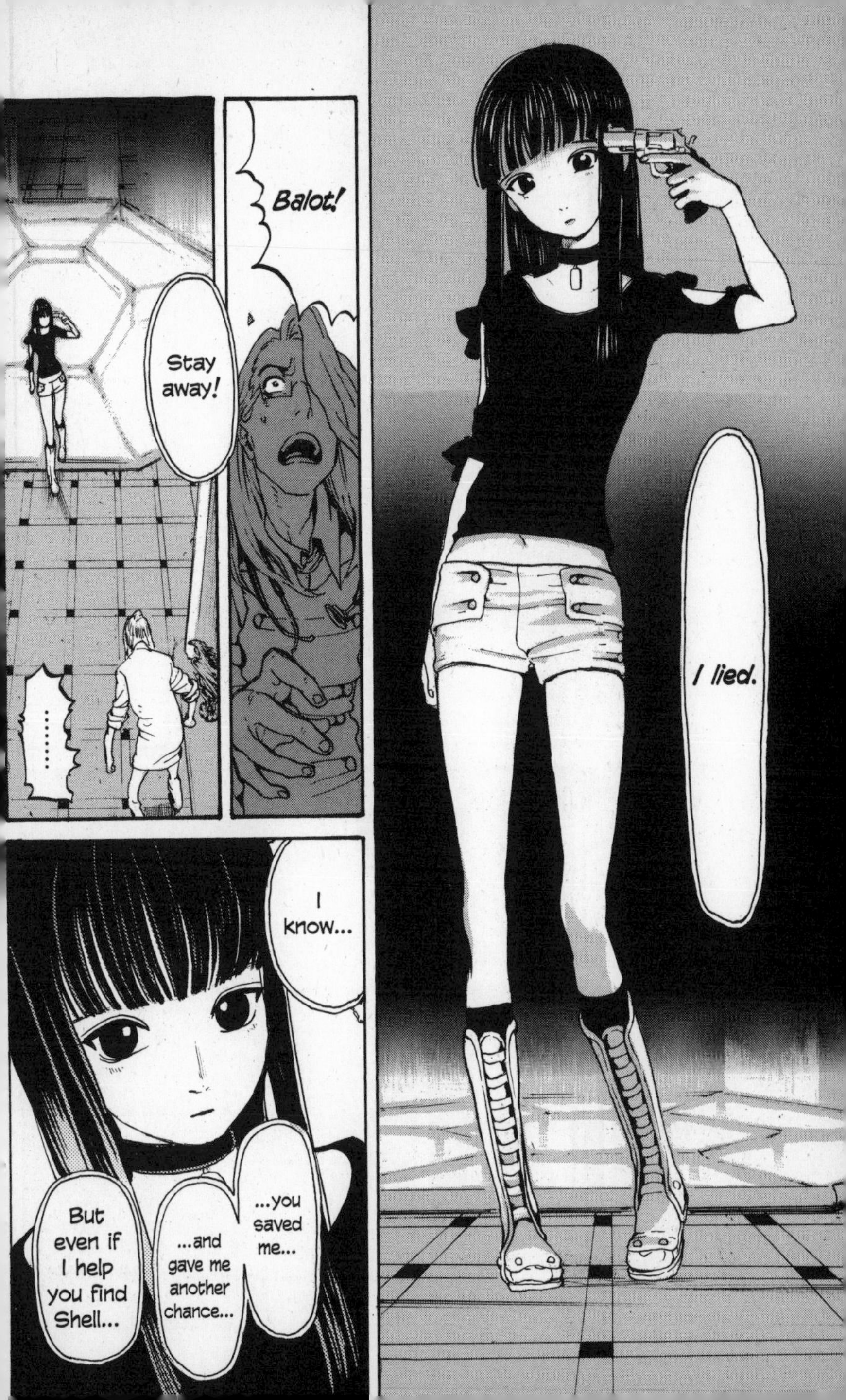
I lied.
Balot!
Stay away!
......
I know...
...you saved me...
...and gave me another chance...
But even if I help you find Shell...

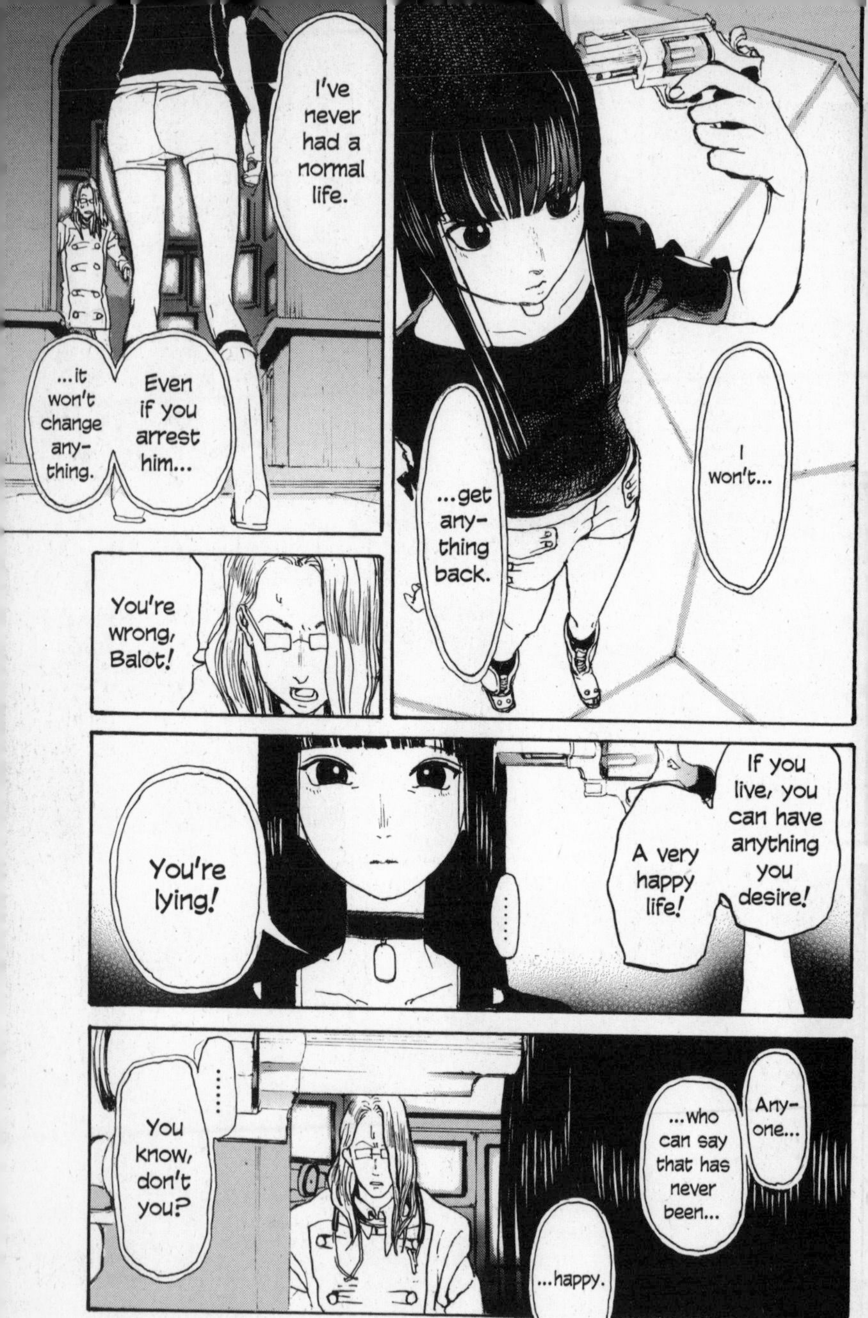

I won't...
...get anything back.
I've never had a normal life.
Even if you arrest him...
...it won't change anything.
You're wrong, Balot!
If you live, you can have anything you desire!
A very happy life!
......
You're lying!
Anyone...
...who can say that has never been...
...happy.
......
You know, don't you?

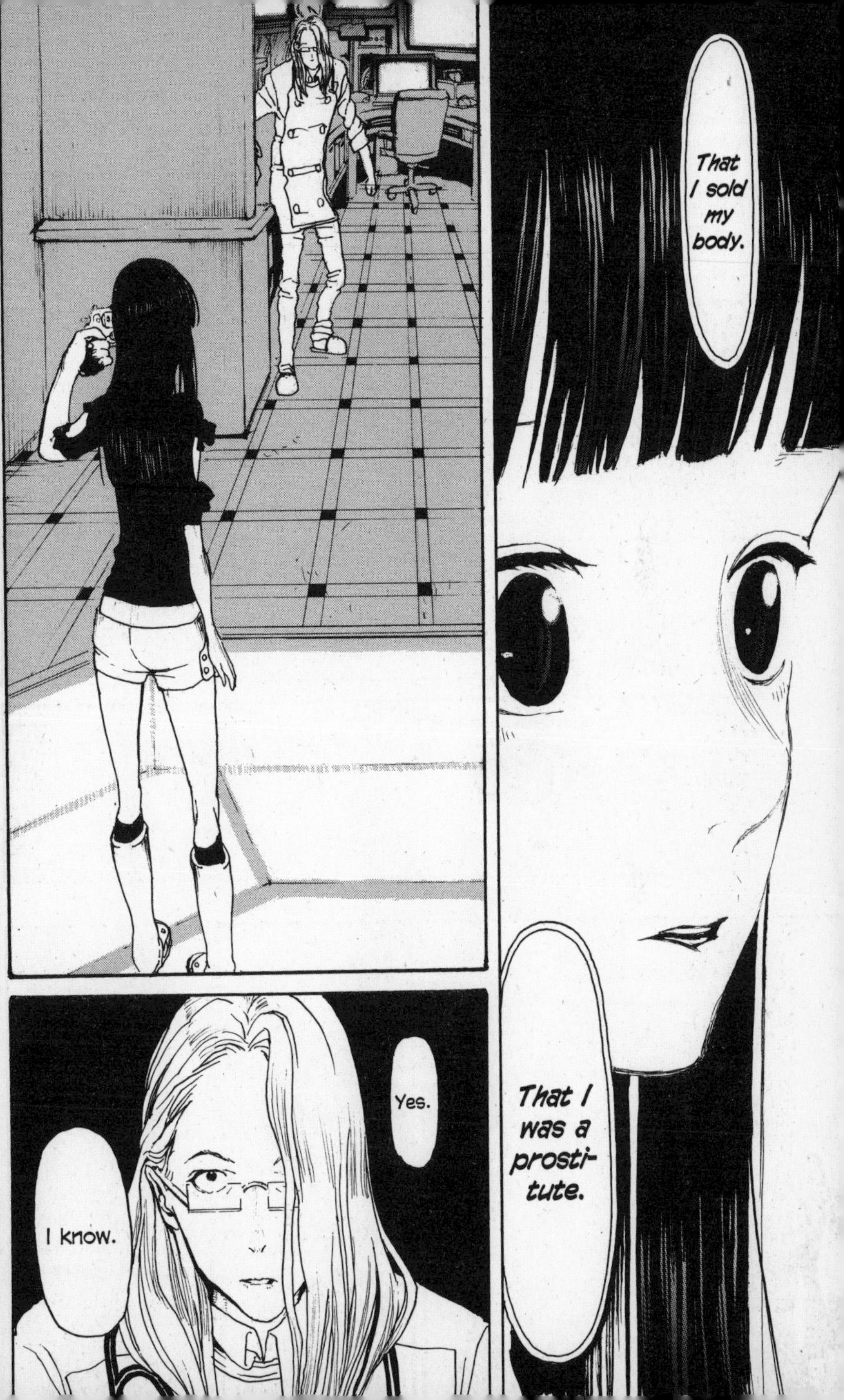
That I sold my body.
That I was a prostitute.
Yes.
I know.

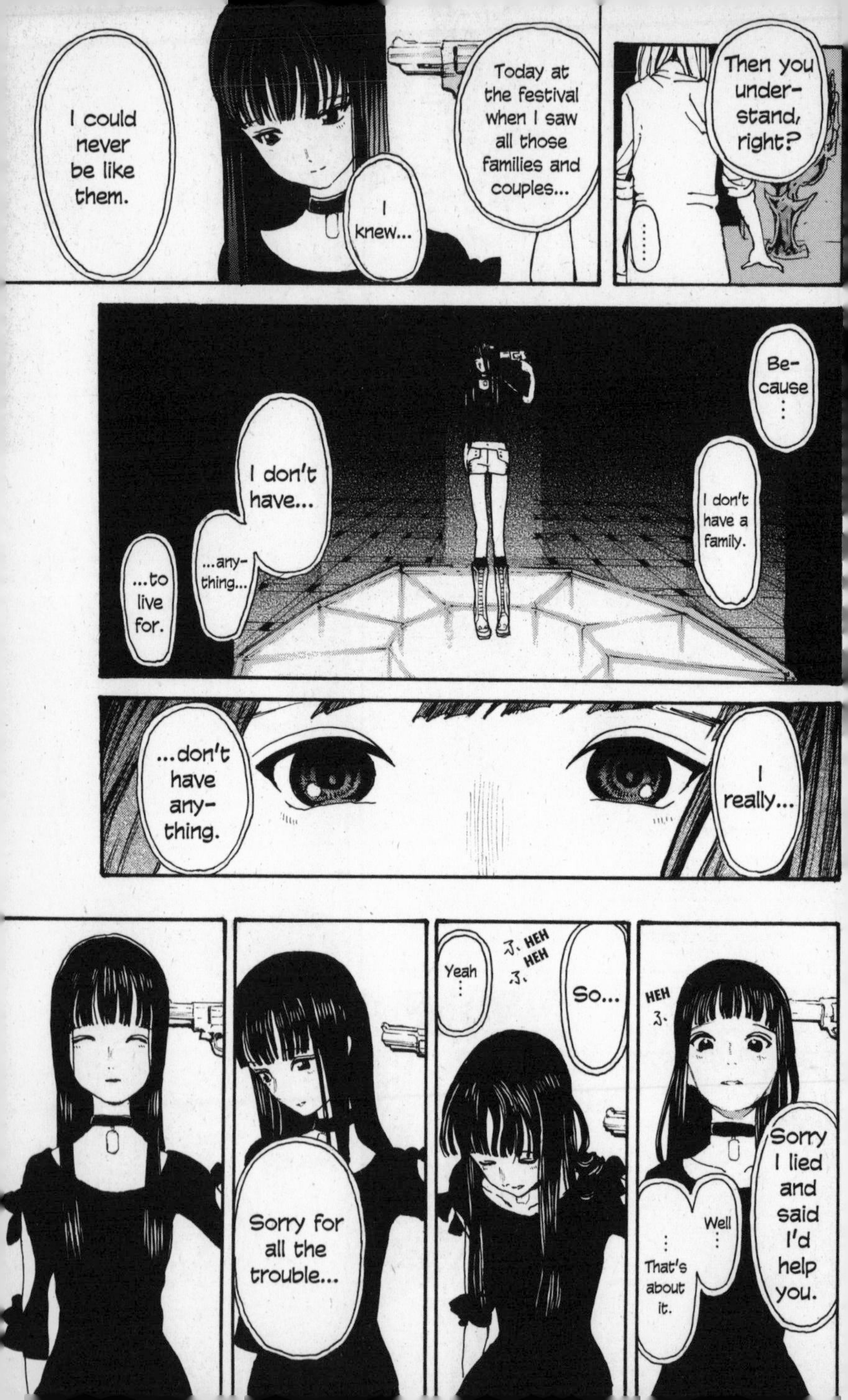
Then you under-stand, right?
......
Today at the festival when I saw all those families and couples...
I knew...
I could never be like them.
Be-cause...
I don't have a family.
I don't have...
...any-thing...
...to live for.
I really...
...don't have any-thing.
HEH ふ
Sorry I lied and said I'd help you.
Well... ...That's about it.
So...
ふ、HEH HEH ふ、
Yeah...
Sorry for all the trouble...

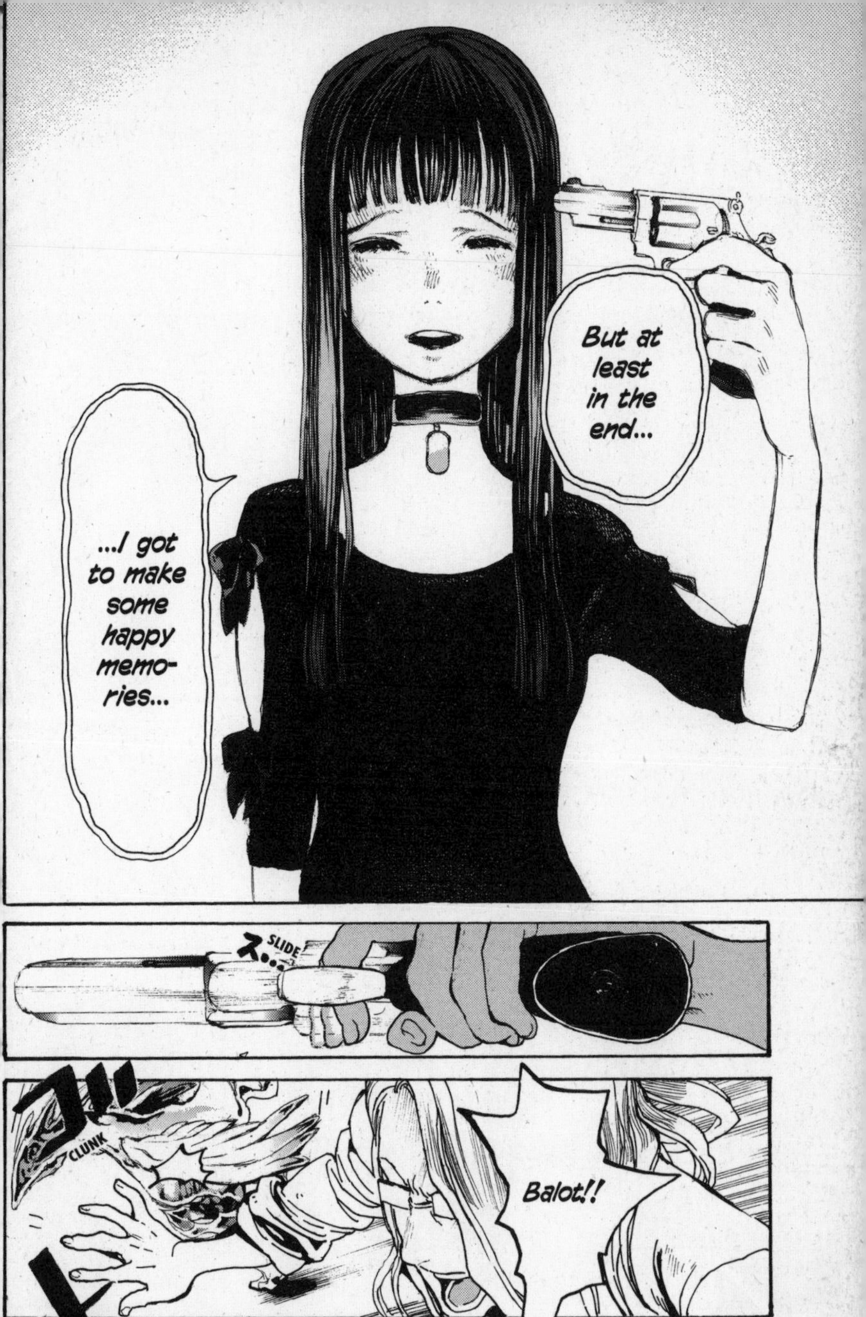
But at least in the end...
...I got to make some happy memories...
SLIDE
Balot!!
CLUNK

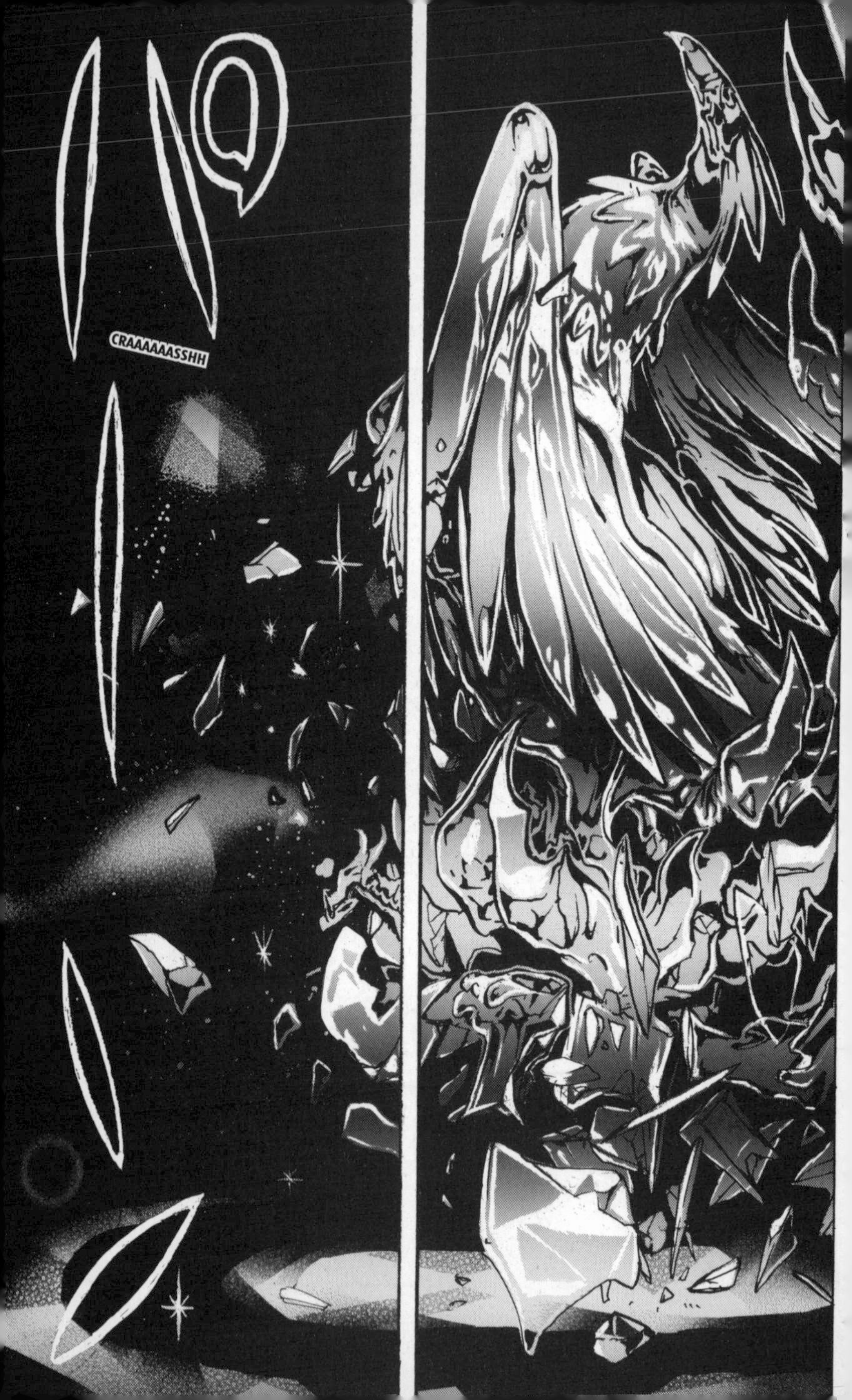
CRAAAAAASSHH

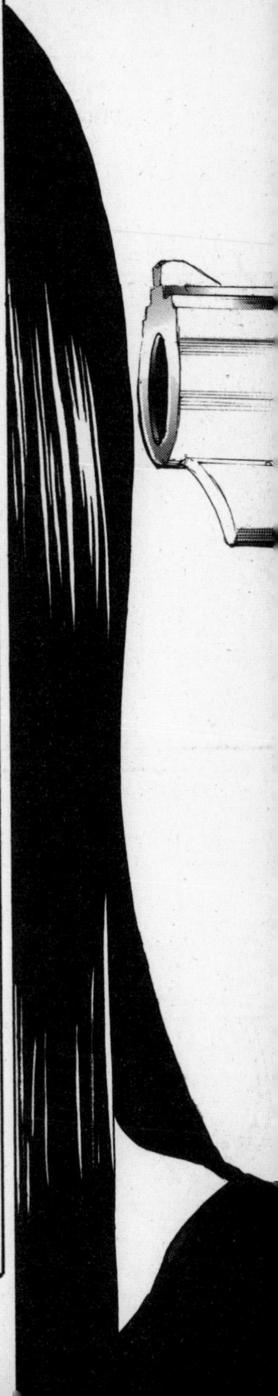

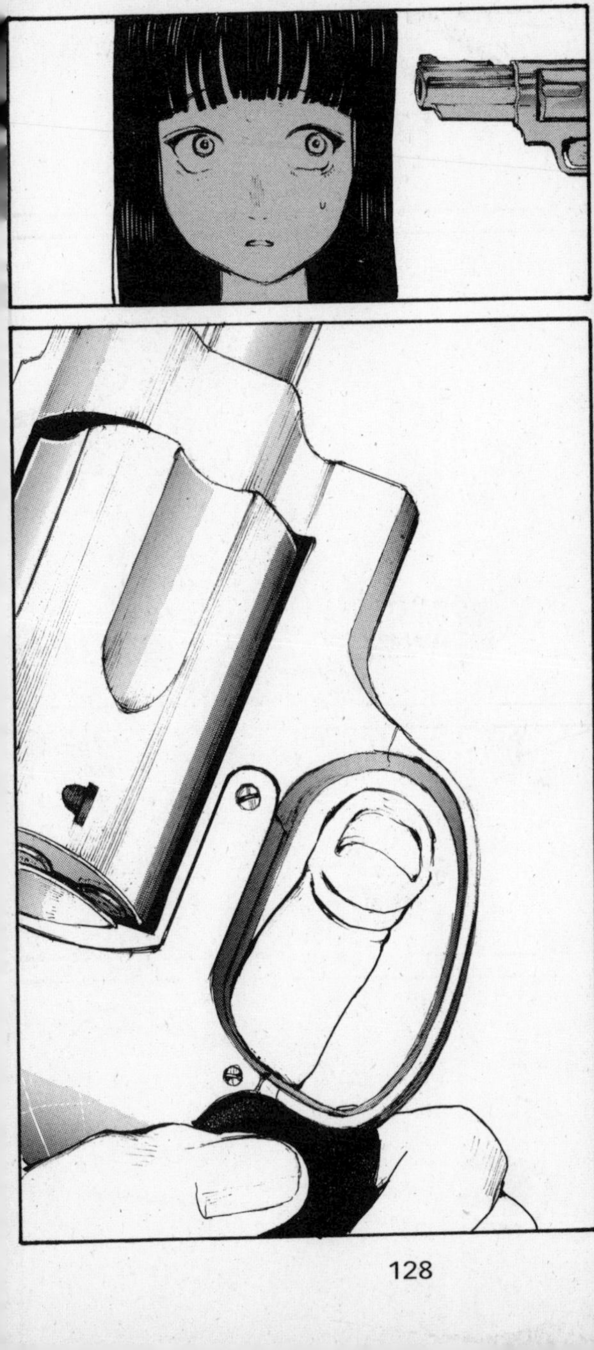

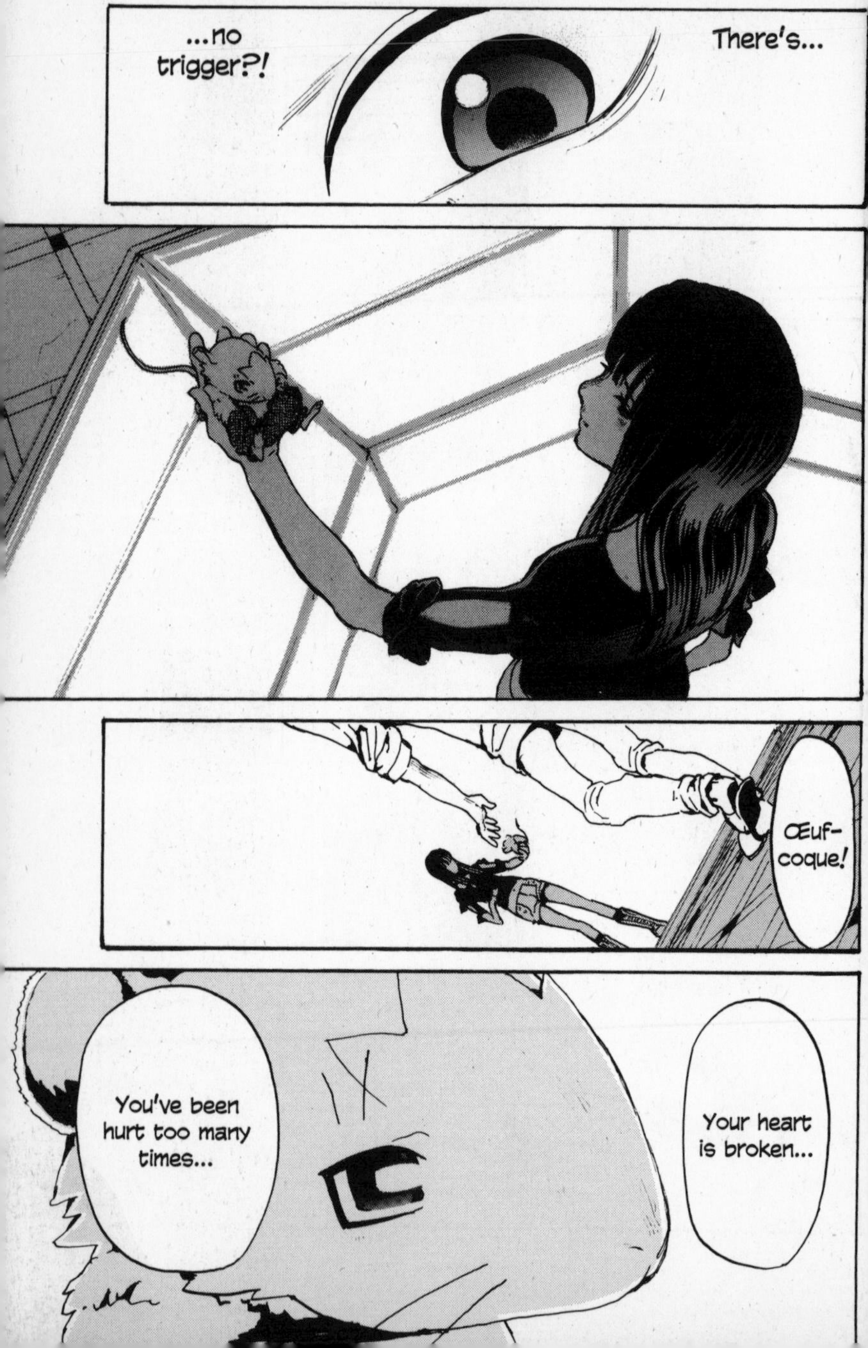
There's...
...no trigger?!
Œuf-coque!
Your heart is broken...
You've been hurt too many times...

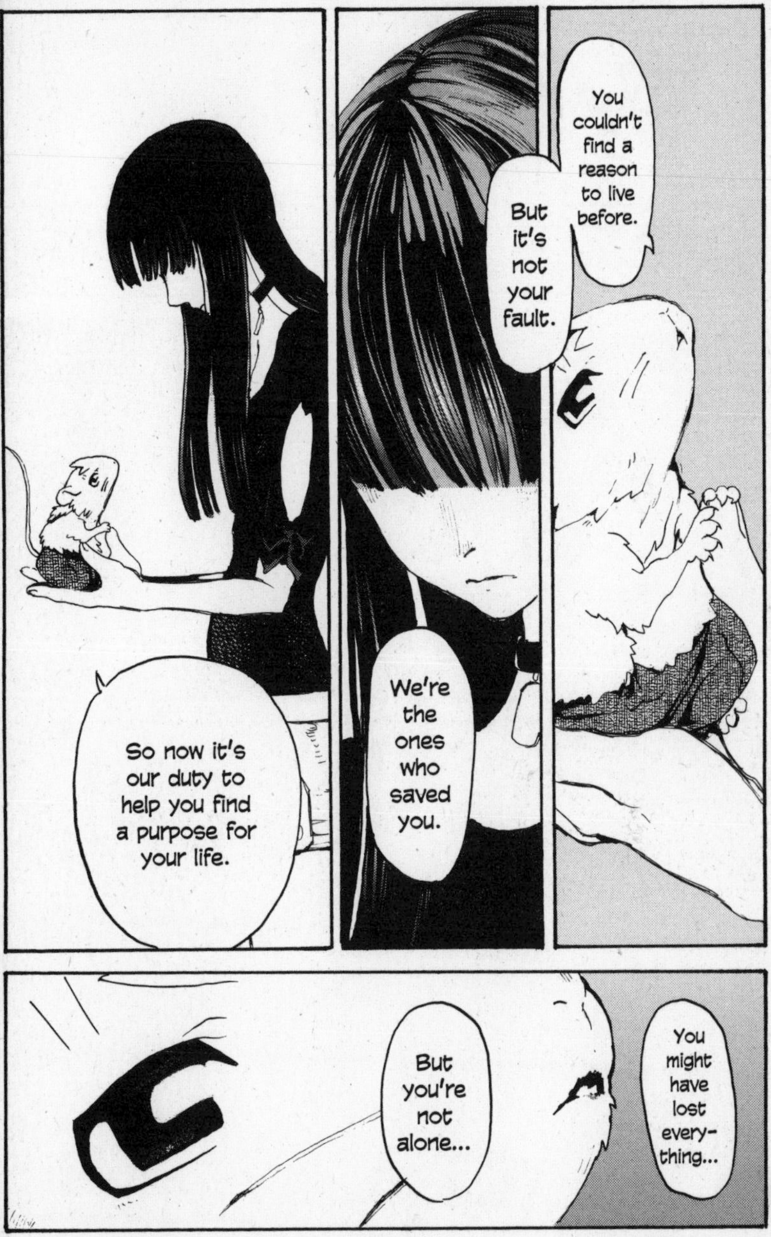
You couldn't find a reason to live before.
But it's not your fault.
We're the ones who saved you.
So now it's our duty to help you find a purpose for your life.
You might have lost every-thing...
But you're not alone...

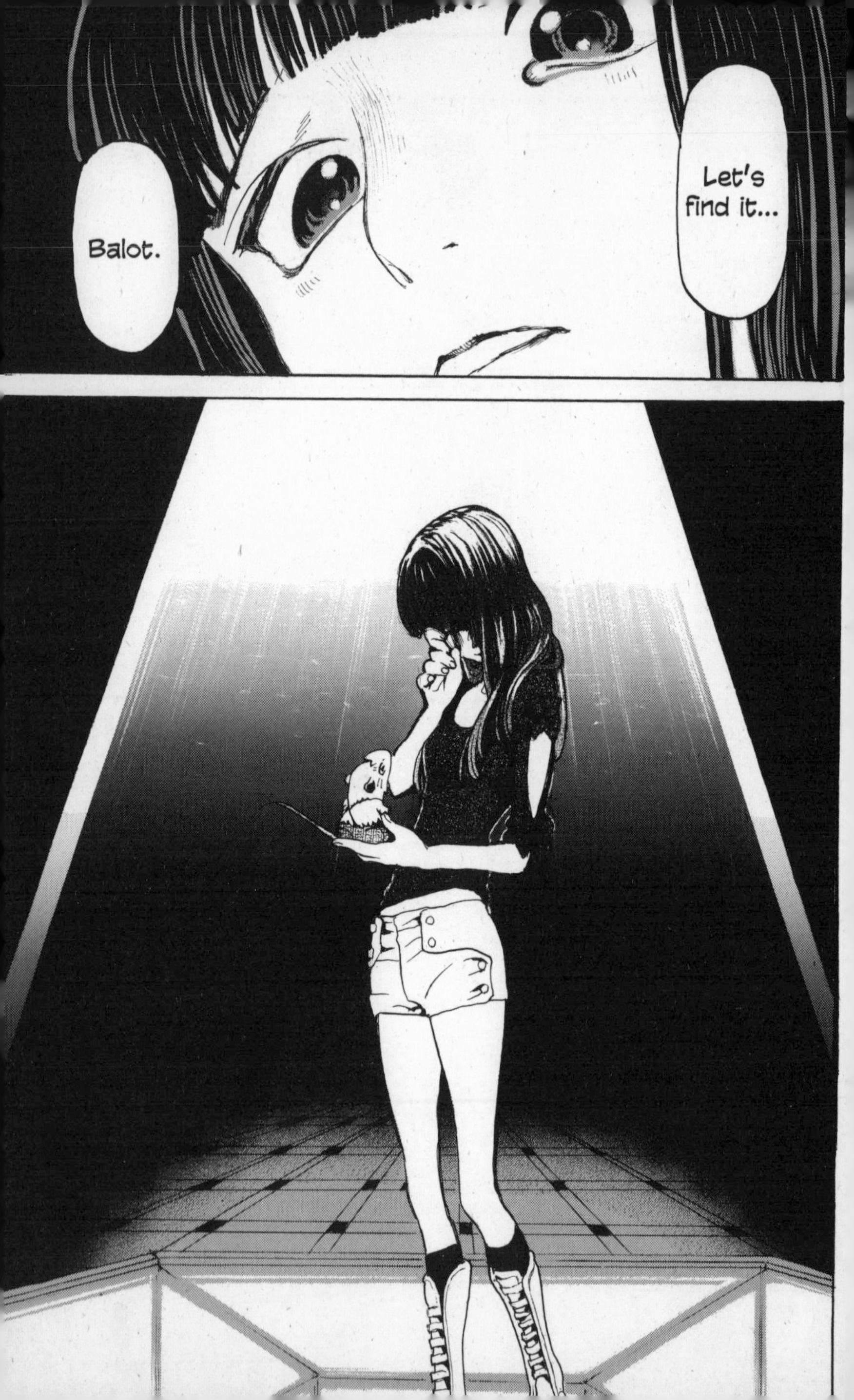
Let's find it...
Balot.

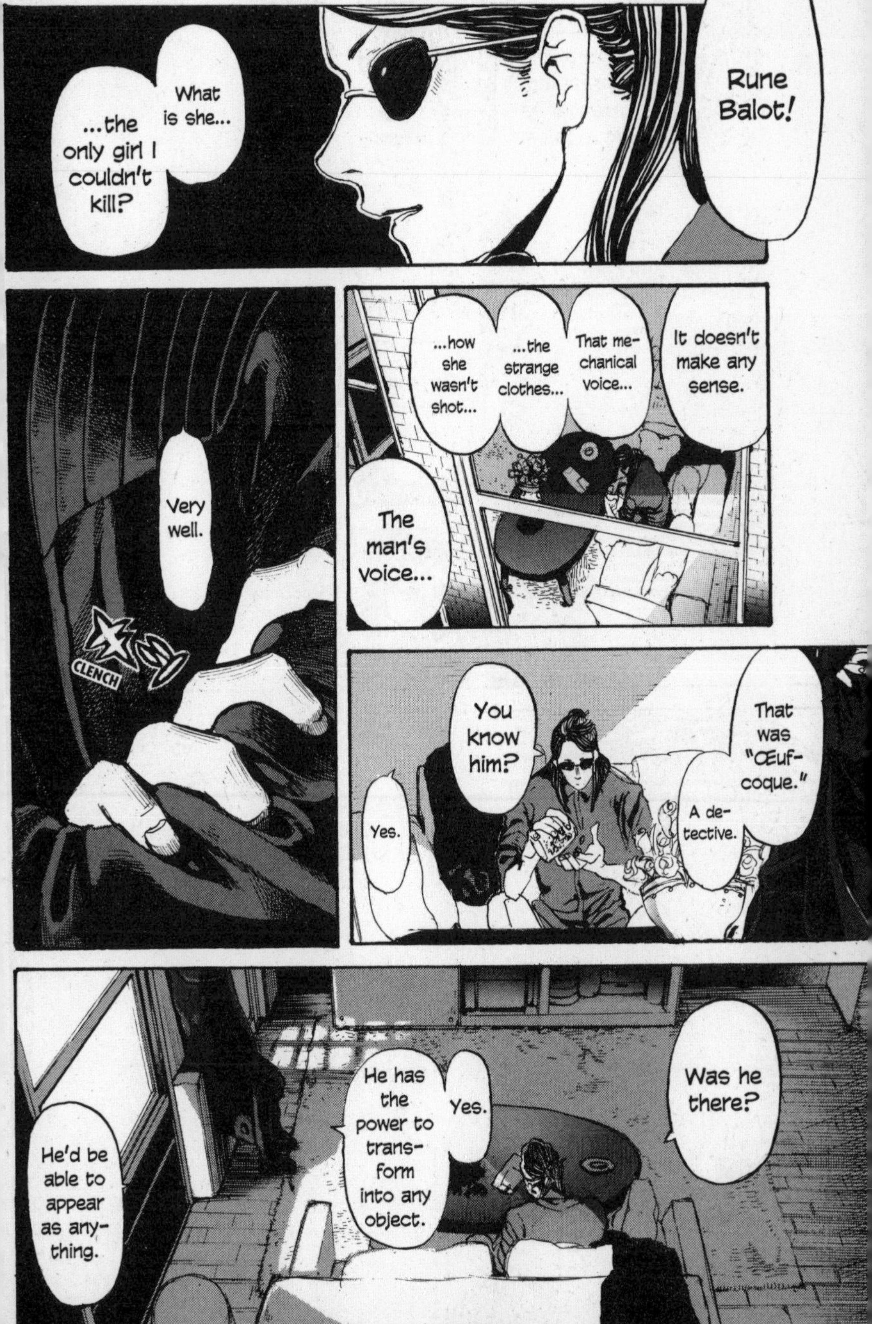
Rune Balot!
What is she...
...the only girl I couldn't kill?
It doesn't make any sense.
That mechanical voice...
...the strange clothes...
...how she wasn't shot...
The man's voice...
That was "Œuf-coque."
A detective.
You know him?
Yes.
Very well.
CLENCH
Was he there?
Yes.
He has the power to transform into any object.
He'd be able to appear as anything.

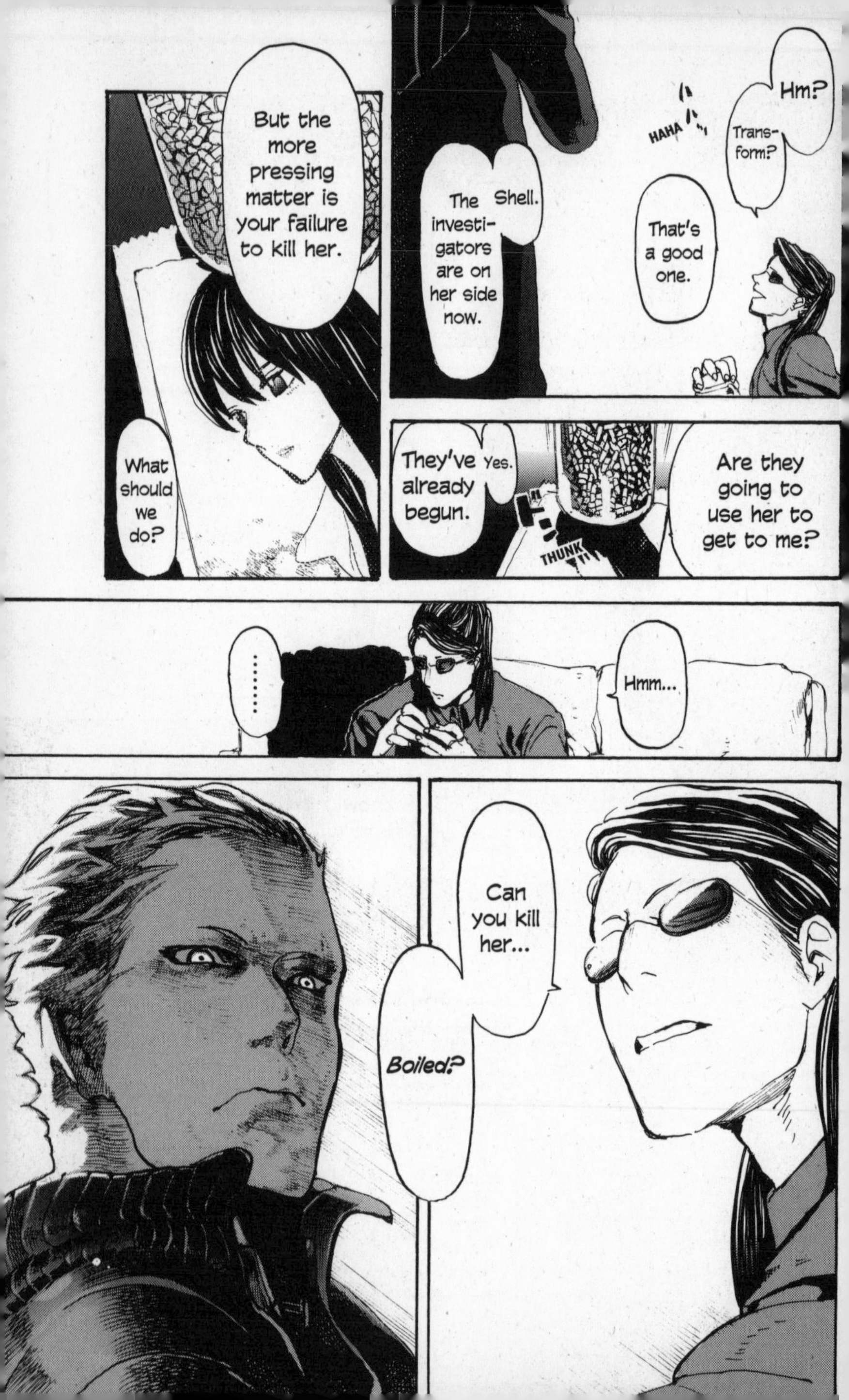
Hm?
Trans-form?
HAHA
That's a good one.
Shell.
The investigators are on her side now.
Are they going to use her to get to me?
Yes.
They've already begun.
THUNK
But the more pressing matter is your failure to kill her.
What should we do?
Hmm...
......
Can you kill her...
Boiled?

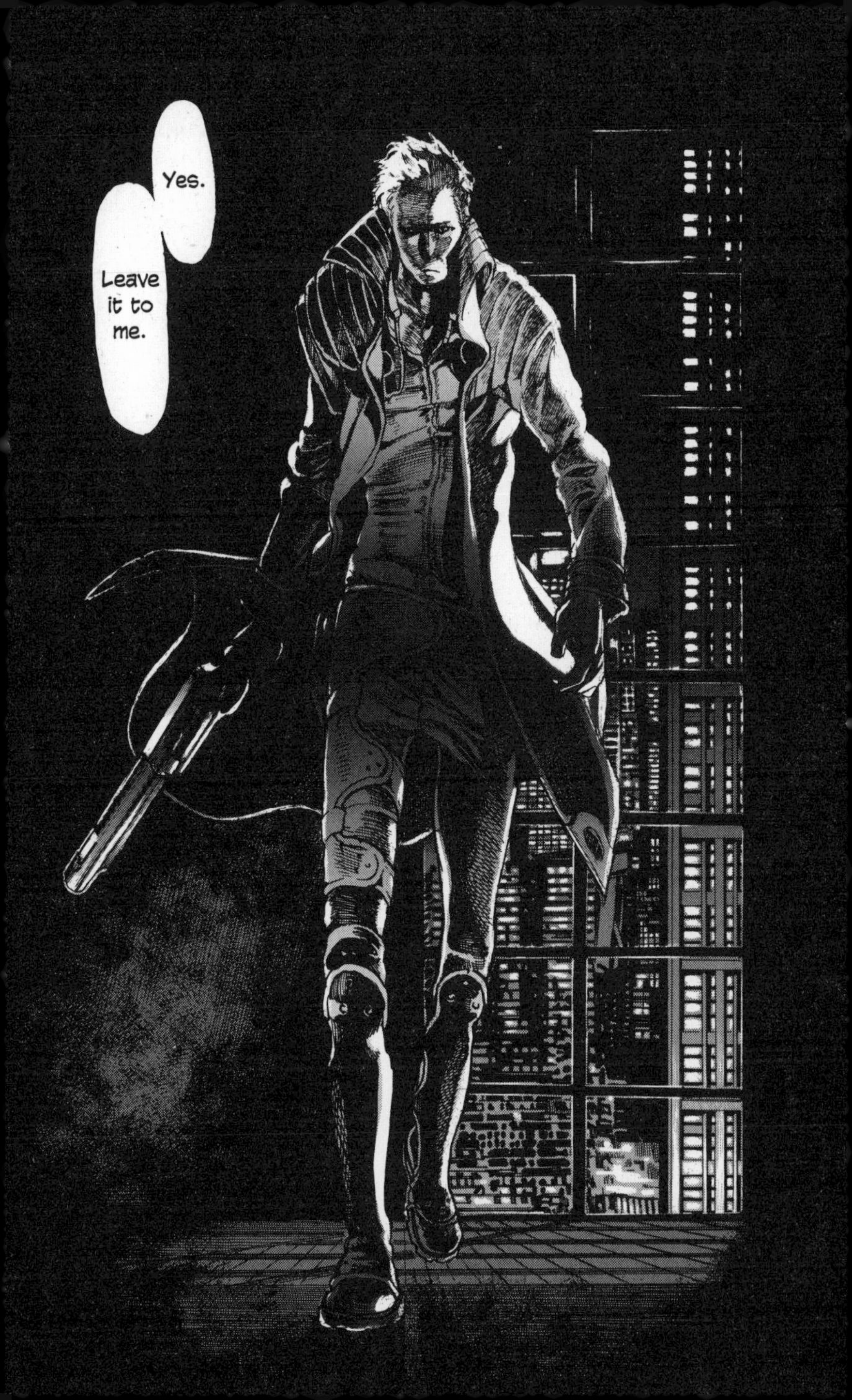
Yes.
Leave it to me.

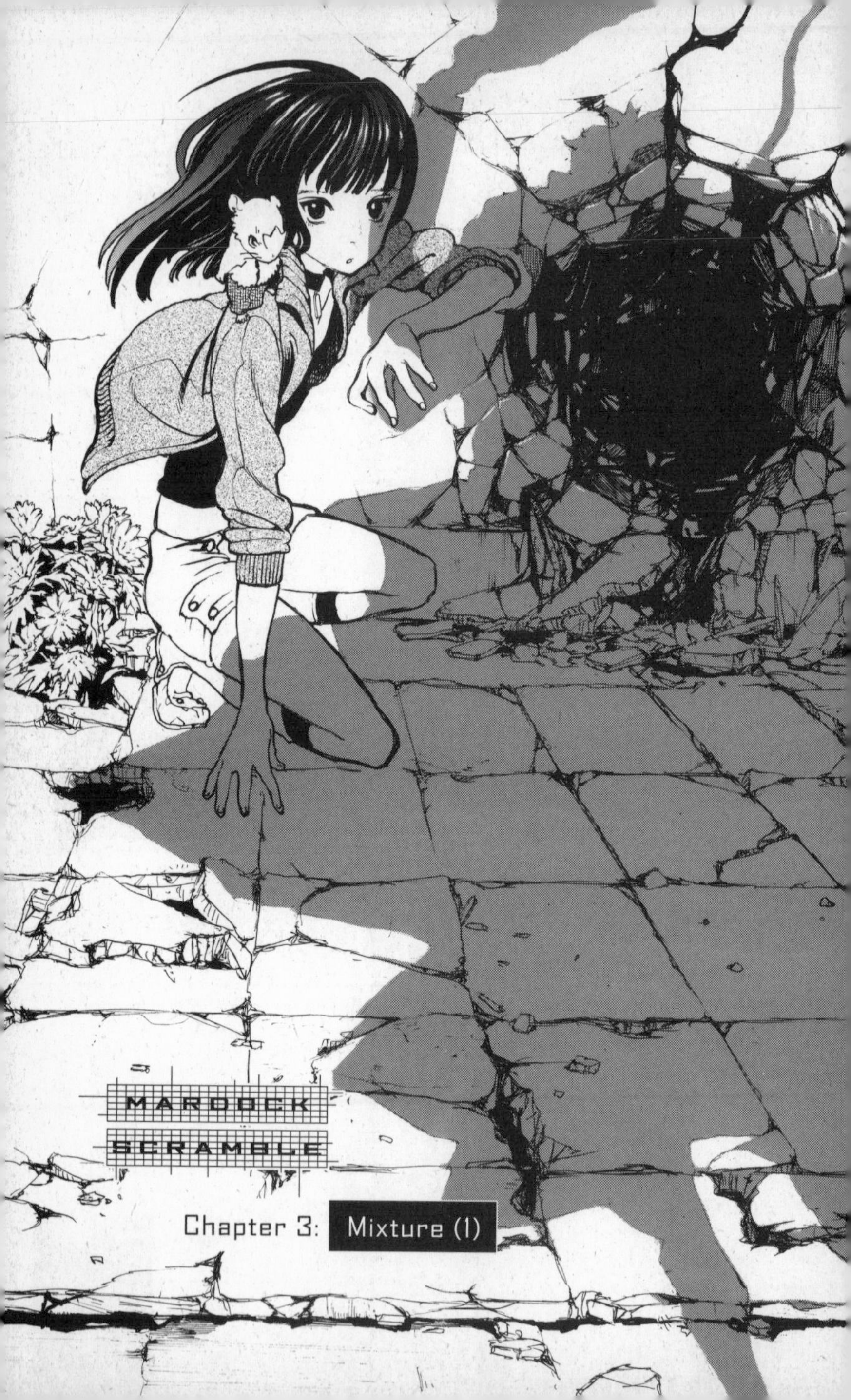
MARDOCK
SCRAMBLE
Chapter 3: Mixture (1)

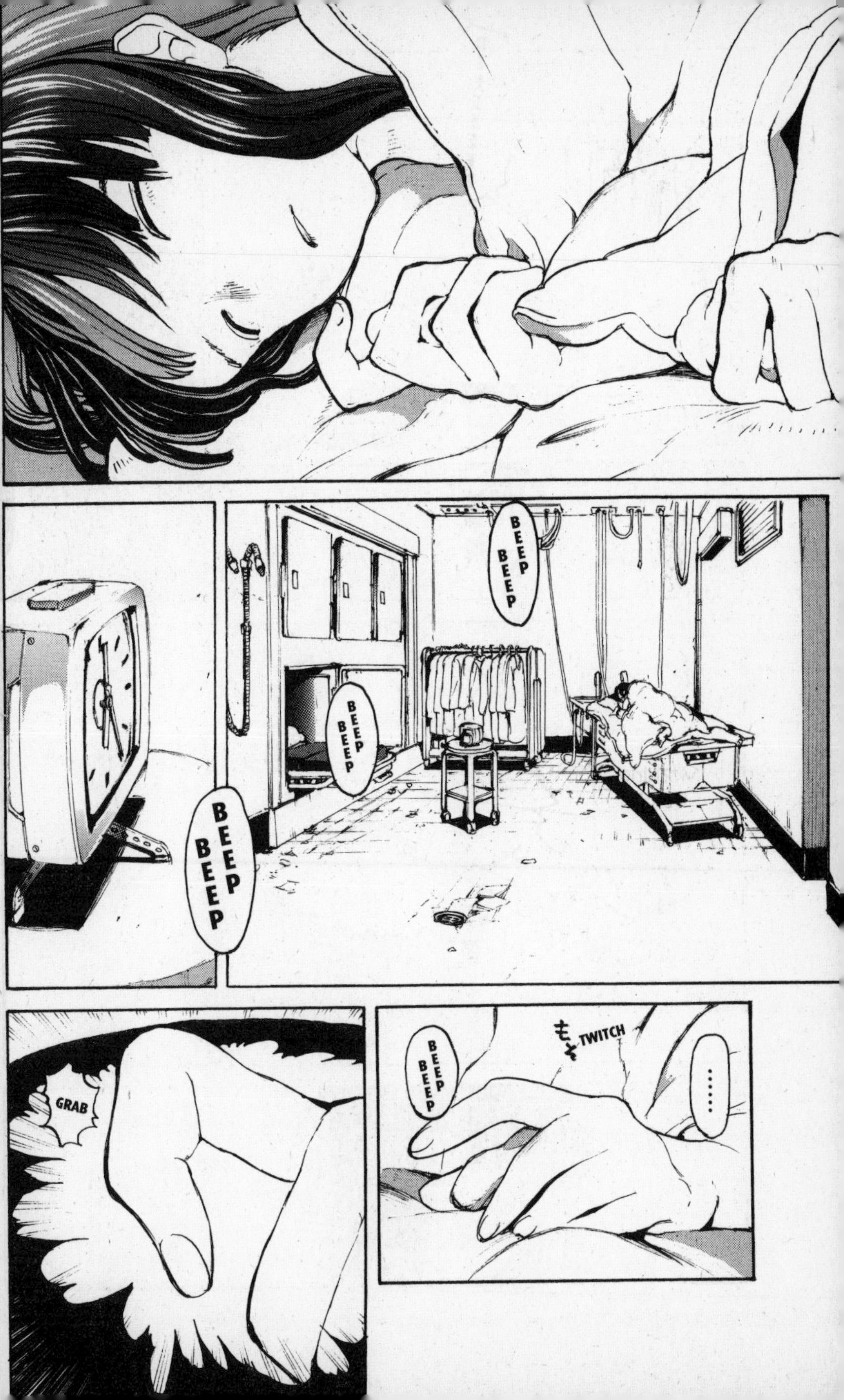
BEEP BEEP
BEEP BEEP
BEEP BEEP
......
TWITCH
BEEP BEEP
GRAB

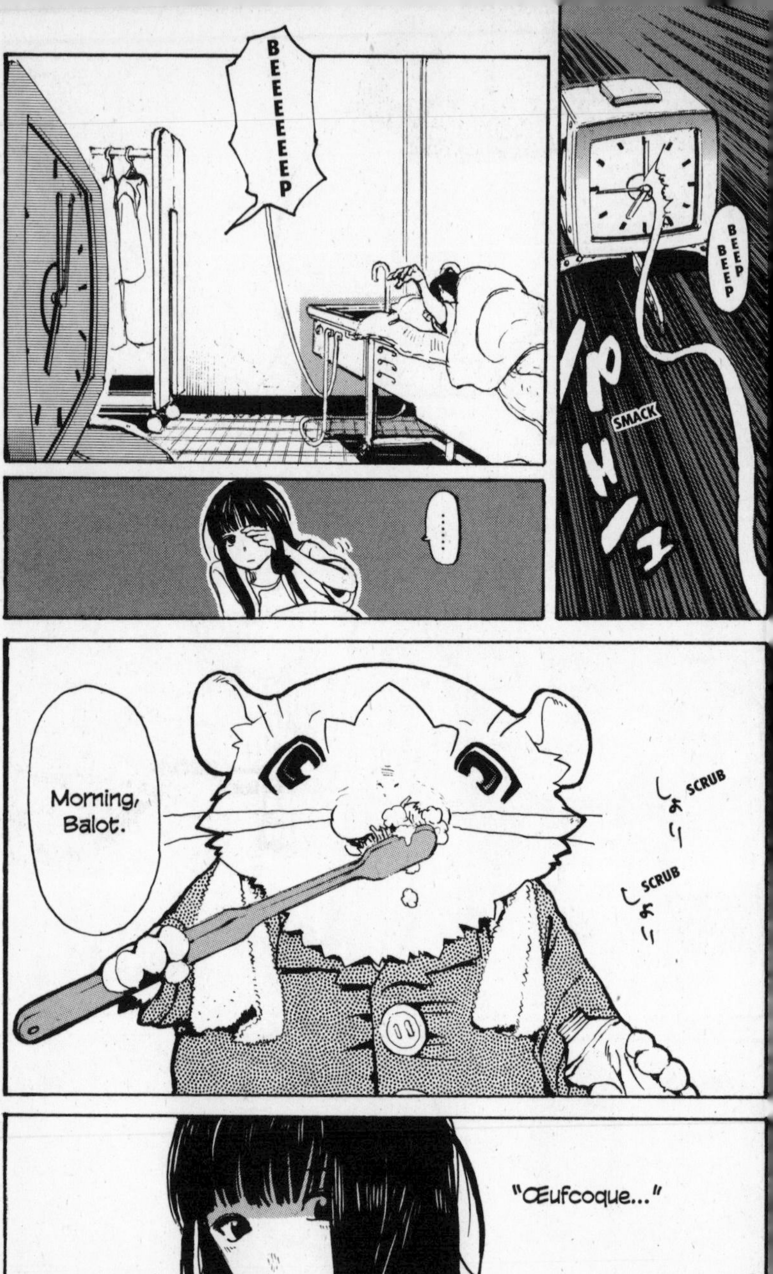

BEEP BEEP
SMACK
BEEEEEEEP
......
Morning, Balot.
SCRUB
SCRUB
"Œufcoque..."

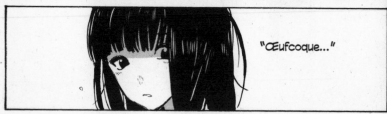

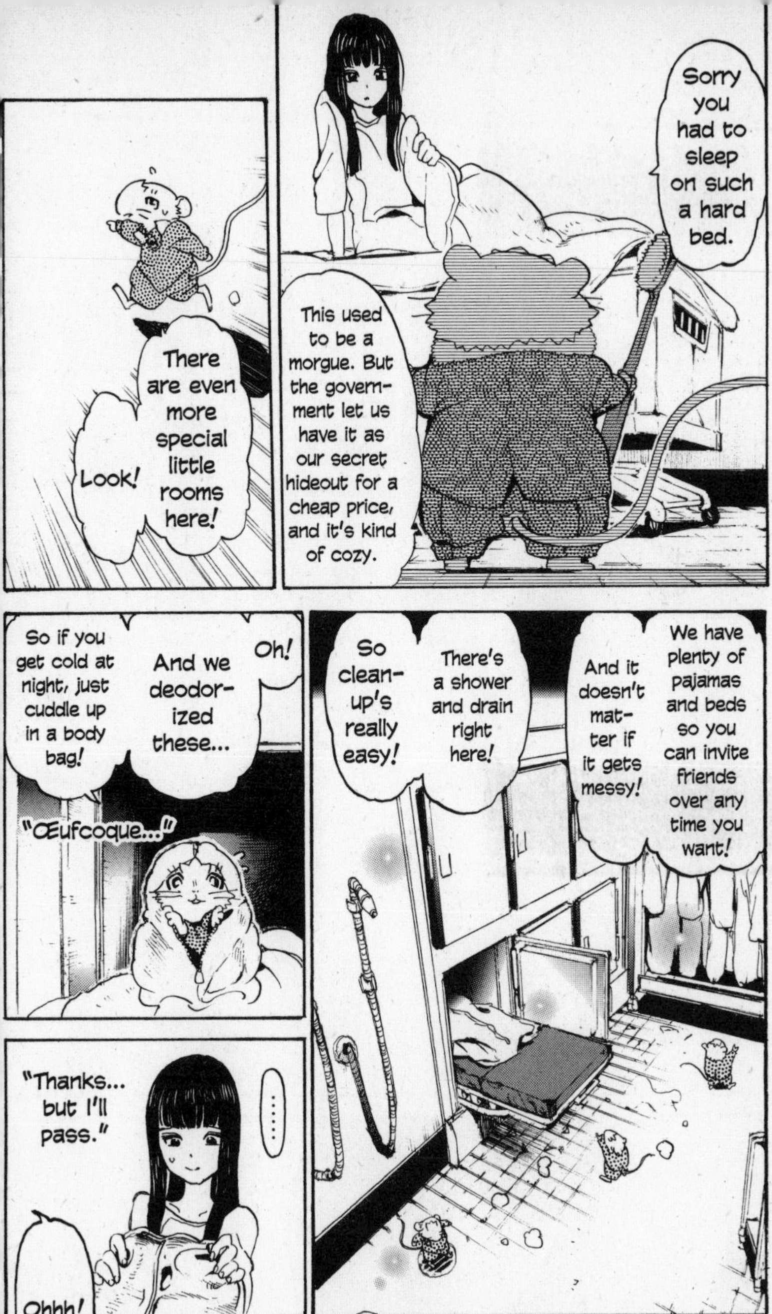
Sorry you had to sleep on such a hard bed.
This used to be a morgue. But the government let us have it as our secret hideout for a cheap price, and it's kind of cozy.
There are even more special little rooms here!
Look!
We have plenty of pajamas and beds so you can invite friends over any time you want!
And it doesn't matter if it gets messy!
There's a shower and drain right here!
So clean-up's really easy!
Oh!
And we deodorized these...
So if you get cold at night, just cuddle up in a body bag!
"Œufcoque..."
......
"Thanks... but I'll pass."
Ohhh!

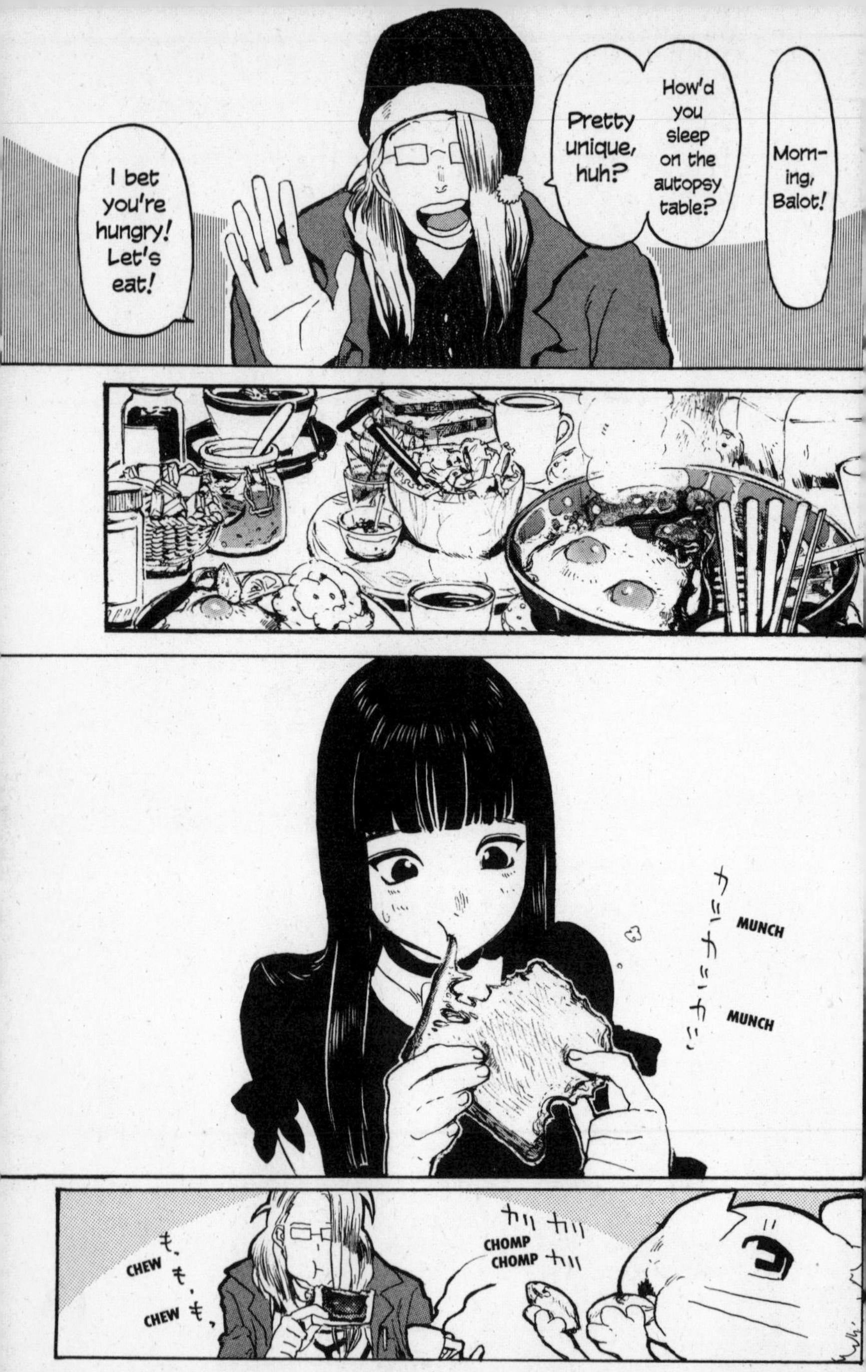
Morn-ing, Balot!
How'd you sleep on the autopsy table?
Pretty unique, huh?
I bet you're hungry! Let's eat!
MUNCH
MUNCH
CHOMP CHOMP
CHEW
CHEW

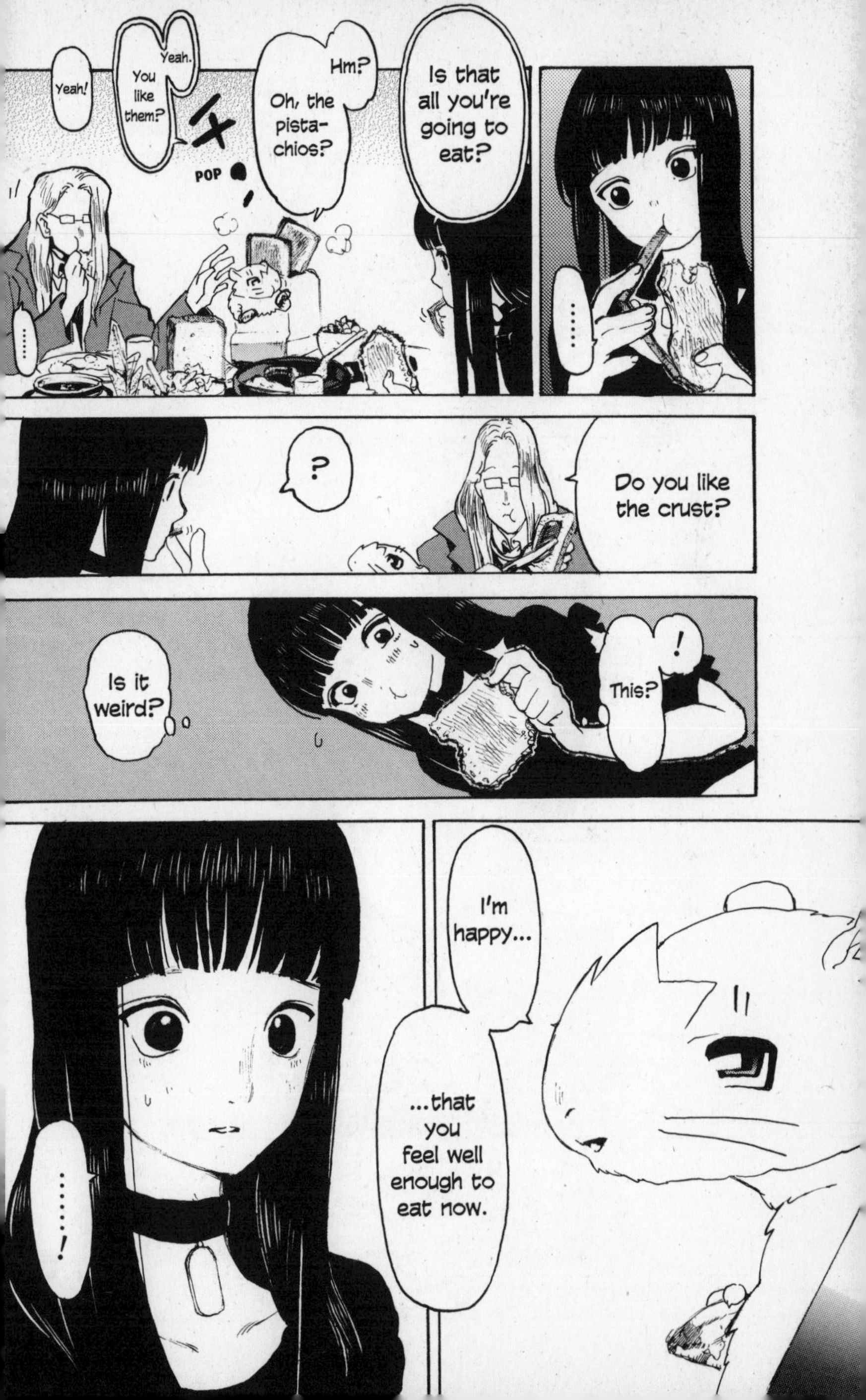
......
Is that all you're going to eat?
Hm? Oh, the pistachios?
Yeah. You like them?
Yeah!
POP
......
Do you like the crust?
?
!
This?
Is it weird?
I'm happy...
...that you feel well enough to eat now.
......!

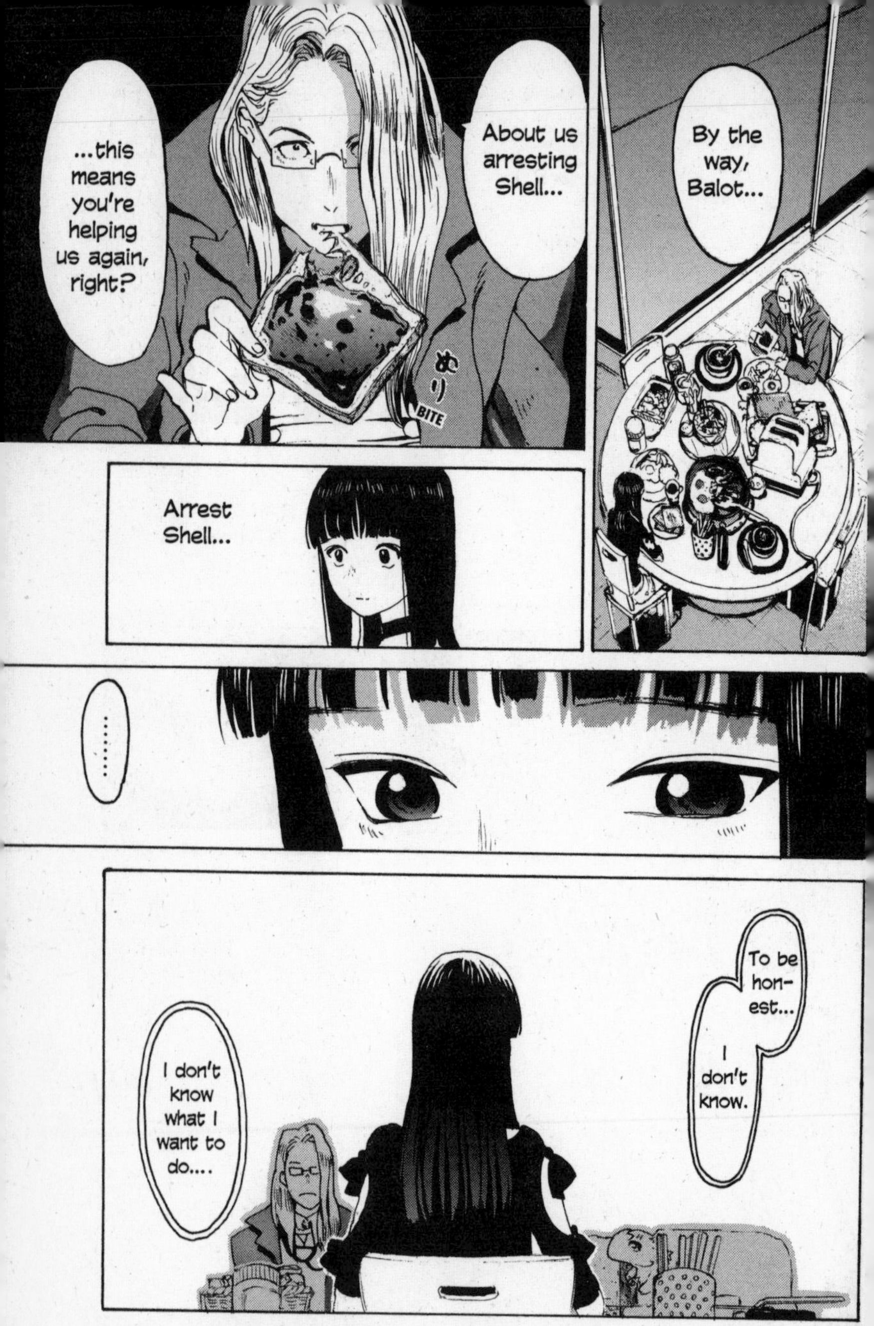
By the way, Balot...
About us arresting Shell...
...this means you're helping us again, right?
ぬり
BITE
Arrest Shell...
......
To be hon-est...
I don't know.
I don't know what I want to do....

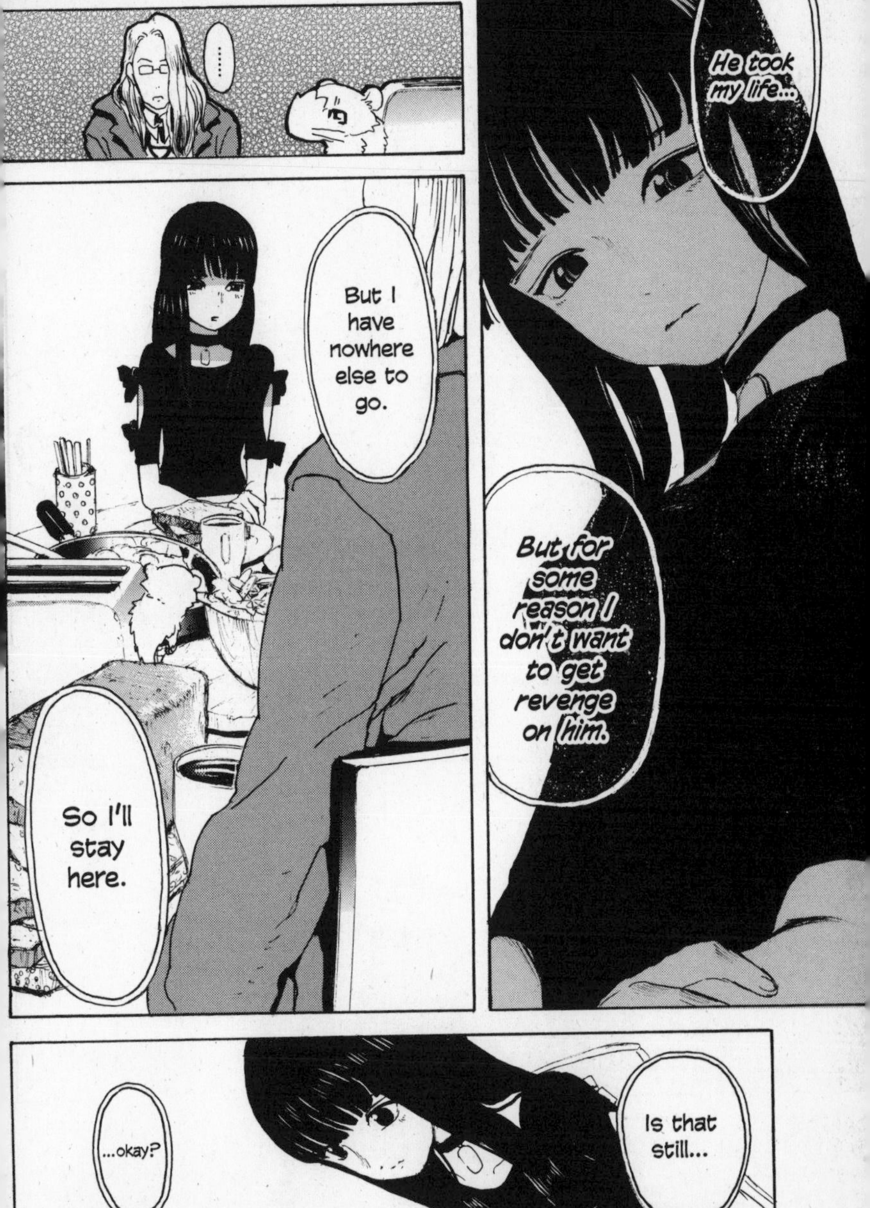
He took my life...
But for some reason I don't want to get revenge on him.
......
But I have nowhere else to go.
So I'll stay here.
Is that still...
...okay?

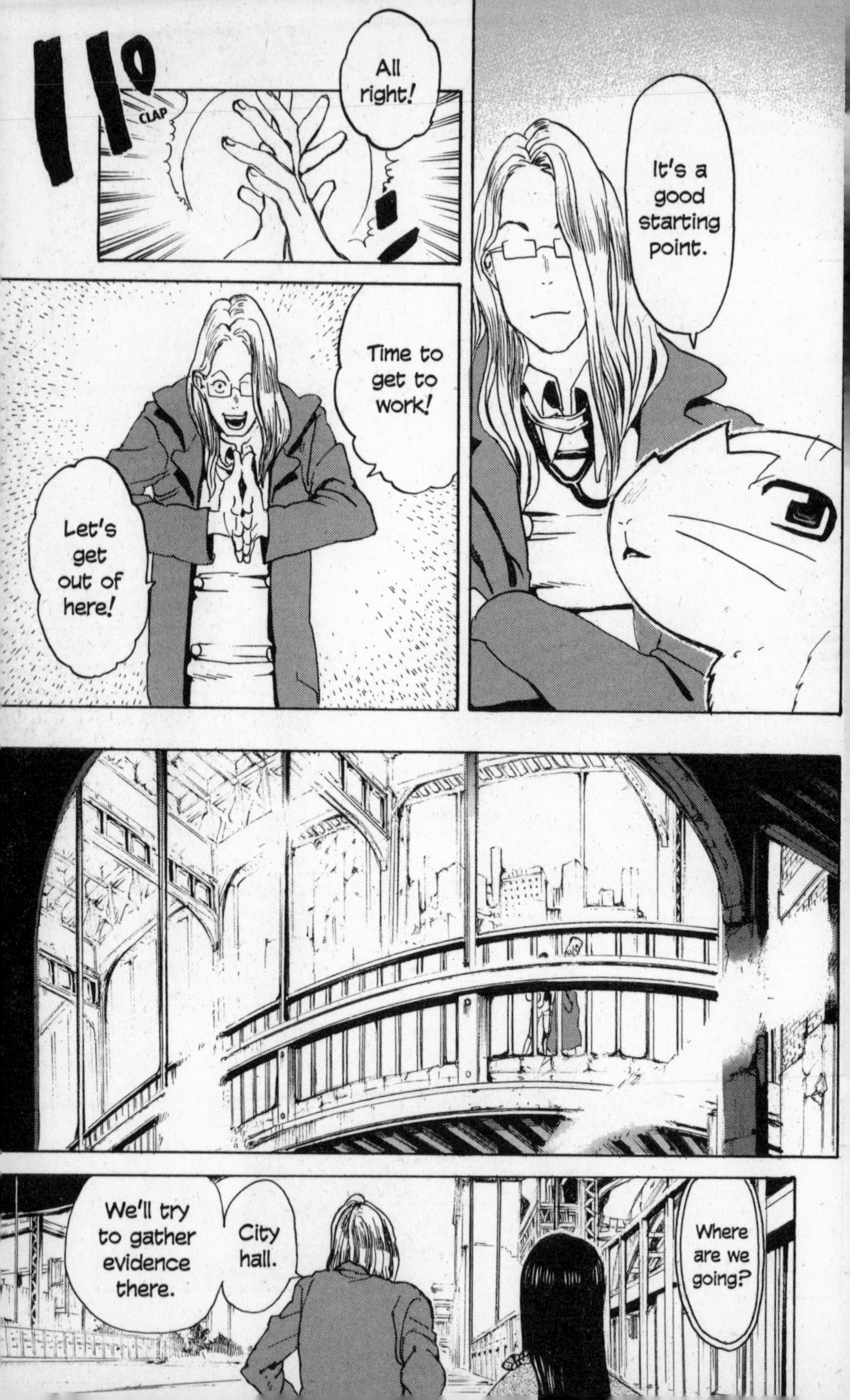
It's a good starting point.
All right!
CLAP
Time to get to work!
Let's get out of here!
Where are we going?
City hall.
We'll try to gather evidence there.

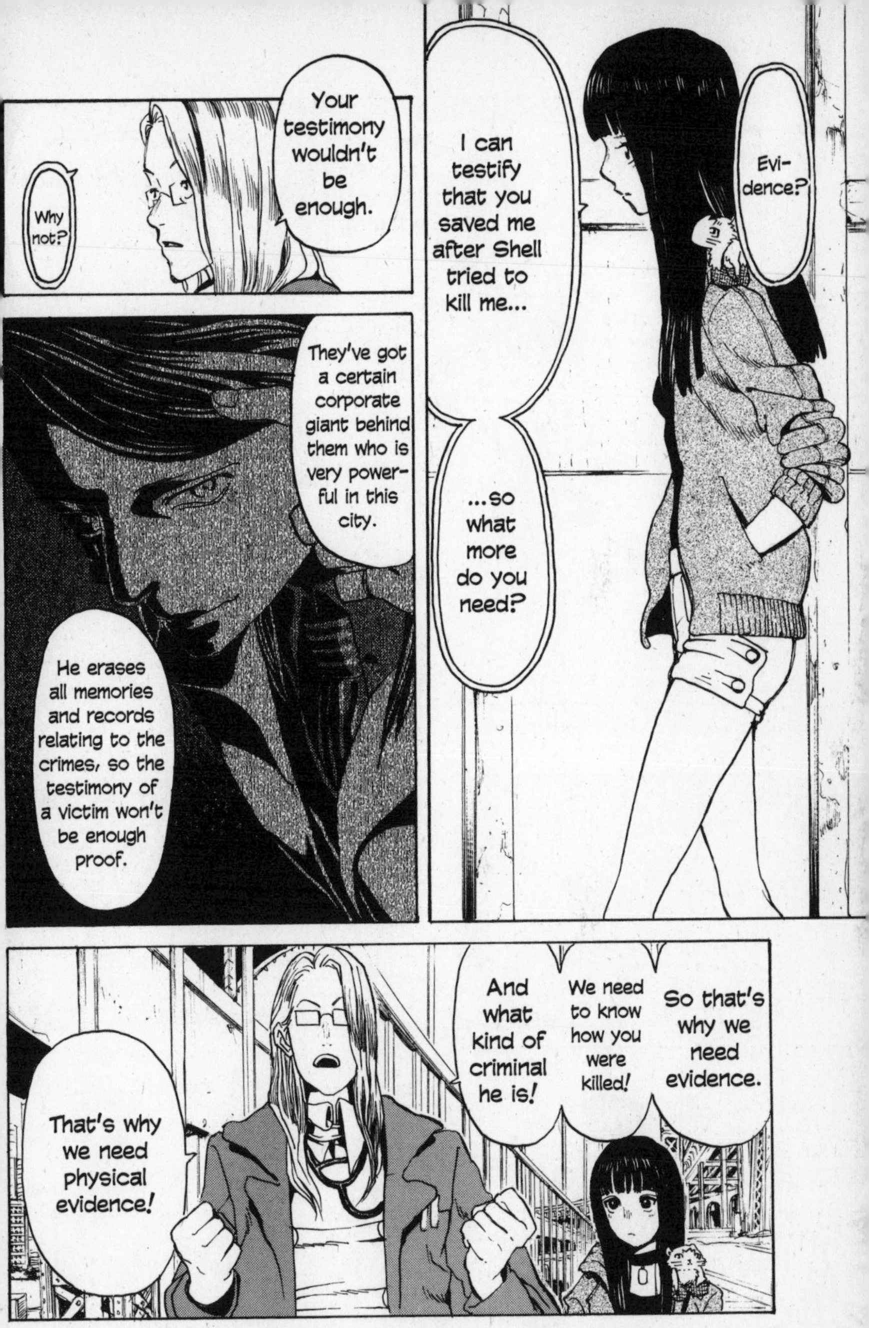
Evi-dence?
I can testify that you saved me after Shell tried to kill me...
...so what more do you need?
Your testimony wouldn't be enough.
Why not?
They've got a certain corporate giant behind them who is very power-ful in this city.
He erases all memories and records relating to the crimes, so the testimony of a victim won't be enough proof.
So that's why we need evidence.
We need to know how you were killed!
And what kind of criminal he is!
That's why we need physical evidence!

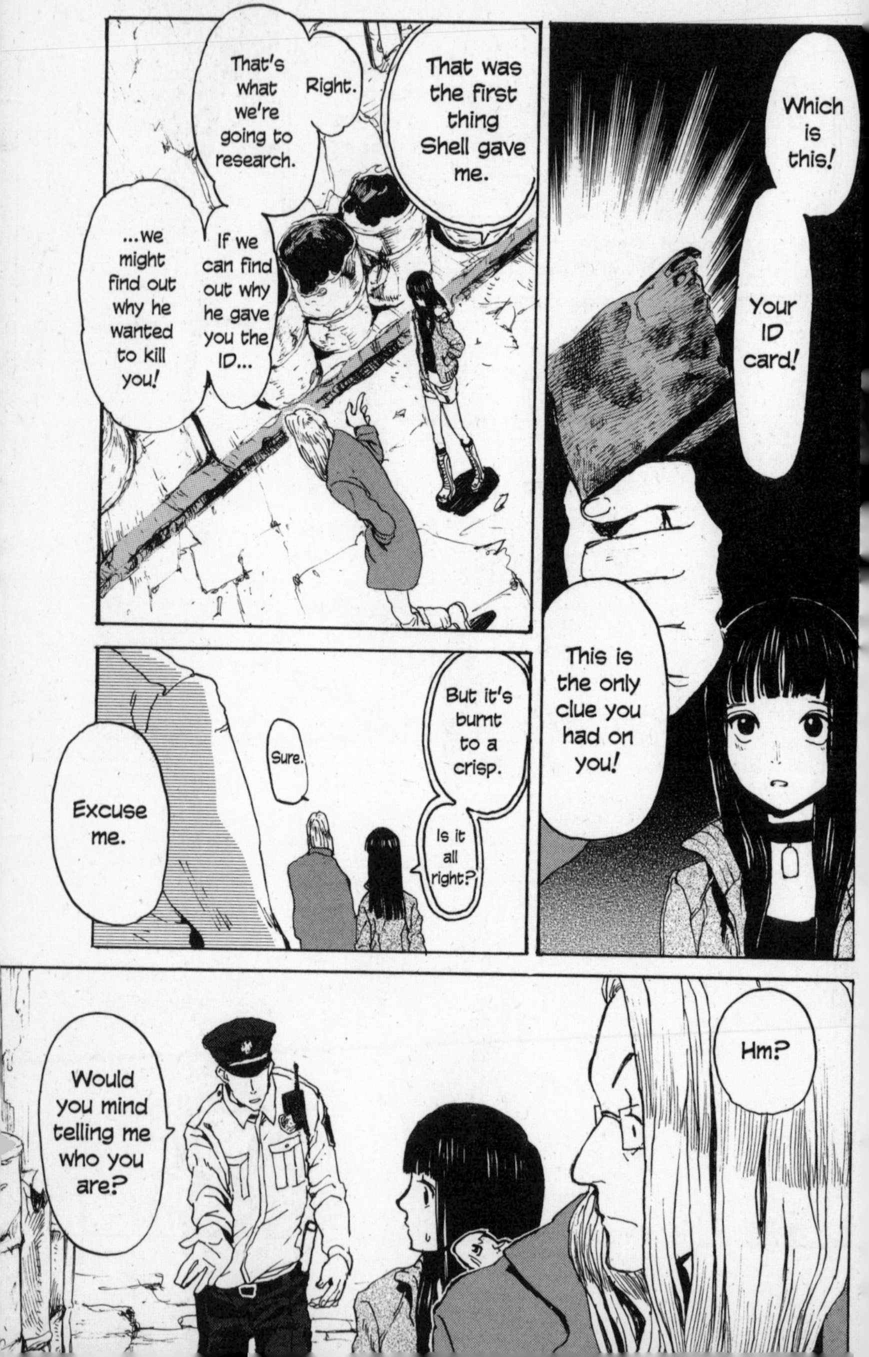
Which is this!
Your ID card!
This is the only clue you had on you!
That was the first thing Shell gave me.
Right.
That's what we're going to research.
If we can find out why he gave you the ID...
...we might find out why he wanted to kill you!
But it's burnt to a crisp.
Is it all right?
Sure.
Excuse me.
Hm?
Would you mind telling me who you are?

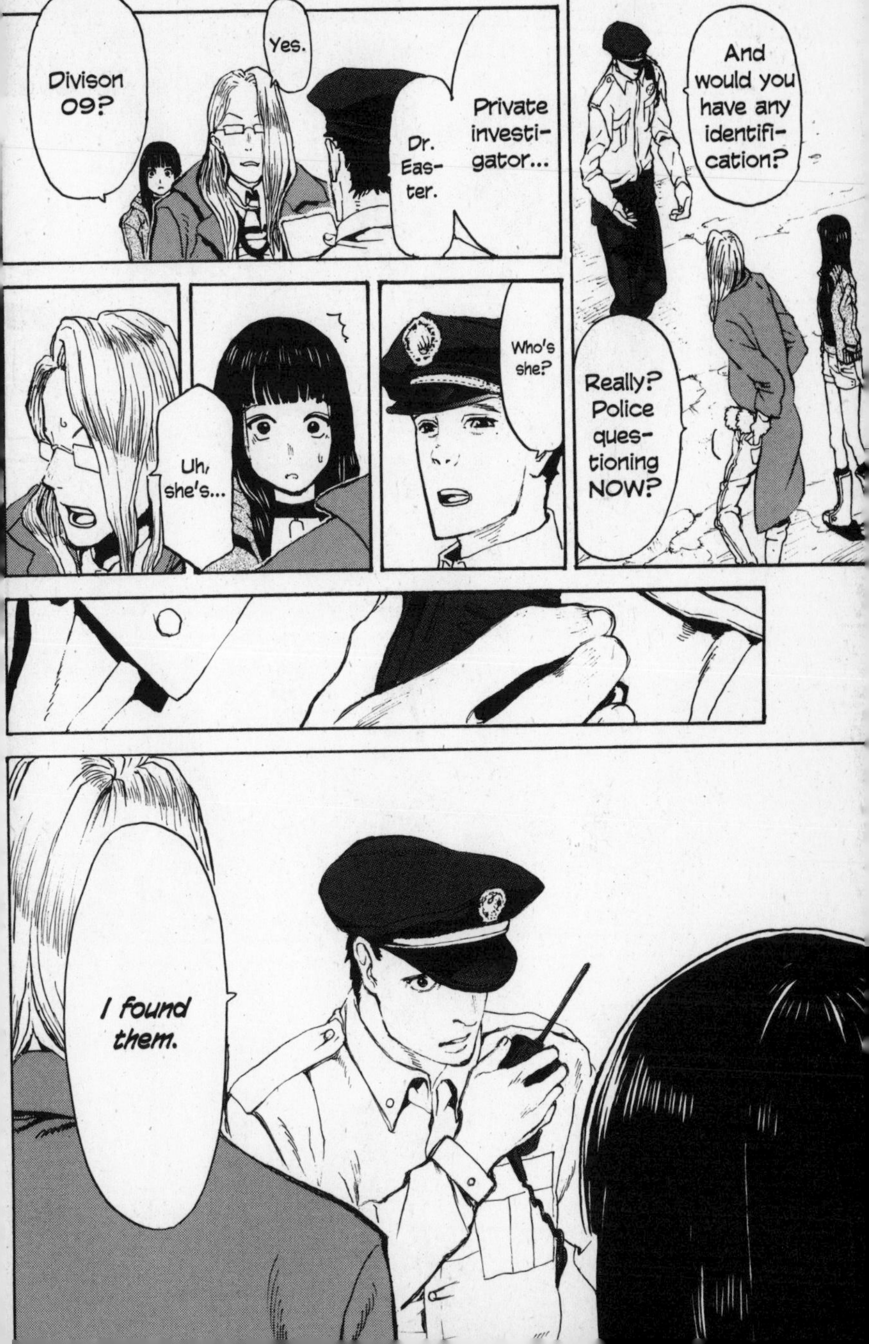
And would you have any identification?
Really? Police questioning NOW?
Private investigator...
Dr. Easter.
Divison 09?
Yes.
Who's she?
Uh, she's...
I found them.

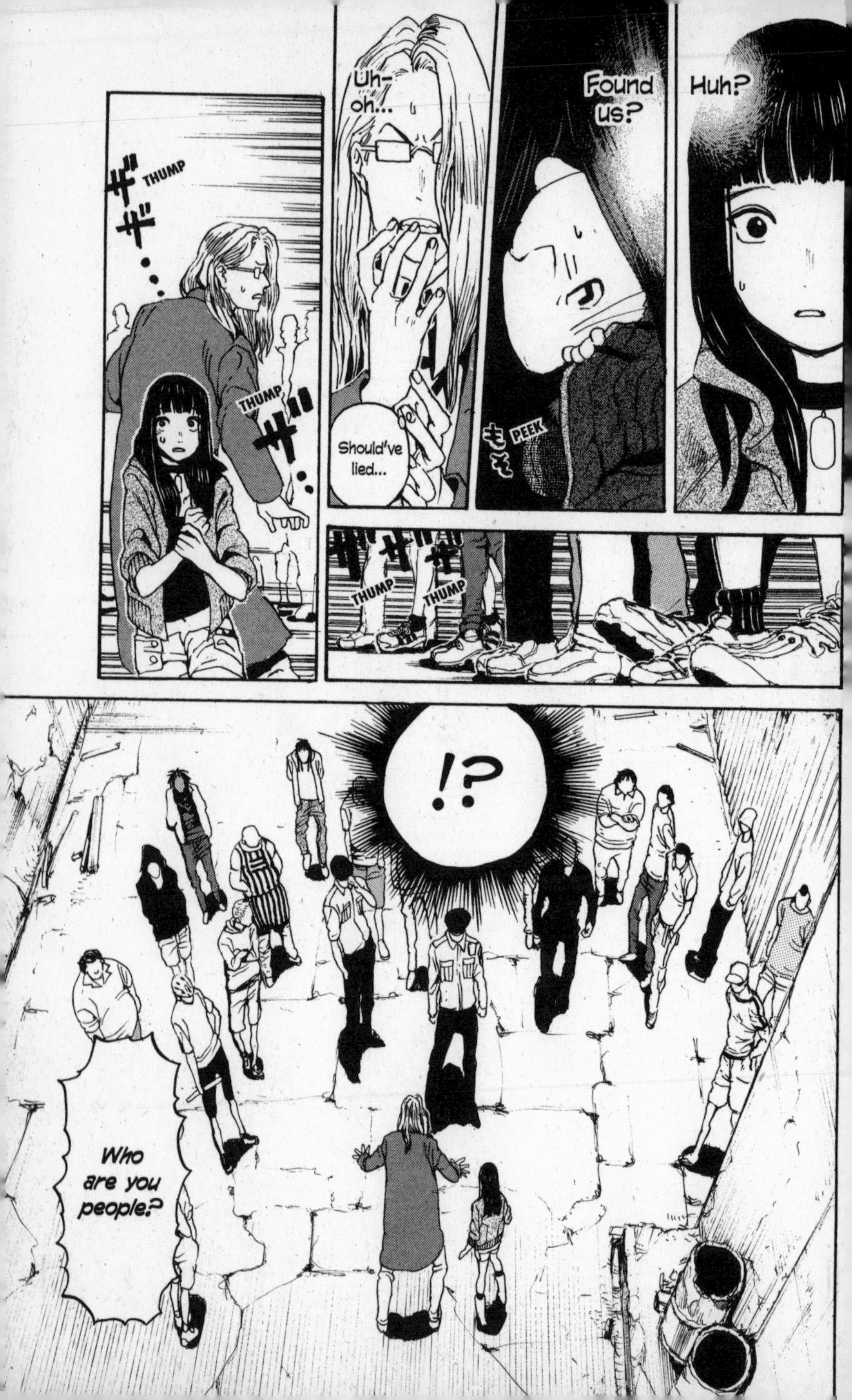
Huh?
Found us?
PEEK
Uh-oh...
Should've lied...
THUMP
THUMP
THUMP
THUMP
!?
Who are you people?

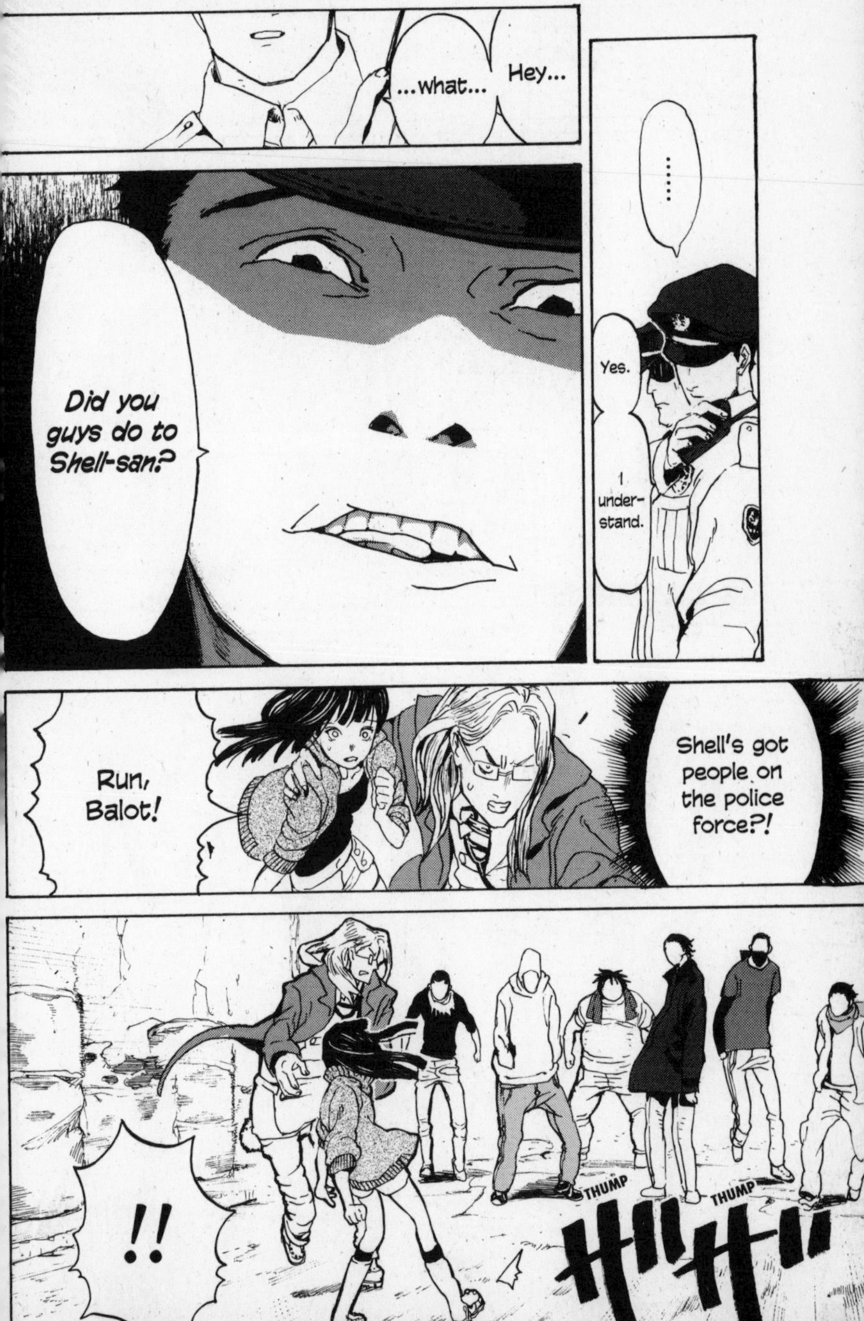
……
Yes.
I understand.
Hey...
...what...
Did you guys do to Shell-san?
Shell's got people on the police force?!
Run, Balot!
THUMP
THUMP
ザッザッ
!!

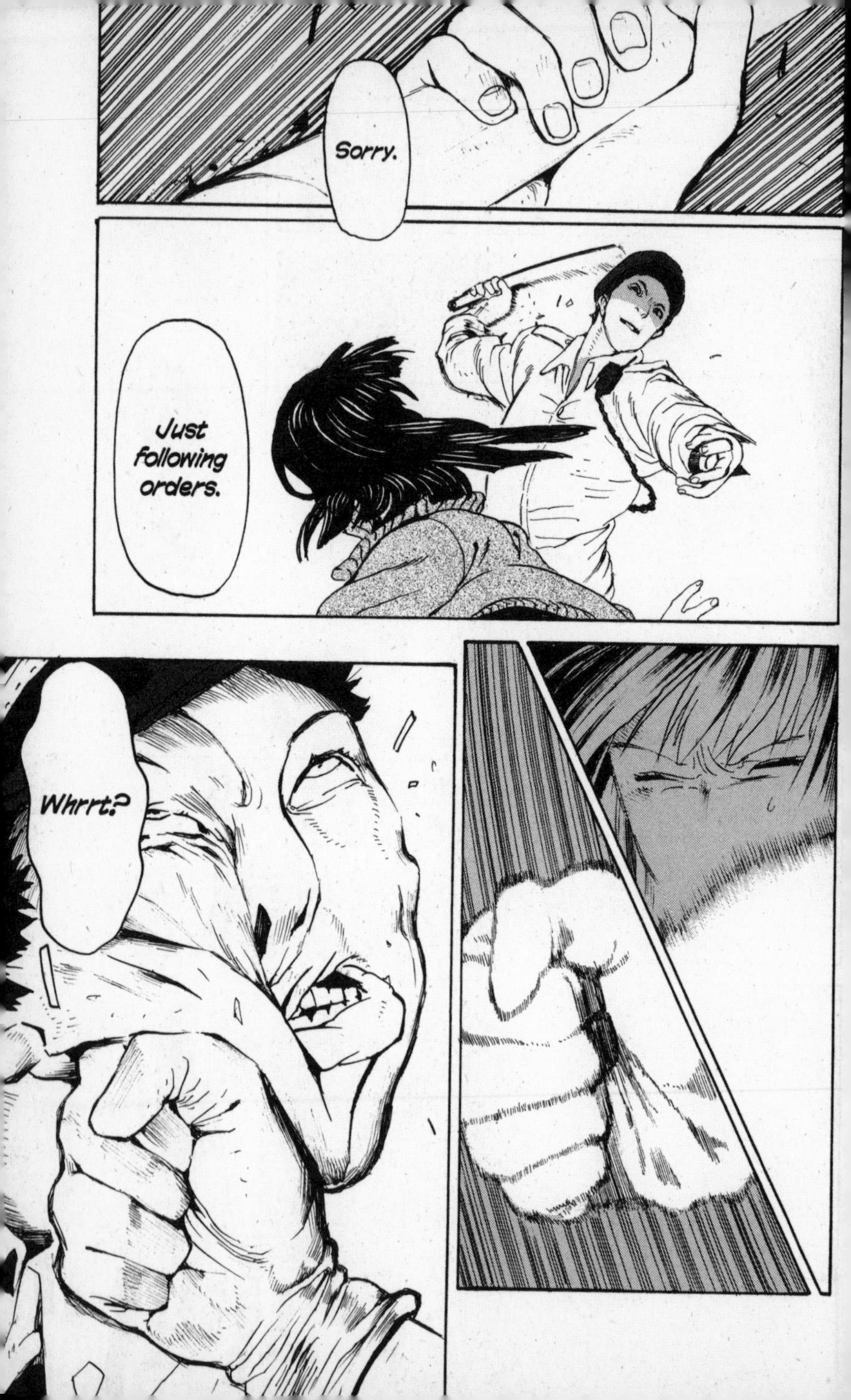
Sorry.
Just following orders.
Whrrt?

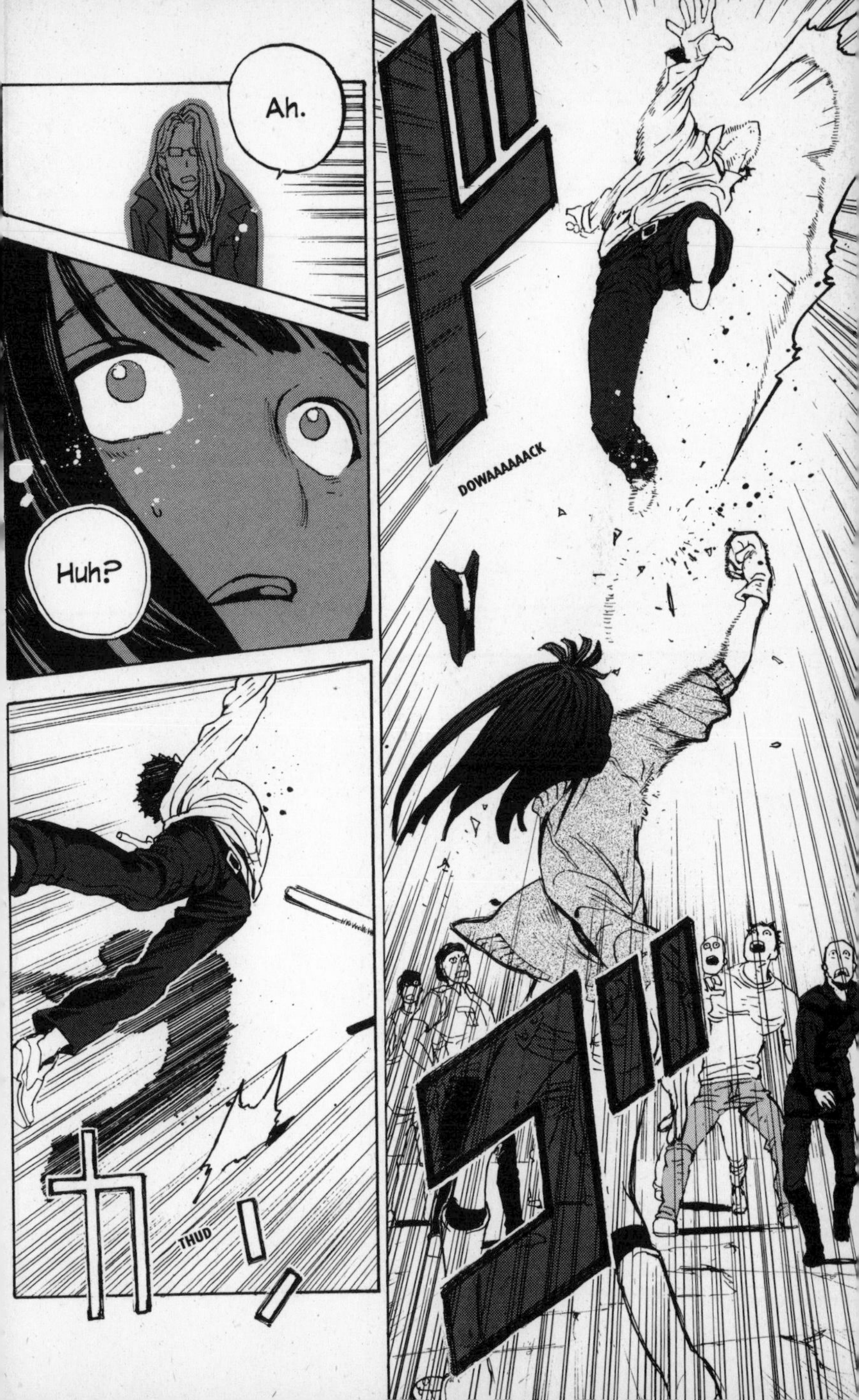
DOWAAAAACK
Ah.
Huh?
THUD

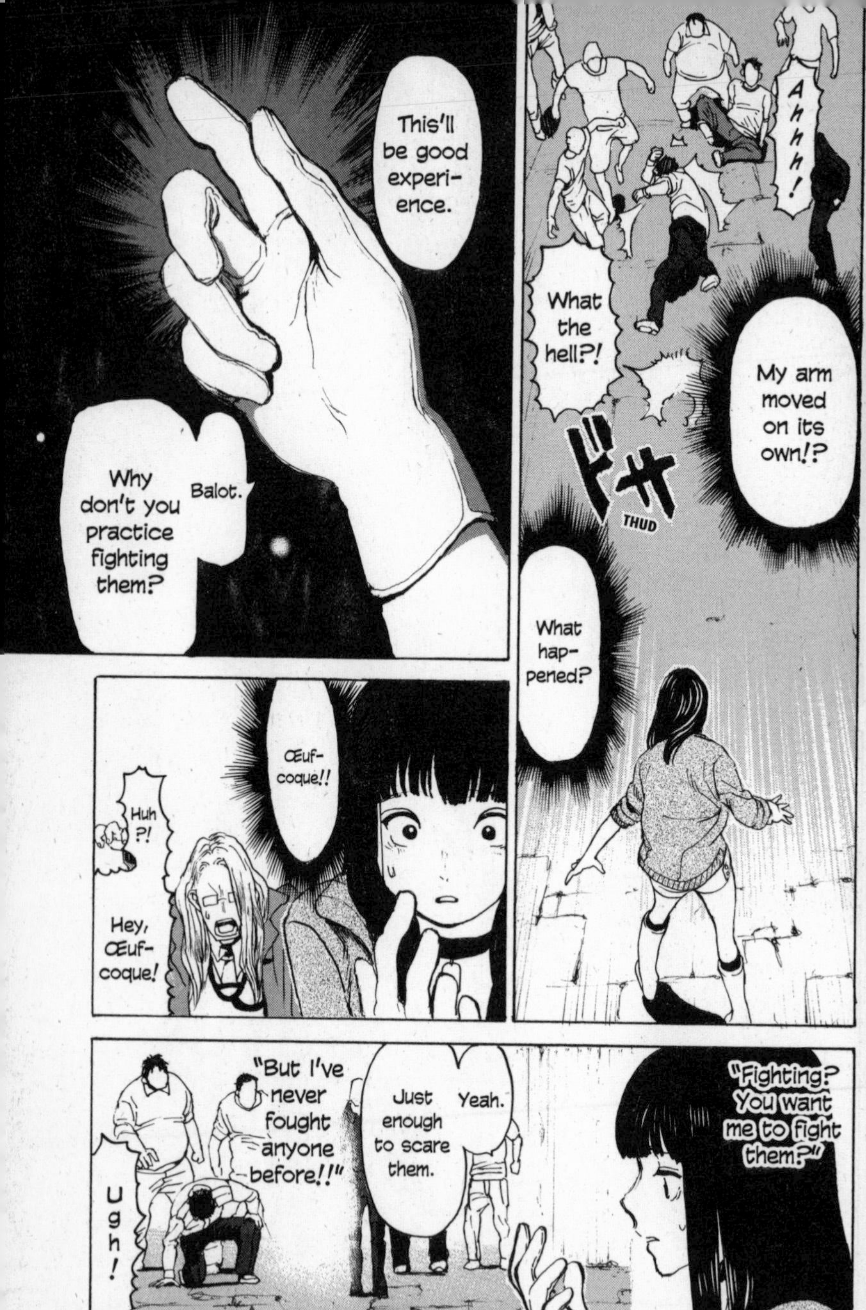
Ahhh!
What the hell?!
My arm moved on its own!?
ドサ
THUD
What happened?
This'll be good experience.
Balot.
Why don't you practice fighting them?
Œuf-coque!!
Huh?!
Hey, Œuf-coque!
"Fighting? You want me to fight them?"
Yeah.
Just enough to scare them.
"But I've never fought anyone before!!"
Ugh!

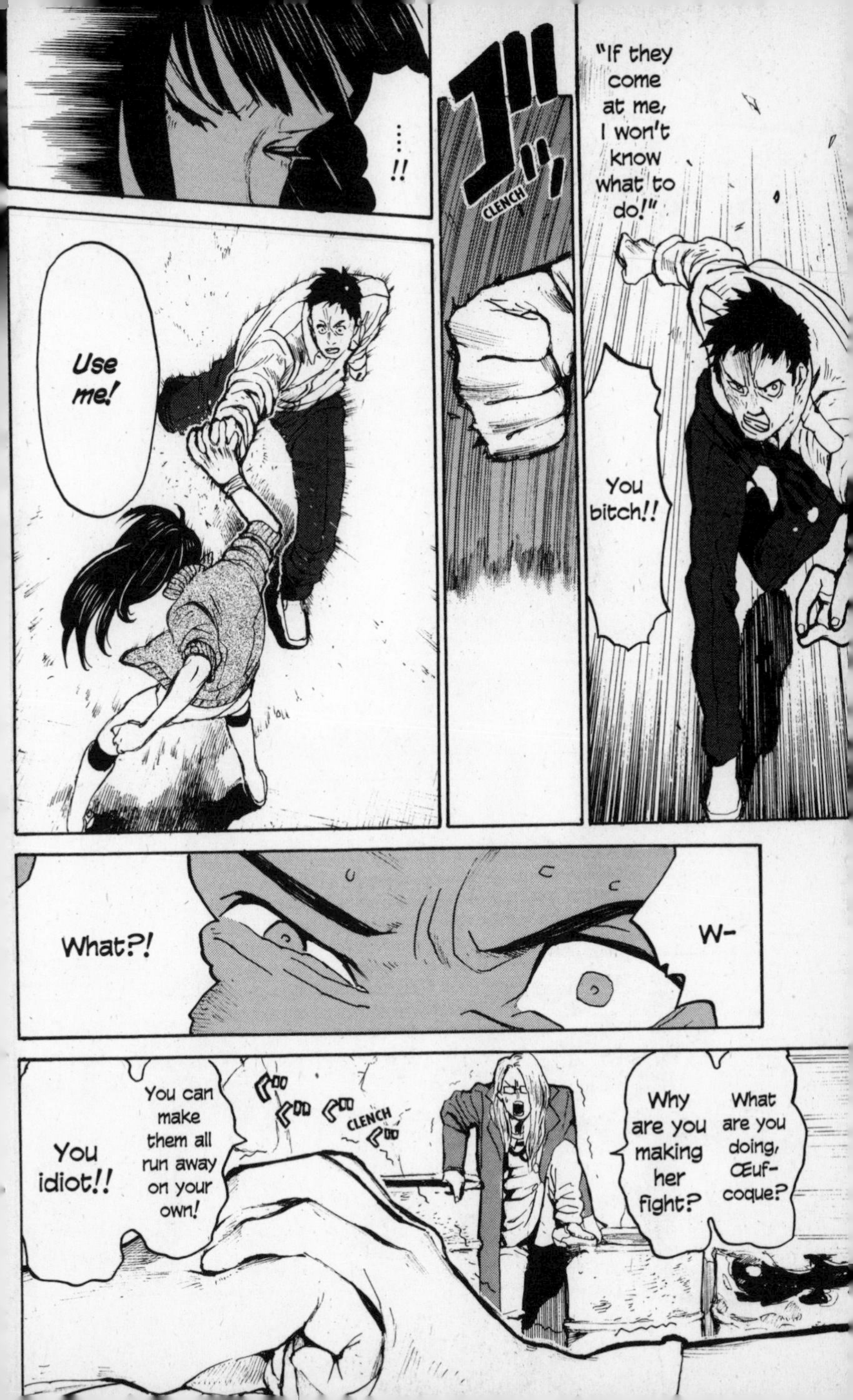

"If they come at me, I won't know what to do!"
You bitch!!
CLENCH
....!!
Use me!
W-
What?!
What are you doing, Œuf-coque?
Why are you making her fight?
CLENCH
You can make them all run away on your own!
You idiot!!

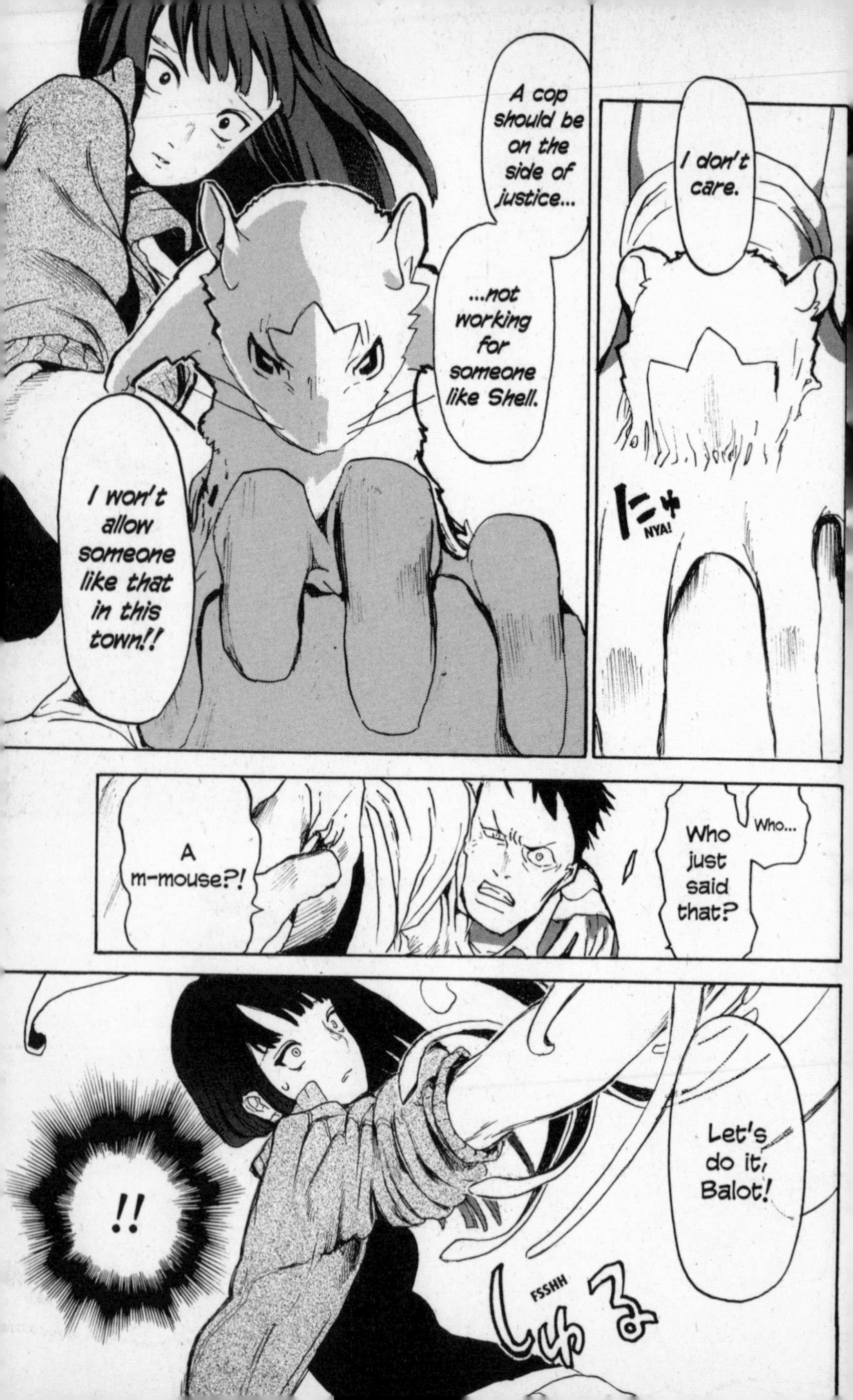
I don't care.
にゅ
NYA!
A cop should be on the side of justice...
...not working for someone like Shell.
I won't allow someone like that in this town!!
Who...
Who just said that?
A m-mouse?!
Let's do it, Balot!
FSSHH
しゅる
!!

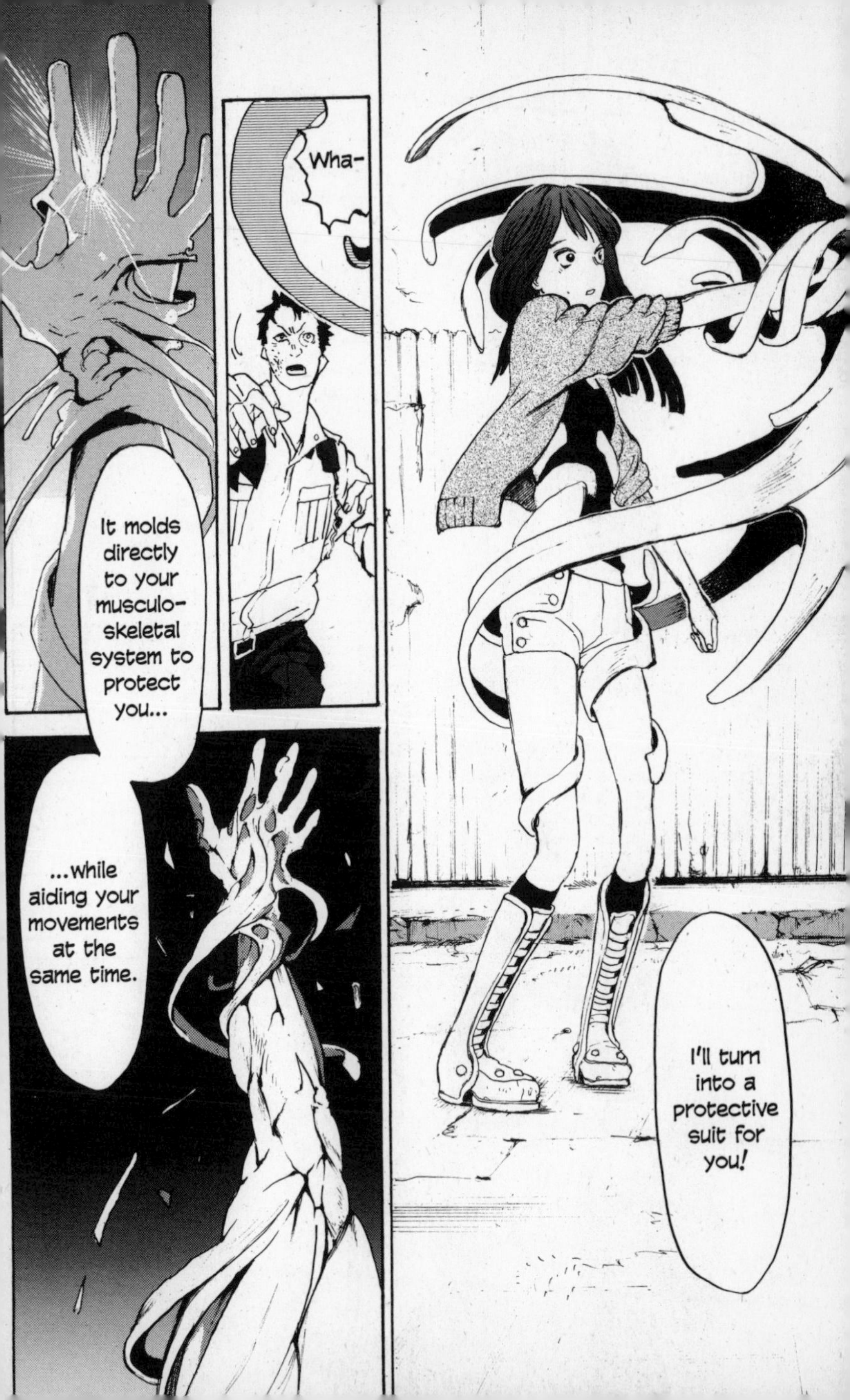
I'll turn into a protective suit for you!
Wha-
It molds directly to your musculo-skeletal system to protect you...
...while aiding your movements at the same time.

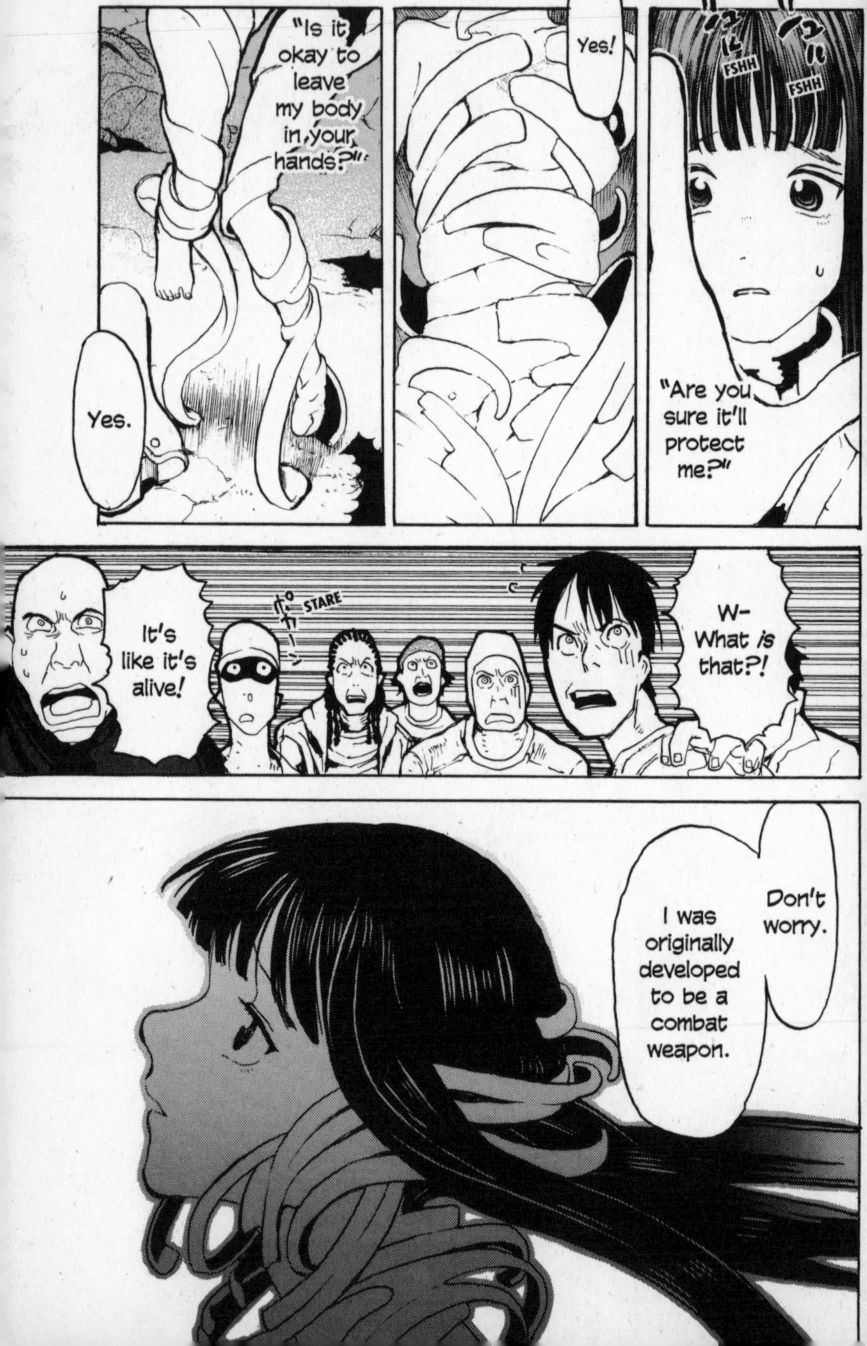
FSHH
FSHH
"Are you sure it'll protect me?"
Yes!
"Is it okay to leave my body in your hands?"
Yes.
W- What *is* that?!
STARE
It's like it's alive!
Don't worry.
I was originally developed to be a combat weapon.

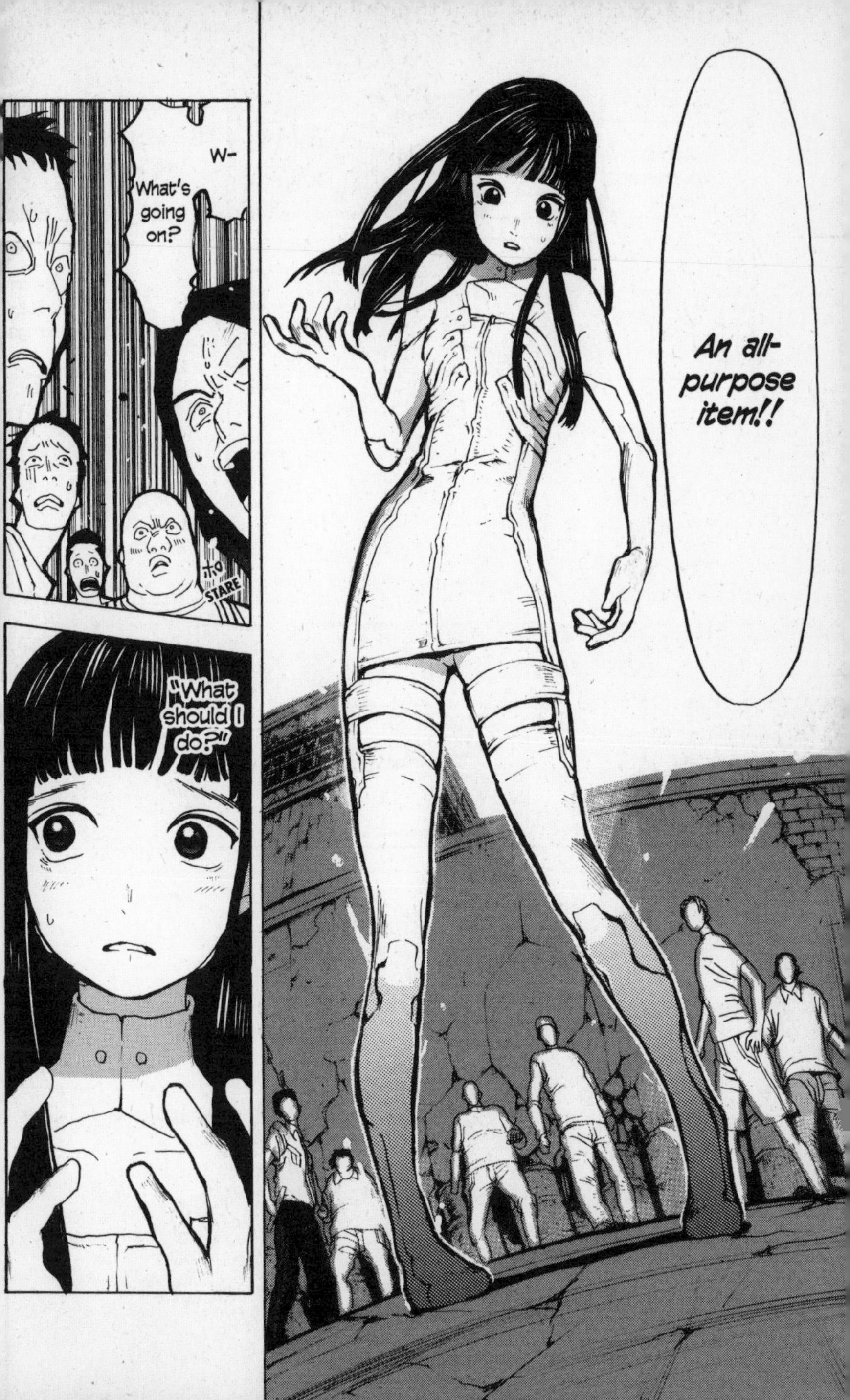
An all-purpose item!!
W-
What's going on?
STARE
"What should I do?"

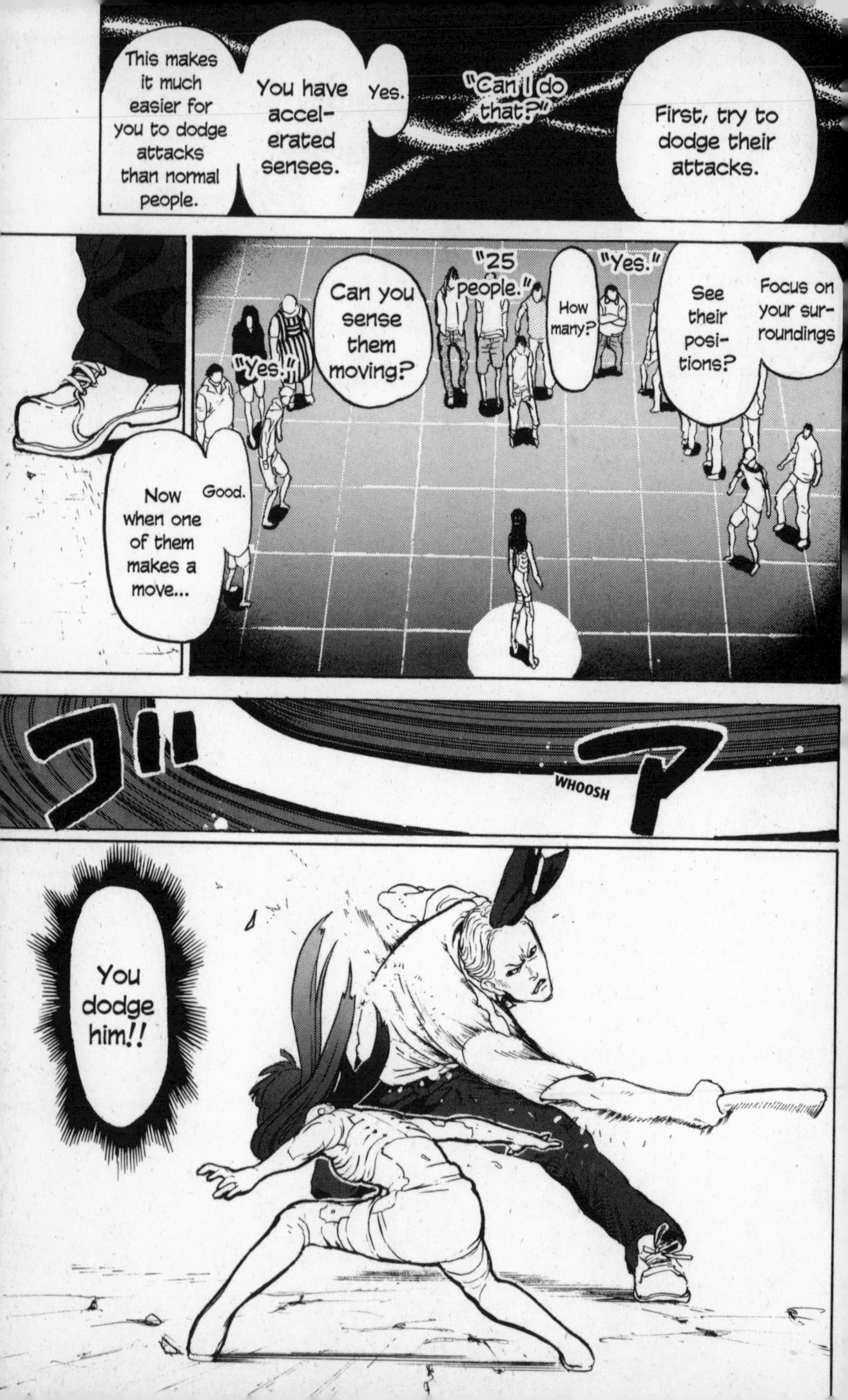
First, try to dodge their attacks.
"Can I do that?"
Yes.
You have accel-erated senses.
This makes it much easier for you to dodge attacks than normal people.
Focus on your sur-roundings
See their posi-tions?
"Yes."
How many?
"25 people."
Can you sense them moving?
"Yes."
Good.
Now when one of them makes a move...
ゴア
WHOOSH
You dodge him!!

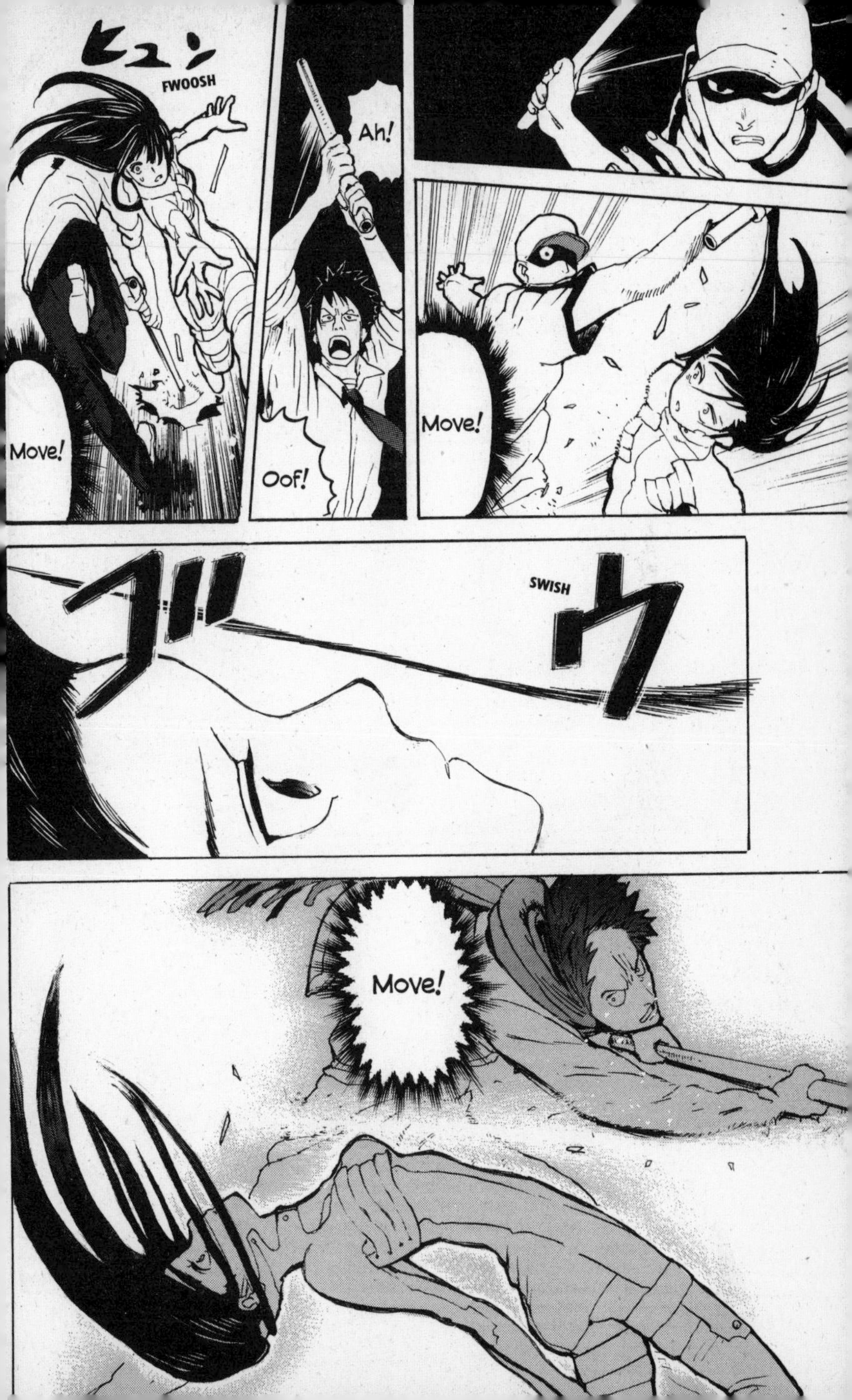
Move!
Ah!
Oof!
ヒュン
FWOOSH
Move!
SWISH
Move!

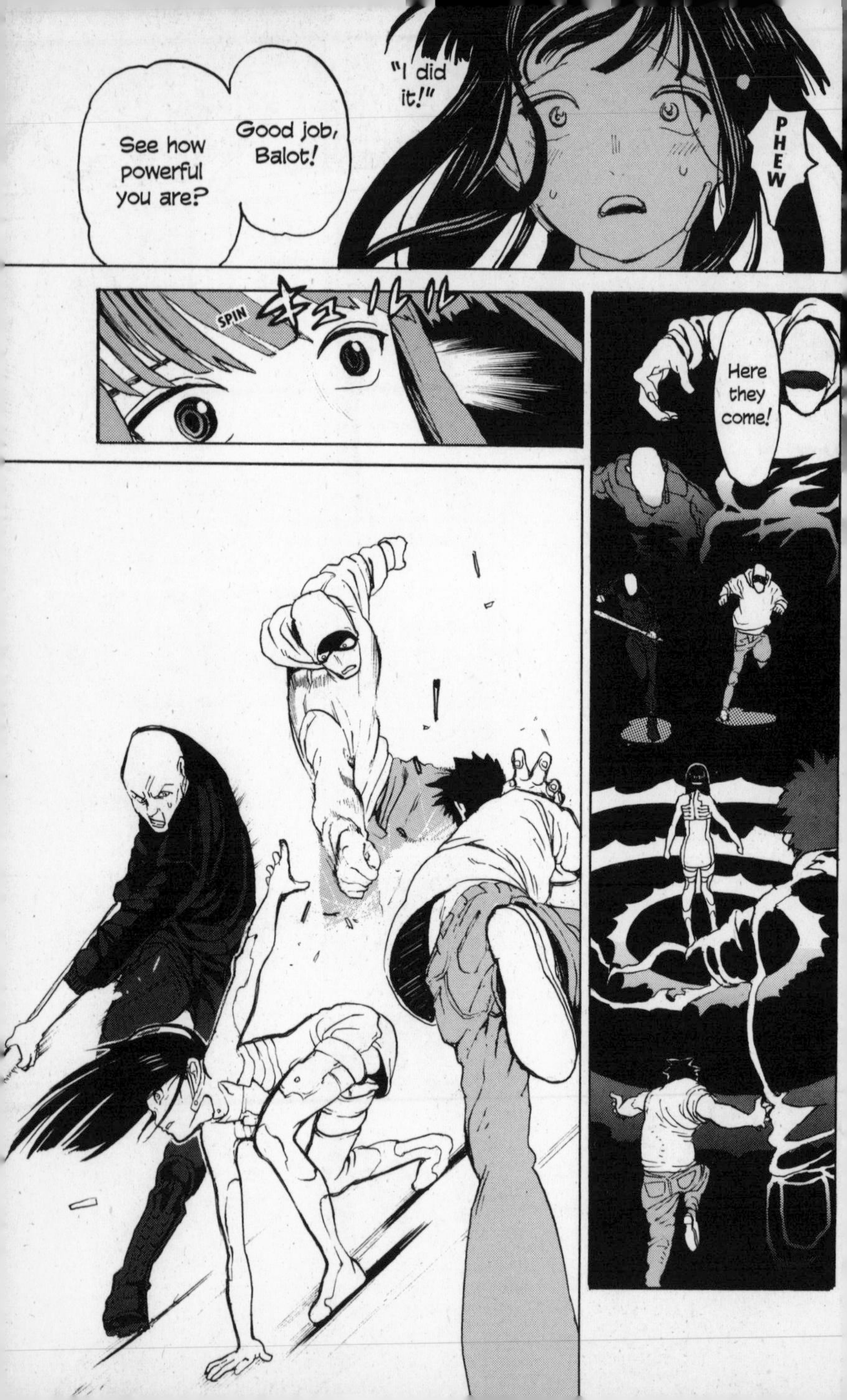
PHEW
"I did it!"
Good job, Balot!
See how powerful you are?
Here they come!
SPIN

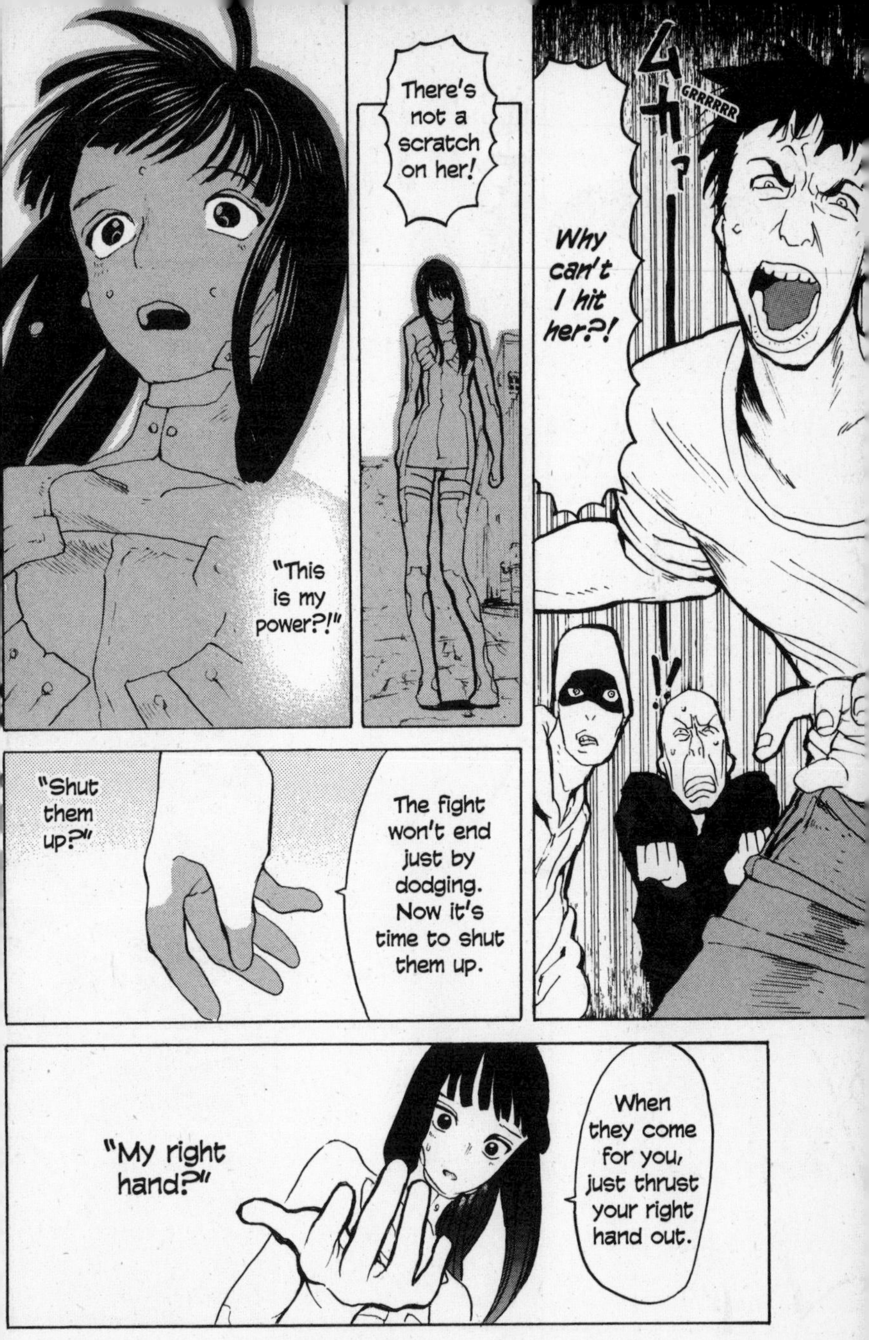
GRRRRRR
Why can't I hit her?!
There's not a scratch on her!
"This is my power?!"
The fight won't end just by dodging. Now it's time to shut them up.
"Shut them up?"
When they come for you, just thrust your right hand out.
"My right hand?"

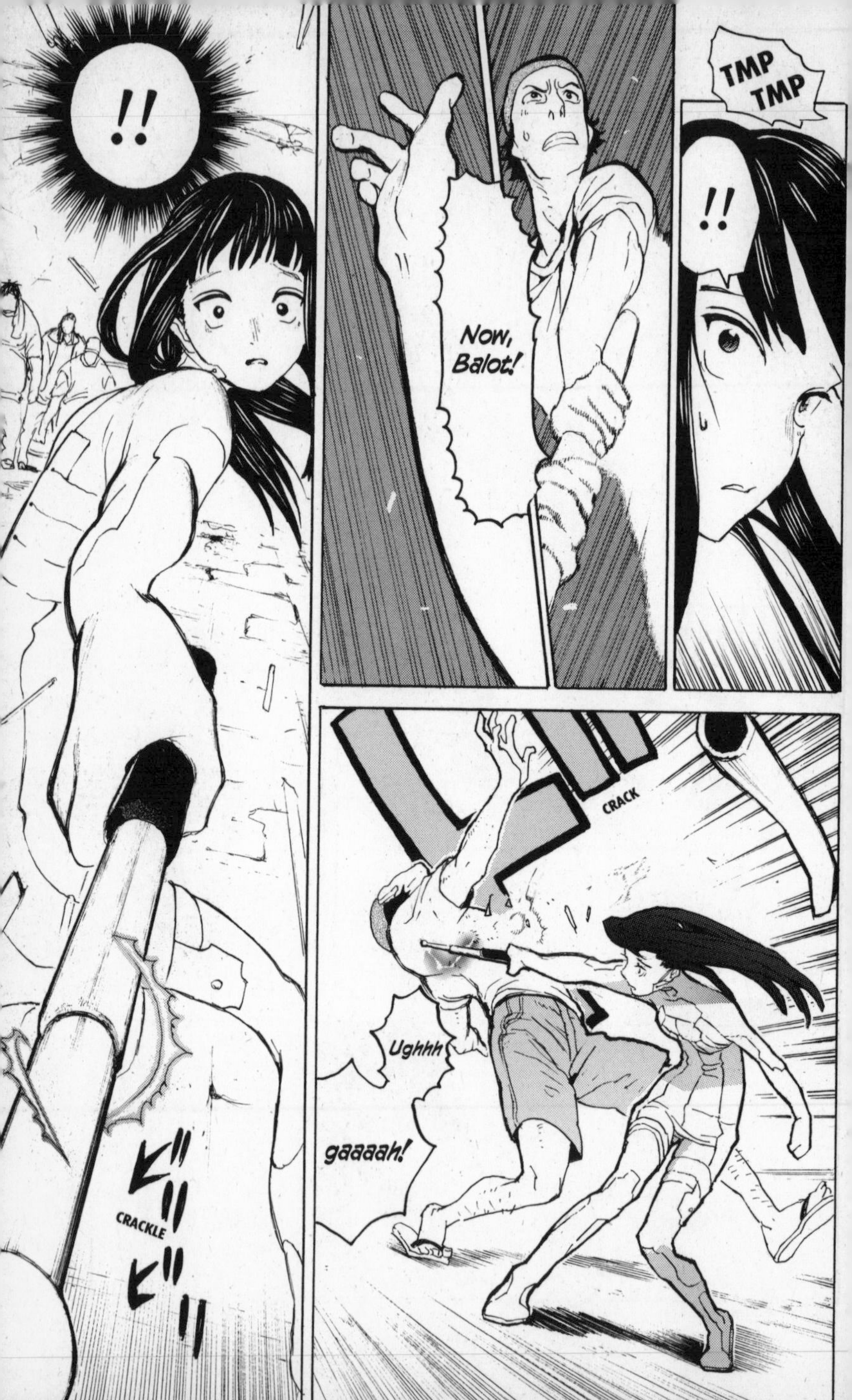
TMP TMP
!!
Now, Balot!
CRACK
Ughhh gaaaah!
!!
CRACKLE

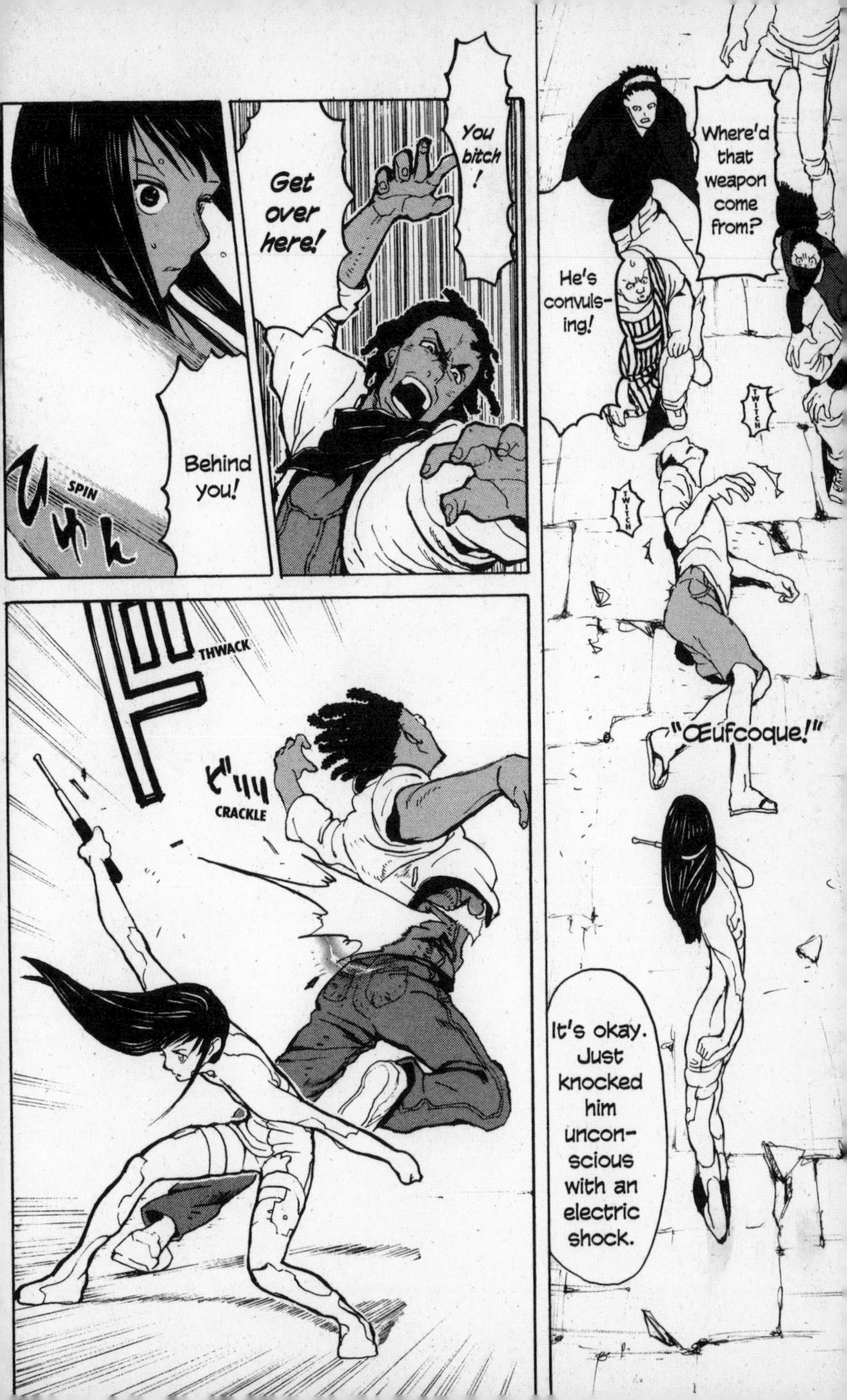
Where'd that weapon come from?
He's convulsing!
TWITCH
TWITCH
"Œufcoque!"
It's okay. Just knocked him unconscious with an electric shock.
You bitch!
Get over here!
Behind you!
SPIN
THWACK
CRACKLE

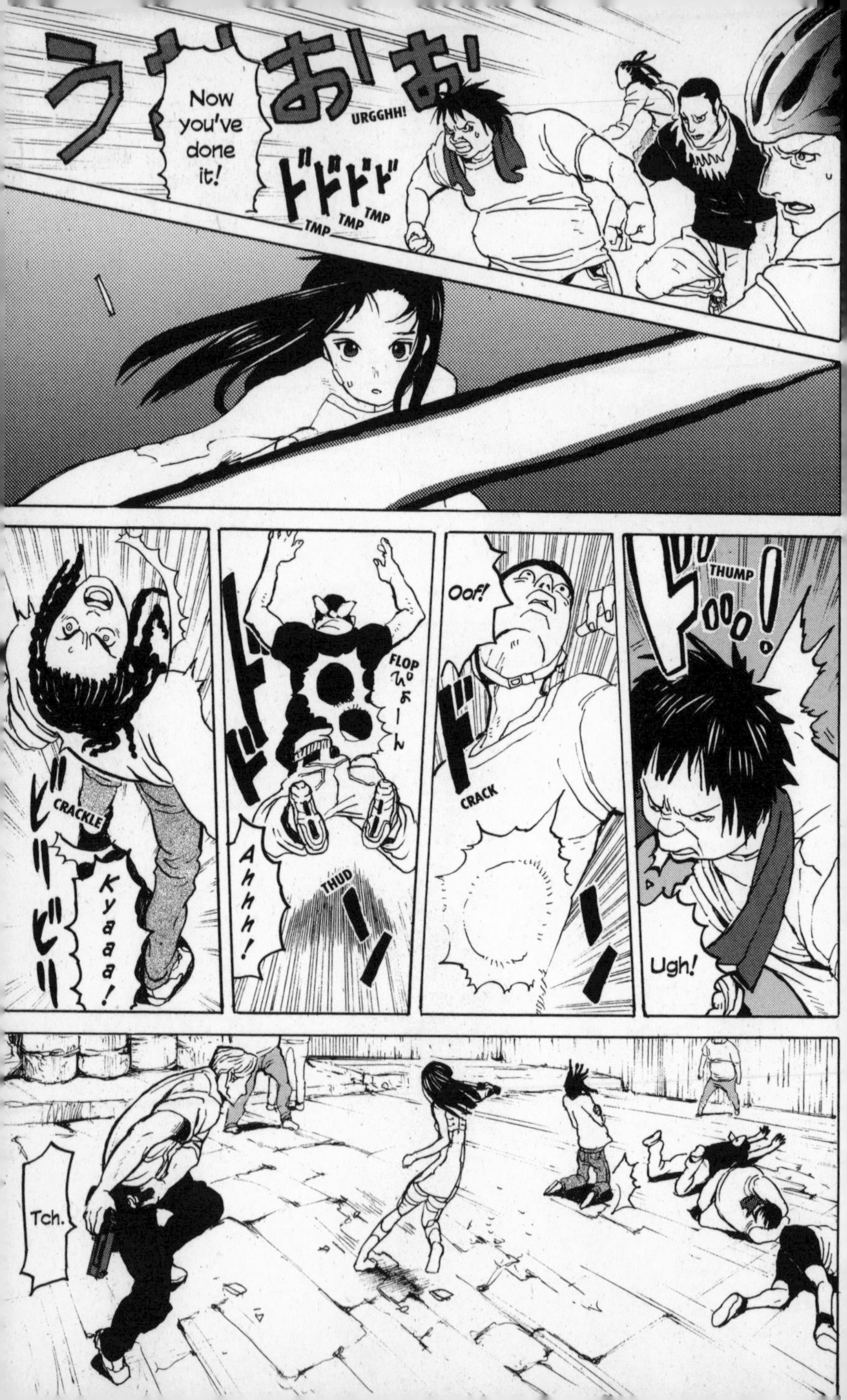
URGGHH!
うおおお
Now you've done it!
ドドドド
TMP TMP TMP
ドーン!
THUMP
Ugh!
Oof!
ド
CRACK
FLOP
ぴよーん
ド
Anhh!
THUD
CRACKLE
ビリリ
Kyaaa!
Tch.

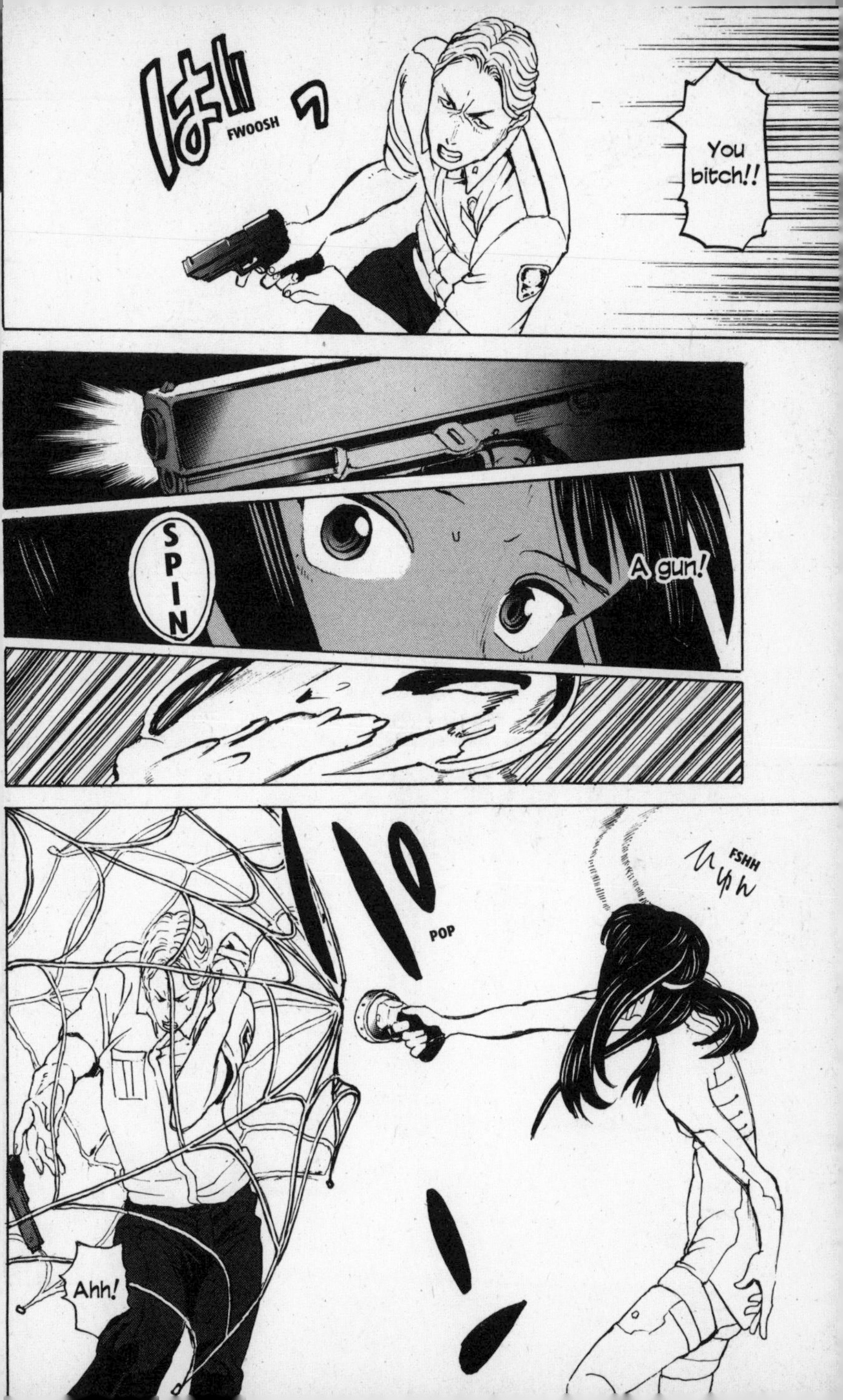
You bitch!!
FWOOSH
A gun!
SPIN
FSHH
POP
Ahh!

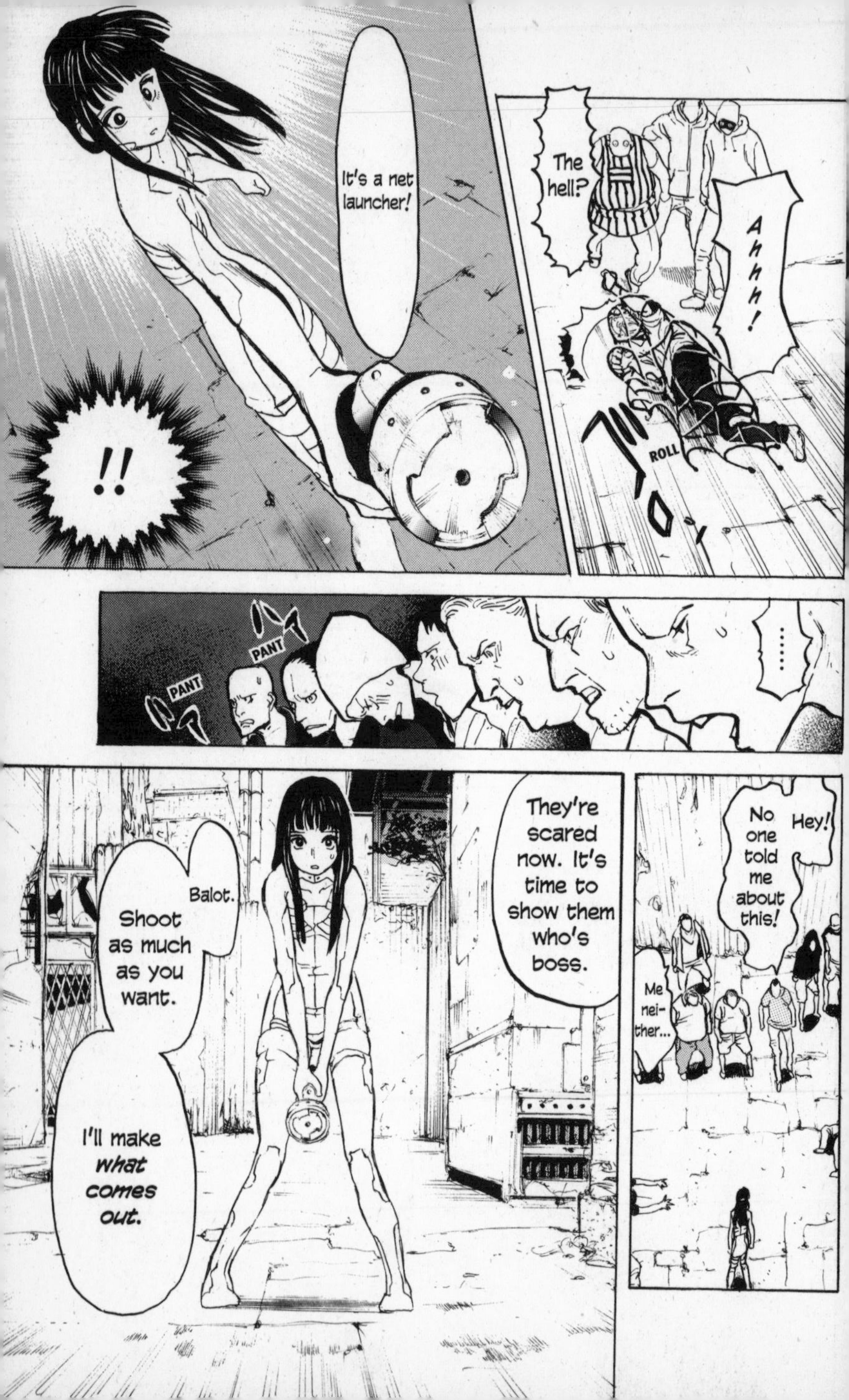
The hell?
Ahhh!
ROLL
It's a net launcher!
!!
......
PANT
PANT
Hey!
No one told me about this!
Me neither...
They're scared now. It's time to show them who's boss.
Balot. Shoot as much as you want.
I'll make *what* comes out.

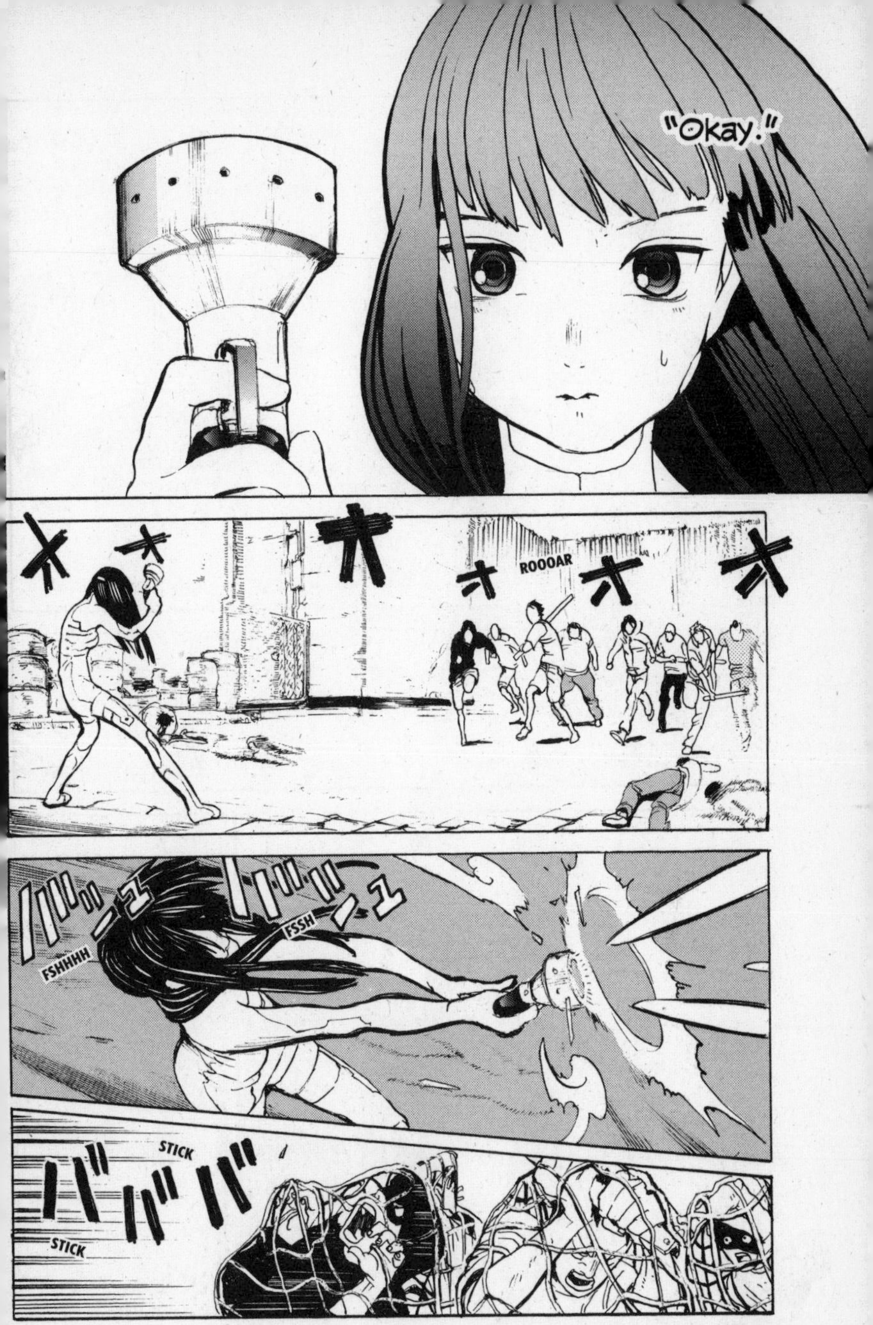
"Okay."
ROOOAR
FSSH
FSHHHH
STICK
STICK

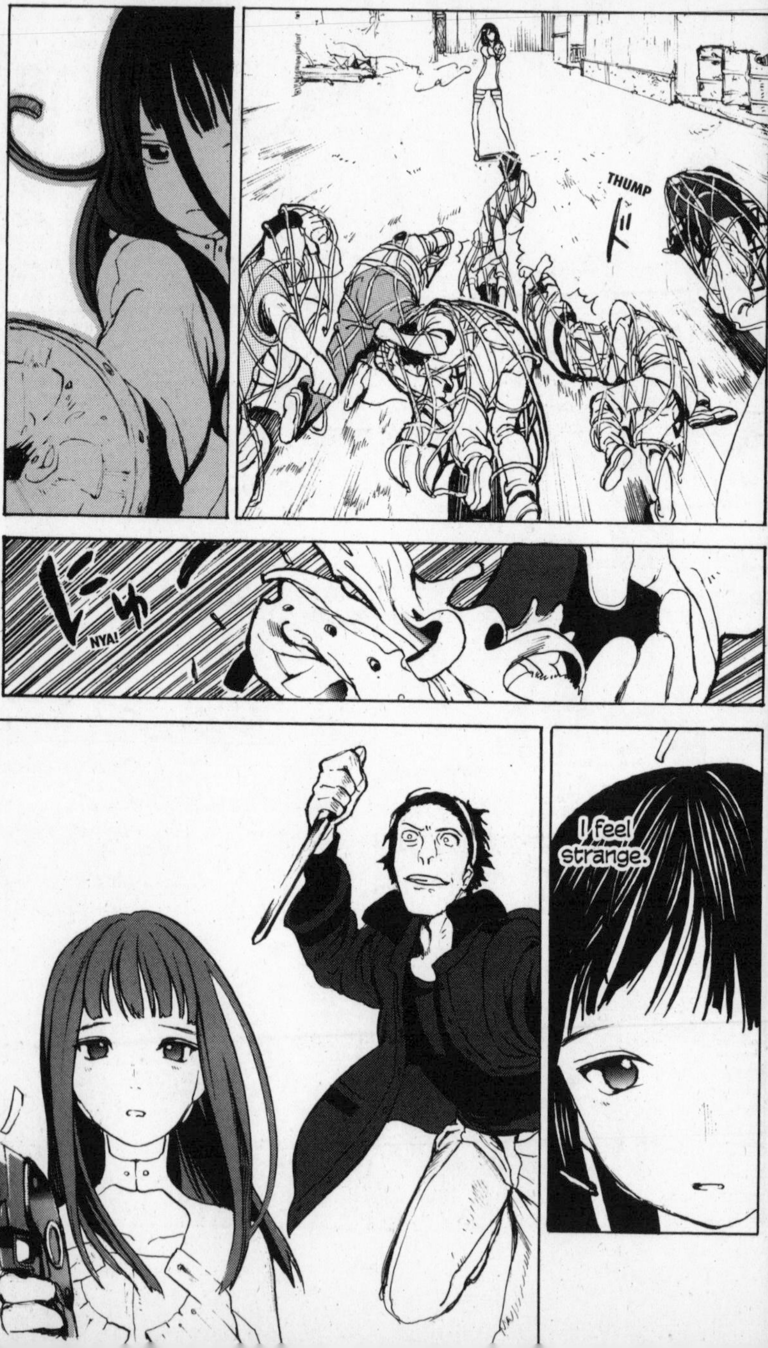
THUMP
ド
にゅ
NYA!
I feel strange.

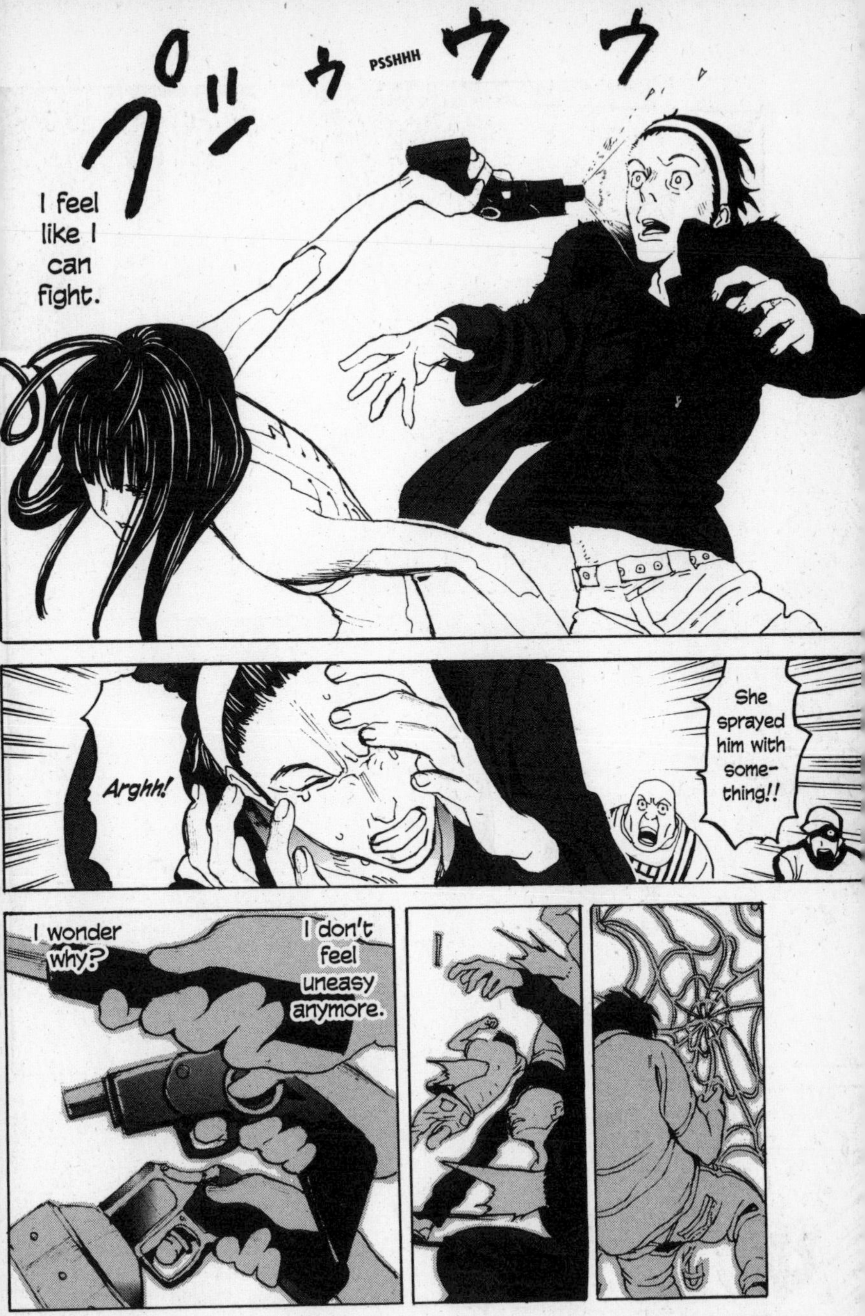
PSSHHH
I feel like I can fight.
She sprayed him with some-thing!!
Arghh!
I don't feel uneasy anymore.
I wonder why?

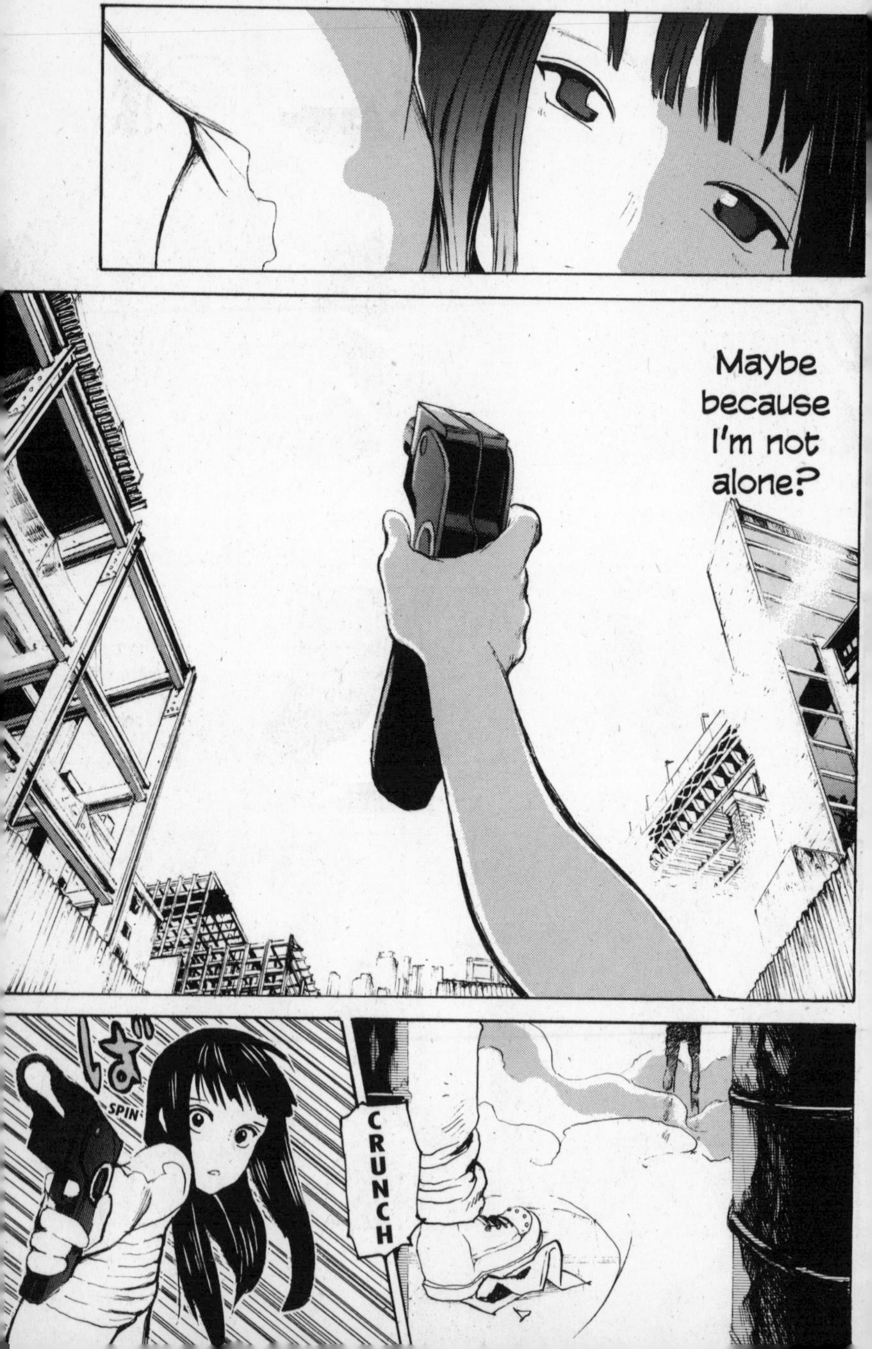
Maybe because I'm not alone?
CRUNCH
SPIN

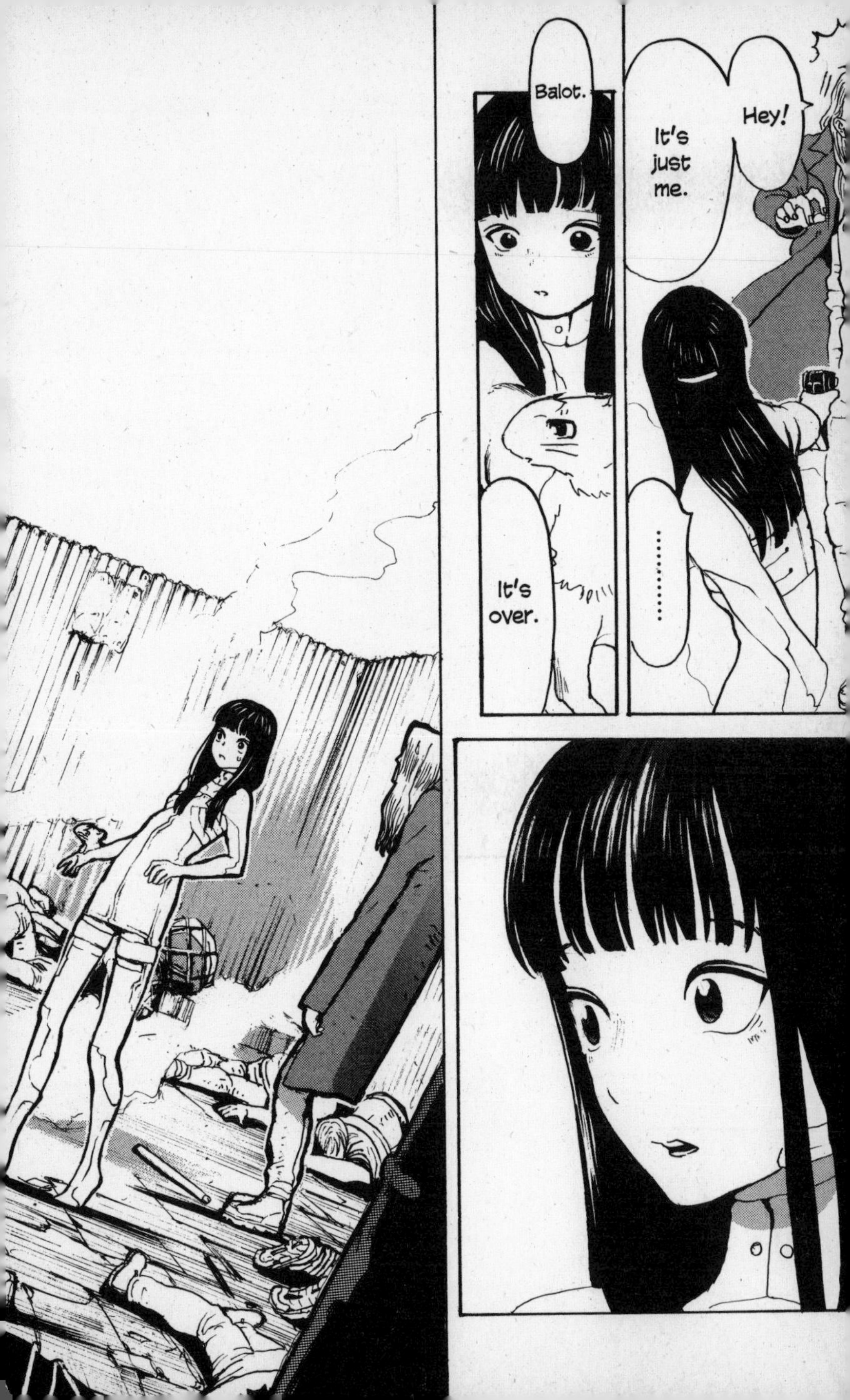
Hey!
It's just me.
......
Balot.
It's over.

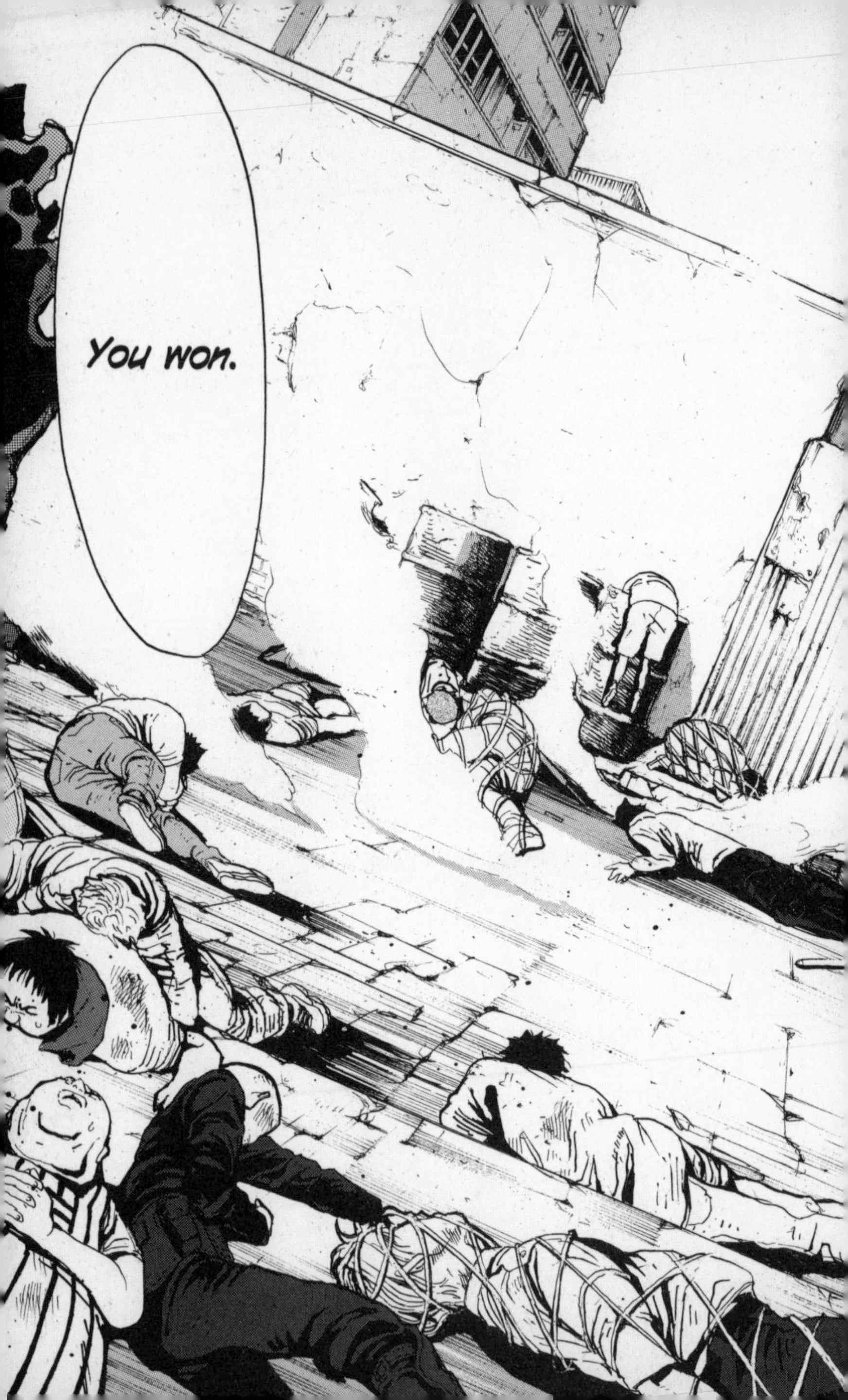
You won.

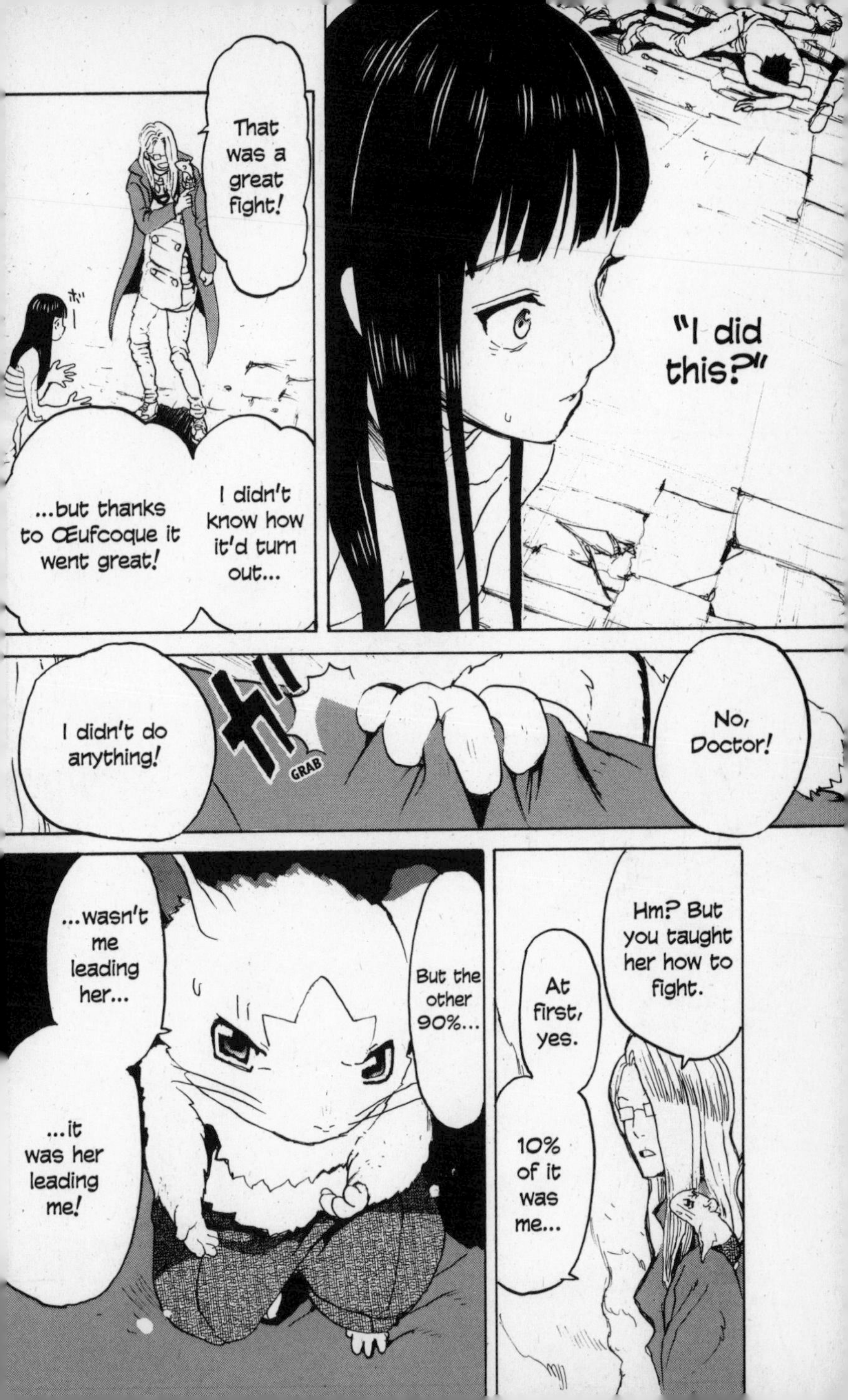
"I did this?"
That was a great fight!
I didn't know how it'd turn out...
...but thanks to Œufcoque it went great!
No, Doctor!
GRAB
I didn't do anything!
Hm? But you taught her how to fight.
At first, yes.
10% of it was me...
But the other 90%...
...wasn't me leading her...
...it was her leading me!

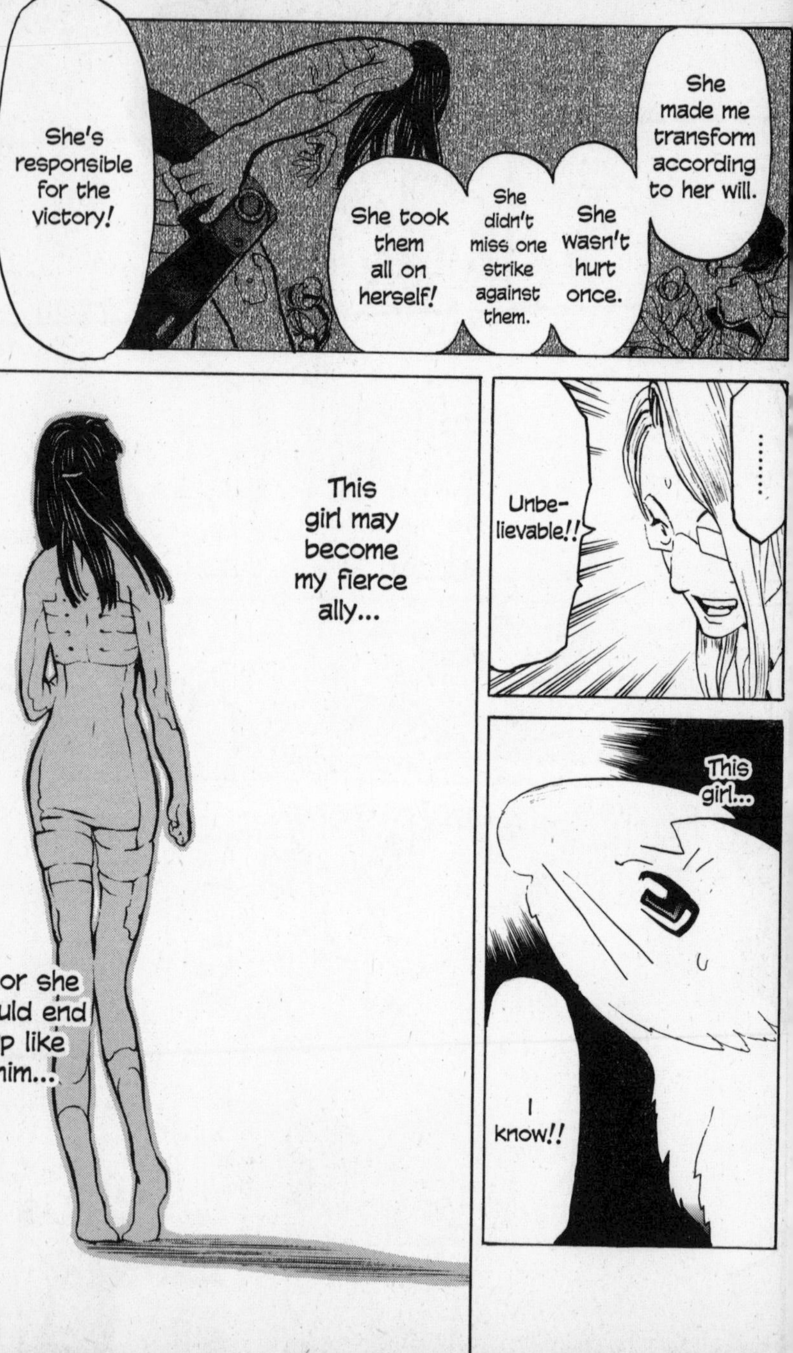
She made me transform according to her will.
She wasn't hurt once.
She didn't miss one strike against them.
She took them all on herself!
She's responsible for the victory!
......
Unbe-lievable!!
This girl...
I know!!
This girl may become my fierce ally...
...or she could end up like him...

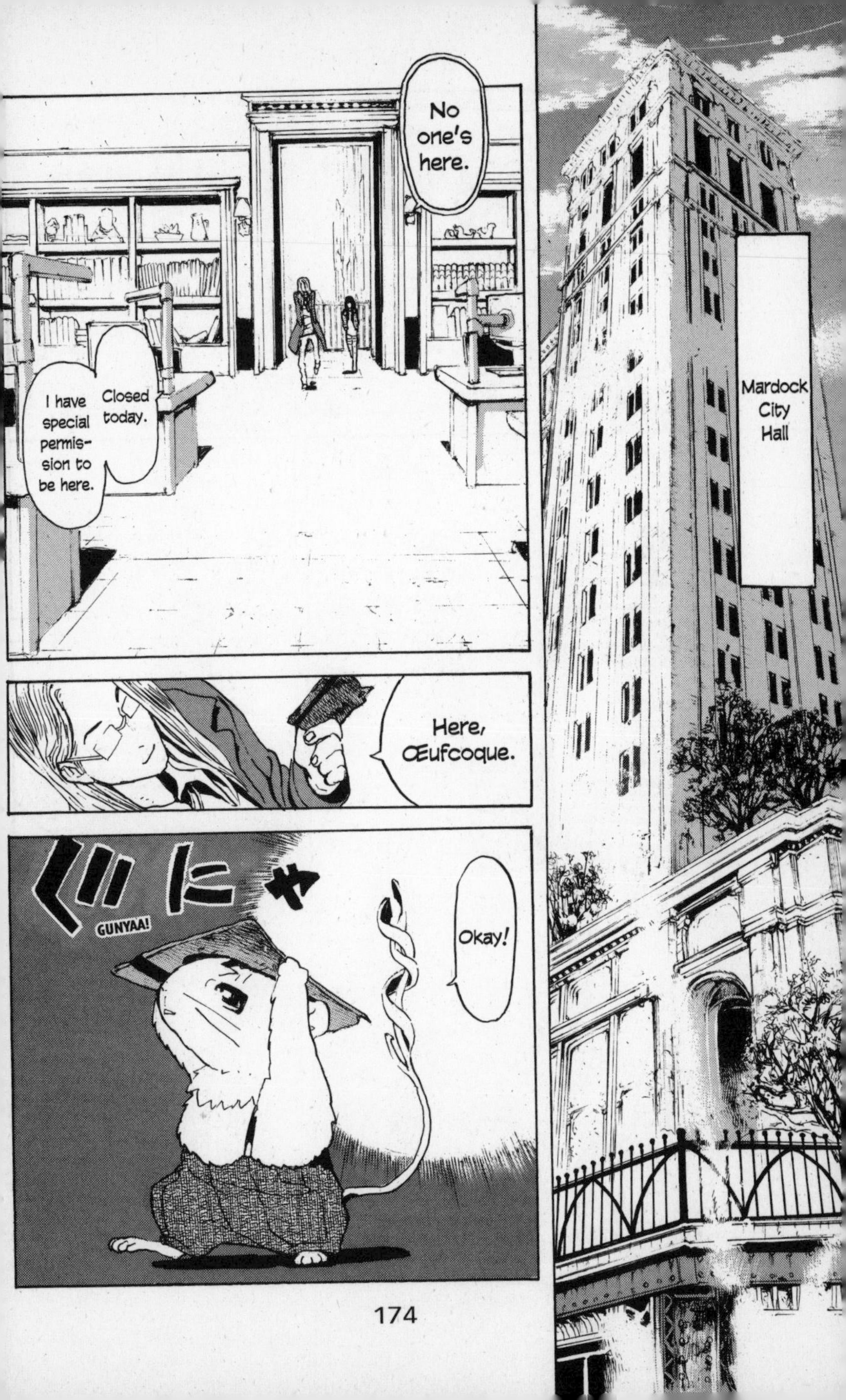
Mardock City Hall
No one's here.
Closed today.
I have special permis-sion to be here.
Here, Œufcoque.
Okay!
ぐにゃ
GUNYAA!

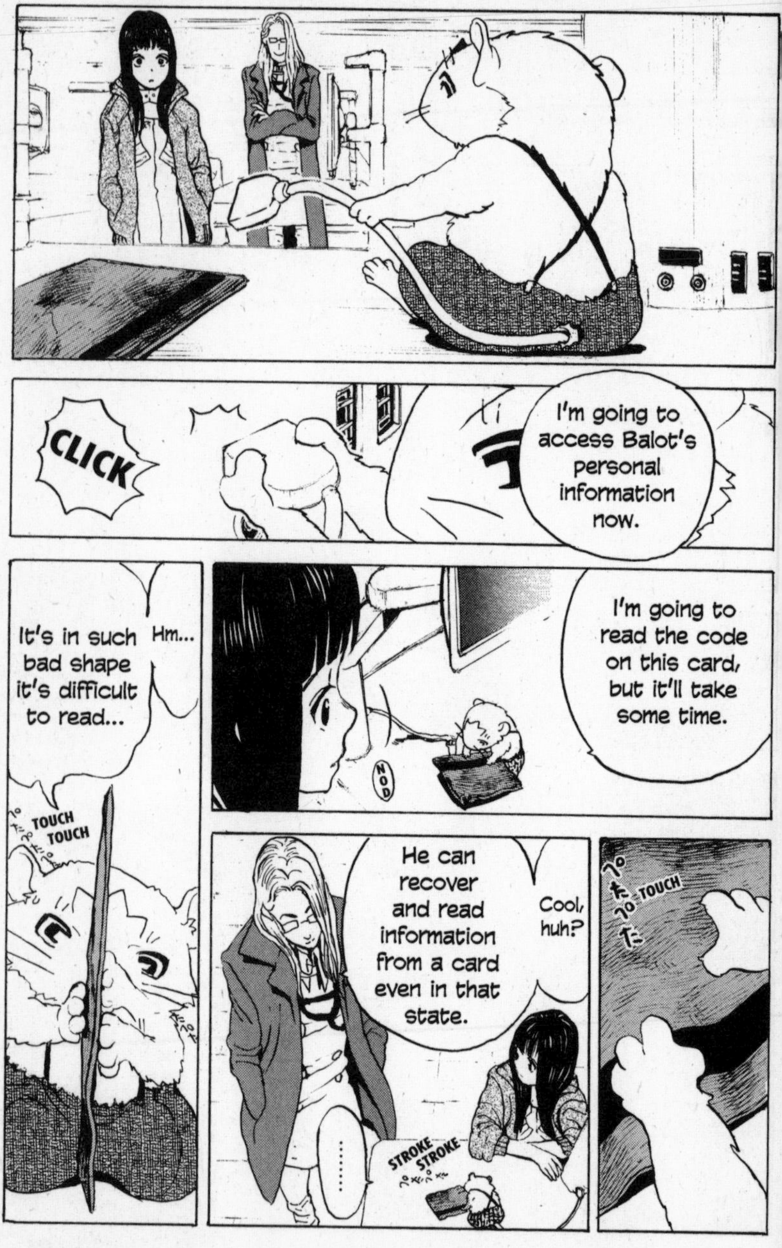
I'm going to access Balot's personal information now.
CLICK
I'm going to read the code on this card, but it'll take some time.
NOD
TOUCH
Cool, huh?
He can recover and read information from a card even in that state.
STROKE STROKE
......
Hm...
It's in such bad shape it's difficult to read...
TOUCH TOUCH

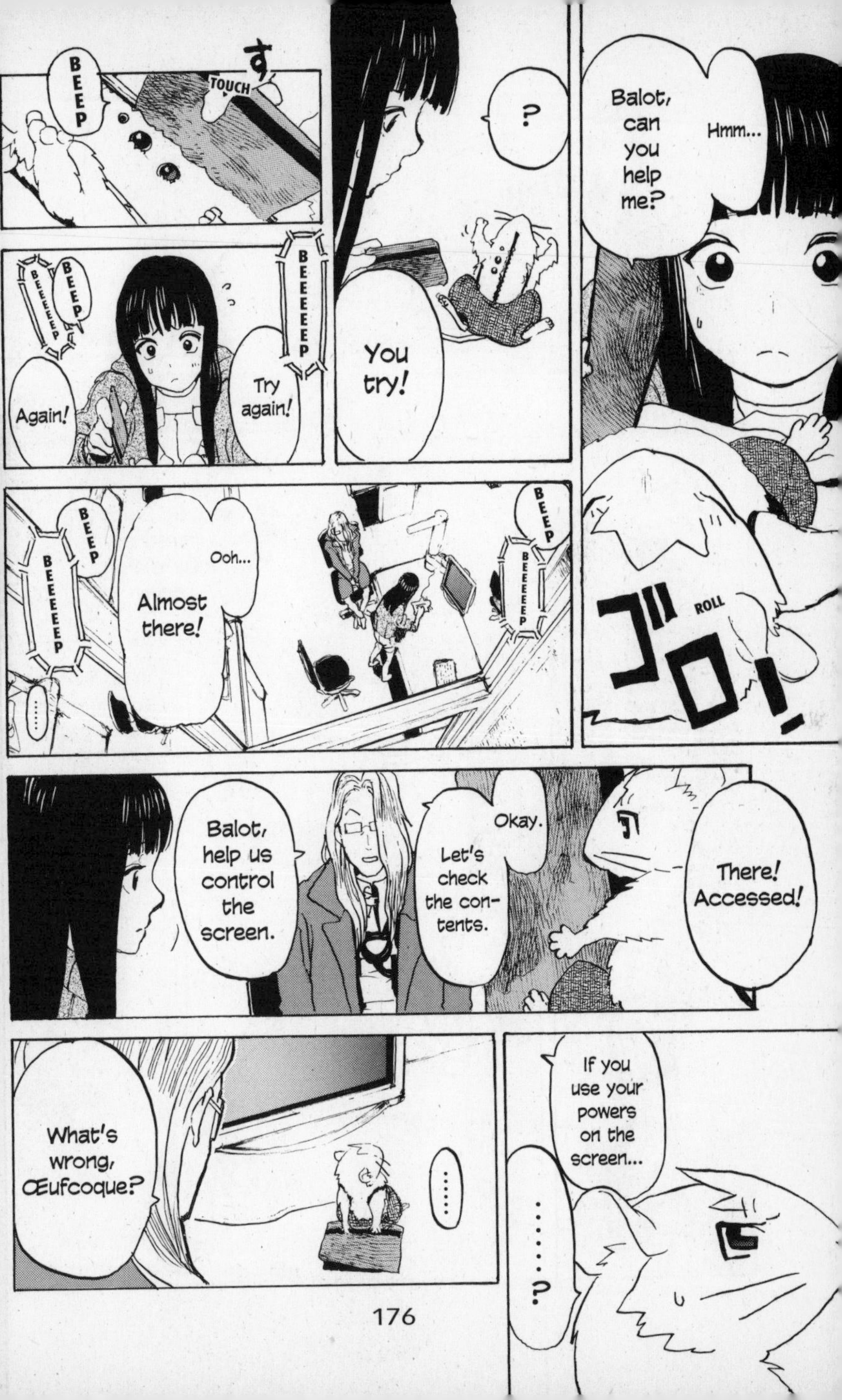
Hmm...
Balot, can you help me?
ROLL
ゴロ
?
You try!
TOUCH
す
BEEP
BEEEEEEP
Try again!
BEEP
BEEEEEEP
Again!
BEEP
BEEEEEEP
Ooh...
Almost there!
BEEP
BEEEEEEP
......
There! Accessed!
Okay.
Let's check the contents.
Balot, help us control the screen.
If you use your powers on the screen...
......?
......
What's wrong, Œufcoque?

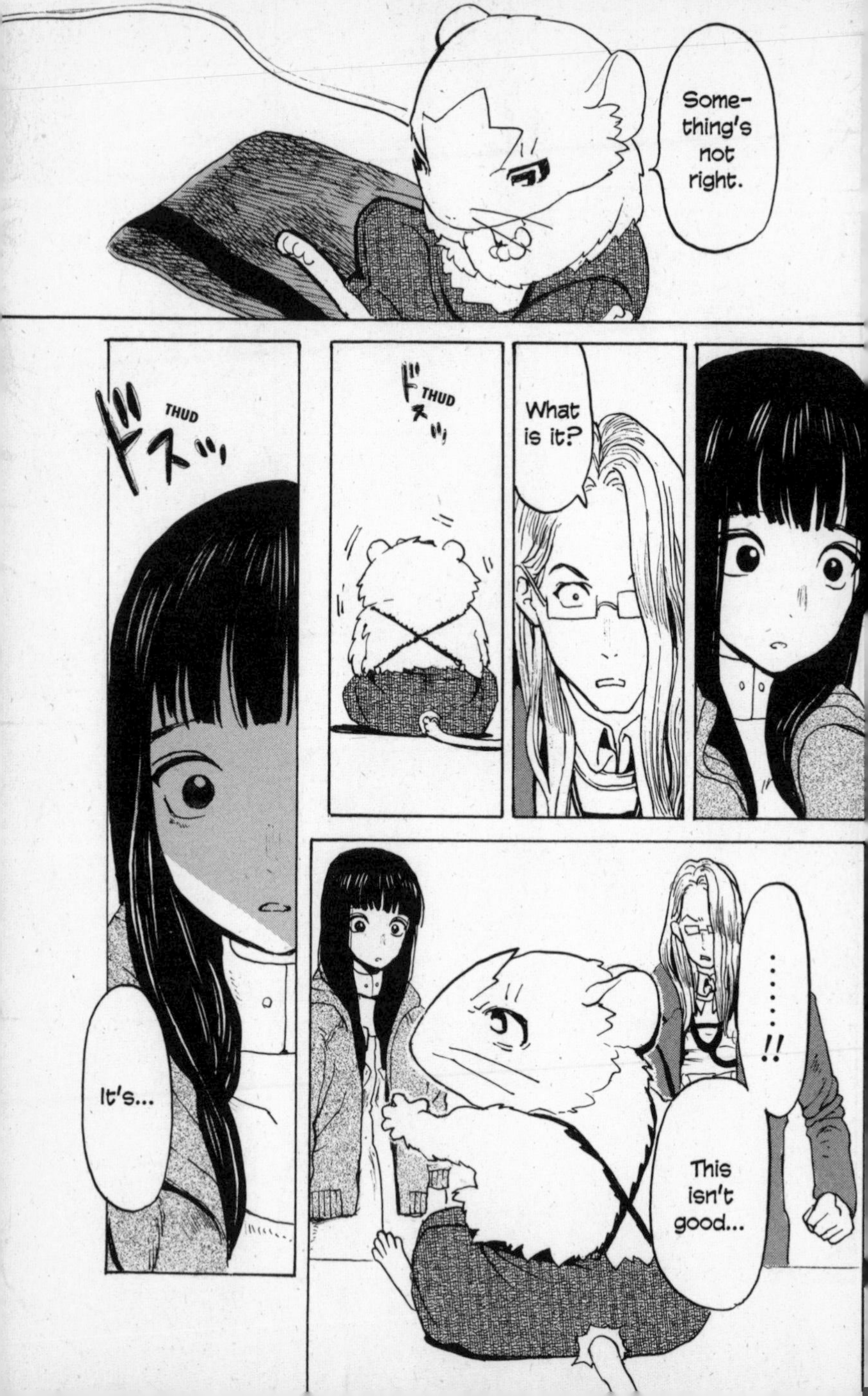
Some-thing's not right.
What is it?
ドスッ
THUD
......!!
This isn't good...
ドスッ
THUD
It's...

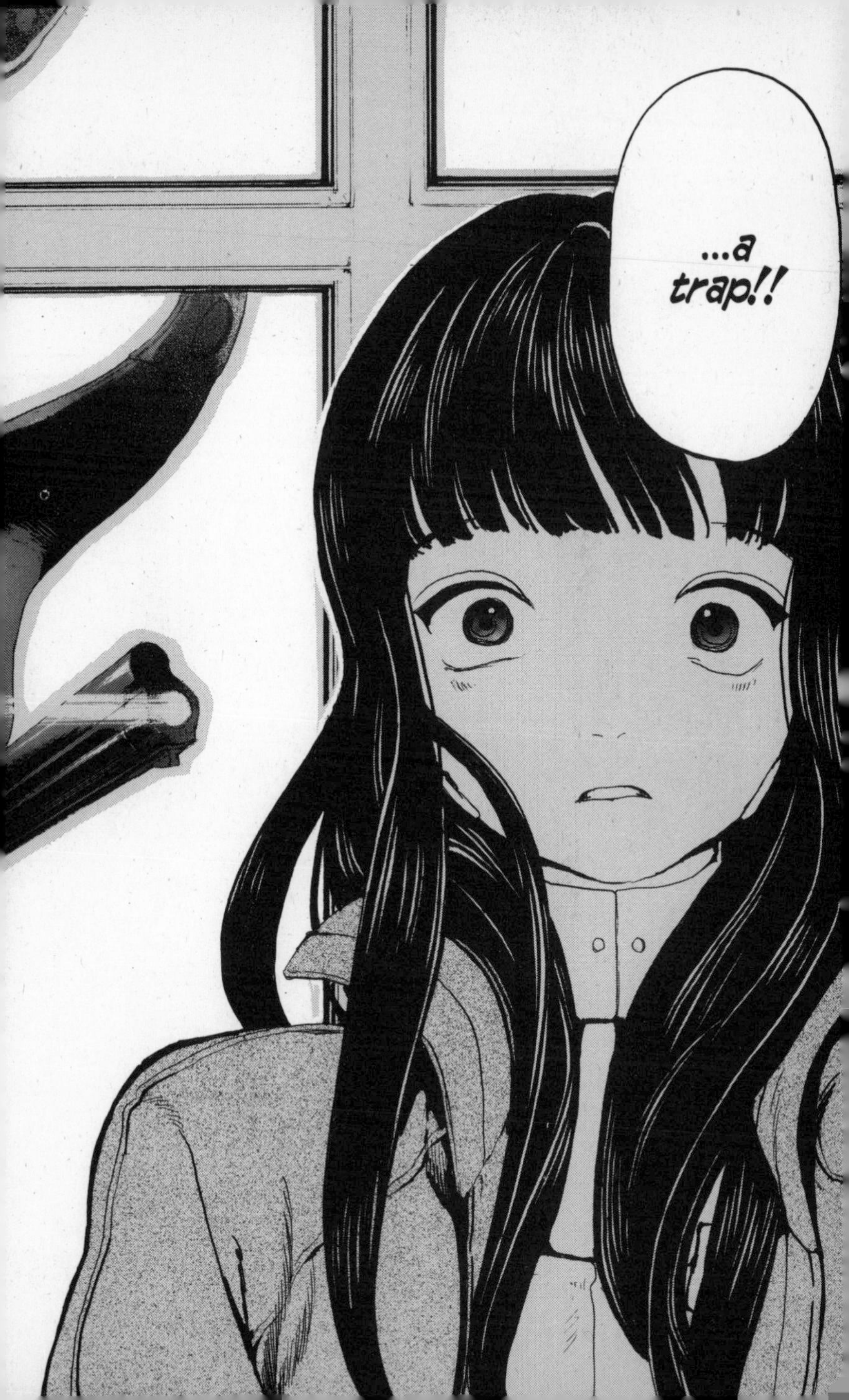
...a trap!!

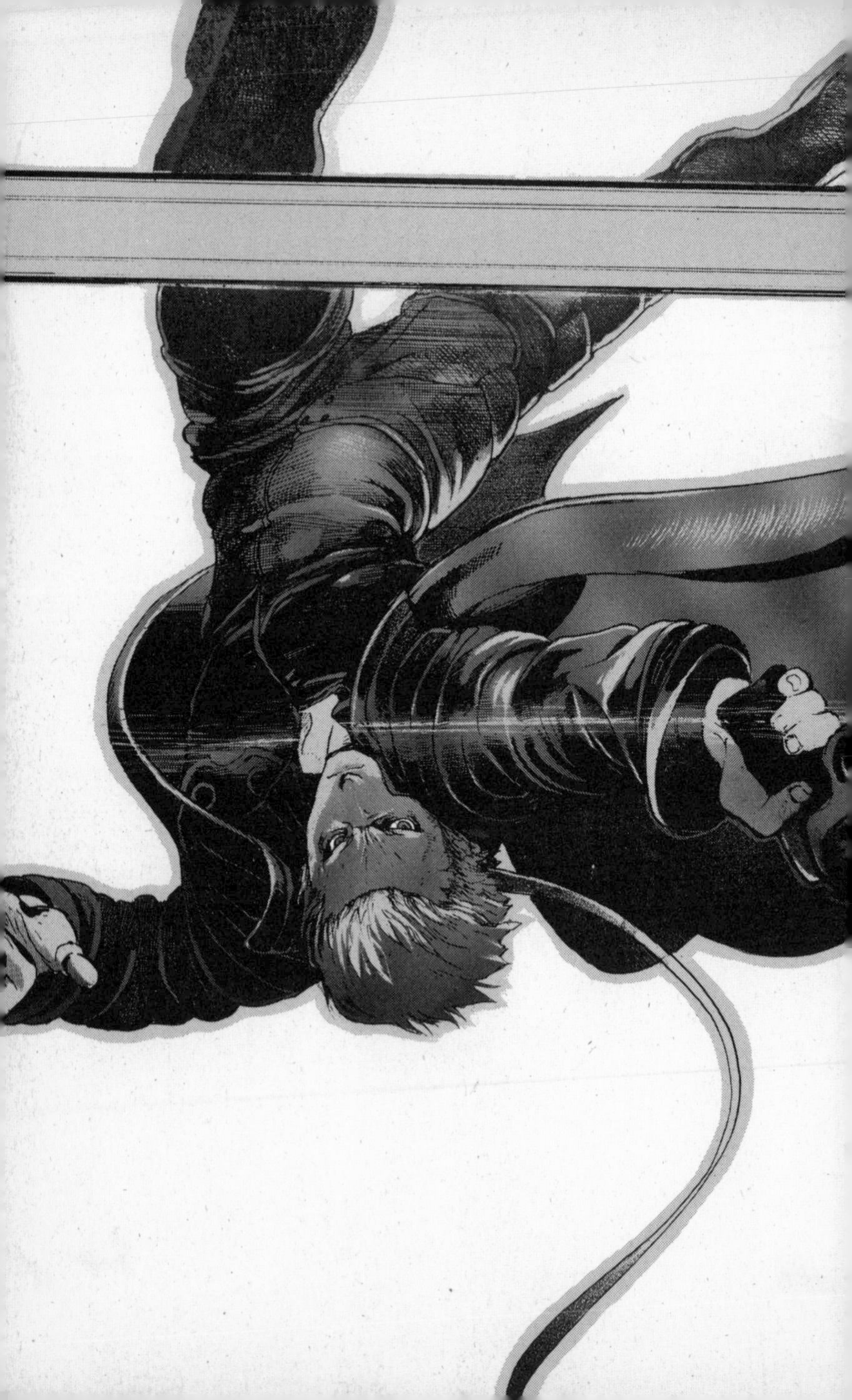

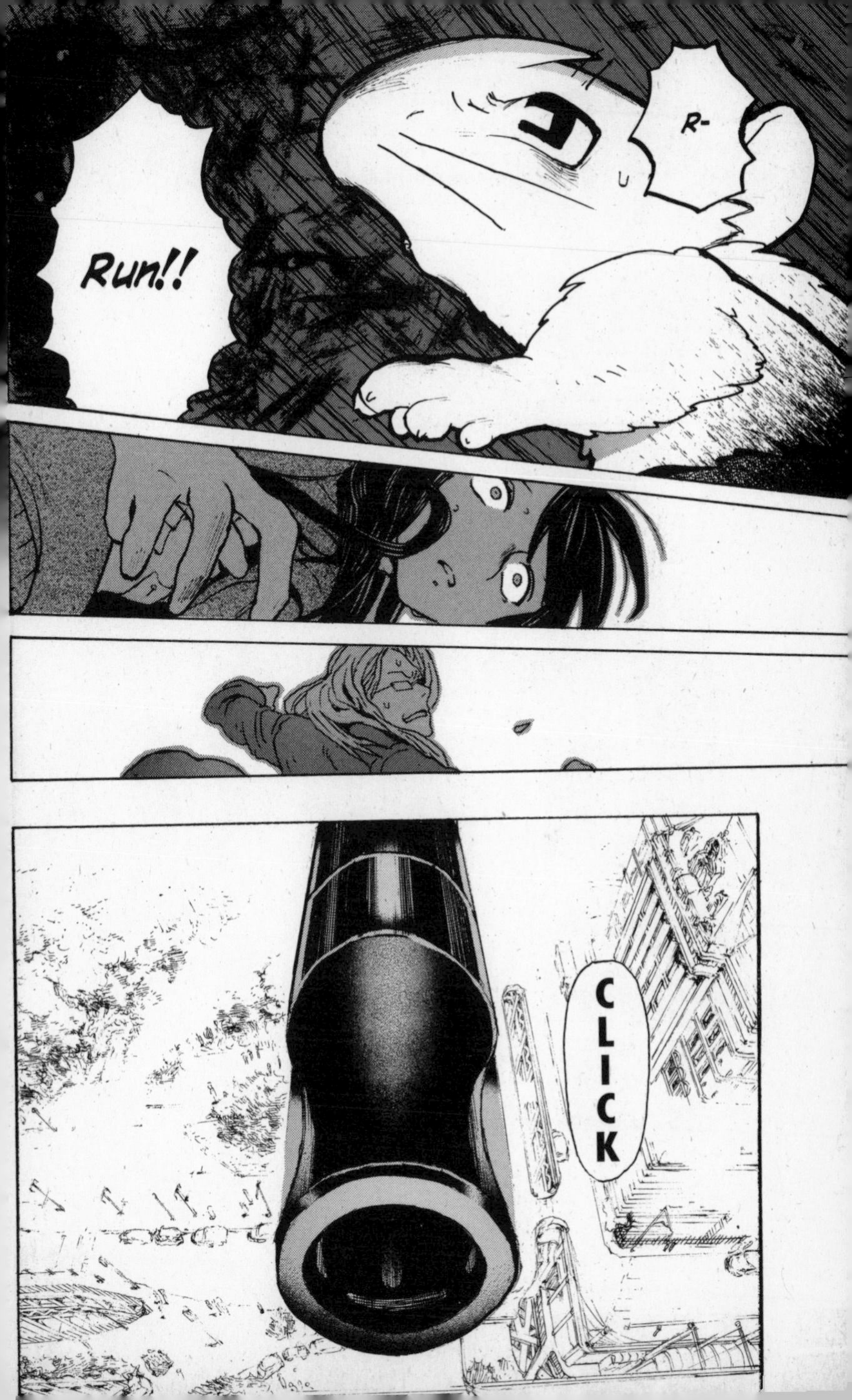
R-
Run!!
CLICK

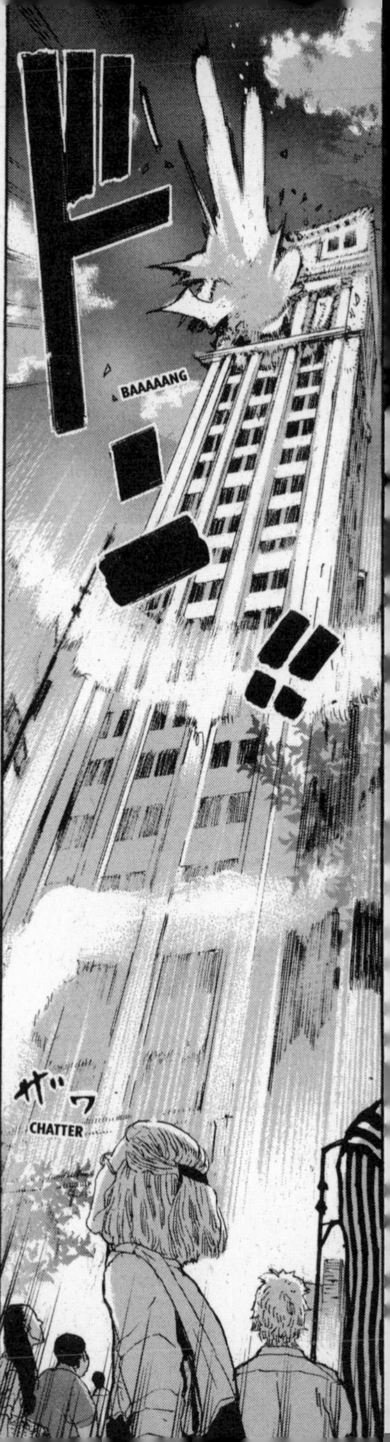
ドー!!
BAAAAANG
ザワ
CHATTER......
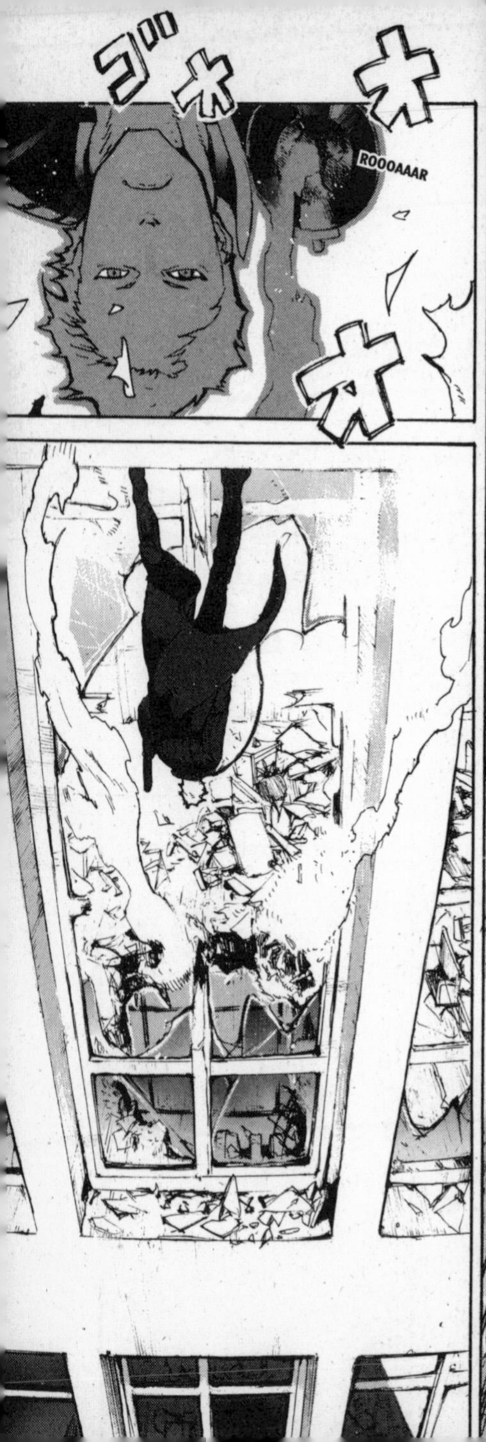
ゴオオオ
ROOOAAAR

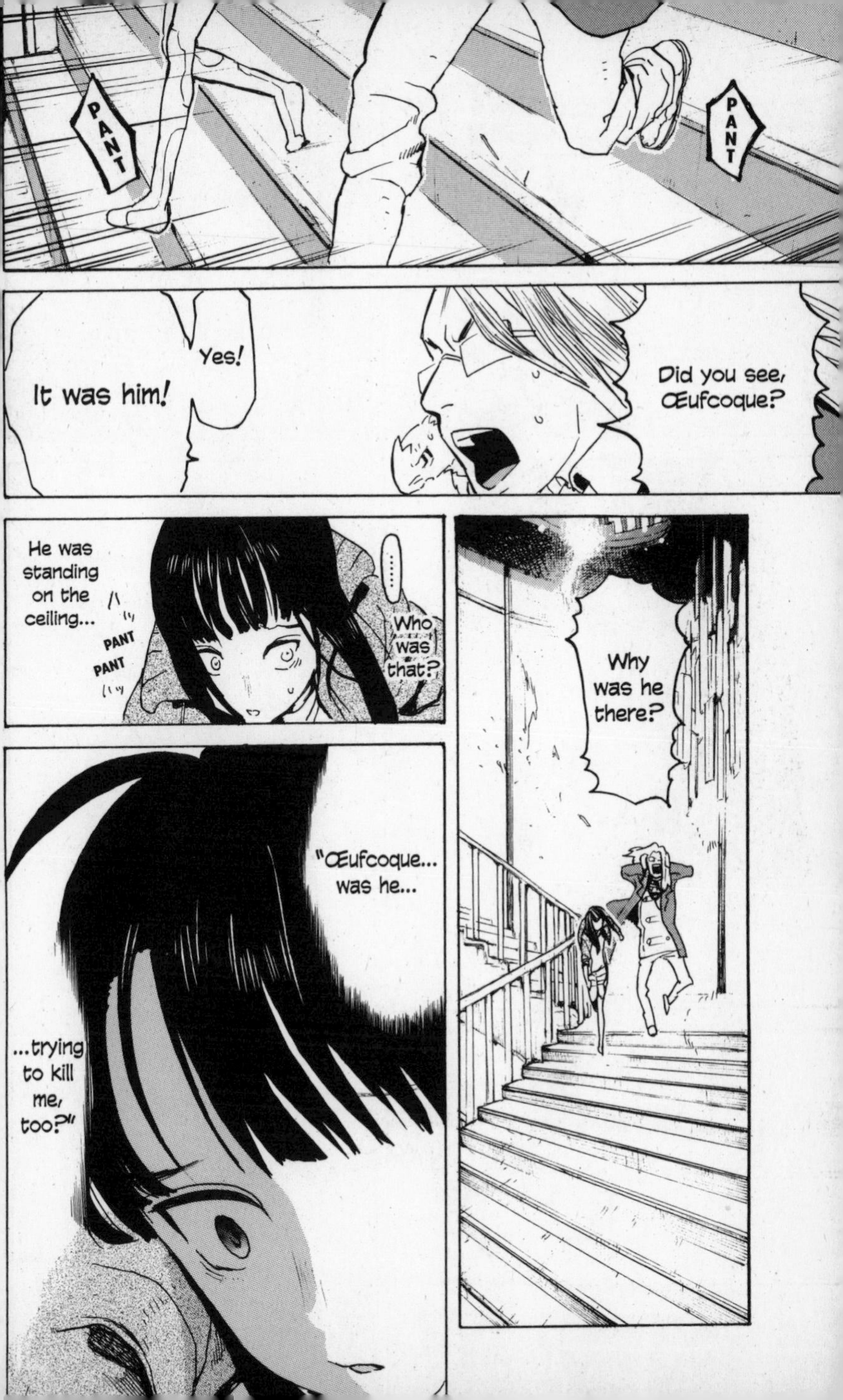
PANT
PANT
Did you see, Œufcoque?
Yes!
It was him!
Why was he there?
......
Who was that?
He was standing on the ceiling...
PANT PANT
"Œufcoque... was he...
...trying to kill me, too?"

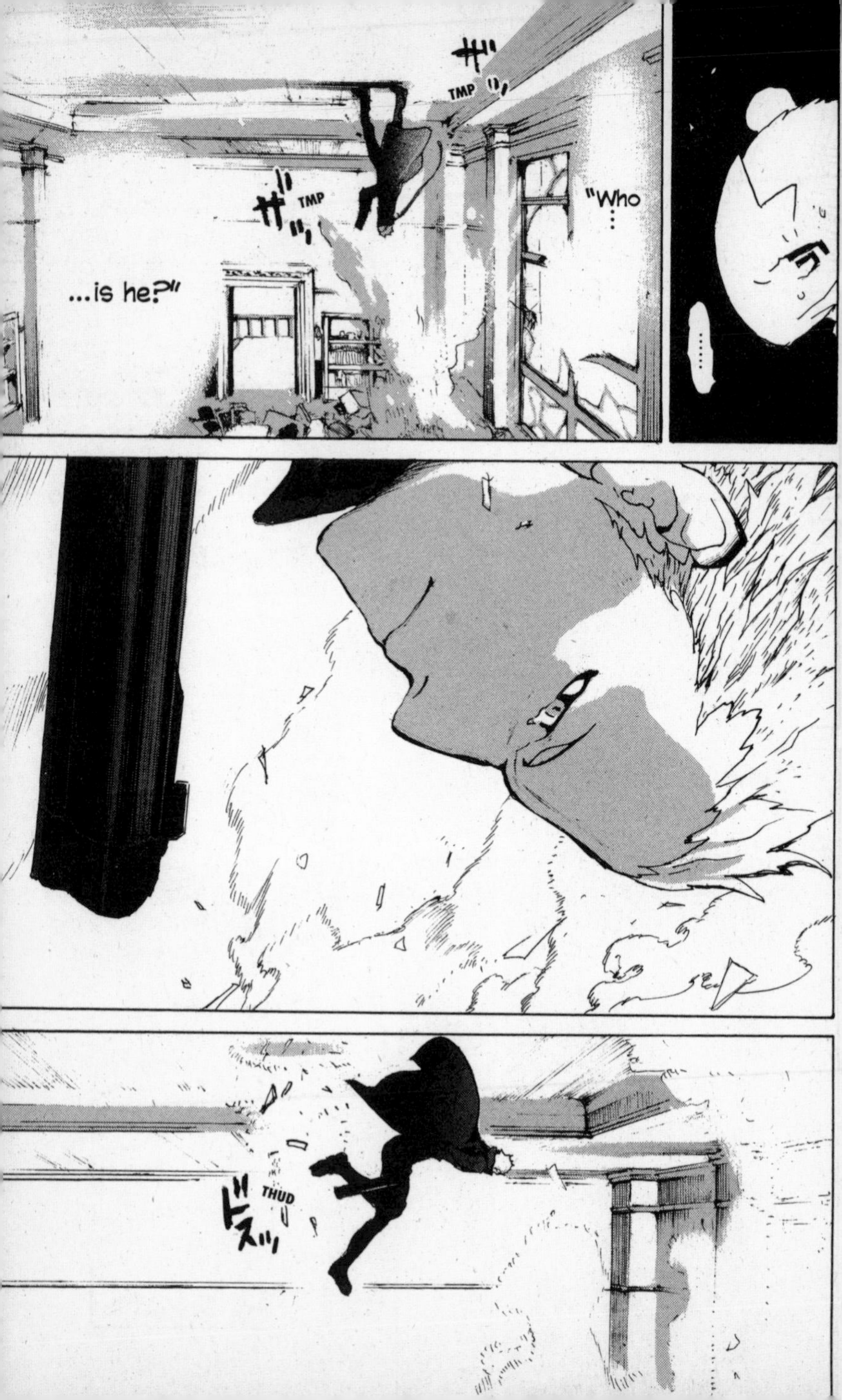
......
ザッ
TMP
ザッ
TMP
"Who
...
...is he?"
ドスッ
THUD

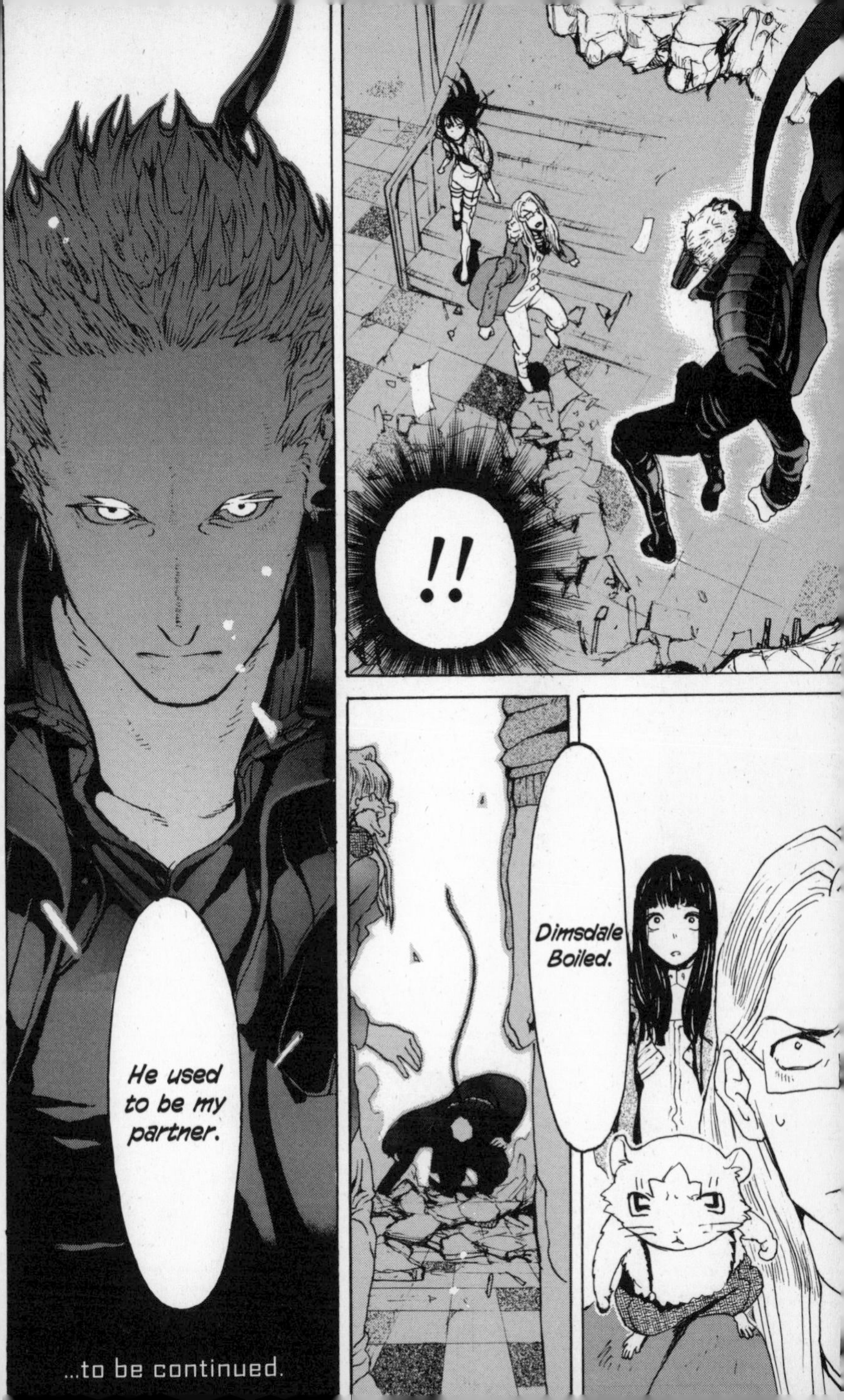
!!
Dimsdale Boiled.
He used to be my partner.
...to be continued.

The following pages are a sample
I produced in winter 2008
for my first meeting with Tow
Ubukata-sensei.

I drew it before it was serialized,
so it is the first time I drew
"Mardock Scramble."

It's a fight scene between Balot
and Pussyhand, but you can see
just how differently Balot turned
out.

I hope you enjoy reading it.

Yoshitoki Oima

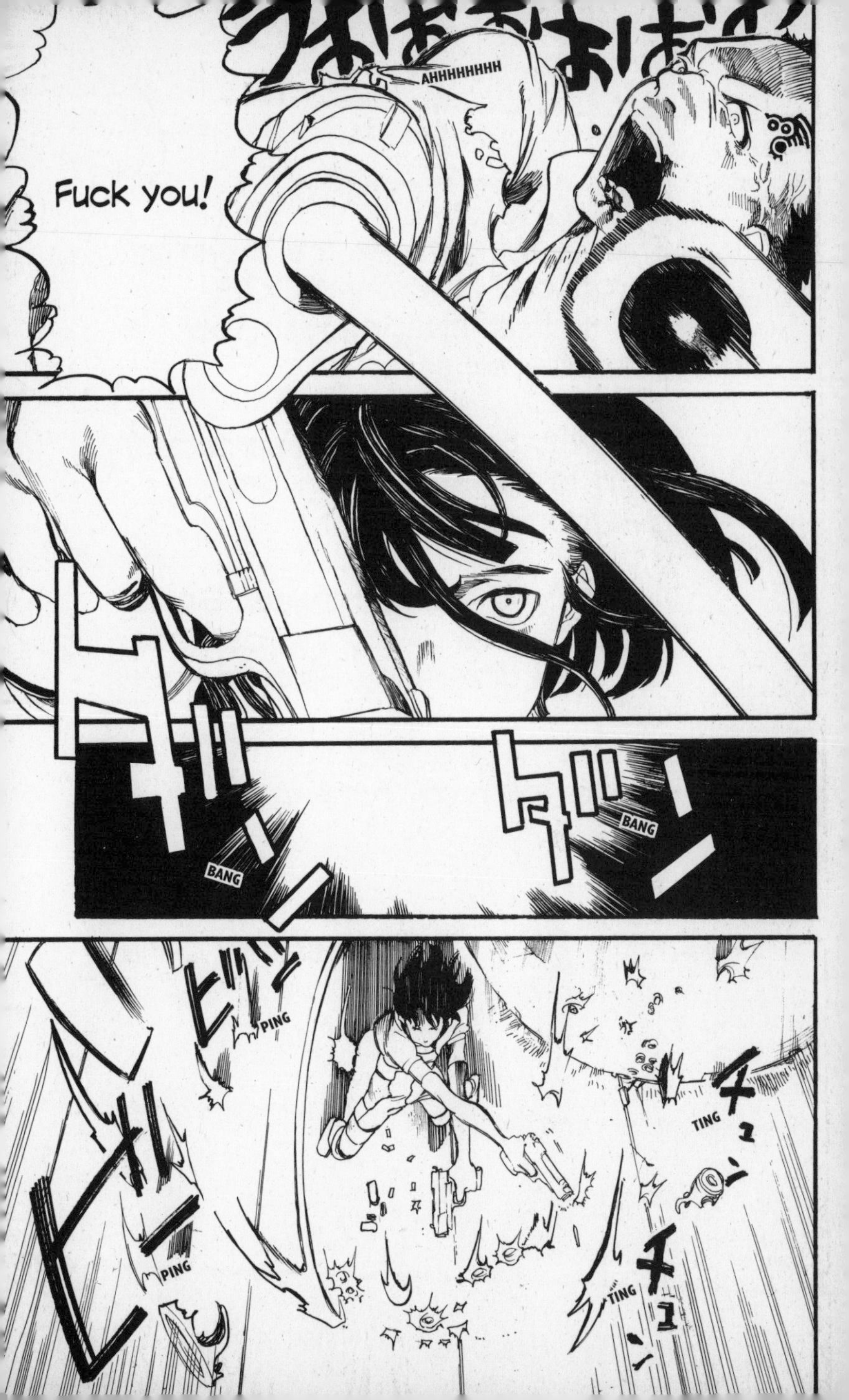
AHHHHHHHHH
Fuck you!
BANG
BANG
TING
PING
TING
PING

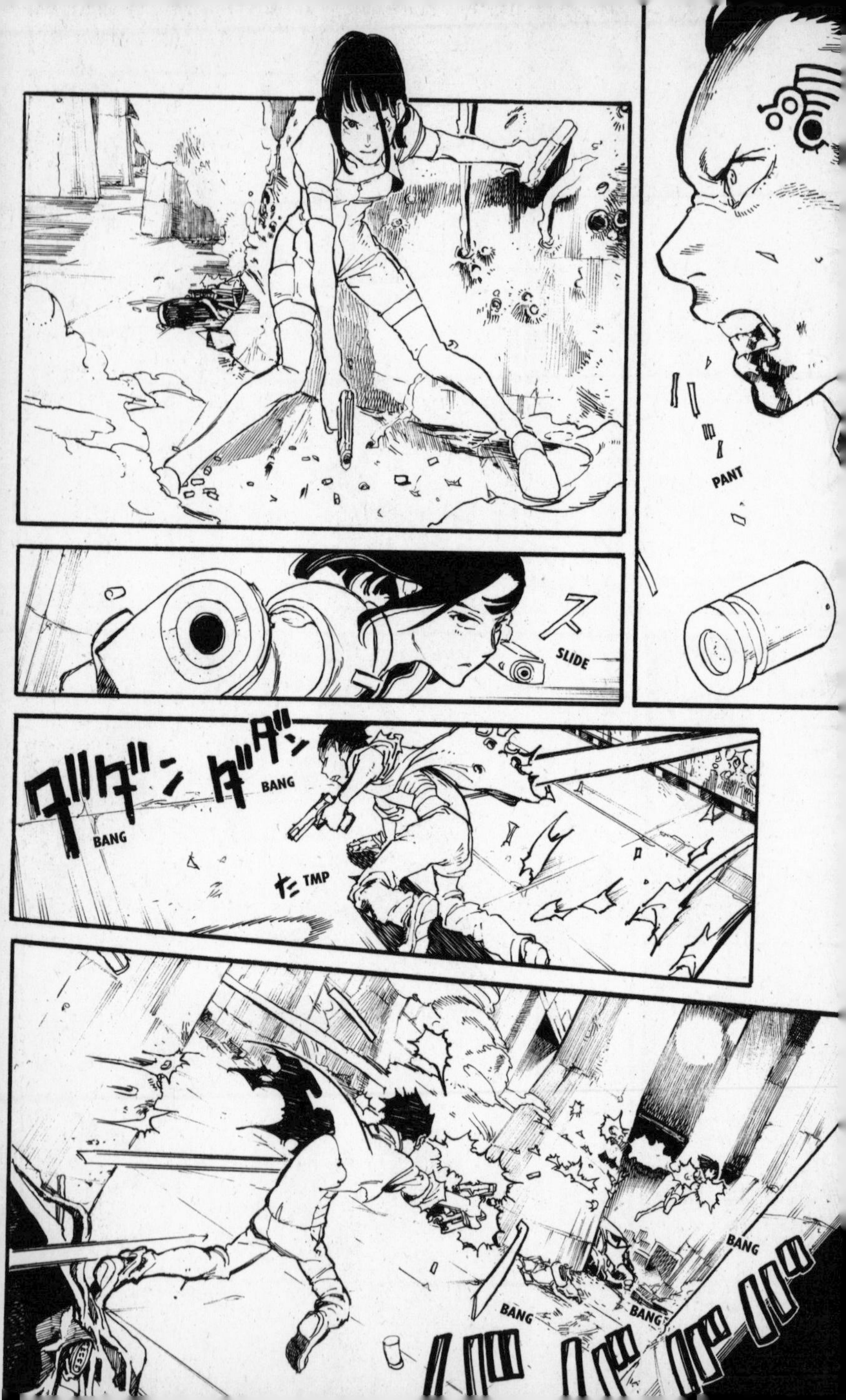
PANT
ス
SLIDE
ダダン
BANG
ダダン
BANG
た
TMP
BANG
BANG
BANG

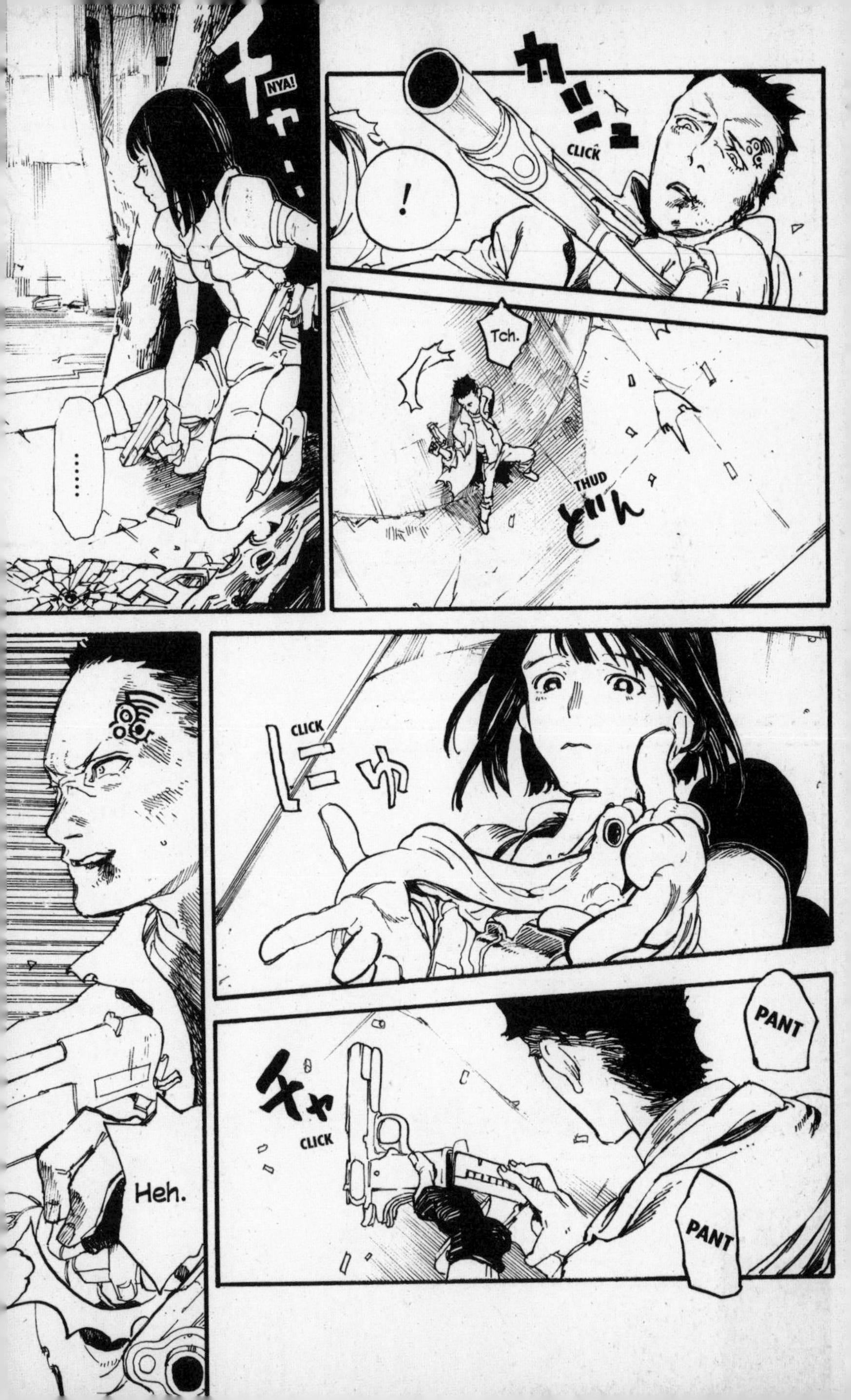

CLICK
!
Tch.
THUD
NYA!
……
CLICK
PANT
CLICK
PANT
Heh.

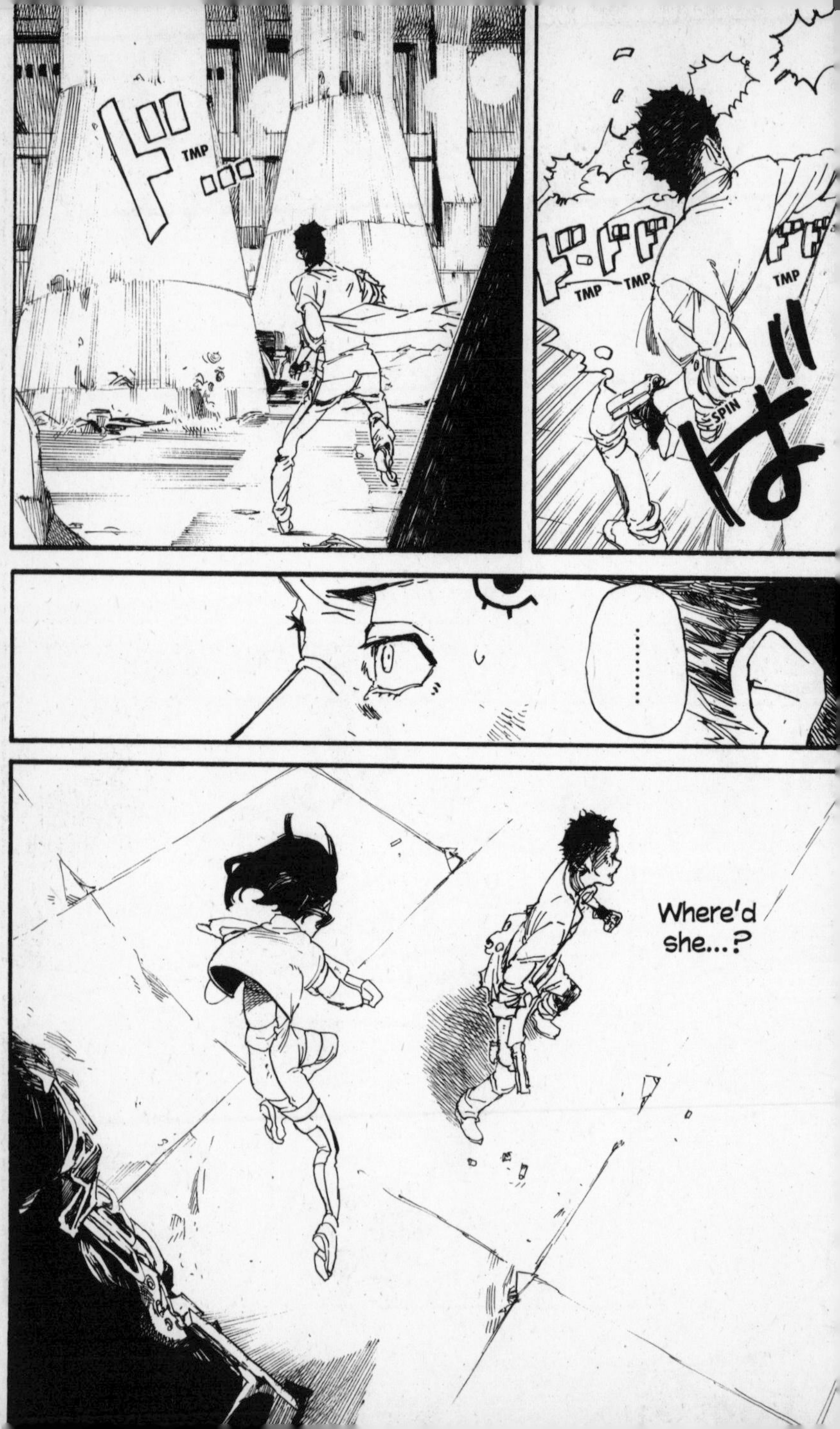
TMP
TMP
TMP
SPIN
TMP
......
Where'd she...?

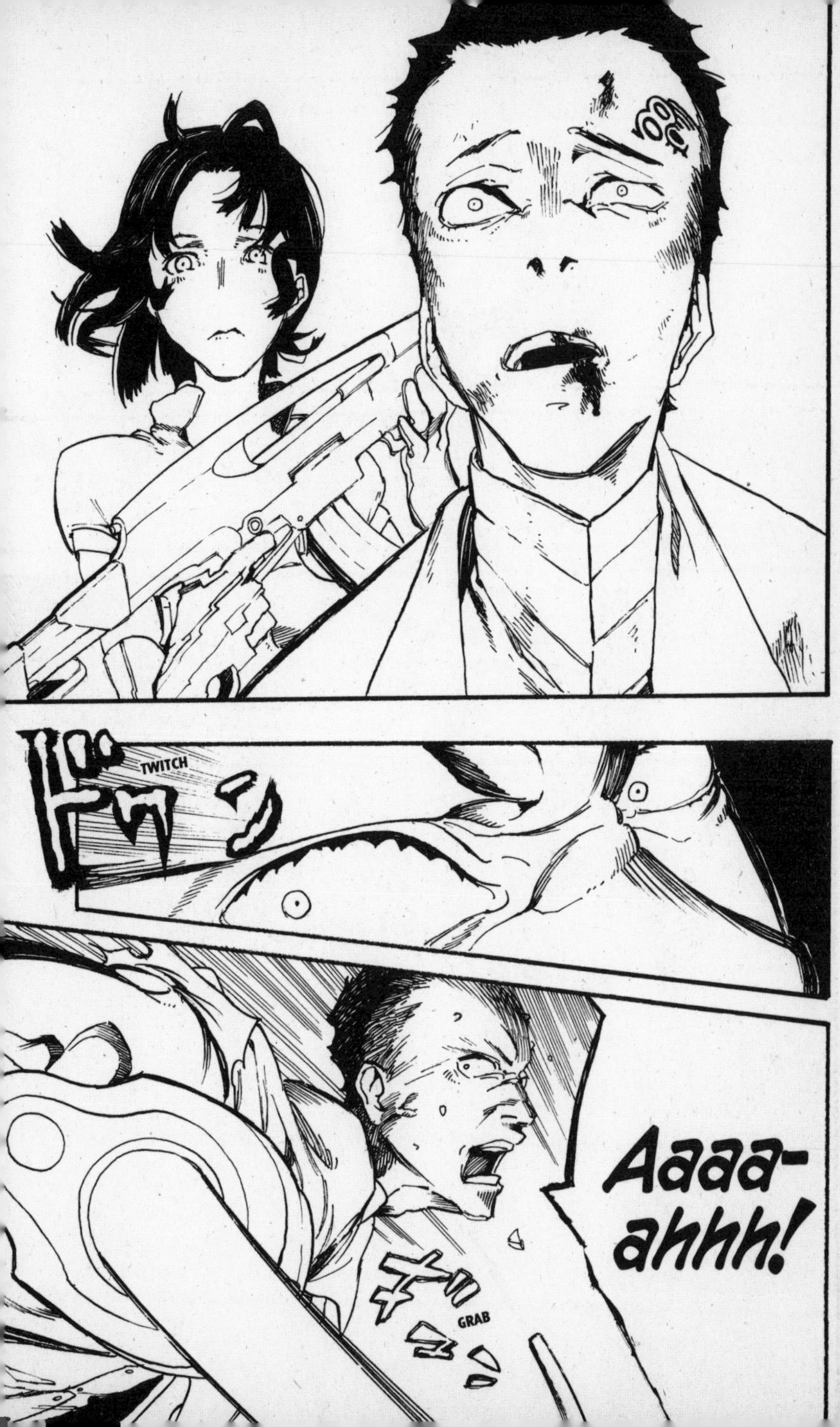
TWITCH
Aaaa-ahhh!
GRAB

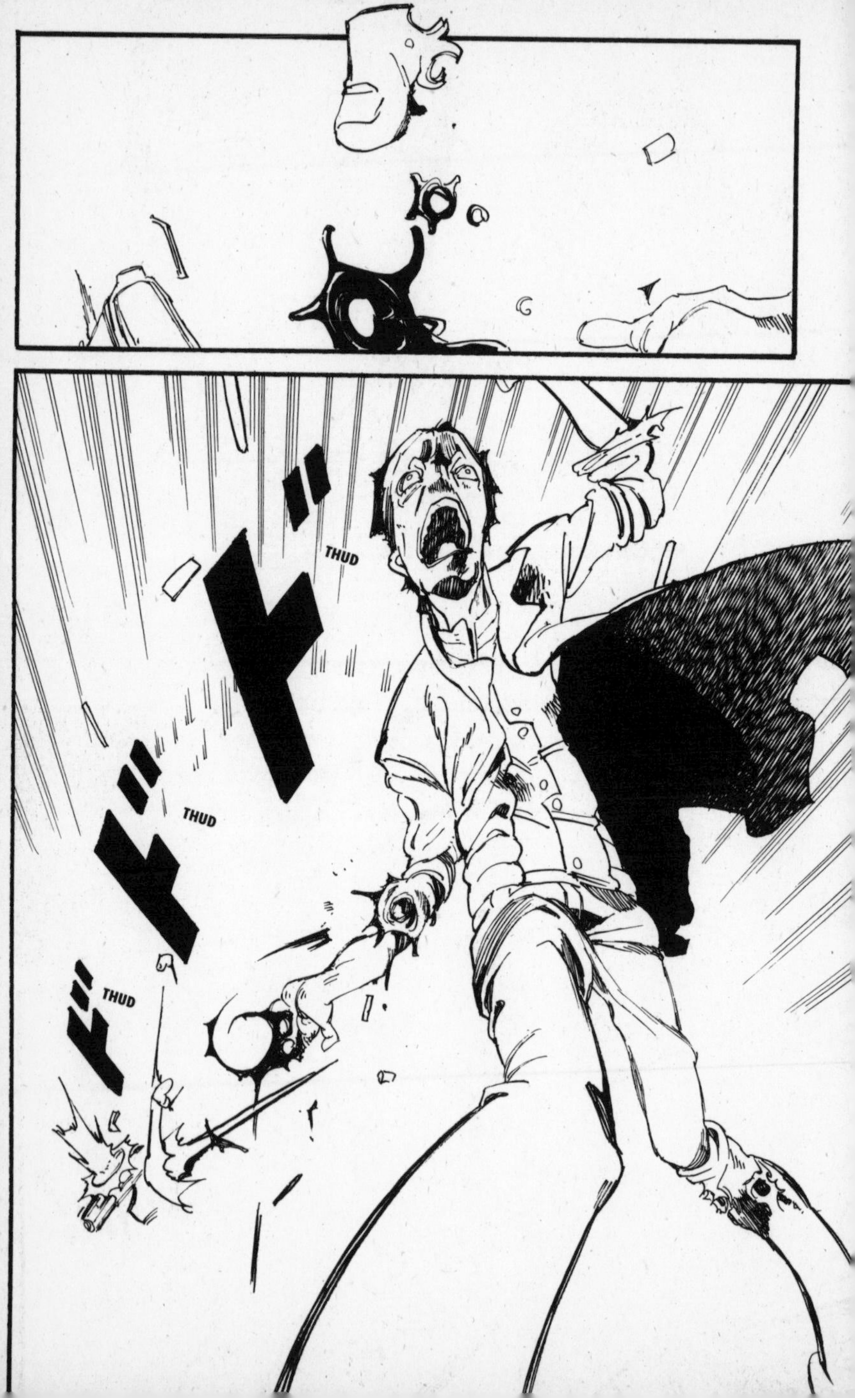
ド
THUD
ド
THUD
ド
THUD

Preview of

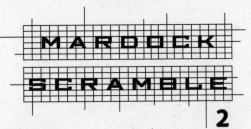

MARDOCK SCRAMBLE 2

We're please to present you a preview from *Mardock Scramble*, volume 2. Please check our website (www.kodanshacomics.com) to see when this volume will be available in English. For now you'll have to make do with Japanese!

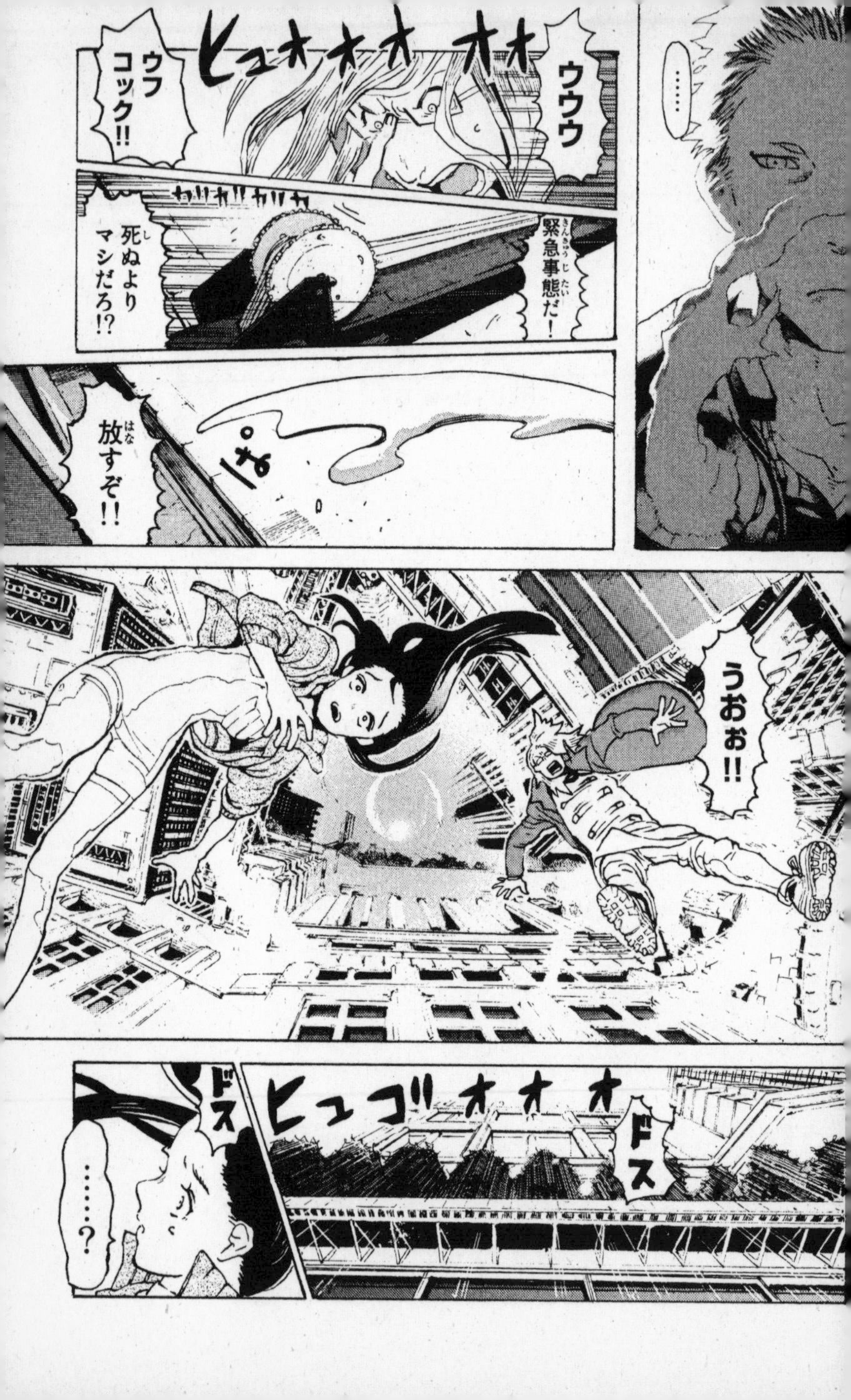
……
ウウウ
ヒュオオオ オオ
ウフ コック!!
緊急事態だ!
カリカリカリカ
死ぬより マシだろ!?
ぱっ
放すぞ!!
うおぉ!!
ヒュゴッオオ オ
ドス
ドス
……?

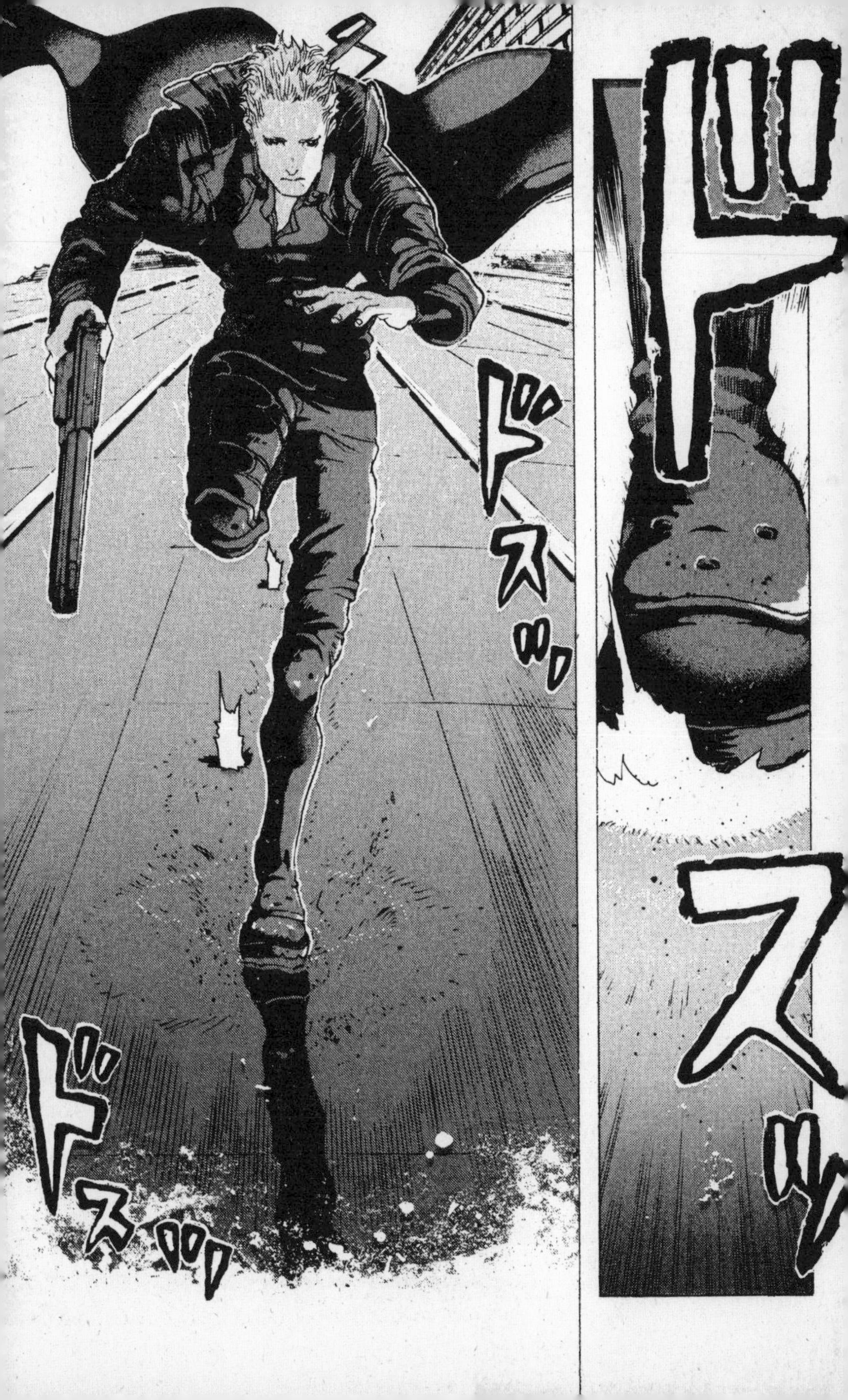
ドスッ
ドスッ
ドスッ

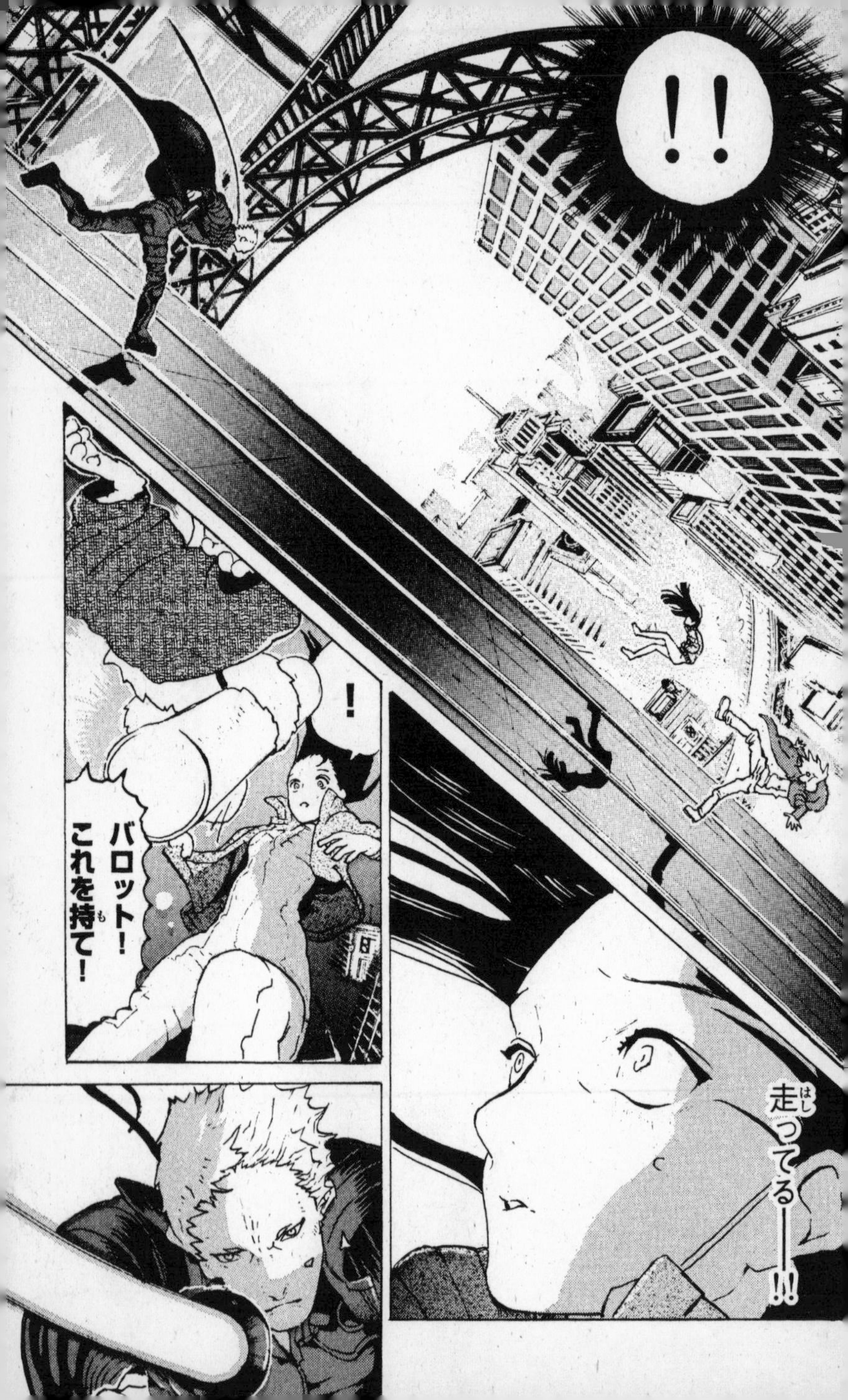
!!
走(はし)ってる――!!
!
バロット！
これを持(も)て！

ボア
!
!!
わ…わ…
発煙筒(めくらまし)だ
放(はな)すなよっ!!

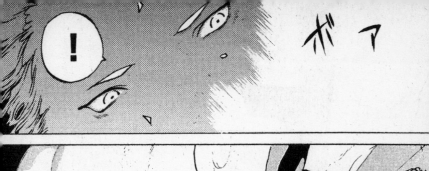

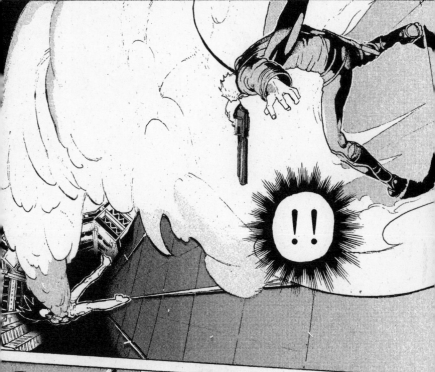

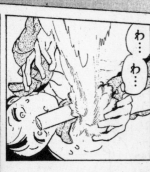

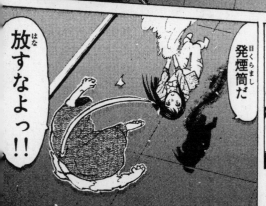

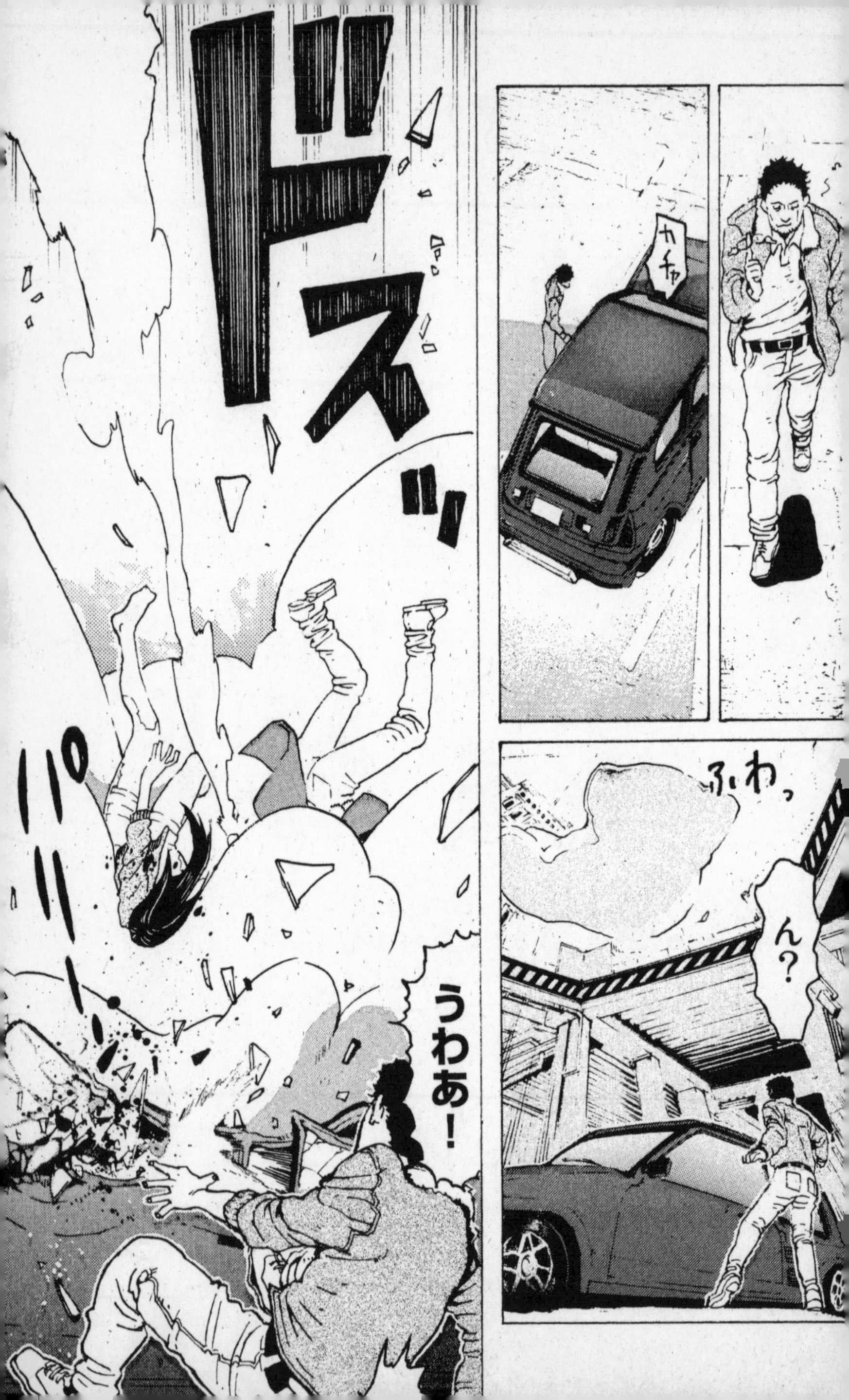
カチャ
ふわっ
ん?
ドスッ
パリー
うわぁ!

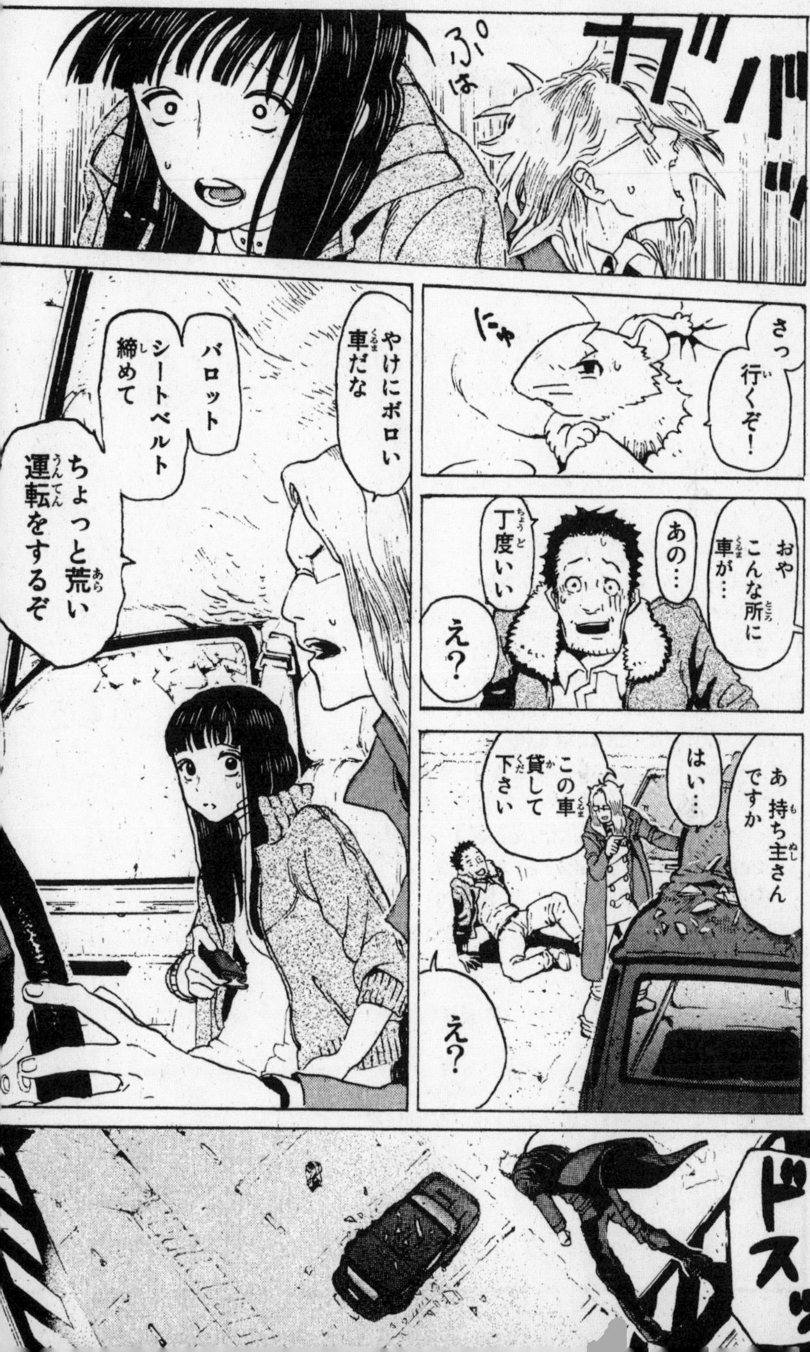
ガバッ
ぷは
さっ 行くぞ!
にゃ
おや こんな所に車が…
あの…
丁度いい
え?
あ 持ち主さんですか
はい…
この車貸して下さい
え?
やけにボロい車だな
バロット シートベルト締めて
ちょっと荒い運転をするぞ
ドスッ

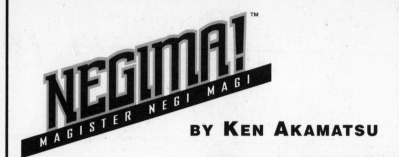

NEGIMA!
MAGISTER NEGI MAGI

BY KEN AKAMATSU

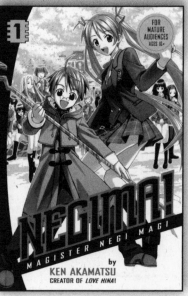

Negi Springfield is a ten-year-old wizard teaching English at an all-girls Japanese school. He dreams of becoming a master wizard like his legendary father, the Thousand Master. At first his biggest concern was concealing his magic powers, because if he's ever caught using them publicly, he thinks he'll be turned into an ermine! But in a world that gets stranger every day, it turns out that the strangest people of all are Negi's students! From a librarian with a magic book to a centuries-old vampire, from a robot to a ninja, Negi will risk his own life to protect the girls in his care!

FOR MATURE AUDIENCES AGES 16+

Ages: 16+

Special extras in each volume! Read them all!

VISIT WWW.KODANSHACOMICS.COM TO:
• View release date calendars for upcoming volumes
• Find out the latest about new Kodansha Comics series

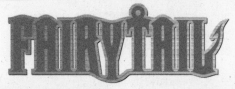
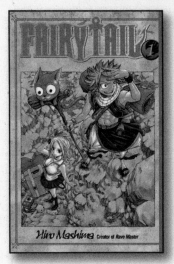
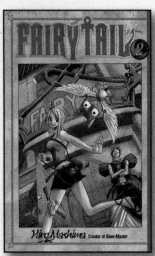

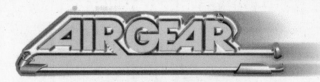

BY OH!GREAT

Itsuki Minami needs no introduction— everybody's heard of the "Babyface" of the Eastside. He's the strongest kid at Higashi Junior High School, easy on the eyes but dangerously tough when he needs to be. Plus, Itsuki lives with the mysterious and sexy Noyamano sisters. Life's never dull, but it becomes downright dangerous when Itsuki leads his school to victory over vindictive Westside punks with gangster connections. Now he stands to lose his school, his friends, and everything he cares about. But in his darkest hour, the Noyamano girls give him an amazing gift, one that just might help him save his school: a pair of Air Trecks. These high-tech skates are more than just supercool. They'll enable Itsuki to execute the wildest, most aggressive moves ever seen—and introduce him to a thrilling and terrifying new world.

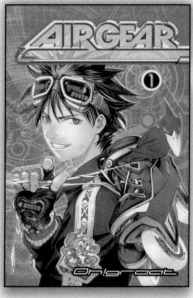

Ages: 16 +

Special extras in each volume! Read them all!

VISIT WWW.KODANSHACOMICS.COM TO:
- View release date calendars for upcoming volumes
- Find out the latest about new Kodansha Comics series

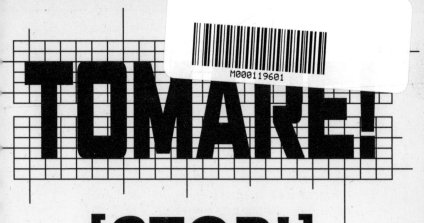

[STOP!]

You are going the wrong way!

Manga is a completely different type of reading experience.

To start at the *beginning*, go to the *end*!

That's right! Authentic manga is read the traditional Japanese way—from right to left, exactly the opposite of how American books are read. It's easy to follow: Just go to the other end of the book, and read each page—and each panel—from the right side to the left side, starting at the top right. Now you're experiencing manga as it was meant to be.